QuickBooks® Desktop 2019

Comprehensive

Trish Conlon

MA, Point Loma Nazarene University

LABYRINTH
LEARNING™

QuickBooks Desktop 2019: Comprehensive

Copyright © 2019 by Labyrinth Learning

LABYRINTH
LEARNING™

Labyrinth Learning
PO Box 2669
Danville, CA 94526
800.522.9746
On the web at lablearning.com

President
Brian Favro

Product Manager
Jason Favro

Development Manager
Laura Popelka

Production Manager
Debra Grose

Senior Editor
Alexandra Mummery

Junior Editor
Alexandria Henderson

Editorial Team
Pam Hillman and
Donna Bacidore

Composition
Happenstance Type-O-Rama

Indexing
Valerie Haynes Perry

Cover Design
Mick Koller, SuperLab Design

PRINT ITEM: 1-64061-042-1
ISBN-13:   978-1-64061-042-2

Manufactured in the United States of America

GPP   10 9 8 7 6 5 4 3 2 1

Contents in Brief

Table of Contents

Chapter 9
Job Costing, Creating Estimates, and Time Tracking 309

Chapter 10
Customizing and Integrating in QuickBooks 353

Preface

QuickBooks® Desktop 2019: Comprehensive provides essential coverage of QuickBooks Pro 2019. Topics covered include basic accounting principles, backing up files, creating companies, working with vendors, working with customers, banking with QuickBooks, customizing QuickBooks, classes, the accounting cycle, physical inventory, payroll, estimates and time tracking, balance sheet accounts, budgets, closing the books, adjusting entries, and more.

For almost two decades, Labyrinth Learning has been publishing easy-to-use textbooks that empower educators to teach complex subjects quickly and effectively. The instructional design enables students to gain confidence, develop practical skills, and compete in a demanding job market. We know your time is stretched thin, and, to help, we provide complimentary comprehensive support materials, assessment and learning management tools, and eLearning components to create true learning solutions for a variety of instructor-led, self-paced, and online courses.

This textbook is designed to help address the various challenges faced by learners and educators in computerized accounting courses.

Our goal is to simplify the entire learning experience and help every learner develop the practical, real-world skills needed to be successful at work and in school. Using a combination of text, videos, and assessments, we begin with fundamental concepts and take learners through a systematic progression of exercises to reach mastery. We're delighted with the results, and we hope that you are, too!

Key Themes

We had conversations with dozens of educators at community colleges, vocational schools, and other learning environments in preparation for this textbook. We listened and have adapted our learning solution to match the needs of a rapidly changing world, while keeping these common themes in mind:

Keep it about skills. Our content focus is on critical, job-ready topics and tasks, with a relentless focus on practical, real-world skills and common sense as well as step-by-step instruction to ensure that learners stay engaged from the first chapter forward. We've retained our method of exercise progression to ensure mastery—an approach that has been successfully developing skills for more than 20 years.

Keep it simple. Our integrated solutions create an engaging experience built on a dynamic instructional design that brings clarity to even the most challenging topics. We've focused our content on the things that matter most and have presented it in the easiest way for today's learners to absorb.

How to Use This Book

Our comprehensive learning solution includes an interactive ebook that delivers learning content in an engaging manner. Features include elements such as videos, self-assessments, slide shows, and more. The ebook also supports highlighting, note-taking, and searching. Every print purchase now includes the ebook.

Every textbook purchase comes with the following:

- *eLab Course Management System:* This robust tool provides additional learning content for students, such as chapter overviews and automatically graded reports and tests. We've expanded our eLab QuickGrader technology to provide automated grading of all reports generated in Apply Your Skills exercises. eLab can be fully integrated with a school's LMS, making course management even easier.

- *Instructor resources:* This course is also supported on the Labyrinth website with a comprehensive instructor support package that includes detailed lesson plans, PowerPoint presentations, a course syllabus, test banks, additional exercises, and more.

- *Learning Resource Center:* Files needed to complete exercises in this textbook can be found within eLab or on the Learning Resource Center at: **labyrinthelab.com/lrc**

We're excited to provide this innovative approach with you, and we'd love you to share your experience with us at: **lablearning.com/share**

Visual Conventions

This book uses visual conventions and typographic cues to guide learners through the chapters. Some of the cues are indicated here:

Cue	What It Does
`Type this text`	Text to type at the keyboard is shown in this typeface.
Action words	Important action words in exercise steps are shown in boldface.
petty cash	Glossary terms are highlighted with a light yellow background.
Tip! Note! Warning!	Tips, notes, and warnings are called out with special icons.
NEW! 2019	Features new to this edition of the software are indicated with this icon.
QG	Exercises that can be used with eLab's Quick Grader solution are indicated with this icon.
Command→Command→Command	Multistep commands are presented like this.
Customer Center→Income Tracker	Reference steps present shortcut steps for executing certain tasks. Do not complete reference steps unless directed to in an exercise.

It is recommended that learners set their screen resolutions to 1024 × 768. This will help ensure that their screens most closely match the provided illustrations. Multiple factors, including screen resolution, DPI setting, monitor size, and window size, can affect the appearance of the QuickBooks screen and buttons.

The QuickBooks Certified User Exam and This Text

This textbook has been certified by and carries the ProCert logo, distinguishing this courseware as a trusted and critical part of preparing for a certification exam. This solution meets all course objectives to prepare students to take the QuickBooks Certified User (QBCU) exam.

The following table maps the QBCU objectives to this textbook:

OBJECTIVE		TEXT LOCATION
1	**QuickBooks Setup**	
1.1	What information is required before setting up a QuickBooks file	p. 145 A Setup Checklist
1.2	How to start a new company data file in QuickBooks (EasyStep Interview)	p. 144 Advanced Setup/Easy Step Interview *and* pp. 148–149 DYS 5-1
1.3	How to keep the lists and preferences from an old file while removing old transactions	p. 144 Using an Existing QuickBooks File as a Template for a New File
1.4	How to customize the Home Page	pp. 12–14 The Insights Tab
1.5	How to set up lists (customers, vendors, items, etc.); this includes understanding which names and items should appear on which lists	pp. 33–36 Working with the Item List
2	**QuickBooks Utilities and General Product Knowledge**	
2.1	How to navigate or move around QuickBooks (use Home Page, menus, icon bar, etc.)	pp. 10–14 Working with the QuickBooks Window
2.2	How to back up and restore a data file	p. 7 Opening and Restoring QuickBooks Files *and* pp. 14–16 Backing Up and Updating Your Company File
2.3	How to determine the release number and how to update QuickBooks	p. 15 Verifying the QuickBooks Release Number
2.4	How to use QuickBooks in a single-user and multi-user mode	p. 162 Working with QuickBooks in a Multi–User Environment
2.5	What versions and editions of QuickBooks are available for a specific year (Desktop version)	pp. 2–3 Editions of QuickBooks *through* Determining the Edition
2.6	How to password protect QuickBooks	p. 162 Setting Passwords
2.7	How and why to use preferences	pp. 150–152 Editing Your QuickBooks Preferences
3	**List Management**	
3.1	How to manage lists (customers, vendors, items, etc.); list management includes:	
	3.1.1 Adding new entries	pp. 63–65 Creating a New Vendor
	3.1.2 Deleting entries	pp. 64–65 Deleting a Vendor
	3.1.3 Editing entries	pp. 63–65 Editing an Existing Vendor
	3.1.4 Merging entries	pp. 64–65 Merge Duplicate Vendors

(cont'd.)

(cont'd.)

(cont'd.)

Acknowledgements

Many individuals contribute to the development and completion of a textbook. This book has benefitted greatly from the feedback and suggestions provided by the following educators and other professionals:

Pete Bada, *NVCC*

Lisa Briggs, *Columbus State Community College*

Dwayne Briscoe, *Bookkeeping-Results, LLC*

Hoa Burrows, *Miami Dade College*

Kathy Camp, *Conway Adult Education Center*

David Campbell, *Northern Virginia Community College*

Amy Chataginer, *William Carey University*

Janine Clover, *Southeastern Community College*

Paul Croitoru, *Wilbur Wright College*

Sarah Dixon-Hackey, *North Dakota State College of Science*

Kerry Dolan, *Great Falls College Montana State University*

Doris Donovan, *Dodge City Community College*

Valorie Duvall, *South Plains College*

Jesse Fink, *Touro College*

Shmuel Fink, *Touro College*

Debbra Finney, *Turlock Adult School*

Roger Fulk, *Upper Valley Career Center – Adult Workforce Division*

Helen Hall, *Quik-help.com*

Maggie Hilgart, *Mid-State Technical College*

Diann Hammon, *JF Drake State Community and Technical College*

Pam Hillman, *Gateway Technical College*

Nancy Howard, *Mt. Hood Community College*

Jenny Jones, *Bluegrass Community and Technical College*

Ruby Kowaney, *Venice Skills Center*

Myles Lambert, *Brookdale Community College*

Vicki Maheu, *San Diego Community Colleges, Continuing Education*

Steven Manske, *Mission College*

Giselinda Mathieu, *Goodwill Workplace Training and Assistance Center*

Deb Niedermeyer, *Montana State University*

Patti Norris, *Central Oregon Community College*

Veronica Paz, *Indiana University of Pennsylvania*

Roxanne Phillips, *CCCOnline*

Karla Robinson, *Kellogg Community College*

Philip Slater, *Forsyth Technical Community College*

Randy Watkins, *Contra Costa College*

Sheree White, *Palm Beach County School District*

Peter Young, *San Jose State University*

About the Author

Trish Conlon (BS, Biology; MA, Education) has been a QuickBooks educator since 1998 and has authored QuickBooks texts for Labyrinth Learning since 2004. She earned her BS from Washington State University and her MA from Point Loma Nazarene University. She has a Teaching License in Finance & Business and Management & Administration from Oregon, a Teaching Credential in Finance & Business from California, and a Certificate in Online Teaching from the University of California San Diego (Extension) and is a QuickBooks Pro Advisor.

1

Introducing QuickBooks Pro

QuickBooks has become the software of choice for many owners of small- to medium-sized businesses. No doubt, this is due to the ease of use and helpful features the software offers. In this chapter, you will explore the various editions of QuickBooks and determine which is right for you. You will also discover what goes on behind the scenes and why it is important to have a basic understanding of accounting. Finally, you will be introduced to a few QuickBooks basics that are vital to your success as a QuickBooks user.

LEARNING OBJECTIVES

▸ Identify basic accounting concepts
▸ Identify the attributes of QuickBooks editions
▸ Define features of the QuickBooks window
▸ Open a portable company file
▸ Back up and restore a company file

Getting to Know QuickBooks Pro

QuickBooks is a software program that allows companies to:

- Keep track of customers, vendors, employees, and other important entities
- Process sales transactions and cash receipts
- Process purchase transactions and payments to vendors
- Run payroll
- Track and sell inventory
- Run end-of-period financial reports
- Track assets (what you own) and liabilities (what you owe)
- Keep track of bank accounts
- Collaborate with accountants easily and efficiently

Each year, Intuit introduces a new version of QuickBooks with new and improved features. As you work through this book, you will see these new aspects of the software called to your attention with a special icon.

 This is how you will be able to identify new or improved QuickBooks features.

Editions of QuickBooks

There are two main varieties of QuickBooks: Desktop and Online. Within each, there are several editions of QuickBooks. Careful evaluation is required to select the edition that best suits your business. Every edition performs basic tasks required for small-business bookkeeping but will differ in terms of capabilities. For example, the Premier and Enterprise editions of QuickBooks are better suited for the manufacturing industry.

This book assumes use of QuickBooks Pro. The trial version of the software defaults to the Accountant edition. To ensure your screens and steps match the book and that your files, particularly exported reports used for automatic grading in eLab (if applicable in your course), are as intended, *you must toggle to the Pro edition of the software every time you start QuickBooks*. Toggle to Pro by going to File→Toggle to Another Edition and choosing QuickBooks Pro.

Intuit also creates a QuickBooks edition for Mac users, which is similar to the Windows-based version in functions, although not in look. The downloadable files associated with this book are not compatible with the Mac or international versions of QuickBooks.

Determining the Edition

QuickBooks Pro works well, and can be customized, for different types of companies in a variety of industries, including nonprofit organizations. Ideally, your company should have fewer than twenty employees and less than $1 million in annual revenue to utilize QuickBooks Pro (these are not strict rules but rather guidelines).

Desktop editions include QuickBooks Pro, multiple QuickBooks Premier editions, and QuickBooks Enterprise.

An advantage to choosing one of the industry-specific QuickBooks Premier editions is that it will provide more industry-specific functionality; for example, running a donor contribution report for a nonprofit business or tracking profitability by product.

QuickBooks Enterprise Solutions is aimed at larger companies, allows for more users, and has more advanced inventory capabilities.

If you need the flexibility of immediate access, then an online edition would be a better choice. Online editions use the Internet via a desktop or mobile device such as smartphone, tablet, or laptop. It is a monthly subscription-based service, allowing you access to your company's Quick-Books file from any computer with access to the Internet.

Online editions include Self-Employed, Simple Start, Essentials, and Plus. Other advantages to choosing online include automatic remote backup, up-to-date company files, and a lack of technological problems associated with desktop product installation and support. Keep in mind that not all features are available in QuickBooks Online. It is best to compare the different editions on the Intuit website to see which versions are available. Browse the company's website at intuit.com.

You can determine the version and edition you are currently running from the Help menu.

 Help→About QuickBooks Desktop Pro 2019

Types of Tasks

There are many tasks you can perform with QuickBooks. They can be broken down into two main categories: those that affect the accounting behind the scenes (activities such as bill paying and company setup) and those that do not (lists and reporting). The following table lists the four basic types of tasks covered in this book:

QUICKBOOKS TASKS AND THEIR FUNCTIONS	
Task	**Function**
Lists (database)	These lists store information about customers, vendors, employees, services, products, payment methods, and more.
Activities	Activities affect what happens behind the scenes. Activities are entered on forms such as invoices or bills.
Company Setup	This task walks you through the basic steps to set up a new company in QuickBooks.
Reports	QuickBooks provides many preset reports and graphs that are customizable.

Accounting Basics

QuickBooks is quite intuitive, but you could find yourself running into problems if you don't understand the accounting basics on which QuickBooks is based. Having the basic knowledge as explained in this book will help you set up your company more effectively and provide a better picture of the health of the business.

What Is GAAP?

GAAP stands for Generally Accepted Accounting Principles (GAAP). These principles are accounting rules used in the United States to prepare, present, and report financial statements for a variety of entities. The organization that creates the rules is called the Financial Accounting Standards Board (FASB). Publicly owned companies need to follow these rules unless they can show that doing so would produce information that is misleading. It is wise for the small-business owner to adhere to GAAP as well.

As GAAP attempt to achieve basic objectives, they have several basic assumptions, principles, and constraints (described below). Throughout the book you will see reminders of how GAAP apply to tasks that you are completing in QuickBooks via the "Flashback to GAAP" feature.

GENERALLY ACCEPTED ACCOUNTING PRINCIPLES (GAAP)

Principle	Description
Business entity principle	The business is separate from the owners and from other businesses. Revenues and expenses of the business should be kept separate from the personal expenses of the business owner.
The assumption of the going concern	The business will be in operation indefinitely.
Monetary unit principle	A stable currency is going to be the unit of record.
Time-period principle	The activities of the business can be divided into time periods.
Cost principle	When a company purchases assets, it should record them at cost. An item worth $750 bought for $100 is recorded at $100.
Revenue principle	Publicly traded companies must record when the revenue is realized and earned, not when cash is received (accrual basis of accounting).
Matching principle	Expenses need to be matched with revenues during the same accounting period. This principle allows for a better evaluation of the profitability and performance (how much did you spend to earn the revenue?).
Objectivity principle	A company's statements should be based on objectivity.
Materiality principle	When an item is reported, its significance should be considered. An item is considered significant when it would affect the decision made regarding its use.
Consistency principle	The company uses the same accounting principles and methods from year to year.
Prudence principle	When choosing between two solutions, the one that will be least likely to overstate assets and income should be selected.

An Accountant's Worst Nightmare (or Greatest Dream?)

Picture yourself as an accountant who has just received a QuickBooks file from a client. The client has no idea how accounting works, and, to him, debit and credit are just types of plastic cards he carries in his wallet. In his file you find duplicate accounts in the Chart of Accounts, accounts created as the wrong type, items posted to incorrect accounts, accounts payable inaccuracies, and payroll inaccuracies (to name just a few problems).

Now, as an accountant, you can consider this a nightmare because you will have to run numerous diagnostics to find all the mistakes (which could have been easily avoided if your client learned how to use QuickBooks properly in the first place) or a dream because your billable hours will increase at a rapid rate.

This scenario is exactly the reason why you, as the client, need to learn what happens behind the scenes in QuickBooks, as well as how to use the day-to-day functions of the software. By having a better understanding of the accounting and how to do things properly in the program, you will reduce the number of hours your accountant will have to spend and, thereby, save yourself the accountant fees in the end!

Appendix A, "Need-to-Know Accounting," provides a good overview of fundamental accounting principles, including an explanation of T-accounts (also called T-charts). If you want to delve even deeper, Labyrinth's *Accounting Basics: An Introduction for Non-Accounting Majors* is an excellent text that will provide you with all the accounting fundamentals you might need.

Introducing Behind the Scenes

Throughout this book you will see a special section called "Behind the Scenes" whenever you are learning about an activity performed within QuickBooks. This section will go over the accounting that QuickBooks performs for you when you record a transaction. Please note that the account names used in this feature use QuickBooks, rather than traditional accounting, nomenclature.

Accrual vs. Cash Basis Accounting

Companies can choose to implement one of two methods for keeping their books. QuickBooks makes it easy for you to produce reports utilizing either method, and your data entry will be the same regardless of which method you choose.

The two main types of accounting methods are:

- Accrual basis: Income is recorded when cash is earned, and expenses are recorded when incurred.

- Cash basis: Income is recorded when cash is actually received, and expenses are recorded when paid.

Following a Transaction Path

Think of an old-fashioned scale; in order to balance, each side has to have the same weight. Accounting works in a similar way. If you have an amount in one account, there eventually has to be the same amount balanced in another account.

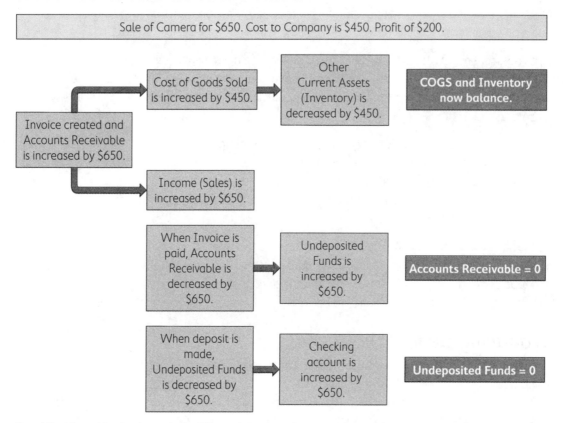

| Sale of Camera for $650. Cost to Company is $450. Profit of $200. |

QuickBooks will calculate the profit and display the result when you run the Profit & Loss report. All of this is done behind the scenes. You can follow some of it by going into the Chart of Accounts and looking at these accounts as you proceed with the process of invoicing, collecting, and depositing.

Managing Basic QuickBooks Files

Before you begin working with a QuickBooks file, you need to understand some basic file-management operations. This section covers the different types of QuickBooks files and how to open and restore QuickBooks portable company files.

Types of QuickBooks Files

There are three different types of files in which you can store your QuickBooks data: company files, backup files, and portable company files.

- The working file is the **company file** that has the file extension **.QBW**. It is not compressed and should be stored on a hard drive. This file contains all of your company data.

- A **portable company file** is a compressed company file and is a convenient way to send your company information by email. Its file type is **.QBM**. It will be de-compressed upon opening automatically. It is not a backup!

- A **backup file** is created when you select the Backup option and is used to store a copy of your data in case your main file becomes corrupted and needs to be restored. A backup file has a **.QBB** extension. Validation of the file's integrity is performed during a backup.

Two other QuickBooks file types play important support roles for your company data. A network data file has a file extension of **.ND**, and it contains important configuration data. A transaction log has a file extension of **.TLG**, and it can help you to recover any data entered after the last backup operation you have performed.

Your company file can be stored anywhere on your computer. The QuickBooks default storage location is the QuickBooks folder for the current version you are using.

Warning! Even though .ND and .TLG files do not allow you to work with your company information, do not delete them. Doing so can affect the integrity of your company data.

Opening and Restoring QuickBooks Files

Through the File menu, you can open a QuickBooks company file or restore a backup or portable file. The last company file that was open when you exited QuickBooks is the file that will open automatically when you next start QuickBooks. When you enter transactions, they are saved automatically to the QuickBooks working company file.

The company file should be backed up periodically. You can also create a portable file for easy transport via email or USB drive. You cannot "open" a backup or portable company file for use; it must be restored.

Warning! When you are opening or restoring older file versions, you will be asked to update the file to the newer version. QuickBooks will make a copy of the file first. After you update, you will not be able to open this file in an older version of QuickBooks.

 File→Open or Restore Company

How to Use This Book and the Student Files

You may be curious about the large number of student exercise files that come with this book and how using this book as a learning tool compares to working with your own company file. The following questions and answers should help to set you in the right direction!

Why is there a different company file for each exercise?

When you are learning QuickBooks, it is much easier to follow the instructions if your screen matches the illustrations in the book (or your instructor's screen). Having a fresh file at the beginning of each chapter helps ensure that mistakes naturally made by students learning new material do not compound and cause a disconnect between student files and the example illustrations. This is why we don't recommend using one file that continues from chapter to chapter.

Tip! A fresh company file for each chapter also means that the chapters in this book can be completed in any order.

Is this how I will work in QuickBooks in "real life"?

No, using a separate file for each type of task (e.g., working with vendors, customers, inventory, etc.) is *not* how you will operate in "real life." In the real world, you will have *one* company file only. The multiple company files are for training purposes only.

Do I have to complete the chapters in the order presented in the book?

No, this book is entirely modular, and you can approach the chapters in any order you choose. For instance, some people feel that the discussion of how to create a company should come first (i.e., after Chapter 1), rather than where it is placed in this book. Chapters may be worked through in any order. Fresh company files provided for each chapter make this possible.

Why do portable company files take so long to restore? What can I do while waiting for a file to restore?

Portable company files are compressed files that QuickBooks must "inflate" before you can use them. Think of the "space bags" you may have seen on an infomercial. Using a vacuum to remove all of the air from a space bag, you can fit some thirty sweaters into a shoebox. (Okay, this is a stretch, but hopefully you get the idea!) This is akin to QuickBooks creating a portable company file. Opening the seal and letting the air back in is like what happens when you restore a portable company file. It takes time for QuickBooks to prepare the portable company files just as it takes time for air to seep back into a space bag so the sweaters can return to their normal volume. If you are using an old computer system or a USB drive, the process will take longer than it will if you have a newer system.

Many users are not happy about waiting for the restore process to occur, but it is a necessity if you have chosen this file option. You may want to begin a chapter by restoring the portable company file first so you can read the concepts discussions while it restores.

What if I want to work with "real" company files rather than portable company files?

You can download either company files or portable company files for this course. Remember that company files will take longer to download and will use more space on your storage drive. On the plus side, you need not restore them in order to use them. For every portable company file there is also a regular company file—except for the Develop Your Skills exercise in Chapter 1, as the first task teaches you how to restore a portable company file.

If you are using portable company files, they will need to be restored, and you will be provided with a name for the company file that you are creating. However, if you are using the company files, you will simply open them from your file storage location, and there is no need to save them with a different name.

Note! Follow the exercise directions based on the file type you are using.

How do I save as a PDF?

Many instructors request students to save reports as PDF files. This makes it easier to submit your work and saves paper. To save a report as a PDF, first create and display the report. Next, click the Print button on the report toolbar and choose to Save As PDF.

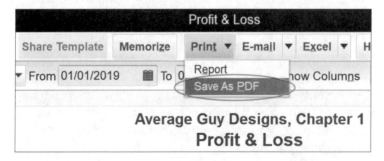

DEVELOP YOUR SKILLS 1-1

In this exercise, you will restore a QuickBooks portable company file. Even if you choose to download the company files, you will use a portable company file for this exercise.

Before You Begin: *Visit the Learning Resource Center at* labyrinthelab.com/lrc *to retrieve the exercise files for this course before beginning this exercise. Two versions of the files are available—portable company files and company files. The password for all files, unless otherwise stated, is* Password1. *Leave the company file open unless otherwise instructed.*

1. Start QuickBooks 2019.

   You may see one of two editions of QuickBooks installed on your computer: Pro or Premier. This book works with both of these editions, so choose whichever edition is installed. This book assumes use of the Pro edition.

   A splash screen displays the version of QuickBooks you are launching and opens the program window. If this is the first time you have used the QuickBooks installation on this computer, you will see a QuickBooks Setup window.

Toggle to QuickBooks Pro

If you are using the trial version of the software provided with this course, your version of QuickBooks is likely showing the Accountant edition. You must toggle to Pro now and every time you start QuickBooks.

2. Choose **File→Toggle to Another Edition**.
3. Click in the circle to the left of *QuickBooks Pro* and then click **Next**.
4. Click **Toggle**.

Restore a Portable Company File

5. Choose **File** and then choose the **Open or Restore Company** command.

> *Note!* In the future, a menu bar command like this will be written as Choose **File→Open or Restore Company**.

6. Choose **Restore a Portable File** and then click **Next**.
7. Navigate to your file storage location, click the **DYS_Chapter01 (Portable)** file, and then click **Open**.
8. Click **Next** and then save the file to your storage location as: **DYS_Chapter01 Average Guy Designs**

   It may take a few moments for the portable company file to open. If asked to update the file, choose Update Now.

   Intuit provides maintenance releases throughout the lifetime of the product. These updates may require you to update your student exercise files before you begin working with them.

9. Type **Password1** and click **OK**.

10. Click **OK** to close the QuickBooks Desktop Information window and then close the Accountant Center window and New Feature tour windows, if necessary.

For the rest of the Develop Your Skills exercises in this book, you can restore a portable company file or open a company file. This exercise showed you how to restore a portable company file. Use this process, as applicable, moving forward. Leave the company file open for the next exercise.

Working with the QuickBooks Window

If you have ever worked with a Windows-based PC, you will probably be familiar with many screen elements, such as the title bar and quick-sizing buttons. In addition, many Windows-based programs utilize menus, toolbars, icon bars, a Ribbon, and tabs, and you will also see these in QuickBooks.

Viewing the QuickBooks Window

The QuickBooks window features many components designed to help you complete all the tasks necessary to manage your business effectively.

Click a menu item on the menu bar to see a drop-down menu of options specific to that item.

The title bar shows the company name and the QuickBooks version/edition you are using.

Alerts and reminders can be easily accessed from the far-right corner of the menu bar.

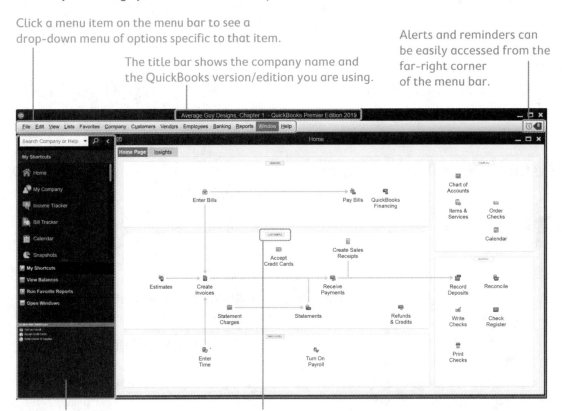

The icon bar is docked on the left side by default. Use the icons to access Centers, personal shortcuts, apps, and services. Use the View menu to move or hide the icon bar.

Click the buttons at the top of each section on the Home Page to go to that Center. For example, click the word *Customers* to open the Customer Center. The Home window is displayed in a restored-down state.

Flowing Through the Home Page

The workflow diagram on the Home Page is indicated by arrows going from one task icon to another. It is important to follow the diagram so as not to run into trouble. Here are some examples of potential trouble spots:

- If you choose Write Checks rather than Pay Bills (for a bill that has already been entered), the accounting behind the scenes will still show the bill as not paid, and expenses will be overstated.

Occasionally, you might need to use Write Checks, such as when you handwrite a paper check to pay for something unbilled or make any payment not entered as a bill.

- If you choose Record Deposits rather than Receive Payments (for an invoiced amount), the accounting behind the scenes will still show the invoice as not paid, and income will be overstated.

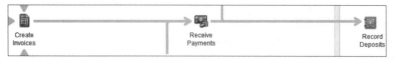

Occasionally, you might use Record Deposits, such as when you receive a tax refund.

- Sales tax errors can also occur by not following the proper flow outlined on the Home Page.

The QuickBooks Icon Bar

The icon bar provides a quick way to access QuickBooks centers, snapshots, shortcuts, apps, and services. It is docked on the left side of the QuickBooks window by default but can be moved to the top of the window or hidden altogether using the View menu.

> **Note!** All commands accessible on the icon bar and Home Page can be found through the menu bar, but the opposite is not true.

QuickBooks Calendar

The QuickBooks Calendar allows you to keep up with deadlines. This feature also integrates a To-Do list so you can keep track of your calendar and tasks in one handy place. The Calendar can be accessed via the Company menu or via the icon bar.

The To-Do list is displayed to the right of the calendar.

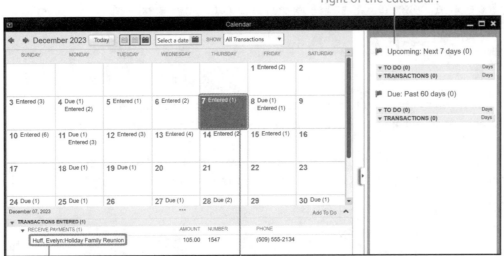

Details of what took place on that day can be viewed in a panel at the bottom of the window.

The calendar will display how many transactions have been entered and are due on a specific day.

The Open Window List and Working with Multiple Monitors

You may wish to display the Open Window List at the top of the icon bar to keep track of all the windows you have open. The active window will always appear at the top of the list. This list is not open by default.

If you need to keep one window active (such as a report) while performing other tasks or viewing other reports, you can extend QuickBooks over several monitors.

You can expand the QuickBooks screen over three monitors. For instance, you can have a report display on one monitor, an invoice on the second monitor, and a customer's record on the third monitor. An icon will appear on the title bar of each window to move the window to another monitor.

 View→Switch to Multi-Monitor Mode | Ctrl + Alt + M

The Insights Tab

The Insights tab on the Home Page offers a comprehensive and easy-to-understand overview of your business.

With the Insights tab:

- You always know how your business is doing, as you are provided quick access to real-time data.
- You can customize your Home Page with your company logo and information.
- You can compare data from multiple years.

- You can view your best customers.
- You can view several quick charts.

See your Profit & Loss trending in an instant.

Customize the display using the Gear tool.

Easily upload a company logo.

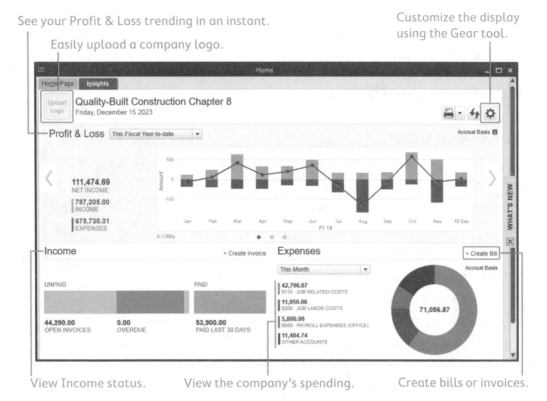

View Income status.

View the company's spending.

Create bills or invoices.

DEVELOP YOUR SKILLS 1-2

In this exercise, you will have a chance to explore the QuickBooks window.

1. Click the **Vendors** [VENDORS] button in the Vendors area of the Home Page.

   The Vendor Center will open, from where you can work with the vendors on your list, manage various vendor transactions, and create new vendors.

2. Choose **Lists→Chart of Accounts** from the menu bar to see the list of accounts for this company.

3. Click the **Snapshots** icon from the icon bar, scrolling down if necessary, to open the Company Snapshot window.

4. Choose **View→Open Window List** from the menu bar and then click **Chart of Accounts** from the Open Windows list.

   The Chart of Accounts window becomes active and is pulled to the front of the other windows. All the windows have their own set of quick-sizing buttons (Minimize, Restore/Maximize, Close), which can be used to control the display of each window and display the name of the window on the title bar.

5. Click the **Close** [x] button for the Chart of Accounts window.

6. Choose **Window→Close All**.

   This command will close all open windows! Notice that the Home Page is closed because it is a window, but the Open Window List/icon bar is still displayed.

7. Open the Home Page by choosing **My Shortcuts** from the icon bar, and then clicking **Home**.

8. Choose **View→Hide Icon Bar**.

Exit and Reopen QuickBooks

9. Choose **File→Exit**; if necessary, click **No** on the Automatic Backup window.

10. Open QuickBooks, following the directions for the version of Windows you are using.

11. Type the password **Password1** and click **OK**. Click **No** in the Set Up an External Accountant User window, if necessary.

    Notice that QuickBooks opens the file that you were last working on and that the icon bar is not visible.

12. Close the Accountant Center window, if necessary.

13. Maximize the QuickBooks program window, if necessary.

14. Choose **View→Left Icon Bar** to display the icon bar.

15. Mouse over the Pay Bills task icon to display the ToolTip for that icon.

16. Leave QuickBooks open with the Home Page displayed for the next exercise.

Backing Up and Updating Your Company File

Because the company file contains all your company's transactions and financial data, it is important to do timely backups. This process also verifies the integrity of the file.

QuickBooks saves all activities and actions automatically. There is no need to perform a save. There isn't even an option to do so! The backup operation will back up the entire file.

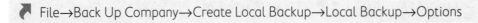 File→Back Up Company→Create Local Backup→Local Backup→Options

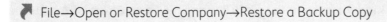 File→Open or Restore Company→Restore a Backup Copy

Backup Location

Do not back up your company file to the same hard drive as where the company file is stored. Choose an alternate backup location such as a network drive, external hard drive, USB drive, cloud storage, or the QuickBooks' online backup option. If you back up your file to a USB drive or some other removable media, make sure to store the backup drive in another physical location. It is wise to store the backup drive off-site in the event of a fire or water damage at the place of business.

> ✔ *Best Practice*
>
> Back up at least weekly at a minimum. You should back up daily if you have a lot of transactions on a daily basis. Having a current backup to restore in the event of a serious crash could get you back up and running quickly.

Protecting Your Data Online

To ensure the security of your QuickBooks data in the event of human error, a natural disaster, or a computer crash, you may wish to use Intuit Data Protect. This online subscription service encrypts and backs up automatically each day to secure servers, for a monthly fee. It allows you to recover your data in the event you lose your working company file. You can also use the service to back up any of your other important files.

 File→Back Up Company→Setup/Activate Online Backup

When to Save a Backup Copy

In QuickBooks, you can choose when to back up your company file. QuickBooks allows you to choose among three options:

- Save it now

- Save it now and schedule future backups

- Schedule only future backups

The future backup options make it easy to back up your company file on a regular basis without having to remember to physically issue the command. You can select a specific day of the week and time to have the backup run automatically.

If you choose scheduled backups, make sure the backup location is available to QuickBooks at the scheduled times. For instance, ensure that you have your USB flash drive attached if that is your backup location. Once a backup has been created, you can restore it, if necessary. It will restore back to the date that the backup was created.

Updating Your QuickBooks Company File

Earlier in this chapter you learned about the different versions of QuickBooks that are available for purchase each year. Intuit releases free QuickBooks updates throughout the life of the version. These updates are available for download and may include such things as a new service, maintenance release, new feature, or something else relevant to your company. Eventually, Intuit will announce that it will no longer support an older version of QuickBooks.

The easiest way to stay abreast of these updates is to have QuickBooks automatically check for and download them for you through the Help menu.

 Help→Update QuickBooks Desktop: Options tab

Verifying the QuickBooks Release Number

You can find the release number for your current version of QuickBooks by tapping the F2 key. This will launch a Product Information window that displays the release number and additional information such as the license and product numbers.

DEVELOP YOUR SKILLS 1-3

In this exercise, you will create a backup copy of your company file.

1. Choose **File→Back Up Company→Create Local Backup**.

2. Verify that Local Backup is selected and then click **Options**.

3. Click **Browse** and browse to your file storage location in the Browse for Folder window.

4. Click **OK** and then click **Use This Location**, if necessary.

   If you have chosen to save the file to the same drive on which the company file is stored, QuickBooks will display a warning window.

5. Click **Next**, choose **Save It Now**, and then click **Next** again.

6. Ensure that the correct file storage location is displayed and then click **Save**.

7. Click **OK** to acknowledge the information window that tells you a backup file has been created.

8. Choose **File→Exit** to close QuickBooks and the company file.

Self-Assessment

Check your knowledge of this chapter's key concepts and skills using the Self-Assessment quiz here, in your ebook, or in your eLab course.

1. QuickBooks Pro would be a good software program for a company with 100 employees.   True   False

2. Performing an activity within QuickBooks affects what happens behind the scenes in the program.   True   False

3. In the cash basis of accounting, you record the expenses when they are accrued.   True   False

4. A portable company file is the same as a backup file.   True   False

5. It's best to store your QuickBooks company file on your computer hard drive.   True   False

6. To use a QuickBooks backup file, you must restore it first.   True   False

7. All commands accessible on the Home Page can be found through the menu bar as well.   True   False

8. The icon bar can be either displayed or hidden in your QuickBooks window.   True   False

9. Updates or maintenance releases are available for QuickBooks for a small fee.   True   False

10. In which location should you NOT back up your company file?
    A. A USB flash drive
    B. With Intuit's Online Backup service
    C. A drive where your main company file is stored
    D. An external hard drive

11. In the event of data loss, what type of file helps you recover any data entered after the last backup operation?
    A. Transaction log
    B. Backup
    C. Portable company
    D. Network

12. To use QuickBooks portable company files, what must you do first?
    A. Restore the files.
    B. Replace the files.
    C. Reuse the files.
    D. Open the files.

13. Which account is decreased when a sale of a product is made?
    A. Sales (Income Account)
    B. Inventory (Other Current Asset)
    C. Cost of Goods Sold
    D. Expense Account

Reinforce Your Skills

In the majority of the Reinforce Your Skills exercises, you will be working with a company called Electrical Energy. This business is an S corporation that provides electrical contracting services to general contractors and individual customers. Emily Holly is the president of the business. You will assist Emily in a variety of QuickBooks tasks as you work your way through these exercises. The password for all files unless otherwise stated is Password1. Leave the company file open unless otherwise instructed. If you are using the trial software on your computer or in a lab at school, remember to toggle to the Pro edition every time you start QuickBooks.

REINFORCE YOUR SKILLS 1-1

Find Your Way Around QuickBooks

In this exercise, you will take a look at Emily's QuickBooks company file. You will begin by restoring a portable company file.

1. Start QuickBooks 2019 and toggle to Pro, if necessary.
2. Choose **File→Open or Restore Company**.
3. Choose to **Restore a Portable File** and then click **Next**.
4. Navigate to your file storage location and then double-click to select **RYS_Chapter01 (Portable)**.
5. Click **Next** and then save the file to your storage location as: **RYS_Chapter01 Electrical Energy**
6. Type **Password1** and click **OK**. Click **OK** in the QuickBooks Information window, if necessary.

   The company file will open with the Home Page displayed.

Navigate in the Company File

7. Click the **Items & Services** task icon in the Company area of the Home Page to display the Item List window.
8. Click the **Calendar** icon on the icon bar to display the Calendar window.
9. Choose **Vendors→Enter Bills** from the menu to prepare for entering a bill.
10. Choose **Company→Lead Center** to review any active, hot, converted, etc., leads.
11. Choose **Customers→Customer Center** to see any outstanding balances or run a QuickReport.
12. Choose **View→Open Window List**.

    Notice that all open windows are listed. Clicking on one of them will make that window active. Alternatively, you can click on the Window menu to see a list of open windows.

13. Choose **Window→Close All**.
14. Click **My Shortcuts** on the icon bar and then click **Home** to display the Home Page and leave this company file and QuickBooks open for the next exercise.

Create a Backup File and Schedule Future Backups

In this exercise, you will backup Emily's QuickBooks company file and schedule future backups.

1. Choose **File→Back Up Company→Create Local Backup**.

2. Click **Options** and then, in the Backup Options window, navigate to your file storage location.

3. Ensure **Complete Verification** is selected and click **OK**.

4. Click **Use This Location**, if necessary.

5. Click **Next**, choose **Save It Now and Schedule Future Backups**, click **Next**, and then click **New** to set up the schedule.

6. Follow these steps to schedule a backup:

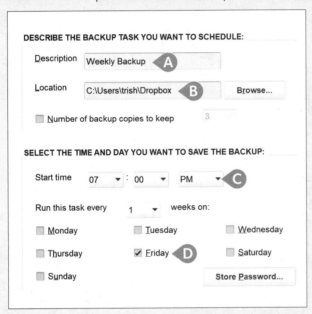

- Ⓐ Type **Weekly Backup** as the Description.
- Ⓑ Navigate to the storage location for your backup. Reminder: This should not be the same location where your company file is stored.
- Ⓒ Choose **7:00 PM**.
- Ⓓ Select **Friday** and then click **OK**. If prompted for a Windows username and password, enter them here. If unknown, click **Cancel**, and your backup will not be scheduled.

   Performing a backup will require a Windows Administrator password. If you are not signed on as Administrator, you will not be able to complete this task. Click OK if you get the Warning message.

7. Click **Finish** and then click **OK**. Click **OK** again to acknowledge the creation of a backup file.

8. Choose **File→Exit** to exit QuickBooks.

Work with T-Accounts

In this exercise, you will use your accounting knowledge. Refer to Appendix A, "Need to Know Accounting," if you need assistance.

1. Open the **Work with T-Accounts** worksheet from your file storage location.

2. Write or type the following account names at the tops of the T-charts:
   - **Bank Service Charges**
   - **Job Income**
   - **Checking**
   - **Accounts Payable**
   - **Construction Equipment**
   - **Capital Stock**

3. Next to each account, write or type the account type (asset, liability, equity, income, or expense).

4. Label the debit and credit side of each T.

5. Write or type **NB** on the appropriate side of the T to indicate the normal balance of each account.

6. Submit your work based on the guidelines provided by your instructor.

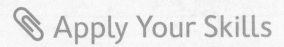
Apply Your Skills

In all of the Apply Your Skills exercises, you will be working with a company called Wet Noses Veterinary Clinic run by Dr. Sadie James, DVM. She is a small-animal veterinarian specializing in dogs and cats. The password for all files unless otherwise stated is Password1. After starting QuickBooks, remember to toggle to Pro as necessary.

APPLY YOUR SKILLS 1-1

Explore QuickBooks and Create a Backup File

In this exercise, you will explore QuickBooks, back up a QuickBooks company file, and schedule future backups.

1. Open the **Explore QuickBooks Worksheet** from your file storage location.
2. Start QuickBooks and toggle to Pro.
3. Open **AYS_Chapter01 (Company)** or restore **AYS_Chapter01 (Portable)** from your file storage location and save your file as: `AYS_Chapter01 Wet Noses Clinic`

   Hint: Choose File→Open or Restore Company, choose Open a Company File, and click Next. Then navigate to the file and click Open.

   Note that you only need to save the file with a different name if you are using a portable company file. If you are working with a company file, you can simply open it from your file storage location and start working.

4. Determine and then enter the version and edition of QuickBooks on the worksheet.
5. Display the Insights tab and change the view to display expenses for this fiscal quarter. Capture your work by pressing the `PrintScrn` key and paste it under the Insights Tab Expenses title on the worksheet.
6. Customize the Insights tab to add the Income and Expense Trend panel. Click the **arrows** to display this new panel and then capture your work and paste it under the Insights Tab Expenses Trend title.
7. Open these windows using any of the methods described in this chapter:
   - Receive Payments
   - Company Snapshot
   - Income Tracker
   - Chart of Accounts
8. Switch back to the Receive Payments window.
9. Capture the screen with the Open Windows list displayed and paste it under the Windows title on the worksheet.
10. Close all windows.
11. Back up the company file and schedule daily backups to occur every Monday through Thursday at 7:00 PM. Capture the Schedule Backup window before clicking **OK** and paste it under the Backup title in the Word worksheet.
12. Save the worksheet file to your storage location as: `CH1-A1 Explore QuickBooks`
13. Close the company file.

Get a Grasp on Accounting Principles

In this exercise, you will use your accounting knowledge to brainstorm the accounts that would be required of a veterinary business.

1. Open the **Get a Grasp on Accounting Principles** worksheet from your file storage location.

2. Think about a veterinary practice. On the worksheet, list the accounts that you feel would be required in the business's Chart of Accounts.

3. In the second column, list the type of account for each.

4. In the third column, state whether the normal balance for the account would be a debit or a credit.

5. Save the worksheet file to your storage location as: **CH1-A2 Get a Grasp**

Extend Your Skills

You have been hired by Arlaine Cervantes to help her with her organization's books. She is the founder of Niños del Lago, a nonprofit organization that provides impoverished Guatemalan children with an engaging educational camp experience. In each chapter, you will sit down at your desk and open a large envelope from her with a variety of documents, as well as go through emails from her. It is your job to sort through the papers and emails and make sense of what you find, entering information into QuickBooks whenever appropriate and answering any other questions in a word-processing document. Remember, you will be digging through papers you just dumped out of an envelope and addressing random emails from Arlaine, so it is going to be up to you to determine the correct order in which to complete the tasks.

In this first chapter, you will determine which edition of QuickBooks is best for Niños del Lago and make other decisions regarding how to use QuickBooks, including devising a backup plan.

Think of the preliminary steps necessary to create and start using QuickBooks to track your new company. Open **EYS_01_Preliminary Steps Worksheet** and complete all fields.

> **Note!** Within the package of exercise files that you have already downloaded, you will find QuickBooks files that you will need to use for Extend Your Skills exercises. Be sure to also check the EYS Miscellaneous Files folder in your file storage location for other additional and necessary files.

2 Working with Customers

Let's face it. The best part of being in business is creating and developing relationships with customers. After all, who doesn't enjoy receiving payment for a job well done? Intuit describes a customer as "any person, business, or group that buys or pays for the services or products that your business or organization sells or provides." When working with QuickBooks, you can consider a customer anyone who pays you funds. This simple definition will help you if you have a unique business, such as a not-for-profit organization that doesn't normally use the term "customer." The job feature is an optional aspect of QuickBooks, but it can be extremely helpful if you have more than one project for a customer, and it enables you to do job costing. In this chapter, you will examine QuickBooks' lists, activities, and reports that allow you to effectively deal with customers.

LEARNING OBJECTIVES

▸ Identify Customer Center features and create new customers and jobs

▸ Create entries and edit various lists

▸ Create invoices and sales receipts and receive payments

▸ Correct errors in customer transactions

▸ Create customer-related reports

📂 Project: Average Guy Designs

Guy Marshall began his graphic design business two years ago and has become quite successful in landing several corporate accounts. He has decided that he needs to start using QuickBooks to track his business finances.

Guy has already completed the initial company setup, and the next step will be for you to set up the company to track customers. You will begin by working with the Customers & Jobs List, which is accessed through the Customer Center. Services need to be added to the Item List so that sales transactions such as invoices and sales receipts can be entered. Information in the Item List allows you to tie the service that is offered to an income account. Finally, you will create reports that will tell you about customer-related transactions.

The Customer Center

The Customer Center is where you will set up all aspects of doing business with each customer. This includes payment terms, sales tax, credit card information, and the ability to track the customer type. In addition, you can track the sales representative who made the sale, if appropriate.

Selecting a customer from the Customer Center will give you access to a lot of information on that customer.

> ✔ **Best Practice**
>
> An excellent way of organizing multiple jobs for a customer is to create each job separately under that customer. When an invoice is created, you then apply it to the specific job, making it easy to track job costs.

Tip! The Customers & Jobs List can be exported to contact management software such as Microsoft Outlook.

Create a new customer or job.

Export the data to Excel and create letters with Word.

Create a new transaction, such as an invoice.

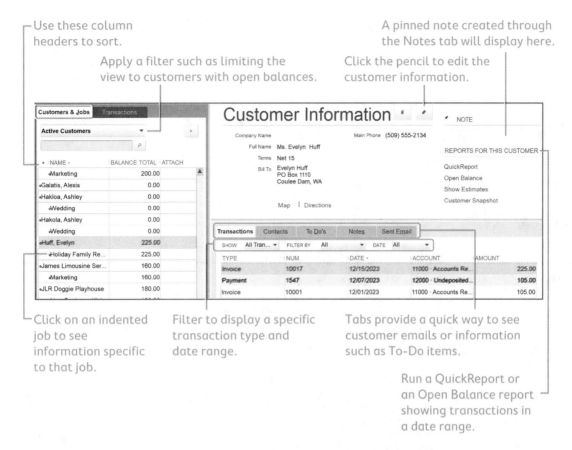

Use these column headers to sort.

Apply a filter such as limiting the view to customers with open balances.

A pinned note created through the Notes tab will display here.

Click the pencil to edit the customer information.

Click on an indented job to see information specific to that job.

Filter to display a specific transaction type and date range.

Tabs provide a quick way to see customer emails or information such as To-Do items.

Run a QuickReport or an Open Balance report showing transactions in a date range.

The more information you enter for each customer, the more flexibility you will have later when you customize and run reports. If you utilize all of the fields, you can sort, group, and filter your reports using those fields.

Creating and Editing Customers and Adding Jobs

Customers must be entered into the Customers & Jobs List, which is integrated into the Customer Center, before a transaction can be created. A new customer or job can be added any time. There is also a Quick Add feature that allows you to add a customer right from an invoice or sales receipt. You can go back later to edit the customer record, adding all the pertinent information.

Creating a New Customer

The more information that you enter for each customer, the better your reports will be. For example, if you track how you acquired the customer (referral, website, or print ad), you can pull a report by this field to determine where most of your customers are coming from. This could be a potential money saver if you see that the print ads are giving you a low customer acquisition rate. Perhaps you would stop paying for these print ads!

Many times, you will have repeat customers. In some cases, you may want to set up separate jobs if there will be many projects for that customer. An example is a customer who might ask for an estimate on an entirely new marketing campaign. This might include web redesign, new brochures, a logo, business cards, and more. In this case, creating a job for the customer would

 **Best Practice**

To have your customer list display in alphabetic order, type entries as last name, first name in the Customer Name field when there is an individual rather than a company as a customer.

allow you to track that job separately as well as enabling job costing. This will allow you to see what your costs are for each job, providing a more accurate picture on your profit/loss reports.

You can also set defaults for specific information for each customer such as the sales tax rate and preferred method of payment.

Tip! If you need to adjust an opening balance for a customer, right-click on the customer name or job and choose Use Register to make the change. It will be reflected in future and past transactions.

↗ Customers→Customer Center: New Customer & Job

↗ Customers→Customer Center: [select customer]→Edit

DEVELOP YOUR SKILLS 2-1

In this exercise, you will add a new customer and job. You will also edit an existing customer. Unless otherwise instructed, keep the Customer Center open. The password for all files unless otherwise stated is Password1. *Leave the company file open unless otherwise instructed.*

1. Start QuickBooks 2019 and toggle to Pro, if necessary.

   If using the trial software provided with this course on your computer or in a lab at school, you must toggle to the Pro edition every time you start QuickBooks.

2. Choose **File→Open or Restore Company**.

3. Open **DYS_Chapter02 (Company)** or restore **DYS_Chapter02 (Portable)** from your file storage location and save the file as: **DYS_Chapter02 Average Guy Designs**

   Note that you only need to save the file with a different name if you are using a portable company file. If you are working with a company file, you can simply open it from your file storage location and start working.

   It will take a few moments for the portable company file to open. You may have to update the file to the latest QuickBooks release after it opens.

4. Type **Password1** and then click **OK**. Close all windows that may be open except for the Home Page. (If the Home Page is not open, click **Home** from the icon bar.)

5. Click **Customers** [CUSTOMERS] on the Home Page and then click the **New Customer & Job** button and choose **New Customer**.

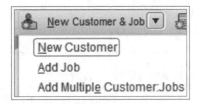

Tip! Whenever a letter in a word found on a menu bar or in a window is underlined, you can press [Alt] + the letter as a shortcut.

6. Enter this information in the Address Info tab:
   - Customer Name: **Lite Foot Dance Company**

   Because you are not entering an opening balance, you do not need to change the date for the As Of field.
   - Company Name: **Lite Foot Dance Company** (you can use keyboard shortcuts to copy/paste)
   - Full Name: **Mr. Hernando Diaz**
   - Job Title: **Owner**
   - Main Phone: **(650) 555-6379**

7. Address Details Invoice/Bill To: **541 Humboldt Ave.** `Enter` **Bayshore, CA 91547**

   Before typing the address, position your cursor at the end of the last line of text in the Invoice/ Bill To: box and press `Enter`.

8. Click **Copy>>** to copy the address to the Ship To field, which saves it as the default shipping address, and click **OK**.

   You can add additional shipping addresses by clicking the Add ➕ button to the right of the shipping address.

9. Click the **Payment Settings** tab and add this information:
   - Payment Terms: **Net 30**
   - Preferred Payment Method: **Cash**

10. Click the **Additional Info** tab and select **Referral** from the Customer Type list.

Tip! Tracking how customers were acquired can serve as a valuable marketing tool.

11. Click **OK** to complete the New Customer record and leave the Customer Center open.

Add a Job for a Customer

It is not always necessary to create jobs for customers. An appropriate example would be a customer such as an event planner, who is hired by various companies or private individuals to plan an event. In a case like this, you can create multiple jobs under the customer so that you can track each job individually and also provide this information to the customer.

DEVELOP YOUR SKILLS 2-2

In this exercise, you will create two new jobs for the Lite Foot Dance Company. The company frequently runs dance productions, and you decide to set up each production as a separate job so that you can track each job independently.

1. From the Customer Center, choose **Lite Foot Dance Company**, click the **New Customer & Job** button, and choose **Add Job**.

2. Type **Dance Explosion Tickets** in the Job Name field and click **OK**.

   Notice the right side of the window says Job Information *rather than* Customer Information.

3. To create a second job, choose **Lite Foot Dance Company**, click the **New Customer & Job** button, and choose **Add Job**.

4. Type **Flash Ballroom** in the Job Name field and click **OK**.

   Leave the Customer Center open.

Edit an Existing Customer

A customer record can be edited at any time. Any changes made to a customer record will be reflected in future and past transactions.

DEVELOP YOUR SKILLS 2-3

In this exercise, you will correct the spelling of a customer name and mark the customer as a referral.

1. Locate and then click to select **DC Athetic Club LLP** in the Customers & Jobs list.
2. Click the **Edit Customer** 🖉 button and correct the name to read: **DC Athletic Club LLC**

   You will need to correct this in four separate places in the Edit Customer window. You can also double-click on a customer to edit the record.

3. Click the **Additional Info** tab and select **Referral** as the Customer Type.
4. Click **OK** to accept the change and leave the Customer Center open.

Delete a Customer

On occasion, it is appropriate to delete a customer. An example would be a customer for whom you did an estimate and more than six months have passed with no order. You can delete a customer or job from the Customers & Jobs List as long *as you have not used it in a transaction.* If you have used it in a transaction, you can make it inactive, but you cannot delete it until after you close the books for a period and clean up your company's data.

DEVELOP YOUR SKILLS 2-4

In this exercise, you will delete a customer who has never given you any business. You will also mark another customer who is out of business as inactive. This will enable you to retain any transactions but not have the customer show up in the active list.

1. Locate **Johnson, Mary**, right-click, and choose **Delete Customer:Job**. Confirm by clicking **OK**.
2. Right-click on **Galatas, Alexis** and then choose **Make Customer:Job Inactive** and leave the Customer Center open.

   If you choose the Active Customers drop-down arrow ▾ and select All Customers, you will see the inactive customers listed with an "X" next to their names and jobs. Switch back to Active Customers to hide the Inactive Customers.

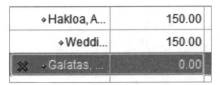

Merge Duplicate Customers

There may be some occurrences in which a customer or job was entered more than once with different spellings. If there are existing transactions under each instance of the customer, you can merge the two, selecting the correct spelling during the process. However, if there are jobs under each customer, you must move the job rather than merge the customer. There are some things to consider when deciding to merge:

- You cannot merge more than two customer names at one time.

- Merging customers or jobs cannot be reversed.

- You cannot merge a customer and a vendor because they are on different lists.

- If there are jobs under both names, you must either delete the jobs from one name or move the jobs from one name to the other name first.

DEVELOP YOUR SKILLS 2-5

In this exercise, you will fix the duplicate entry for Ashley Hakola by moving the job under the misspelled name and then merging the two names. Because this list is sorted by name, you will have to first put the list in its original order before you can move the job.

1. Click on the **diamond** ◈ at the top of the Customers & Jobs list to sort the list in its original order.

   If you don't see the diamond, the list is already sorted in the original order. You will receive a warning telling you to click the diamond if it's not in original order. The diamond heading will disappear once sorted.

   Because you can't repeat the same job name for a customer, you must edit the job first.

2. Double-click on the Job Name for **Hakloa, Ashley:Wedding** (under the misspelled customer).

3. Click after the word *Wedding* in the Job Name; type **, Petrello** and then click **OK**.

4. Mouse over the ◈ to the left of **Wedding, Petrello**, under Hakloa, Ashley, and drag the job under *Hakola, Ashley*. You will see a dashed line as you drag.

5. Double-click **Hakloa, Ashley**.

   Now you will edit the incorrect entry.

6. Type **Hakola, Ashley** as the Customer Name.

   The name must be typed exactly as it appears in the customer record it will be merged with. You can correct any other information that is wrong in the first customer record.

7. Click **OK**.

   QuickBooks displays a message asking whether you would like to merge the duplicate list entries. Remember, clicking Yes is a permanent action!

8. Click **Yes** to permanently merge the two entries.

9. Close the Customer Center window and leave the company file open.

The Income Tracker

This view will give you an overall picture of customer activity at a glance.

Customize to remove Estimates and/or Time & Expenses from this view.

Filter by a specific customer or job.

Click a column heading to sort by that column.

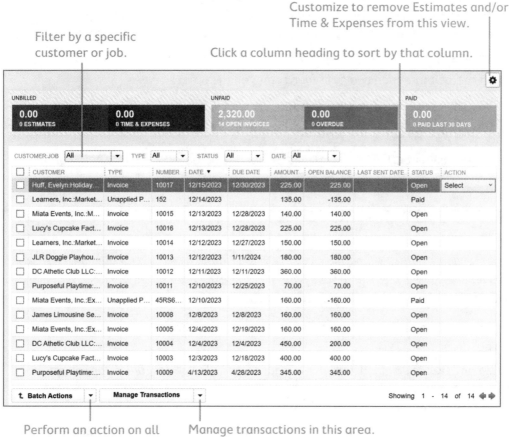

	CUSTOMER	TYPE	NUMBER	DATE ▼	DUE DATE	AMOUNT	OPEN BALANCE	LAST SENT DATE	STATUS	ACTION
☐	Huff, Evelyn:Holiday...	Invoice	10017	12/15/2023	12/30/2023	225.00	225.00		Open	Select ∨
☐	Learners, Inc.:Market...	Unapplied P...	152	12/14/2023		135.00	-135.00		Paid	
☐	Miata Events, Inc.:M...	Invoice	10015	12/13/2023	12/28/2023	140.00	140.00		Open	
☐	Lucy's Cupcake Fact...	Invoice	10016	12/13/2023	12/28/2023	225.00	225.00		Open	
☐	Learners, Inc.:Market...	Invoice	10014	12/12/2023	12/27/2023	150.00	150.00		Open	
☐	JLR Doggie Playhou...	Invoice	10013	12/12/2023	1/11/2024	180.00	180.00		Open	
☐	DC Athletic Club LLC:...	Invoice	10012	12/11/2023	12/11/2023	360.00	360.00		Open	
☐	Purposeful Playtime:...	Invoice	10011	12/10/2023	12/25/2023	70.00	70.00		Open	
☐	Miata Events, Inc.:Ex...	Unapplied P...	45RS6...	12/10/2023		160.00	-160.00		Paid	
☐	James Limousine Se...	Invoice	10008	12/8/2023	12/8/2023	160.00	160.00		Open	
☐	Miata Events, Inc.:Ex...	Invoice	10005	12/4/2023	12/19/2023	160.00	160.00		Open	
☐	DC Athletic Club LLC:...	Invoice	10004	12/4/2023	12/4/2023	450.00	200.00		Open	
☐	Lucy's Cupcake Fact...	Invoice	10003	12/3/2023	12/18/2023	400.00	400.00		Open	
☐	Purposeful Playtime:...	Invoice	10009	4/13/2023	4/28/2023	345.00	345.00		Open	

Perform an action on all selected customers/jobs.

Manage transactions in this area.

 Customers→Income Tracker

The QuickBooks Lead Center

The QuickBooks Lead Center provides you with a tool to track potential sales leads. Within the Lead Center, you can create tasks and track them, input contact and location information, and keep notes.

 Customers→Lead Center

DEVELOP YOUR SKILLS 2-6

In this exercise, you will explore the Lead Center and add Mark Kingston as a customer lead. You will add a task to contact a vendor on Mark's behalf to see whether Mark's request for 1,000 specialty-order party favor boxes can be fulfilled monthly.

1. Choose **Customers→Lead Center**.
2. Click **New Lead**.

3. Add the information below to create the lead:
   - Name: **Kingston, Mark**
   - Main Phone: **(203) 555-9991**
   - Main Email: **Kingston.Mark@email.com**

4. Click **OK** and then click **To Do** at the bottom of the window.

5. Fill in this information to enter the task:
   - Type: **Task**
   - Priority: **High**
   - With: **Vendor: Graphic Supply Shoppe**
   - Due Date: **11/15/2023**
   - Details: **Speak to Customer Rep: Can they fulfill monthly order of 1,000 high gloss 4x4-inch boxes in various colors?**

6. Click **OK** to close the Add To Do window.

   The task will not be displayed because the To-Do item is linked to the vendor and not directly to this lead.

Add a Second Task and Run the To-Do Report

7. Ensure **Kingston, Mark** is selected, click **To Do**, and then add this information to enter the task:
   - Type: **Call**
   - Priority: **High**
   - With: **Lead**
   - Due Date: **11/17/2023**
   - Details: **Call Mark with status update of box research.**

8. Click **OK** to close the Add To Do window.

   The call will be displayed because the To-Do item was associated directly with the customer.

9. Click **Reports** at the bottom of the window to launch the To Do Notes report.

   You can also see a To-Do list by going to the Company menu or viewing the calendar.

10. Close all windows and click **Home** on the icon bar. Leave the company file open.

Working with the Item List

As you saw from your work with the Customers & Jobs list, lists are the way QuickBooks stores various data that is necessary for many of the behind-the-scenes activities to occur. There are lists that store the services and products you sell, accepted payment methods, price levels, sales tax, and even the messages that appear on a customer's invoice. You might say that they, as well as the Chart of Accounts, are the backbones of QuickBooks.

Many lists are automatically created for you based on the type of company you set up, including the Chart of Accounts. Some of these lists are used to populate forms such as invoices or bills. Once the company file is created, list entries can be edited or new ones created. You can also mark a list entry as inactive rather than deleting it.

Accessing and managing these lists will differ slightly depending on whether the list is integrated into a QuickBooks center (Customers & Jobs, Vendors, and Employees) or is accessible via the List menu.

 Lists→Item List: Item

Creating Items

Before you can create an invoice, the services or products you sell must be entered into the Item List. Although there are other types of items, in this section you will just learn how to create items for service and non-inventory parts. An item is defined in QuickBooks as something that a company buys, sells, or resells in the course of business.

When creating an item, you will also select the income account to which it should be assigned. When an invoice is created with that item selected, it will automatically affect the proper income account.

TYPES OF ITEMS	
Item Type	**Description**
Service	Services you charge for or purchase (e.g., one-hour photo session, website design, specialized labor, consulting hours, or professional fees)
Non-inventory Part	A product that you purchase but don't resell, sell but do not purchase, or purchase and resell but don't stock or track as inventory
Inventory Part	Goods you purchase, track as inventory, and resell
Other Charge	Used for things like shipping charges, markups, or other line items that appear on your invoices
Subtotal	Totals all items above it on a form up to the last subtotal; use it to apply a percentage discount or surcharge to many items
Group	Quickly enters a group of individual items on an invoice
Discount	Subtracts a percentage or fixed amount from a total or subtotal; do not use for an early payment discount
Payment	Records a partial payment at the time of sale; reduces the amount owed on an invoice
Sales Tax Item	Calculates a single sales tax at a specific rate that you pay to a single tax agency (may not appear in all businesses)
Sales Tax Group	Calculates and individually tracks two or more sales tax items that apply to the same sale; customer sees only the total sales tax (may not appear in all businesses)

Service Items

Service items are used in QuickBooks to track services that you both sell to customers and purchase from vendors. If the item is not in the Item List, it can't be bought or sold through an invoice or bill. Service items can also be used on timesheets and paychecks to track time.

Non-inventory Items

Non-inventory part items are things that a business buys but doesn't stock as inventory. Some companies will use purchase orders to obtain non-inventory items to track items that are used in their businesses but not resold to customers, such as paper and printer ink. You can also purchase non-inventory items through the Enter Bills window by utilizing the Items tab. In order to track both purchase and sales information for an item, you need to identify that the item is "used in assemblies or is purchased for a specific customer:job" in the New or Edit Item window.

Using Subitems

If you wish to track your items in a more detailed fashion, you can use subitems. They can be created for any item on your Item List and can be useful on reports to determine aspects of your business such as profitability. You might use subitems in your company file to:

- Differentiate between broad categories of products/services and individual items within them

- Manage pricing levels for volume discounts

- Differentiate between measurements

- Track multiple vendors for an item

When using subitems, you state an item with no price for the main item, and then you can list prices for the subitems beneath it or leave them blank if you wish to apply pricing directly on sales forms.

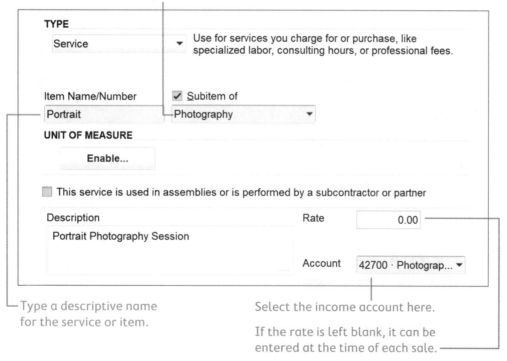

In this exercise, you will create three new items. Guy is now offering photography services and will add it as a service item. He is also adding specialty paper as a non-inventory item so he can track his cost of goods for a photography job. You will start by creating the service item. You will also add an item as the first subitem for Photograph.

1. Choose **Lists→Item List**.

2. Click the **Item** drop-down arrow ▼ at the bottom of the window and choose **New**.

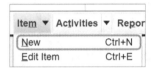

3. Tap ⌨Tab to select the default service item type, *Service*.

4. Add this information to create the item:

   - Item Name/Number: **Photography**
   - Description: **Photography services**
   - Account: **42700•Photography Income**

     It is imperative that you enter the correct account here! An item directs the flow of dollars from the sales input form to the account indicated here. You are skipping the rate field so that you can enter a rate quoted to the customer directly on the sales form.

5. Click **OK** and leave the Item List open.

Create a Non-Inventory Part

6. Click the **Item** button, choose to create a new **Non-inventory Part**, using the following information:

   - Item Name/Number: **Paper**
   - Description: **Specialty paper**
   - Price: **29.95**
   - Account: **615** (then ⌨Tab to fill in 61500•Job Materials and click **OK**)
     Leave the Item List open.

Create a Subitem

7. Click the **Item** button, choose to create a new **Service** item, using the following information:

   - Item Name/Number: **Portrait**
   - Click in the checkbox to choose **Subitem Of**
   - Subitem Of: **Photography**
   - Description: **Portrait photography session**
   - Account: **42700•Photography Income**

8. Click **OK**.

   The item is indented under Photography.

9. Close the Item List window and leave the company file open.

Creating Invoices

Once you have set up your initial Customers & Jobs List and the Item List, you can begin entering sales transactions. In this section, you will learn to create invoices and use Accounts Receivable, which is the account debited when invoices are created. When you create an invoice, you *must* specify a customer because Accounts Receivable (along with the customer's individual sub-register) will be debited by the transaction.

Invoicing a customer is also known as a customer making a purchase "on account."

After you select your customer from the drop-down list at the top of the form, all of the relevant information you entered in that customer's record will fill into the appropriate fields on the Create Invoices window.

Additional tools are available on the Formatting, Send/Ship, and Reports tabs.

From the Main tab, you can email invoices, print, attach files, delete and receive payments, and more.

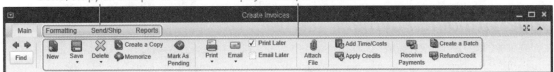

Select items and enter descriptions and quantities in this area. The amount is automatically calculated.

The default template is Intuit Service Invoice, but other templates are available that can be customized.

Change or set the payment terms for a customer here.

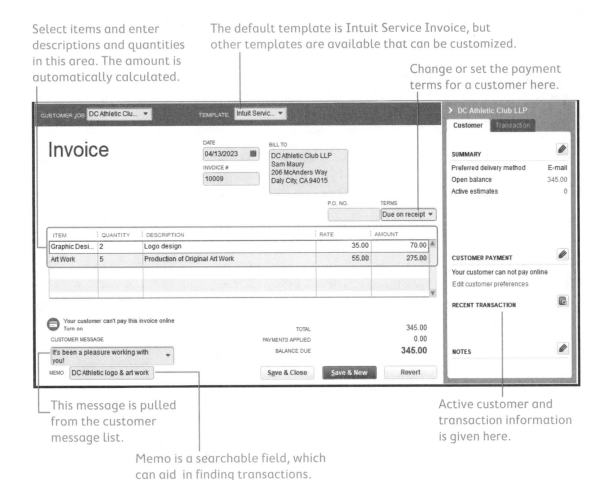

This message is pulled from the customer message list.

Active customer and transaction information is given here.

Memo is a searchable field, which can aid in finding transactions.

Entering Customers Not Already on the Customers & Jobs List

When you type a new entry into a field that draws from a list, QuickBooks gives you the opportunity to add the record to the list. You can choose to Quick Add the new record (the name will be entered into the list without accompanying information, which you can add at a later date) or to complete a full setup (a New Customer window appears in which you can type all of the relevant information).

Form Templates

When you first install QuickBooks, Intuit provides you with various templates, such as the Intuit Service Invoice, Intuit Product Invoice, Intuit Professional Invoice, and Intuit Packing Slip. You can continue to use these invoices as they are, create custom invoices to meet your specific needs, or download templates from the QuickBooks website. In this section, you will work with one of the default invoice forms—the Intuit Service Invoice.

Understanding Payment Terms

Payment terms dictate an agreement between buyer and seller as to when and how much is to be paid for a product or service. In the case of a "Net 30" payment term, the net (or entire) amount of the invoice is due in thirty days. By default, if payment terms are not stated for a customer or on an invoice, QuickBooks will set the payment due date to be ten days from the date of sale.

Invoice Status Tracker

 In QuickBooks 2019, you can easily track the status of invoices right from the Create Invoices window.

One of the most helpful new features in QuickBooks 2019 (in my humble opinion...) is the ability to track the status of your invoices right from the Create Invoices window. If you click the "See History" link to the right of "Invoice," it will produce a window that shows the invoice's history.

The dates that are tracked with this new feature are:

- Date created
- Due Date and Past Due Status
- If it has been emailed and whether it has been viewed by the recipient
- The date payment was received
- The date the funds were deposited in your account

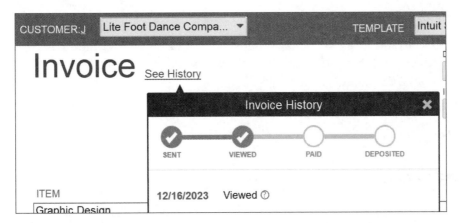

When you click the See History link in the Create Invoices window, you can see the current status of the invoice to aid you in managing your receivables.

Invoices can be mailed directly from the Create Invoices window. If you are set up to collect credit card payments through QuickBooks, there will be a link in the email to make it easy for the customer to click and pay you.

Going Behind the Scenes

Behind the Scenes is a special feature in this book that allows you to take a peek at the accounting that QuickBooks is doing for you when you enter information into forms. In the following illustration, you will find the first instance of the "Behind the Scenes" feature. Remember that the names used in this feature are the account names QuickBooks uses, not traditional accounting nomenclature. If you would like to learn more about basic accounting principles and what the "behind the scenes stuff" is all about, check out Appendix A in this book.

BEHIND THE SCENES

When creating invoices, QuickBooks takes care of all of the accounting for you. Following is an illustration of the accounting that goes on behind the scenes for the first invoice you will create in the following exercise:

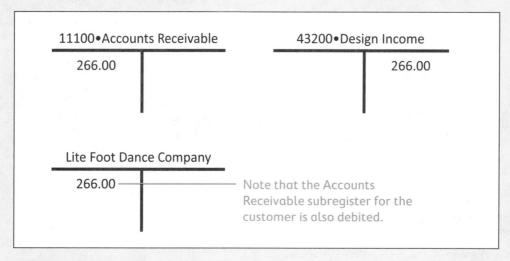

Note that the Accounts Receivable subregister for the customer is also debited.

Customers→Create Invoices

DEVELOP YOUR SKILLS 2-8

In this exercise, you will create invoices for customers. Hernando Diaz has just emailed you to ask you to do a job for his company, Lite Foot Dance Company. You have agreed to a rate of $38/hour and to grant him payment terms of "Net 15." You've already set up the job.

1. Click the **Create Invoices** 📄 task icon in the Customers area of the Home Page.
2. Click the **Customer:Job** drop-down arrow ▼ at the top of the window and then choose **Lite Foot Dance Company:Dance Explosion Tickets**.

Notice that the customer's address and terms fill in for you from the underlying list.

3. Enter this information to complete the invoice:

> **Tip!** When you type in a date field, you do not need to include the slash marks. QuickBooks will format the date properly for you once you move to the next field.

- Date: **121623**
- Invoice #: **10018**
- Terms: **Net 15**
- Item: **g** (*Graphic Design* will fill in; tap Tab)
- Quantity: **7**
- Description: Replace *Graphic Design* with **Branding and logo design for new dance studio**
- Rate: **38** (click **OK** in the Price Level/Billing Rate Level window, if necessary)
- Customer Message: **Thank you for your business.**
- Memo: **Lite Foot: Graphic Design**

QuickBooks automatically calculates the total amount. Because the rate was left blank when this item was created, you needed to enter the rate. QuickBooks recalculates the amount once you've moved to another field.

Notice the Customer and Transaction tabs that appear to the right of the Invoice. You can edit the customer record or see any prior transactions using these tabs.

4. Click **Save & New**, click **Yes** to save the new Payment terms, close the Check Spelling on Form window, and leave the company file open.

Because you changed the terms, you will have a choice, once you save the invoice, of changing them permanently for this customer or just for this invoice. QuickBooks will warn you every time the date of a transaction is more than 30 days in the future. If you would like to turn the date notification off, you can edit the Accounting Preferences.

BEHIND THE SCENES BRIEF

11000•Accounts Receivable DR 266.00; **43200•Design Income CR <266.00>**

> **Note!** The Accounts Receivable subregister for the customer is also debited. In this feature, *DR* indicates a debit and *CR* indicates a credit. CR amounts display with brackets.

Create an Invoice for a New Customer

A new customer, Mary Jones, has stopped by Average Guy Designs' office to pick up a project you just completed for her. You will add her as a new customer "on the fly" while creating the invoice for her. Your insertion point should be in the Customer:Job field at the top of a new invoice. If this is not the case, choose Create Invoices under the Customer tab.

5. In the Customer:Job field, type **Jones, Mary** and then tap Tab .

6. Click **Quick Add** in the Customer:Job Not Found window.

Since you chose Quick Add, you will need to edit the Customer later to fill in additional information.

7. Tap Tab to go to the Date field and then type: **121823**

You can also tap the + or - keys to move the date forward or backward one day at a time.

8. Enter this information to complete the invoice and leave the invoice # as 10019:

- Terms: **Net 15**
- Item: **A** (then $\boxed{\text{Tab}}$ to accept *Art Work*)
- Quantity: **6**
- Rate: **45** (dismiss the Price Levels window, if necessary)
- Customer Message: **It's been a pleasure working with you!**
- Memo: **Jones: Art Work**

  Memos are searchable fields and can be displayed on reports. It's a good idea to use them and be consistent in how you enter the memo. In this case, the customer's name was used and the type of service bought.

  BEHIND THE SCENE BRIEF

  11000•Accounts Receivable DR 270.00; **43200•Design Income CR <270.00>**

9. Click **Save & Close**; click **Yes** in the *Information Changed* window to accept the Terms, close the *Spelling* window, if necessary, and leave the company file open.

   Saying yes to this prompt will update the customer's record with the payment terms you entered.

Receiving Payments

After you have created invoices and a payment is received, entering it through the Receive Payments window will be the next step. Using Receive Payments will credit accounts receivable and the appropriate customer subregister. The other half of the equation (the account to be debited) depends on how you treat the payments received.

> **Tip!** It is very important to use the Received Payments window. If you don't, the invoices will remain open, and your income and amounts in accounts receivable will be overstated. When you receive payments, there will be a number notification on the Record Deposits task icon. This serves as a reminder to deposit the payment in the bank.

Record Deposits

Options for Accepting Payments

You have several options of receiving payments in QuickBooks to match the ways your customers are actually paying you. You can also add forms of payments such as gift cards.

The Undeposited Funds Account

When you receive payments through an invoice or sales receipts, these funds are grouped into the Undeposited Funds asset account. QuickBooks automatically creates this Other Current Asset account for you. It is a self-reconciling account, meaning that after you deposit the funds using the record deposit or make deposit task, Undeposited Funds will be affected automatically.

The default setting is for all payments received and cash sales to be placed in the Undeposited Funds account. It is a Cash and Cash Equivalent account.

Let's look at accounting scenarios that result when you receive payments.

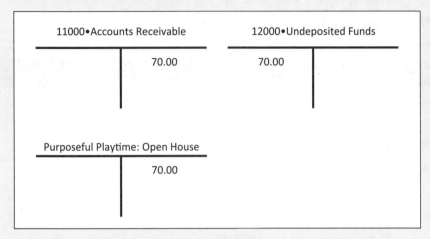

Using the Undeposited Funds account when receiving a payment

Receiving a customer payment directly into a bank account

Customers→Receive Payments

DEVELOP YOUR SKILLS 2-9

In this exercise, you will record payments received from invoiced customers. You have just received a credit card payment from Purposeful Playtime for the Open House job.

1. Click the **Receive Payments** task icon in the Customers area of the Home Page.

2. Enter this information to complete the payment:

   • Received From: **Purposeful Playtime:Open House**

   • Payment Amount: **70** (then Tab)

   Notice that when you type the amount, it is automatically applied to the invoice listed with the same amount. If no invoices match the amount, it would be applied to invoice(s) beginning with the oldest one.

   • Date: **121823**

   • Payment Method: **Credit Debit**

   The Enter Card window will open with Visa as the default.

- Card number: **8977554621339667**
- Exp date: **04**, and then ⌷Tab⌷ and type: **25**; click **Done**.

Note!⟋ The Card Security Code (CSC) cannot be saved. That would violate the Payment Applications Best Practices guidelines by the Payment Card Industry (PCI) for software providers.

- Memo: **Purposeful: Open House**

3. Click **Save & New**.

BEHIND THE SCENES BRIEF

12000•Undeposited Funds DR 70.00; **11000•Accounts Receivable CR <70.00>**

Receive a Partial Payment

Guy just received a check from Lucy's Cupcake Factory for $100 to apply to the oldest outstanding invoice. You will receive this payment.

4. Enter this information to complete the partial payment:

- Received From: **Lucy's Cupcake Factory:Marketing**
- Payment Amount: **100**
- Date: **121923**
- Method of payment: **Check**
- Check #: **2548**
- Memo: `Lucy: Marketing`

By choosing to leave this as an underpayment, when you receive the next payment from this customer, the Receive Payments window will show that there is a balance due of $300.00 for invoice #10003.

Partial payment applied to oldest invoice

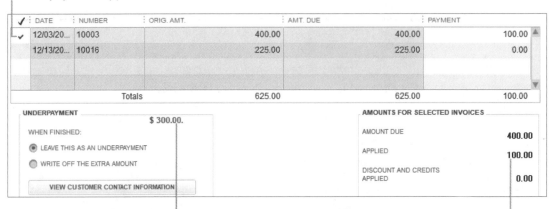

✓	DATE	NUMBER	ORIG. AMT.	AMT. DUE	PAYMENT
✓	12/03/20...	10003	400.00	400.00	100.00
	12/13/20...	10016	225.00	225.00	0.00
	Totals		625.00	625.00	100.00

UNDERPAYMENT $ 300.00.

WHEN FINISHED:
◉ LEAVE THIS AS AN UNDERPAYMENT
○ WRITE OFF THE EXTRA AMOUNT

VIEW CUSTOMER CONTACT INFORMATION

AMOUNTS FOR SELECTED INVOICES
AMOUNT DUE 400.00
APPLIED 100.00
DISCOUNT AND CREDITS APPLIED 0.00

Balance due and option of how to treat underpayment   Amount applied

BEHIND THE SCENES BRIEF

12000•Undeposited Funds DR 100.00; **11000•Accounts Receivable CR <100.00>**

5. Click **Save & Close** when you have ensured that you have entered all information correctly and leave the company file open.

Selecting the Correct Form for Customer Sales

There are three main ways of recording customer sales and charges. Choosing the appropriate form can depend on when payment is received.

COMPARING CUSTOMER FORMS	
Form	**When to Use**
Invoices	Use this when a customer does not make a payment at the time of service and/or receipt of product. The invoice amount is held in Accounts Receivable.
Sales Receipts	Use this when a customer makes a payment at the time of service and/or receipt of product. Accounts Receivable is not affected. This form is a combination of the Create Invoices and Receive Payments windows.
Statements	If you have a customer for whom you do multiple jobs throughout the month, you can gather the charges and send one statement for all of them. The statement will show previous account balances, new charges, and payments for a specific time period.

The customer does not need to be entered if you use a sales receipt. However, you may still want to enter the customer so that it produces more meaningful sales reports. You can use the Quick Add method of adding a new customer on the fly.

If you use this form, by default the payment will still be placed in the Undeposited Funds account (a holding account for payments received but not yet deposited).

Create a Sales Receipt for a Customer

When a customer pays at the time of sale and there is no need to create an invoice, you can generate a Sales Receipt for the customer. Remember, a Sales Receipt does not affect Accounts Receivable but will still affect Undeposited Funds.

BEHIND THE SCENES

The behind-the-scenes accounting that occurs when you enter cash sales is a hybrid of the two transactions (Creating Invoices and Receiving Payments) with the elimination of the middleman—Accounts Receivable.

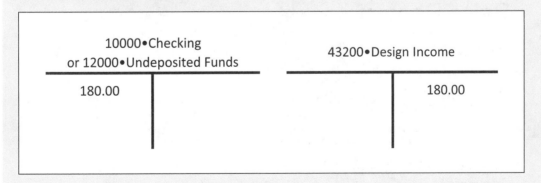

In this exercise, you will receive payment at the time of the sale. Ashley was in the area so she stopped by your office to pick up the art work you created for her. Because she is prepared to pay with cash, you will enter a sales receipt instead of an invoice.

1. Click the **Create Sales Receipts** 📑 task icon in the Customers area of the Home Page.

   The Enter Sales Receipts window opens with the insertion point in the Customer:Job field.

2. Use this information for the sale:

   • Customer Job: **H** (select **Hakola, Ashley:Wedding**)

   • Date: **122023**

   • Method of Payment: **Cash**

   • Item: **a** (then Tab to accept *Art Work*)

   • Qty: **4**

   • Rate: **45**

   • Customer Message: **Thank you for your business.**

   • Memo: **Hakola: Wedding, Art Work**

BEHIND THE SCENES BRIEF
12000•Undeposited Funds DR 180.00; **43200•Design Income CR <180.00>**

3. Click **Save & New**; close the Check Spelling on Form window.

   Your insertion point should be in the Customer:Job field of a new Enter Sales Receipt window.

Record a Sales Receipt Without a Specified Customer

Because Accounts Receivable is not affected when you enter a cash sale, you can create a sales receipt without choosing a customer. This may come in handy if you sell something to someone just once and don't need that customer listed in your Customers & Jobs List or if you provide services in a different capacity. In this exercise, Guy worked with another photographer to take photos at a company party.

4. Use this information to complete the sales receipt:

ⓐ Choose **Check** as the form of payment

ⓑ Date: **122223**

ⓒ Check No.: **1894**

ⓓ Item: **ph** (choose **Photography**)

   Note the Sale No. increments automatically.

ⓔ Rate: **200** (click **Save & Close**)

12000•Undeposited Funds DR 200.00; **42700•Photography Income CR <200.00>**

This transaction will debit Undeposited Funds *and credit* Photography Income, *but there will be no customer tracked. The purpose of selecting a customer for a sales receipt is to ensure that you can produce meaningful customer reports, such as* Sales by Customer Summary, *if they are important to your business.*

Adjusting Customer Transactions

It is inevitable that you will need to deal with errors or modifications to transactions. It is very important that you do this properly to ensure that everything behind the scenes is correct.

Editing an Existing Transaction

To edit an existing transaction in QuickBooks, you simply open the window where the transaction is recorded and make the changes. You do need to think about the implications of any modifications that you make, though. Many transactions are tied to others, and a change to one can affect another. For instance, if an invoice has been paid, both the invoice and the payment are linked in QuickBooks.

✔ Best Practice

After a transaction has been cleared during the reconciliation process, it should not be changed. Because each situation may require a different solution, you may want to check with an accountant.

Voiding vs. Deleting Transactions

QuickBooks allows you to either void or delete a transaction you no longer need recorded. In most cases, you will want to void a transaction so that you can keep a record of it. This will remove everything from behind the scenes and yet leave evidence that the transaction existed.

Locating Transactions in QuickBooks

QuickBooks provides two methods for you to choose from in order to locate transactions in your company file.

The Find Feature

The Find feature helps you locate a transaction if you don't know all of the information about it from within the form itself. There are two options within Find:

- **Simple** to perform basic searches

- **Advanced** to perform more complex searches, utilizing filters to help to sort through all of your data

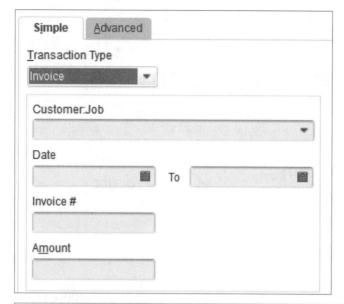

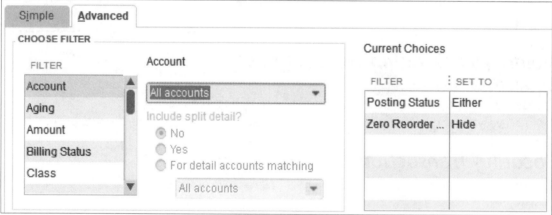

Simple and Advanced Find—Rather than scroll through hundreds, if not thousands, of customers or invoices, use Find. Simple gives you a way to search when you know the customer, while Advanced is more powerful and will give better results when you're not sure of the customer.

The Search Feature

Search is a more powerful feature accessed above the icon bar. It allows you to search the entire company file for the following types of information:

- Forms/transactions (invoices, estimates, and so on)

- People and companies (customers, vendors, employees, and other names)

- List entries (items, tax items, and so on)

- Amounts and dates
- Menu commands (QuickBooks opens the menu and highlights the command for you)
- Specific text within notes, descriptions, memos, and transactions

You can modify your key word(s) here.

Use these links to see the invoice or perform a task.

Edit customer information and view payments.

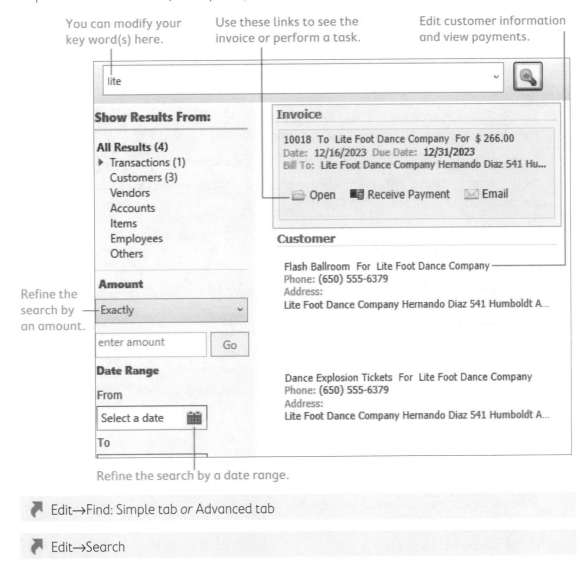

Refine the search by an amount.

Refine the search by a date range.

↱ Edit→Find: Simple tab *or* Advanced tab

↱ Edit→Search

Fixing Errors

The following table outlines a common customer-related error, the effects of the error behind the scenes, and how to correct the error.

A COMMON ERROR AND ITS FIX

Error	Effect Behind the Scenes	The Fix
An invoice is entered but the Receive Payments window is not used when the payment is deposited.	Your income will be double-stated and Accounts Receivable for the customer is not "cleared out."	Delete the deposit and then enter the transaction properly using the Receive Payments window.

Remember that if you need to choose between two solutions, pick the one that is less likely to overstate assets and income.

DEVELOP YOUR SKILLS 2-11

In this exercise, you will search for and edit an invoice containing an incorrectly entered rate for an item.

1. Choose **Edit→Search**, resizing the window, if necessary, and then click the **Update Search Information** link to bring in any new information.

2. Click in the search field at the top of the window; type **lite** and then tap ⏎ Enter.

3. Mouse over the **10018** Invoice transaction displayed for **Lite Foot Dance Company** until the buttons appear and then click **Open**.

4. Change the rate for the Branding and logo work to: **35**

5. Click **Save & Close**; click **Yes** to record the transaction with the changes and close the spelling window, if necessary.

6. Close the Search window and leave the company file open.

Receive Payment for an Invoice

Guy has just received a check from Mary Jones for $270. Rather than go directly to Make Deposits, you will enter the payment using Receive Payments. If you did incorrectly use the Make Deposits window, you would have stated the income twice! Then you would need to delete the deposit and use Receive Payments. You will use Find to locate Mary Jones' invoice.

7. Choose **Edit→Find** and ensure the Simple tab is displayed.

8. Ensure Transaction Type is **Invoice**, choose **Jones, Mary** from the **Customer:Job** drop-down list, and then click **Find**.

   There will be one transaction listed and it is highlighted.

9. Click **Go To** and then click **Receive Payments** from the ribbon at the top of the Create Invoices window.

10. The Customer Payment window will be prefilled. Enter this information to receive the payment:
    - Date: **122323**
    - Payment method: **Check**
    - Check #: **470**
    - Memo: **Jones: Payment 10019**

    ### BEHIND THE SCENES BRIEF

    12000•Undeposited Funds DR 270.00; **11000•Accounts Receivable CR <270.00>**

11. Click **Save & Close** and note that the invoice is now marked Paid.

12. Close the Create Invoices window and then close the Find window. Leave the company file open.

Running Customer-Related Reports

There are many ways to access the various preset reports in QuickBooks. We will focus on three methods in this section. The first will be the Report Center, where you see a listing of all the reports and can select date ranges prior to viewing report. The second will be the Reports Menu, where reports are grouped by category, such as Company & Financial or Accountant & Taxes. The third will be a QuickReport, which can be run from within the Customer or Vendor Information window.

The Report Center

Like other QuickBooks windows, there are several tabs to select from. When you first open the Report Center, you will be on the Standard tab. From here you can select a category to see associated reports and also change the date range. Reports can be customized and also memorized, making it easier to run next time. Some of the basic functions that the tabs allow you to do include:

- Run a memorized report
- View reports marked as favorite
- View recently run reports
- Run reports created by contributors

Reports Menu

This option might be quicker after you are familiar with the categories of reports in QuickBooks. When you are in the report, you will have the same options to customize, print, export, and more. You will also see additional report types such as Scheduled Reports and Commented Reports.

QuickReport

A QuickReport can be run from the various center and list windows. QuickReports show all transactions recorded in QuickBooks for a particular center or account. You will use this report to get a quick snapshot of all customer transactions for James Limousine Service in the Develop Your Skills exercise.

FLASHBACK TO GAAP: TIME PERIOD

Remember that it is implied that the activities of the business can be divided into time periods.

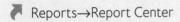 Reports→Report Center

Customers→Customer Center: [select customer]→QuickReport

In this exercise, you will help Guy create customer reports. One helpful report is the Open Invoices report that displays all unpaid invoices. You will produce this for Average Guy Designs, but first you will produce a QuickReport for James Limousine Service.

1. Click the **Customers**  button on the Home Page to open the Customer Center; choose **James Limousine Service**.

   You must always select the list item on which you wish to run a QuickReport.

2. Click the **QuickReport** link at the right of the Customer Center window.

3. Type **a** to select **All dates**. Resize the window to see all of the transactions, if necessary.

   A customer QuickReport can also display all transactions for a selected customer within a designated date range.

4. Close the QuickReport and the Customer Center windows.

Create an Open Invoices Report

5. Choose **Reports→Report Center**.

6. Select **Customers & Receivables** and then locate and click **Open Invoices**.

7. Click the **Dates:** drop-down arrow ▼, choose **All**, and then click **Run**.

   QuickBooks will display the Open Invoices report, which shows all unpaid invoices.

Tip! You can change your view from Carousel (the default) to List View or Grid View at the top of the Report Center window.

8. Close the Open Invoices report and the Report Center and leave the company file open.

Sales Reports

Running sales reports will help you to stay on top of your company's sales. Sales reports are grouped by customer, item, and sales by rep (if sales reps have been set up). You can also view sales information by job if you have jobs set up for your company.

 Reports→Sales

In this exercise, you will run a report showing the dollar value of sales based on item.

1. Choose **Reports→Sales→Sales by Item Summary**.

2. Type **a** to set **All** as the date range for the report.

   The report will show totals and percentages broken down by services you sold. This could prove to be an important report to look at to determine which services are best sellers.

3. Close the report, choosing not to memorize it.

4. Leave the company file open if you choose to go on to Tackle the Tasks or close it if you are finished working in QuickBooks.

Tackle the Tasks

Now is your chance to work a little more with Average Guy Designs and apply the skills that you have learned in this chapter to accomplish additional tasks. You will use the same company file you used in the Develop Your Skills exercises throughout this chapter. Enter the following tasks, referring back to the concepts in the chapter as necessary. If you are using the trial software for this course on your computer or in a lab at school, you must toggle to the Pro edition every time you start QuickBooks.

Add Customers	Add the following customers: York, Olivia, 1021 Miller St., Medford, OR 97504; (541) 555-8921; Referral; Due on Receipt (There are no jobs for this customer.) Masters Manufacturing, James McDonald, 575 Industrial Way, Eureka, CA 95501; (707) 555-6722; From Advertisement; Net 15; Job: Outside Signage Tim's BBQ Palooza, Tim Laughlin, 8 College Drive, Berkeley, CA 94608; (510) 555-4419; Referral; Net 30; Job: Menu Design
Create Items	Service item: Print; Description: Print Layout Services; $40; 48800•Print Layout Income. Service item: Video; Description: Basic Video Editing Services; $55; 48900•Video Editing Income (you will need to set up a new account, scroll up to find Add New). Service item: Adv. Video; Description: Advanced Video Editing Services; $75; 48900•Video Editing Income. Service item: Branding; Description: Comprehensive Branding Plan; $400; 43200•Design Income.
Create Invoices	Olivia York; 12/23/2023; 5 hours of Print Layout Services; Thank you for your business.; York: Print Layout Masters Manufacturing:Outside Signage; 12/26/2023; 8 hours of Print Layout Services; Thank you for your business.; Masters: Print Layout Tim's BBQ Palooza:Menu Design; 12/27/2023; Comprehensive Branding Plan; It's been a pleasure working with you!; Tim's: Branding
Receive Payments (remember to choose the correct job)	Receive full payment for invoice #10018 from Hernando Diaz of Lite Foot Dance Company: Dance Explosion; check #1632; 12/27/2023; Lite Foot: Payment 10018. Receive full payment for invoice #10013 from JLR Doggie Playhouse; check #872; 12/29/2023; JLR: Payment 10013. Receive $200 payment for invoice #10003 from Lucy's Cupcake Factory: Marketing; check #341; 12/29/2023; leave as underpayment; Lucy's: Payment 10003. Receive $50 payment for invoice #10014 from Learners, Inc.: Marketing MasterCard # 9565332412894455; exp. 03/2025; Date: 12/30/2023; Learners: Payment 10014.
Generate Reports	Create a report that will show the contact information for all of your customers.

Self-Assessment

Check your knowledge of this chapter's key concepts and skills using the Self-Assessment quiz here, in your ebook, or in your eLab course.

1. A customer is a person or a company to whom or which you issue funds. *True* *False*

2. You can delete a customer from the Customers & Jobs List as long as that customer hasn't been used in a transaction. *True* *False*

3. If you want to invoice a customer for a service, the service must first be set up as an item. *True* *False*

4. When you use a sales receipt to bill a customer, Accounts Receivable is debited. *True* *False*

5. Invoicing a customer is also known as a customer making a purchase on account. *True* *False*

6. You can enter customers "on the fly" in the Create Invoices window. *True* *False*

7. When you void a transaction, every trace of it is removed from behind the scenes, but evidence that the transaction existed remains in QuickBooks. *True* *False*

8. To use the QuickBooks' Find feature, you must know the transaction date. *True* *False*

9. If an invoice is entered but the Receive Payments window is not used when the payment is deposited, your income will be double-stated. *True* *False*

10. The Invoice Status Tracker shows you how many days an invoice is overdue. *True* *False*

11. Which account is debited when invoices are created?
    A. Accounts Payable
    B. Accounts Receivable
    C. Checking
    D. Income Account

12. Which type of account is the Undeposited Funds account?
    A. Asset
    B. Liability
    C. Equity
    D. Income

13. Which QuickBooks form would you use if a customer is making a purchase on account?
    A. Enter Sales Receipts
    B. Create Sales Form
    C. Enter Invoice Receipt
    D. Create Invoices

14. Which type of information can you find using the QuickBooks Search feature?
    A. Forms/transactions
    B. Amounts and dates
    C. Menu commands
    D. All of these options

Reinforce Your Skills

Emily Holly's company, Electrical Energy, has expanded enough for her to hire you as a QuickBooks coordinator. The coordinator now has to catch up on some transactions, adding a new service, adding a customer, editing a customer, and making changes to a transaction. The password for all files unless otherwise stated is Password1. Leave the company file open unless otherwise instructed. If you are using the trial software on your computer or in a lab at school, remember to toggle to the Pro edition every time you start QuickBooks.

REINFORCE YOUR SKILLS 2-1

Manage Your Customers & Jobs List

In this exercise, you will create and edit Customers & Jobs List entries for Emily.

1. Choose **File→Open or Restore Company**.
2. Open **RYS_Chapter02 (Company)** or restore **RYS_Chapter02 (Portable)** from your file storage location and save your file as: **RYS_Chapter02 Electrical Energy**
3. Choose **Customers→Customer Center**.
4. Double-click **Campbell, Heather** to open it for editing.
5. Change the customer's name to: **Cohen, Heather**

   You will have to change the name in four locations. This customer's name will change in all of the transactions that Heather was involved in, as well as in all of her future transactions.

6. Click **OK** to accept the change and then leave the Customer Center open.

Add a New Customer

7. Click the **New Customer & Job** button and then choose **New Customer**.
8. Use the following information to set up the new customer:
   - Customer Name: **Chai, Linda**
   - First: **Linda**
   - Last: **Chai**
   - Main Phone: **(914) 555-4433**
   - Mailing Address: **PO Box 7762** [Enter] **Greenburgh, NY 10607**
   - Type: **Referral: Residential**
   - Terms: **Net 15**
9. Click **OK** to accept the new record and leave the Customer Center open.

Add a Job to a Customer

10. Click the customer you just created, **Chai, Linda**, to select it.

11. Choose **New Customer & Job→Add Job**.

12. Type **New Home** as the name of the job; click **OK**.

13. Close the Customer Center window and leave the company file open.

REINFORCE YOUR SKILLS 2-2

Create a New Non-Inventory Subitem

In this exercise, you will create a two-sided subitem for an existing item so you can use it on a sales form. You will select an expense account and an offsetting income account for this item. This is necessary as the item needs to be purchased and then resold to the customer and still affect the correct accounts.

1. Choose **Lists→Item List** and then choose **Item→New**.

2. Enter this information to create a new subitem:

- Type: **Non-inventory Part**
- Item Name/Number: **Gate Handle**
- Subitem: **Electric Gate**
- Click the checkbox for **This item is used in assemblies or is purchased for a specific customer:job**
- Description on Purchase Transactions: **Replacement Gate Handle**
- Expense Account: **51400•Job Materials Purchased**
- Tax Code: **Non**
- Income Account: **45100•Job Income**

3. Click **OK** to accept the new item and close the window.

4. Close the Item List and leave the company file open.

REINFORCE YOUR SKILLS 2-3

Enter Sales Transactions

In this exercise, you will create invoices for Electrical Energy.

1. Choose **Customers→Create Invoices**.

2. Choose **Chai, Linda:New Home** as the Customer:Job.

3. Use this information to complete the invoice:

- Date: **041623**
- Template: **Intuit Service Invoice Template**
- Invoice #: **Chai 01**
- Item: **01.1 Plans**
- Qty: **15**
- Description: **New Home Plan**

- Rate: **80**
- Customer Message: **Thank you for your business.**
- Memo: `Chai: New Home Plan`

4. Click **Save & New** to record the transaction.

5. Click **Yes** on the Future Transactions window, and then click **Add** on the Check Spelling on Form window.

Enter a Job "On the Fly" for a Customer in an Invoice

Now you will enter a new job for a customer while creating an invoice.

6. Use this information to complete the Invoice and add the Customer:
   - Customer:Job: **Akiyama, Hiroki** (choose **Quick Add**)
   - Date: **041823**
   - Invoice #: **Akiy 01**
   - Item: **08.20 Repair**
   - Qty: **1**
   - Rate: **350**
   - Customer Message: **Thank you for your business.**
   - Memo: `Akiyama: Circuit Repair`

7. Click **Save & Close** to record the transaction, click **Yes** on the Future Transactions window, and then leave the company window open.

REINFORCE YOUR SKILLS 2-4

Receive Payments

In this exercise, you will receive the payment for the invoice you created earlier.

1. Choose **Customers→Receive Payments**.

2. Choose **Chai, Linda:New Home** from the Received From field and use this information to complete the payment:
   - Amount: **1200**
   - Date: **042423**
   - Payment Method: **Check**
   - Check number: **1574**
   - Memo: `Chai: New Home`

3. Click **Save & Close**, click **Yes** in the Future Transactions window, and leave the company file open.

   Notice the Record Deposits notification appear.

Find a Transaction

You realized that the amount recorded on the invoice for Hiroki Akiyama was incorrect, and you need to edit the transaction. In this exercise, you will use the QuickBooks Find feature to locate the transaction.

1. Choose **Edit→Find** and use the following information to complete the Find:
    - Leave Transaction Type as Invoice
    - Customer:Job: **Akiyama, Hiroki** (click **Find**)

    The invoices for the customer will be displayed in the bottom of the window.
2. Double-click the invoice dated **04/18/2023** in the bottom portion of the window.

    The Invoice window will open.
3. Change the amount to **325** and tap ⎡Tab⎤ to recalculate.
4. Click **Save & Close**, click **Yes** to record the changes, click **Yes** in the Future Transactions window, close the Find window, and leave the company file open.

Run Customer-Related Reports

In this exercise, you will run three reports for Emily, beginning with a QuickReport.

1. Click the **Customers** button on the Home Page to open the Customer Center.
2. Click **Willow Gardens** to select it.
3. Click the **QuickReport** link at the far-right side of the window.
4. Set the date range to **All**.

    You will see a report that shows all of the transactions for Willow Gardens.
5. Choose **Window→Close All** and leave the company file open.
6. Choose **Reports→Customers & Receivables→Customer Phone List**.
7. Double-click **Akiyama, Hiroki**.

    QuickBooks will open an Edit Customer window, from where you can make any changes to the customer's information.
8. Add Hiroki's Main Phone number, **(914) 555-5124**, and then click **OK**.
9. Close the report and then choose **Reports→Company & Financial→Income by Customer Summary**.
10. Change the Dates to **All**.
11. Close the company file and choose not to Memorize the Report.

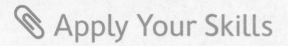

Apply Your Skills

The Wet Noses Veterinary Clinic advertising campaign was a success and the company has acquired new customers. It has also added new services. In this exercise, you will be creating new customers and adding those services. You will also perform daily tasks like creating invoices, receiving payments, and running reports. The password for all files unless otherwise stated is Password1. *After starting QuickBooks, remember to toggle to Pro as necessary.*

APPLY YOUR SKILLS 2-1 QG

Set Up Customers and Jobs

In this exercise, you will be setting up some new customers and creating jobs.

1. Choose **File→Open or Restore Company**.

2. Open **AYS_A1_Chapter02 (Company)** or restore **AYS_A1_Chapter02 (Portable)** from your file storage location and save your file as: **AYS_A1_Chapter02 Wet Noses Clinic**

3. Open the **Customer Center**.

4. Use this information to set up three customers for Wet Noses Veterinary Clinic:

   Customer 1 information:

   • Customer Name: **York, Edison**
   • Main Phone: **(425) 555-4401**
   • Address: **7931 NE 176th St.** Enter **Bothell, WA 98011**
   • Terms: **Due on Receipt**
   • Account Number: **D22**
   • Type: **From Advertisement**
   • Job: **Dog-Scruffy**

   Customer 2 information:

   • Customer Name: **Reeves, LaShonda**
   • Main Phone: **(425) 555-3953**
   • Address: **11908 100th Pl. NE** Enter **Kirkland, WA 98034**
   • Terms: **Due on Receipt**
   • Account Number: **C94**
   • Type: **Referral**
   • Job: **Dog-Nicky**

   Customer 3 information:

   • Customer Name: **Sanders, Ellie**
   • Main Phone: **(425) 555-7731**
   • Address: **302 Northshore Blvd.** Enter **Bothell, WA 98011**
   • Terms: **Due on Receipt**
   • Account Number: **D34**

- Type: **From Advertisement**
- Job: **Cat-Josie**

5. Run the **Customer Contact List** report, which should include these new customers, and any open balances.

6. Click the **Excel** `Excel ▼` button and export this list to a new worksheet, saving it to your file storage location as: **CH2_A1 Customer Contacts**

7. Close Excel, close the Customer Contact List report, and leave the company file open.

APPLY YOUR SKILLS 2-2 QG

Set Up Service and Non-Inventory Items

In this exercise, you will be creating new items for the company to sell.

1. Use this information to set up two Service Items:

   First item:
   - Item Name: **Boarding**
   - Description: **Overnight Boarding**
   - Rate: **35.00**
   - Account: **46200•Nonmedical Income**

   Second Item:
   - Item Name: **Dental**
   - Description: **Dental Cleaning**
   - Rate: **45.00**
   - Account: **43700•Fee for Service Income**

2. Use this information to set up a Non-Inventory Part:
   - Item Name: **Treats**
   - Description: **Treats for patients — by the box**
   - Rate: **18.43**
   - Account: **46200•Nonmedical Income**

3. Run an **Item Price List** report to include the new items and their prices.

4. Click the **Excel** `Excel ▼` button and export this list to a new worksheet, saving it to your file storage location as: **CH2_A2 Item Price List**

5. Close Excel, close the Item Price List report, and then close the company file.

APPLY YOUR SKILLS 2-3

Record Sales Transactions and Receive Payments

In this exercise, you will be helping Dr. James to record invoices and cash sales. You will enter the sales information and update the Customer's record to capture the custom field information for each pet.

1. Choose **File→Open or Restore Company**.

2. Open **AYS_A3_Chapter02 (Company)** or restore **AYS_A3_Chapter02 (Portable)** and save your file as: **AYS_A3_Chapter02 Wet Noses Clinic**

3. On 06/01/2023, Emily Dallas brought her dog, Cowboy, in for an Exam, Vaccine, and Rabies Vaccine. She also bought two boxes of treats. Create an invoice for these services and items. Terms are Net 30; choose to save the new terms for the customer. Add a customer message and for the memo type: **Dallas: Dog-Cowboy, Exam & Vaccines**

4. On 06/02/2023, Ellie Sanders brought her cat, Josie, in for a New Patient Exam, Feline DHC, and FIV/FeLV, and one box of treats treat. She paid cash, so you will need to create a sales receipt for her. Add a customer message and for the memo type: **Sanders: Cat-Josie, New Patient**

5. On 06/03/2023, Becky Todd brought her dog, Jedi, in for an ACTH Stimulation Test, CBC Chem, and Boarding for three nights. Create an invoice for her. Add a customer message and for the memo type: **Todd: Dog-Jedi, Boarding & Tests**

6. On 06/04/2023, Edison York brought his dog, Scruffy, in for Dental and Boarding for two nights. He paid cash, so create a sales receipt for him. Add a customer message and for the memo type: **York: Dog-Scruffy, Dental & Boarding**

7. Leave the company file open for the next exercise.

APPLY YOUR SKILLS 2-4 QG

Accept Customer Payments for Invoices

In this exercise, you will be receiving payments from customers.

1. On 06/07/2023, you received check #773 for $93.76 from Emily Dallas as payment for invoice #176. For the memo type: **Dallas: Inv. 176**

2. On 06/08/2023, you received check #2310 for $284.21 from the County Animal Shelter as payment for invoice #163. For the memo type: **County Animal – Inv. 163**

3. Run a **Sales by Customer Summary** report for your Customers, from 04/01/2023 through 06/30/2023 (the 2nd quarter).

4. Click the **Excel** Excel ▾ button and export this list to a new worksheet, saving it to your file storage location as: **CH2_A4 Sales by Customer Summary**

5. Close Excel and close the Sales by Customer Summary report.

6. Run the **Open Invoices** report for the date of **06/30/2023** to determine if there are any outstanding invoices for the month.

7. Click the **Excel** Excel ▾ button and export this list to a new worksheet, saving it to your file storage location as: **CH2_A4 Open Invoices**

8. Close Excel, close the Open Invoices report, and then close the company file.

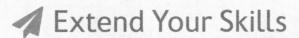

Extend Your Skills

Before You Begin: Open **EYS_Chapter02 (Company)** or restore **EYS_Chapter02 (Portable)** from your file storage location. The password for all users unless otherwise stated is *Password1*.

You have been hired by Arlaine Cervantes to help her with her organization's books. She is the founder of Niños del Lago, a nonprofit organization that provides impoverished Guatemalan children with an engaging educational camp experience. You have just sat down at your desk and opened a large envelope from her with a variety of documents and noticed that you have several emails from her as well. It is your job to sort through the papers and emails and make sense of what you find, entering information into QuickBooks whenever appropriate and answering any other questions in a word-processing document saved as: **EYS_Chapter02_LastnameFirstinitial**. Remember, you are digging through papers you just dumped out of an envelope and addressing random emails from Arlaine, so it is up to you to determine the correct order in which to complete the tasks.

- Sticky note: We now also receive donations from the Hanson Family Trust. Would we set them up as a customer? The information for the trust is 900 SE Commercial St., Salem, OR 97306; (503) 555-9331; contact, Richard Hanson.

- A handwritten note: We will be providing cultural competency training to schools and organizations to raise additional funds for the organization. Can we set up a service item directed to 47250•Service to Outside Orgs? (You will need to set this account up as a subaccount for 47200•Program Income.) Set the amount to zero as it will be entered at the time of "sale."

- Note: How would we set up the students who participate in our program? They don't pay us money, so are they customers or is there another list we can include them on? Enter the following students when you find an answer: Diego Margarita, Maria Prentice, Felipe Valdez, and Rosa Batres.

- Scribbled on a scrap of paper: Provided a Cultural Competency 3-day workshop on 7/9/2019 at St. Martin's Catholic School, received check #3821 for $4,500. Can we enter this receipt of cash into QuickBooks?

- A letter from the House Foundation: They will be providing a $5,000 grant (not yet received) to the organization to complete construction of the dormitories. Set up the new customer, who is located at 552 Sheridan Avenue, Macon, GA 31205.

- Handwritten invoice dated 7/10/2019: Cultural competency workshop to be held at Lakeside Christian School on 7/27/2019 for $1,500. Due Net 15. (They have agreed to pay 50% upfront.)

- Scribbled note from Arlaine: Can you produce a report for me that shows all the donors and customers for Niños del Lago?

- Photocopy of check #1826 from Lakeside Christian School for $750 (50% deposit for upcoming training), with a note of "deposited into checking account on 7/15/2019."

- A handwritten question: I don't have customers, but I do have donors and grants.... How do I set them up if QuickBooks just has customers?

3 | Working with Vendors

Tracking expenses properly is very important for your financial statements as well as for keeping your vendors happy! A vendor is essentially anyone to whom you pay money. However, this does not include employees. A vendor could be the electric company, the organization to which you pay taxes, a merchandise supplier, or subcontractors you pay to do work for your customers. QuickBooks allows you to produce 1099 tax forms for subcontractors at the end of the year. In this chapter, you will examine the QuickBooks lists, activities, and reports that allow you to effectively deal with vendors.

LEARNING OBJECTIVES

▶ Identify features of the Vendor Center and Vendor List

▶ Enter and pay bills

▶ Write and print checks

▶ Correct errors in vendor transactions

▶ Produce vendor and profit & loss reports

📂 Project: Average Guy Designs

Now that Guy Marshall has set up his customers and entered transactions related to them, he needs to set up the Vendor List before he can track expenses. These transactions include entering and paying bills and writing checks. Guy will also learn how to produce reports that will provide relevant vendor information as well as a profit & loss report.

You can access the Vendor List and activities (entering and paying bills) from the Vendor Center, pictured below. When you select a vendor from the Vendor Center, it provides an all-in-one look at that vendor's information, bills, and payments.

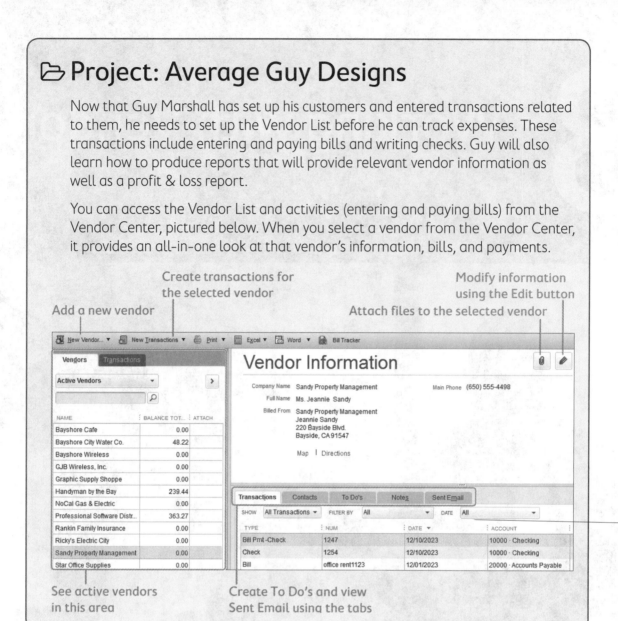

Add a new vendor

Create transactions for the selected vendor

Modify information using the Edit button

Attach files to the selected vendor

See active vendors in this area

Create To Do's and view Sent Email using the tabs

The Vendor Center

The Vendor Center contains the Vendor List, which is used in various forms and reports. Each vendor's record in the list is organized into five tabs: Address Info, Payment Settings, Tax Settings, Account Settings, and Additional Info, where you can create custom fields to store additional data. Keep in mind that the more information you enter for each vendor, the better your customized reports will be because you can sort, group, and filter your reports using information pulled from the vendor records. This list can even be exported to contact management software such as Microsoft® Outlook.

The Vendor List

Setting up the Vendor List is a necessary function and will allow you to customize each vendor so that it makes other functions easier. Some of the customizations available to you are setting Vendor IDs for 1099 vendors, setting default accounts such as Utilities for your Electricity vendor, and storing the type of vendor, such as service provider.

Creating a New Vendor

You can access the Vendor List via the menu or Home Page. Subcontractors should be set up as vendors, not as employees. Vendors can either be created ahead of time or "on the fly" when you are entering a bill for them.

Each tab holds additional fields to track vendor information.

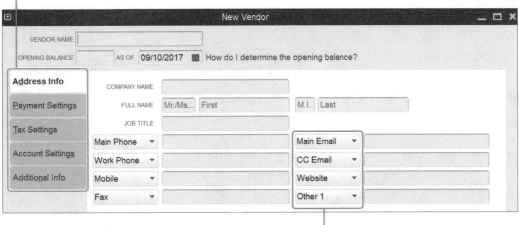

Contact fields on the Address
Info tab are customizable.

 Vendors→Vendor Center: New Vendor→New Vendor

Setting Up Default Expense Accounts for a Vendor

In QuickBooks, when you add a new vendor, you have the option to associate up to three expense accounts with that vendor. These accounts will automatically fill in when you enter a bill for this vendor. By setting up expense account information to be prefilled, tracking expenses is easier and faster.

Once set up, when that vendor is entered in the Enter Bills, Write Checks, or Enter Credit Card Charges windows, QuickBooks will automatically fill in the expense account names for you. You can always choose to override the default accounts that are filled in by changing them in the individual transaction window. If there are fewer than three expense accounts for a vendor, just leave the additional account prefill fields blank.

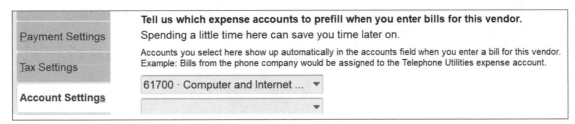

Set up default expense accounts for a vendor here.

Editing an Existing Vendor

Once created, the vendor can always be edited through the Vendor Center. The only item that cannot be edited after you have created and saved a new vendor is the opening balance (it must be adjusted through the accounts payable register). When you change the information for a vendor, including the vendor's name, it will be reflected in both future and past transactions.

Deleting a Vendor

You can delete a vendor from the Vendor List *as long as you have not used it in a transaction*. If you have used it in a transaction, you can make it inactive, but you cannot delete it until after you close the books for a period.

Making a Vendor Inactive

If you have a vendor with whom you are no longer working, you cannot delete the vendor from the associated list if that vendor has been involved in any transactions. What you can do is make the vendor inactive. If you find you need a list entry again for that vendor, you can reactivate it.

Merge Duplicate Vendors

Occasionally, you may find that you have two records created for the same list entry. QuickBooks allows you to merge these duplicate entries into one. You perform the merge by editing one of the entries and changing its name to match the other exactly. The two entries will permanently become one and all prior transactions with the merged list entry will reflect the change in name. Refer to QuickBooks Help in addition to the following regarding merging vendors:

- You can merge up to four vendors at a time.

- You cannot merge vendors with online transactions or direct deposits.

- You can merge vendors only when you are logged in as a QuickBooks "Admin" user.

Warning! Merging list entries cannot be undone!

DEVELOP YOUR SKILLS 3-1

In this exercise, you will manage the Vendor List for Average Guy Designs by adding, editing, merging, and deleting vendors. The password for all files unless otherwise stated is Password1. *Leave the company file open unless otherwise instructed.*

1. Start QuickBooks 2019 and toggle to Pro, if necessary.
2. Choose **File→Open or Restore Company**.
3. Open **DYS_Chapter03 (Company)** or restore **DYS_Chapter03 (Portable)** from your file storage location and save your file as: **DYS_Chapter03 Average Guy Designs**

Edit an Existing Vendor

When this vendor was created, the address and phone number for Graphic Supply Shoppe wasn't available, so you will add it now.

4. Click the **Vendors** [VENDORS] button in the Vendors area of the Home Page.
5. From the list of vendors, double-click **Graphic Supply Shoppe** to open it for editing.

Tip! When you double-click a record on the Vendor List, QuickBooks opens it for editing. You could also single-click the vendor you wish to open and then click the **Edit** button.

6. Enter the following information to edit the vendor:
   - Main Phone: **(212) 555-6743**
   - Address Details Billed From: **302 E 44th St.** [Enter] **New York, NY 10017**

7. Click **Copy>>** to copy the Billed From address to the Shipped From field and then click **OK** to accept the address.

8. Click **OK** to complete the change to the vendor record.

Add a New Vendor

Next you will add a new vendor to the list.

9. Click the **New Vendor** button on the toolbar of the Vendor Center and then choose **New Vendor**.

10. Enter this information to complete the vendor record:
    - Vendor Name: **GJB Wireless, Inc.**
    - Company Name: **GJB Wireless, Inc.**
    - Full Name: **Mr. Amir Dhanu**
    - Job Title: **Business Sales Rep**
    - Main Phone: **(650) 555-1112**
    - Address Details Billed From: **721 Chicago Ave.** [Enter] **Bayshore, CA 91547**

11. Click **Copy>>** to copy the Billed From address to the Shipped From field and then click **OK** to accept the address.

12. From the New Vendor window, click the **Payment Settings** tab and enter the payment information:
    - Account No: **E31W006**
    - Payment Terms: **Net 30**

13. Click the **Additional Info** tab and choose **Service Providers** from the Vendor Type list.

14. Click **OK** to create the new vendor record.

Delete a Vendor

Guy has not purchased anything from Paper Palace yet, and the company has just gone out of business. You will now delete this company from the Vendor List.

15. Click the **Paper Palace** record in the Vendor List to select it.

16. Choose **Edit→Delete Vendor** from the QuickBooks menu bar.

    QuickBooks asks you to confirm the deletion. QuickBooks wants to ensure that you don't delete anything by accident; it will always ask you to confirm deletions.

17. Click **OK** to confirm the deletion.

18. Close the Vendor Center window.

Entering Bills

After you have set up your initial Vendor List, you can begin to enter spending transactions. In this section, you will learn to enter bills and use accounts payable, which is the account credited when bills are entered. When you enter a bill, you *must* specify a vendor because accounts payable will be credited by the transaction.

When entering bills, you need to decide if the expenditure is for an expense or for items that you will add to your inventory, if you are tracking inventory.

The Ribbon shows commands such as Memorize and Pay Bill.

This area provides a snapshot of information for the selected vendor.

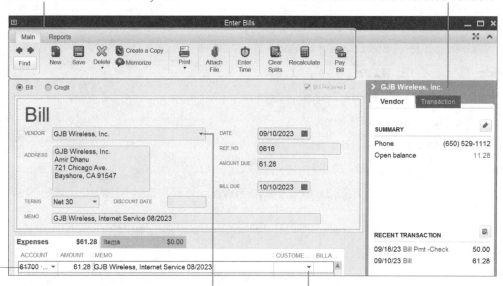

This drop-down arrow ▼ allows you to select an existing vendor, and stored information will fill in.

To pass on an expense to a customer, select the Customer:Job and check the Billable column.

The Importance of Entering Reference Numbers and Memos

When entering a bill, it is very important to enter reference information or the bill number in the Ref. No. field and notes in the Memo fields. The first memo field is for information that will print on a check created when you pay this bill. The second memo field is for internal use and can include any information that you want to track. The memo information displays in reports, is searchable, and can aid you if you are looking for a bill.

Passing on Expenses to Customers

When you enter a bill, you may be purchasing equipment or supplies or incurring a consultant's fee that you want to pass on to the customer. QuickBooks allows you to easily indicate which expenses are to be billed to a customer by providing a "Billable?" column in the Enter Bills window. When you make an item billable to a specific customer, the next time you invoice that customer you will be asked if you'd like to add the outstanding billable time and costs to the invoice.

Billable Time/Costs	✕

ⓘ The customer or job you've selected has outstanding billable time and/or costs.

Do you want to:

◉ Select the outstanding billable time and costs to add to this invoice?

○ Exclude outstanding billable time and costs at this time? (You may add these later by clicking the Add Time/Costs button at the top of the invoice.)

FLASHBACK TO GAAP: COST

Remember that when a company purchases assets, it should record them at cost, not fair market value. For example, if you bought an item worth $750 for $100, the item should be recorded at $100.

The cost of goods sold (COGS) comprises expenses that are directly related to the manufacture or acquisition of products or services that the company sells. Some expenses that might be considered COGS are labor, raw materials, depreciation, and overhead. You cannot pass on the COGS to a customer (it is instead incorporated into the final price of the product), so make sure that you use the proper type of account (expense) if the costs are to be billed to your customer.

BEHIND THE SCENES

When entering bills, QuickBooks takes care of all the accounting for you. Here is an illustration of the accounting going on behind the scenes.

20000•Accounts Payable		63300•Insurance Expense	
	125.49	125.49	

Rankin Family Insurance	
	125.49

QuickBooks credits the subregister for the vendor (Rankin Family Insurance) along with Accounts Payable.

 Vendors→Enter Bills

In this exercise, you will enter bills, track expenses, and enter a vendor "on the fly." You just received a bill for Internet service that you will enter into QuickBooks.

1. Click the **Enter Bills** 🖳 task icon in the Vendors area of the Home Page.

2. Click the **Vendor** drop-down arrow ▼ on the bill and then choose **GJB Wireless, Inc.**

   Look at the form and notice that the vendor's address and terms fill in for you from the underlying list and that the due date is calculated.

3. Enter this information to create a bill:

   • Date: **091023**

   The date will format correctly after you leave this field.

   • Ref. No.: **Inv 0616 08/2023**

   • Amount Due: **61.28**

   • Memo: **GJB Wireless, Internet Service 08/2023**

4. Account column under the Expenses tab: Type **co** and then choose **61700•Computer and Internet Expenses**.

   When you typed co, QuickBooks filled in Computer and Internet Expenses from the underlying list for you (in this case, the Chart of Accounts).

Set Default Accounts for a Vendor

You know that all bills for GJB Wireless, Inc., will use the same expense account, so you will now edit the vendor and set the account prefills right from the Enter Bills window.

5. Click the **Edit** 🖊 button in the history pane of the Enter Bills window to display the Edit Vendor window.

6. Click the **Account Settings** tab and then choose **61700•Computer and Internet Expenses** from the first drop-down list.

7. Click **OK** to save the changes to the vendor record and return to the bill.

8. Change the Terms on the bill to **Net 15**.

   Whenever you make a change to a vendor's information on a form such as the Enter Bills window, QuickBooks asks whether you want to make that change permanent when you save. Otherwise, the new information will appear only on the current form.

9. Click **Save & New** to enter the bill and then click **Yes** to change the default Terms for the vendor. Leave the Enter Bills window open for the next step.

> ### BEHIND THE SCENES BRIEF
>
> 61700•Computer and Internet Expenses DR 61.28; **20000•Accounts Payable CR <61.28>**

Enter a Bill for a Vendor Not on the Vendor List

When you enter a vendor name that is not on the Vendor List, QuickBooks allows you to add it to the Vendor List "on the fly."

10. In the Vendor field at the top of a new bill, type **Rankin Family Insurance** and then tap Tab .

    A Vendor Not Found window will appear.

11. Click **Set Up**.

    You could have chosen to Quick Add the vendor, in which case you could proceed with the bill; however, you would have to return to the Vendor List at a later time and edit the entry to enter all the vendor information in your company file.

12. Enter the following information to create the new vendor:

    - Company Name: **Rankin Family Insurance**
    - Full Name: **Mrs. Mary Rankin**
    - Job Title: **Owner/Agent**
    - Main Phone: **(650) 555-7762**
    - Address Details Billed From: **1456 Pine St.** Enter **Bayshore, CA 91547**

13. Click **Copy>>** and then click **OK** to copy the address to the Shipped From field.

14. Click **OK** to accept the information for the new vendor.

15. Enter this information to create the bill:

    - Date: **091023**
    - Ref. No: **Inv 769 08/2023**
    - Amount Due: **125.49**
    - Memo: **Rankin, Inv 769 08/2023**

      A good practice is to fill in both memo fields; you can copy the memo from the first memo field into the memo field on the expense line, if that is faster for you.

    - Account: Type **ins** and choose **63300•Insurance Expense**

    > **BEHIND THE SCENES BRIEF**
    >
    > 63300•Insurance Expense DR 125.49; **20000•Accounts Payable CR <125.49>**

16. Click **Save & Close** to record the bill.

Paying Bills

When you have entered your bills, you will need to pay them in a timely manner. In QuickBooks, you use the Pay Bills window to debit accounts payable. The other half of the equation (the account that will be credited) depends on the account from which you withdraw funds (or charge, in the case of bill payment by credit card).

Warning! When you have used the Enter Bills window, make sure you use the Pay Bills window to issue the payment—*not* the Write Checks window! If you use the Write Checks window, it will not pay off the bill, thus you will expense the purchase twice and not "clear out" the entry in the accounts payable account.

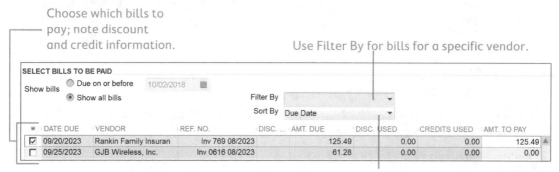

Choose which bills to pay; note discount and credit information.

Use Filter By for bills for a specific vendor.

Use Sort By to see choices for viewing your bills in a chosen order.

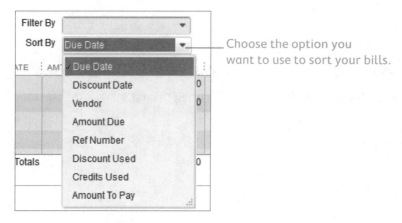

Choose the option you want to use to sort your bills.

Payment Details

At the bottom of the Pay Bills window, you must make three important choices regarding your payment: Payment Date, Payment Method, and Payment Account.

- **Payment Date**—Make sure you select the date you want the payment to be reflected in your bank and Accounts Payable accounts.

- **Payment Method**—You can choose how you will pay the bill. If you choose to pay by check, you must select whether you will print the check later in a batch, or at the time and assign it a check number. If you choose to pay by credit card, you must have a credit card account set up prior to selecting it from the Payment Method drop-down list.

- **Payment Account**—You can select to pay the bill from any bank account you have set up. When you select an account, QuickBooks will show you the ending balance for the account so you can ensure you have enough money to pay the bill. Make sure to select the proper account, as it will be credited behind the scenes!

Bill payment options

The Payment Summary Window

When you have chosen to pay the selected bills in the Pay Bills window, QuickBooks will display a Payment Summary window. There are three options available to you from this window: pay another bill, print checks, or close the window.

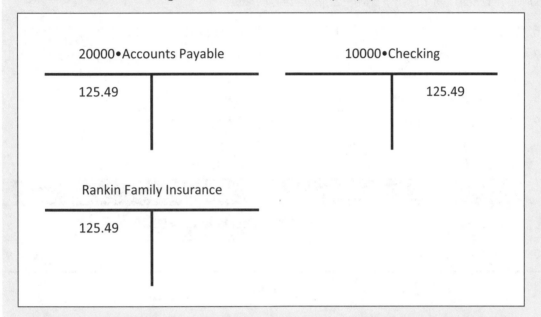

DEVELOP YOUR SKILLS 3-3

In this exercise, you will enter a partial payment for one of the bills because the service hasn't been completed. You will complete this task for Guy by using the Pay Bills window because the bills were originally entered in the Enter Bills window and, therefore, are "sitting" in Accounts Payable.

1. Click the **Pay Bills** task icon in the Vendor area of the Home Page.
2. Click in the checkbox beside the bill due for **Rankin Family Insurance**.
3. In the Payment section at the bottom of window, enter the following:
   - Date: **091823**
   - Method: **Check**
   - Click **To Be Printed**
   - Account: **10000•Checking**

4. Click the **Pay Selected Bills** button.

BEHIND THE SCENES BRIEF

20000•Accounts Payable DR 125.49; **10000•Checking CR <125.49>**

---

5. Click **Pay More Bills** in the Payment Summary window.

Make a Partial Bill Payment

You will now help Guy to pay a partial amount of a bill due.

6. Click in the checkbox beside the bill due for **GJB Wireless, Inc.** to select it.

7. Double-click on **61.28** in the Amt. To Pay column to select it for the GJB Wireless, Inc., bill, type **50**, and tap ⸤Tab⸥.

8. Click the **Pay Selected Bills** button to complete the transaction.

9. Click **Pay More Bills** in the Payment Summary window.

   Take a look at the current bills to be paid in the Pay Bills window. Notice that the bill for GJB Wireless, Inc., is still on the list, but only for the remaining amount due of $11.28.

BEHIND THE SCENES BRIEF

20000•Accounts Payable DR 50.00; **10000•Checking CR <50.00>**

---

10. Close the Pay Bills window.

Writing and Printing Checks

If you are using the cash basis of accounting, you do not have to use the enter bills and pay bills features of QuickBooks—even though they are useful features for managing cash flow. Instead, you can simply write a check to pay for your expenditures when they are due and expense them properly. Additionally, if you handwrite a check for which there was no bill entered into Quick-Books, you will not use the pay bills feature.

Warning! Remember that if you use the Enter Bills feature, you must use the Pay Bills feature for the bills you have entered! If you don't, your expenses will be overstated, funds will remain in Accounts Payable, and your reports will not reflect accurate amounts.

Check to Pay Bills

 When you open the Write Checks window and try to pay a vendor for whom there is an outstanding bill, QuickBooks will display a Check for Bills window.

The Check for Bills feature was actually a "slip-stream" feature implemented in a later release of QuickBooks 2018. However, in QuickBooks 2019, the default is the "Go to Pay Bills" button rather than the "Write your check" one.

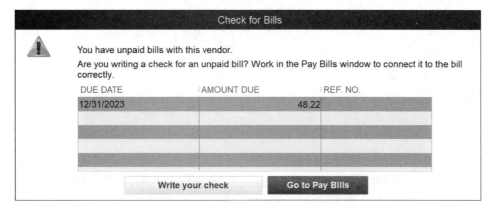

When you try to write a check for a vendor for whom there is an outstanding bill, you will see this window displayed to help you make sure you don't get yourself in trouble!

As with the Pay Bills window, you must decide from which account to issue the check and whether to print the check or add it to a batch for later printing.

The Print Later option sets the check number TO PRINT.

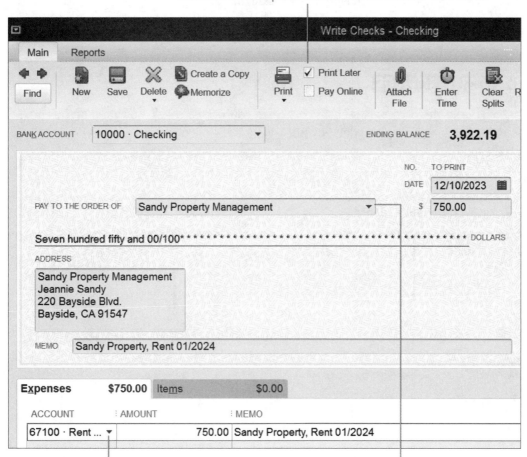

This field allows you to choose the account that the transaction is affecting.

The Pay to the Order of field will prefill the information from the underlying list.

 Banking→Write Checks

Print Checks Setup

To be sure every item prints in the proper location on the checks, you will need to align the checks to your printer. If you change your printer, you will have to realign your checks. It is important to select the check style that matches the checks you have purchased and to print a sample check to ensure proper alignment. Uploading a signature graphic file instead of manually signing each check is a great time-saving feature, although caution should be applied if others have access to the Write Checks feature.

Printing Checks

When you choose to print your checks in the Pay Bills and Write Checks windows, QuickBooks will "hold" all of them in a queue until you are ready to print a batch of them.

Select Checks to Print		
Bank Account 10000 · Checking ▼	**First Check Number** 1247	

Select Checks to print, then click OK.
There are 2 Checks to print for $875.00.

✓	DATE	PAYEE	AMOUNT
✓	12/10/2023	Ricky's Electric City	125.00
✓	12/30/2023	Sandy Property Managem...	750.00

Choose which checks from your batch to print.

BEHIND THE SCENES

The behind the scenes accounting that occurs when you write a check is a hybrid of the two previous transactions (Enter Bills and Pay Bills), with the elimination of Accounts Payable, the middle man.

67100•Rent Expense	10000•Checking
750.00	750.00

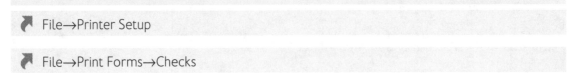

↰ File→Printer Setup

↰ File→Print Forms→Checks

DEVELOP YOUR SKILLS 3-4

In this exercise, you will pay for expenses with both printed and handwritten checks.

1. Click the **Write Checks** 🖋 task icon in the Banking area of the Home Page.
2. Complete the check with this information:
   - Ensure the **Print Later** checkbox on the Ribbon is checked
   - Bank Account: **10000•Checking**
   - Date: **121023**
   - Pay to the Order of: **Sandy Property Management**
   - Amount to Pay: **750**
   - Memo: **Sandy Property, Rent 01/2024**
   - Account: **67100•Rent Expense**

   ### BEHIND THE SCENES BRIEF
   67100•Rent Expense DR 750.00; **10000•Checking CR <750.00>**

3. Click **Save & New** to record this check and leave the Write Checks window open.

Record a Handwritten Check

You may not always be at your computer when you wish to write a check. In this situation, Guy has taken his checkbook while entertaining a client, and you need to record the handwritten check.

4. Click to remove the checkmark from the **Print Later** box, so the check number field can be edited.
5. Enter this information to record the handwritten check:
   - No: **1248**
   - Date: **123023**
   - Pay to the Order of: **Bayshore Cafe** (then Tab and choose **Quick Add**, choose **Vendor**, and then click **OK**)
   - Amount: **37.49**
   - Memo: **Bayshore Cafe, Lunch with Client 12/2023**
   - Account: Type **me** (choose **64300•Meals and Entertainment**)

   ### BEHIND THE SCENES BRIEF
   64300•Meals and Entertainment DR 37.49; **10000•Checking CR <37.49>**

6. Click **Save & Close** to complete the transaction.

Print a Batch of Checks

After you have indicated that checks are to be printed, you need to issue a separate command to print them.

7. Click the **Print Checks** task icon in the Banking area of the Home Page.

> **Note!** If you don't see the Print Checks task icon, use the sizing arrow to make the Home Page larger or choose File→Print Forms→Checks.

8. Enter **1249** as the first check number.

   By default, all of the checks will be selected.

9. Click the checkmark to the left of **Sandy Property Management** to deselect it and then click **OK**.

10. Click the **Printer Name** drop-down arrow ▼ and choose the correct printer or PDF driver.

    At this point you can verify that the correct printer is selected. You can choose a PDF driver to send the checks to a file in order to not waste paper and ink on practice checks.

11. Ensure that **Voucher** is chosen as the check style and then click **Print**. If you choose to print to PDF, click **Save** to choose to save the PDF in your default file location.

    When complete, QuickBooks will display a Print Checks - Confirmation window. Here you have the opportunity to reprint any checks that did not print correctly or to troubleshoot the order in which your checks printed.

12. Click **OK** in the Print Checks - Confirmation window.

    Notice that there are links to help you if your checks do not print correctly.

Editing Vendor Transactions

QuickBooks tries very hard to make sure you don't make errors that will affect what happens behind the scenes, as shown by the Open Bills Exist window that is displayed. However, sometimes users still end up making mistakes that need to be corrected!

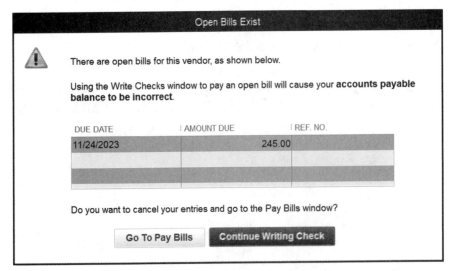

The Open Bills Exist window is displayed when you try to write a check to a vendor for whom you have an outstanding bill.

Fixing Errors

The following table outlines a common vendor-related error as well as an error that occurs in the Write Checks window, the effects of the errors behind the scenes, and how to correct them.

> ## ✔ Best Practice
>
> After a transaction has been cleared during the reconciliation process, it should not be changed. Because each situation may require a different solution, you may want to check with an accountant.

COMMON ERRORS AND FIXES

Error	Effect Behind the Scenes	The Fix
A bill is entered but the Pay Bills window is not used when the payment is made.	Your expenses will be double-stated and Accounts Payable for the vendor is not "cleared out."	Void the check or credit card payment for the expense and then enter the transaction properly using the Pay Bills window.
A "regular" check was cut to pay payroll or sales tax liabilities.	The liability accounts are not cleared out; QuickBooks payroll essentially has a second set of books that are affected only when you pay the liabilities through the proper method.	Void the "regular" check and then process the payment through the proper method (Pay Payroll Liabilities or Pay Sales Tax).

FLASHBACK TO GAAP: PRUDENCE

Remember that if you need to choose between two solutions, pick the one that is less likely to overstate assets and income.

DEVELOP YOUR SKILLS 3-5

In this exercise, you will find and edit a bill. You will start by helping Guy to edit the bill for Ricky's Electric City for 3-D Printer Repair, as it should have been for $225.00 rather than $125.00.

1. Choose **Edit→Find**.
2. Be sure the **Simple** tab is selected and then enter the following information:
   - Transaction Type: **Bill**
   - Vendor: **Ricky's Electric City**
3. Click the **Find** button, single-click the bill for **Repair 3-D Printer** in the results list, and then click the **Go To** button.
4. Change the **Amount Due** on the bill to: **225.00**
5. Click **Save & Close**; click **Yes** to record the transaction with the changes.
6. Close the Find window.

Void a Check and Pay a Bill with a Check

Unfortunately, Guy has already gone straight to the Write Checks window to pay the Bayshore City Water bill and has written a check for this expense. You must fix Guy's mistake by voiding the check and reentering the payment correctly using the Pay Bills window.

By writing a check for an outstanding bill in the Write Checks window, Guy has stated the expense twice and has not cleared the amount from Accounts Payable.

7. Choose **Banking→Write Checks**.

8. Click the **Previous** button, above the Find button, until the check to Bayshore City Water that Guy entered on 11/12/2023 is displayed.

You can look for a transaction by using the Previous and Next buttons if you believe the transaction to be easy to locate. If not, use the Find or Search feature.

9. Choose **Edit→Void Check**.

10. Set the check number to: **VOID 1251**

11. In the Memo field, after VOID:, as an explanation, type: **incorrectly entered, reprocessed through pay bills**

12. Click **Save & Close** to close the Write Checks window and click **No, Just Void the Check** in the QuickBooks window, if necessary.

    You would click Yes if the check was written in the prior period. Because this check was written in the same period, no journal entry is necessary. Since Guy has already sent this check to the vendor, you will want the date and number of the bill payment check to match what he originally entered.

13. Choose **Vendors→Pay Bills** to properly pay the bill.

14. Enter the payment correctly:
    - Click in the checkbox to select the **Bayshore City Water** bill.
    - Payment Date: **111223**
    - Payment Method: **Check**
    - Check No.: Click in the checkbox to select **Assign Account Number**.
    - Account: **10000•Checking**

> **BEHIND THE SCENES BRIEF**
>
> 10000•Checking DR 525.37; **68600•Utilities: 68620 Water CR <525.37>**
> 20000•Accounts Payable DR 525.37; **10000•Checking CR <525.37>**

15. Click **Pay Selected Bills**, enter **1251** in the Assign Check Numbers window, and click **OK**.

16. Click **Done** in the payment summary window.

    Before moving on, think about what you have just completed and make sure you understand the "why" behind it. You have deleted the overstated expenses by voiding the check and have "cleared out" Accounts Payable for Bayshore City Water by processing the payment correctly.

Producing Vendor and Profit & Loss Reports

After you have recorded your vendor-related transactions, QuickBooks has many reports that you can produce to view your data. The general types of reports are:

- List reports

- Summary reports that subtotal your data and provide a summary

- Transaction reports that show each transaction that makes up the subtotal found in a summary report

If you wish to see all transactions grouped by vendor, there are two different reports you can run. The *Vendor Balance Detail* report (found in the Vendors & Payables category) shows only those transactions affecting Accounts Payable (transactions entered and paid as "bills"). The *Expense by Vendor* reports (both summary and detail, found in the Company & Financial category) show transactions made by all payment methods.

QuickZoom

QuickBooks has a great feature called QuickZoom. This feature allows you to zoom through underlying subreports until you reach the form where the data was originally entered. This can be extremely useful if you have questions as to where a figure in a report comes from. You can even edit the source transaction once you have QuickZoomed to it, if you desire.

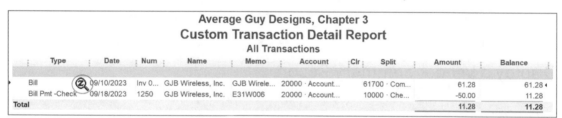

	Type	Date	Num	Name	Memo	Account	Clr	Split	Amount	Balance
	Bill	09/10/2023	Inv 0...	GJB Wireless, Inc.	GJB Wirele...	20000 · Account...		61700 · Com...	61.28	61.28
	Bill Pmt -Check	09/18/2023	1250	GJB Wireless, Inc.	E31W006	20000 · Account...		10000 · Che...	-50.00	11.28
Total									11.28	11.28

The zoom pointer indicates that you can double-click to dive deeper into your data. The number of layers to zoom through depends on the type of report (or graph) with which you started. Here, a double-click would open the Enter Bills window with the transaction for GJB Wireless, Inc., displayed.

The Profit & Loss (P&L) Report

Now that you have recorded both income and expenses, you will be able to run a meaningful profit & loss (P&L) report. It is important to make sure all income and expense transactions are entered so that income is matched to expenses for the period you are reporting. The P&L report will reflect all transactions that have affected income and expense accounts. The profit & loss report is also called an income statement, and these terms can be used interchangeably.

 Reports→Report Center: Company & Financial→Profit & Loss | Reports→Company & Financial→Profit & Loss

FLASHBACK TO GAAP: MATCHING

Remember that expenses need to be matched with revenues from the same accounting period.

In this exercise, you will produce a vendor summary report, a vendor detail report, and a profit & loss report. You will use the QuickZoom feature to drill down into your data to see where the data originated, and you can edit the source transaction after you've QuickZoomed to it. You will start by creating a report that shows what you owe all vendors. Then you will use QuickZoom to see the details of where a balance originated.

1. Choose **Reports→Vendors & Payables→Vendor Balance Detail**.

   You can generate reports through the Report Center or the menu bar with the same result. The report will be displayed with the date range of All selected, as it is the default for this particular report.

2. Place your mouse pointer over the total amount due of 11.28 for GJB Wireless, Inc., until you see the zoom pointer and then double-click.

   A Custom Vendor Transaction Detail report will be displayed that shows the transactions leading to the balance for GJB Wireless, Inc. If the Bill Payments (Check) window appears instead, you zoomed in on the 11.28 to the right of Bill Pmt-Check instead of the Total for GJB Wireless.

3. Place your mouse pointer over the Bill dated 09/10/2023 that you entered for this vendor until you see the zoom pointer and then double-click.

   The Enter Bills window will open with the bill that you entered for this vendor earlier in this chapter. If need be, you could edit the transaction at this point.

4. Choose **Window→Close All,** clicking **No** if asked to memorize any of the reports displayed.

Display a Vendor Summary Report

Now you will create a report that shows a summary of all expenses by vendor, regardless of payment method.

5. Choose **Reports→Company & Financial→Expenses by Vendor Summary**.

6. Type **a** to set the date range to **All**. Resize the report window to see all the data, if necessary.

   The Expenses by Vendor Summary report will be displayed, listing the total amount ever paid or accrued for each active vendor.

7. Close the report, clicking **No** when asked if you want to memorize it.

Create a Profit & Loss Report

Guy would now like to see whether the company had a net income or loss for December based on the transactions entered.

8. Choose **Reports→Company & Financial→Profit & Loss Standard**.

   Remember, you can display all reports available through the Report Center via the menu bar as well.

9. Set the correct date range:
   - From: **120123**
   - To: **123123**

10. Click **Refresh** on the Report toolbar. Resize the report window to see all the data, if necessary.

Average Guy Designs, Chapter 3 Profit & Loss December 2023	Dec 23
▾ Income	
42700 · Photography Income ▸	200.00 ◂
43200 · Design Income	4,345.00
48800 · Print Layout Income	520.00
Total Income	5,065.00
Gross Profit	5,065.00
▾ Expense	
61500 · Job Materials	195.50
64300 · Meals and Entertainment	37.49
64900 · Office Supplies	352.00
67100 · Rent Expense	1,500.00
▾ 68600 · Utilities	
68620 · Water	525.37
Total 68600 · Utilities	525.37
Total Expense	2,610.36
Net Income	2,454.64

You will see a report that shows your total income and expenses for the time period along with the resulting net income (or loss). The date range was set to Custom on the toolbar. QuickBooks gives you the option to set the exact date range you desire in your reports.

11. Close the Profit & Loss report, choosing not to memorize it.

Working with QuickBooks Graphs

QuickBooks provides several graphs along with the preset reports. QuickBooks graphs are accessible through the Reports option on the menu bar or through the Report Center.

Types of QuickBooks Graphs

Following are the six graphs provided by QuickBooks. If you can't find a graph that suits your needs, you always have the option of exporting a report to Microsoft Excel and using Excel's much more advanced charting features to analyze your data.

The graphs provided in QuickBooks include:

- Income and Expense
- Net Worth
- Accounts Receivable

- Sales
- Accounts Payable
- Budget vs. Actual

The Graph Toolbar

The Graph toolbar displays different buttons depending on which graph you have created. Once you have created your graph, you can use the Graph toolbar to do a variety of tasks such as customize your graph by date, choose how to view your data, or print your graph.

For some graphs, there are also buttons at the bottom of the window that allow you to choose how to view the pie chart data at the bottom of the window (e.g., by Income or by Expense).

QuickZooming with Graphs

The QuickZoom feature you used previously in this chapter for reports is also available with graphs. You simply double-click on a portion of a graph (when you see the QuickZoom pointer) to zoom in and see where the data comes from.

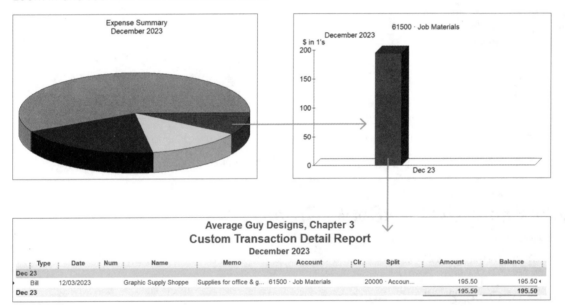

Notice that when you QuickZoom on a pie chart, you see a bar graph. When you Quick-Zoom on a bar graph, you see a report showing where the data originated.

DEVELOP YOUR SKILLS 3-7

In this exercise, you will display an Income and Expense Graph for the month of December 2023.

1. Choose **Reports→Company & Financial→Income & Expense Graph**.
2. Click the **Dates** button on the toolbar and set the correct date range:
   - From: **120123**
   - To: **123123**

3. Click **OK**.

    You will see a bar chart at the top of the window showing both income and expenses. At the bottom you will see a pie chart of the expenses. Next you will change the pie chart to display the income.

4. Click the **Income** button at the bottom of the window.

    The pie chart now shows the distribution of income between accounts.

5. Close all windows, keeping the company file open if you are continuing on to Tackle the Tasks, or close it if you are done with the chapter.

Tackle the Tasks

Now is your chance to work a little more with Average Guy Designs and apply the skills that you have learned in this chapter to accomplish additional tasks. You will use the same company file you used in the Develop Your Skills exercises throughout this chapter. Enter the following transactions, referring to the concepts in the chapter as necessary. If you are using the trial software for this course on your computer or in a lab at school, you must toggle to the Pro edition every time you start QuickBooks.

Add a Vendor	Enter the following vendors:
	Professional Software Distributors; 6439 Washington Square, Wausau, WI 54401; Contact: Abby Gibbs, Manager, (715) 555-9922; Acct #: PR203X; Vendor Type: Supplies; Net 15; Account Settings: 61700•Computer and Internet Expenses
	Handyman by the Bay; 16 Spruce Street, Bayshore, CA 91547; Contact: Bryan Duffy, Manager, (631) 555-1212; Acct #: 20944; Vendor Type: Service Providers; Net 30; Account Settings: 67200•Repair and Maintenance
	Star Office Supplies; 40 Noor Ave., S. San Francisco, CA 94080; Contact: Jim Nadiera, Manager, (650) 555-9999; Acct#: 87340; Vendor Type: Supplies; Net 30; Account Settings: 64900•Office Supplies
Enter Bills	Enter the following bills, making sure to enter a memo for each as well:
	Professional Software Distributors; Dated: 12/26/2023; Amt. $563.27; Ref. No.: Inv 17-222; Acct: 61700•Computer and Internet Expenses
	Handyman by the Bay; Dated: 12/02/2023 Amt. $239.44; Ref. No.: Inv 16-001; Acct: 67200•Repairs and Maintenance
	NoCal Gas & Electric; Dated: 12/15/2023; Amt. $82.37; Ref. No. Inv. 1223-73642; Acct: 68610 Gas & Electric
	Bayshore City Water; Dated: 12/15/2023; Amt. $48.22; Ref. No.: Inv. 9435D1; Due: 12/31/2023; Acct: 68620•Water
Pay Bills	On 12/31/2023, pay all bills due on or before 12/30/2023; Acct.: Checking; check to be printed.
	Choose Pay More Bills, then on 12/31/2023 pay $200 towards the bill for Professional Software Distributors, to be printed.
Write and Print Checks	Write a check on 12/31/2023 to Star Office Supplies for $36.21 for Office Supplies; check #1252.
	Print all checks waiting in the queue; first check #1253.
Generate Reports	Create reports that will answer the following questions:
	• Which bills are due as of 01/09/2024?
	• What is the company's current balance with each vendor?
	• What is the contact information and current balance for each vendor?
	• Did the business have a profit or a loss during December 2023?

Self-Assessment

Check your knowledge of this chapter's key concepts and skills using the Self-Assessment quiz here, in your ebook, or in your eLab course.

1. In QuickBooks, subcontractors are considered vendors.   *True   False*

2. Vendors must be entered into the Vendor List before you can enter a bill for them.   *True   False*

3. You can delete a vendor from the Vendor List as long as it has been used fewer than ten times in transactions.   *True   False*

4. When you use the Enter Bills window in QuickBooks, you MUST specify a vendor.   *True   False*

5. You can choose a payment method from the Pay Bills window.   *True   False*

6. You must use the Enter Bills and Pay Bills features to account for expenses; you CANNOT just write a check.   *True   False*

7. If you use the cash basis of accounting, you MUST use the Write Checks window (not the Enter Bills window) when paying bills.   *True   False*

8. QuickZoom allows you to quickly print a report for a single list record.   *True   False*

9. If you accidently merge two list entries, you can choose to undo the action.   *True   False*

10. You have to enter only your income transactions to create an accurate Profit & Loss report.   *True   False*

11. When you pay a bill, which account is debited?
    A. Accounts Payable
    B. Checking
    C. Accounts Receivable
    D. Telephone Expense

12. Which of the following is NOT one of the five tabs shown when editing a vendor's record?
    A. Payment Settings
    B. Report Settings
    C. Tax Settings
    D. Account Settings

13. What will prevent you from deleting a vendor record from the Vendor List?
    A. You have previously edited the vendor's information.
    B. You entered an account number for the vendor.
    C. You used the vendor in a transaction.
    D. All of these options

Reinforce Your Skills

Emily Holly's company, Electrical Energy, Inc., has purchased supplies and is working with several new vendors. As QuickBooks coordinator you now need to enter vendors, enter and pay bills, and write checks in the Vendor Center. The password for all files unless otherwise stated is Password1. Leave the company file open unless otherwise instructed. If you are using the trial software on your computer or in a lab at school, remember to toggle to the Pro edition every time you start QuickBooks.

REINFORCE YOUR SKILLS 3-1

Manage the Vendor List

In this exercise, you will work with the Vendor List for Electrical Energy, Inc. You will edit an existing vendor, create a new vendor, and delete a vendor. To begin, Ace Hardware has changed its name to Four Brothers Hardware. You will make that change in QuickBooks.

1. Choose **File→Open or Restore Company**.
2. Open **RYS_Chapter03 (Company)** or restore **RYS_Chapter03 (Portable)** from your file storage location and save your file as: **RYS_Chapter03 Electrical Energy**
3. Choose **Vendors→Vendor Center**.
4. Double-click **Ace Hardware** to open it for editing.
5. Change the vendor's name to: **Four Brothers Hardware**

   You will have to change the name in four separate places, including the Vendor Name, Company Name, and Billed From address on the Address Info tab and on the Payment Settings tab in the Print Name on Check As field. This new name will be reflected in all transactions that deal with this vendor—past and present.

6. Click **OK** to accept the change.

Add a New Vendor

Emily has begun to purchase job supplies from a new vendor in Oregon. You will set up the company as a vendor.

7. Click the **New Vendor** button and then choose **New Vendor**.
8. Enter the following information to create a new vendor:
   - Company Name: **Valley Building Supply**
   - Contact Name: **Ms. Carmela Hutch**
   - Job Title: **Owner**
   - Phone: **(914) 555-9438**
   - Fax: **(914) 555-9455**
   - Address: **256 Main Street** Enter **White Plains, NY 10601**

- Account #: **84-976**
- Terms: **Net 15**
- Vendor Type: **Materials**

9. Click **OK** to accept the new vendor record.

Delete a Vendor

10. Click **Computer Suppliers** to select it.
11. Choose **Edit→Delete Vendor**.
12. Click **OK** to confirm the deletion.
13. Close the Vendor Center window and leave the company file open.

REINFORCE YOUR SKILLS 3-2

Enter and Pay Bills

In this exercise, you will enter a bill Emily just received. You will also pay all bills due by a certain date.

1. Choose **Vendors→Enter Bills**.
2. Enter this information to complete the bill:
   - Vendor: **Valley Building Supply**
   - Date: **121923**
   - Ref. No.: **Valley Bldg, 12/2023**
   - Amount: **$100.00**
   - Memo: **Valley Bldg, Plugs and Switches 12/2023**
   - Account: **51400•Job Materials Purchased**
3. Click **Save & Close** to enter the transaction and close the window and click **Yes** in the Future Transactions window, if necessary.

Pay a Bill

4. Open the Pay Bills window by choosing **Vendors→Pay Bills**.
5. Choose **Show All Bills** (you should see one) and select the bill for **Valley Building Supply**.
6. Set the date to **122323** and set the check to be printed from the Checking account.
7. Click **Pay Selected Bills** to record the payment and close the window; click **Yes** in the Future Transactions window, if necessary.
8. Click **Done** in the Payment Summary Window and leave the company file open.

Write and Print Checks

In this exercise, you will write a check for an expense and print the checks you have created.

1. Choose **Banking→Write Checks**.
2. Set the check to print later.
3. Enter this information to complete the check:
   - Date: **122623**
   - Pay to the Order of: **Westchester County** (**Quick Add** it as a **Vendor**)
   - Amount: **$250**
   - Memo: **Business License, 2024**
   - Account: **61000•Business License and Permits**
4. Click **Save & Close** to accept the transaction and close the window; click **Yes** in the Future Transactions window, if necessary.

Print a Batch of Checks

5. Choose **File→Print Forms→Checks**.

   Notice that, by default, QuickBooks selects all checks; you can change this if you need to.

6. Ensure that **Checking** is the bank account and then enter **11353** as the first check number.
7. Click **OK** to move to the Print Checks window.

   At this point you can verify that the correct printer and check style are selected. You can choose to print to PDF to send the checks to a file in order to not waste paper and ink on practice checks.

8. Click **Print**, and if you have chosen to create a PDF file, click **Save** after you have chosen where to save the checks.
9. Click **OK** in the Print Checks - Confirmation window and leave the company file open.

Find and Edit a Transaction

In this exercise, you will use the Find feature to locate a transaction rather than click the Previous button repeatedly. You also will edit the date to ensure accurate record keeping as Emily realized an incorrect date was entered on the April Con Edison bill.

1. Choose **Edit→Find**.
2. Choose **Bill** as the Transaction Type and **Con Edison** as the Vendor.
3. Enter the date range as **04/01/2023** to **04/30/2023** and then click **Find**.

4. Double-click the bill dated **04/16/2023** in the bottom portion of the window.

The Enter Bills window will open; leave it open for the next step.

Edit a Transaction

5. Change the date of the bill to **041023** and add a Memo: **Con Ed, 04/2023**

6. Click **Save & Close**, choose **Yes** to record the change, and click **Yes** in the Future Transactions window, if necessary.

7. Close the Find window and leave the company file open.

REINFORCE YOUR SKILLS 3-5

Create Vendor and P&L Reports

In this exercise, you will run vendor and P&L reports for Electrical Energy, Inc.

1. Choose **Reports→Vendors & Payables→Vendor Balance Summary**.

You should see that you currently owe no vendors.

2. Choose **Reports→Company & Financial→Profit & Loss Standard**.

3. Type **a** to set the date range to **All**.

4. Choose **Window→Close All**, choosing not to memorize either report.

5. Close the company file.

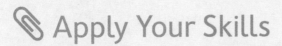

Apply Your Skills

Wet Noses Veterinary Clinic has not had time to maintain its vendor records. You will manage the vendor list, enter and pay bills, write checks, and edit transactions to bring the company QuickBooks file up-to-date. The password for all files unless otherwise stated is Password1. After starting QuickBooks, remember to toggle to Pro as necessary.

APPLY YOUR SKILLS 3-1 QG

Work with the Vendor List

In this exercise, you will manage the Vendor List and create a report of vendors with contact information for Wet Noses Veterinary Clinic.

1. Open **AYS_A1_Chapter03 (Company)** or restore **AYS_A1_Chapter03 (Portable)** from your file storage location and save your file as: **AYS_A1_Chapter03 Wet Noses Clinic**

2. Using the following information, create three new Vendor List entries.

   Vendor 1:
   - Name: **Casey's Consulting**
   - Contact Name: **Ms. Casey Scripps**
   - Job Title: **Owner**
   - Phone: **425-555-9569**
   - Fax: **425-555-9568**
   - Address: **902 Creekview Dr.** Enter **Kirkland, WA 98034**
   - Account No.: **JR154**
   - Terms: **Due on Receipt**
   - Type: **Consultant**

   Vendor 2:
   - Name: **Take a Walk**
   - Contact Name: **Ms. Shannon High**
   - Job Title: **Walker**
   - Phone: **206-555-9433**
   - Fax: **206-555-9434**
   - Address: **13602 75th Ave. NE** Enter **Seattle, WA 98132**
   - Account No.: **VET87**
   - Terms: **Net 15**
   - Type: **Service Providers**

   Vendor 3:
   - Name: **Billy's Van Service**
   - Contact Name: **Mr. Billy Ranch**
   - Job Title: **President**

- Phone: **425-555-4477**
- Fax: **425-555-4478**
- Address: **9501 NE 182nd Pl.** Enter **Bothell, WA 98011**
- Account No.: **BB23**
- Terms: **Net 15**
- Type: **Service Providers**

3. Edit the **Puget Sound Power Company** vendor record to display **Shaunda Jones** as the contact.

4. Add these vendor types to the existing vendor records, adding a new entry to the **Vendor Type List** when necessary:
   - Wyland Broadband: **Service Providers**
   - Northshore Water Company: **Utilities**
   - Oberg Property Management: **Service Providers**
   - Puget Sound Power Company: **Utilities**
   - Seattle Vet Supply: **Suppliers**
   - Whoville Office Supplies: **Supplies**
   - Brian's Pet Taxi: **Service Providers**

5. Run the **Vendor Contact List** report to display your list of vendors with contact information.

6. Click the **Excel** Excel ▾ button and export this list to a new worksheet, saving the worksheet to your file storage location as: **CH3_A1 Vendor Contact List**

7. Close the company file.

APPLY YOUR SKILLS 3-2 QG

Enter and Pay Bills

In this exercise, you will first manage expenses incurred by Wet Noses Veterinary Clinic, run a report showing all unpaid bills, and then pay the bills.

1. Open **AYS_A2_Chapter03 (Company)** or restore **AYS_A2_Chapter03 (Portable)** from your file storage location and save your file as: **AYS_A2_Chapter03 Wet Noses Clinic**

2. On 07/02/2023, Dr. James received a bill from Seattle Vet Supply for **$3,813.58**. It should be broken down by account as follows: $1,773.25 for medical supplies, $1,056.92 for vaccines, and $983.41 for medicines. The Ref. No. is: **Inv 77-9-56** and the memo is: **Seattle Vet, Inv 77-9-56 07/2023**

3. Enter a bill received on 07/08/2023 from Northshore Water Company for **$210.67**. The Ref. No. is **Water Bill, 07/2023** and the memo is: **Northshore Water, Water Bill 07/2023**

4. On 07/18/2023, a bill was received from Puget Sound Power Company for **$241.33**. The Ref. No. is **Power Bill, 07/2023** and the memo is: **Puget Sound Power, Power Bill 07/2023**

5. Enter a bill received on 07/21/2023 from Wyland Broadband for **$159.44**. It should be broken down by account as follows: $55.99 for Internet service and $103.45 for telephone service. The Ref. No. is **Int/Phone 07/2023** and the memo is: **Wyland, Int/Phone, 07/2023**

6. Run the **Unpaid Bills Detail** report for **All** dates to determine which bills are outstanding and to see the total amount payable.

7. Click the **Excel** [Excel ▼] button and export this list to a new worksheet, saving the worksheet to your file storage location as: **CH3_A2 Unpaid Bills**

8. On 07/22/2023, Sadie decided to sit down and pay her bills. Pay all of the bills due on or before 07/22/2023. You will print the checks later.

9. Close the company file.

APPLY YOUR SKILLS 3-3 [QG]

Write Checks, Find and Adjust a Bill, and Print Checks

In this exercise, you will write checks for Dr. James, and you will record an adjusted amount for the bill from Wyland Broadband. Use the Find feature to locate the transaction. Then you will print checks.

1. Open **AYS_A3_Chapter03 (Company)** or restore **AYS_A3_Chapter03 (Portable)** from your file storage location and save your file as: **AYS_A3_Chapter03 Wet Noses Clinic**

2. Dr. James took her employees for a working lunch at **Rose's Cafe** on **07/24/2023**. She wrote a check at the restaurant for **$84.35**, using check number **1418**, for the **Meals and Entertainment** expense. Memo: **Working lunch for staff: 7/2023**

3. Sadie received a bill from **Animal Lovers** for an advertisement for **$135.00** on **07/25/2023**. Because she just paid her bills, she has decided to simply write a check for the expense and will print it later. Memo: **Animal Lovers: Advertisement**

4. Locate the **Wyland Broadband** bill dated **07/21/2023** and increase the Computer and Internet Expenses portion of the bill by $40.00, to **$95.99**, which leads to a revised total due of $199.44.

5. Run the **Vendor Balance Detail** report for July 1 through 31, 2023.

6. Click the **Excel** [Excel ▼] button and export this list to a new worksheet, saving the worksheet to your storage location as: **CH3_A3 Vendor Balance Detail**

7. Print to PDF all checks in the queue using **1419** as the first check number.

8. Close the company file.

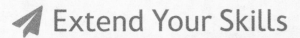 Extend Your Skills

Before You Begin: Open **EYS_Chapter03 (Company)** or restore **EYS_Chapter03 (Portable)** or from your file storage location.

You have been hired by Arlaine Cervantes to help her with her organization's books. She is the founder of Niños del Lago, a nonprofit organization that provides impoverished Guatemalan children with an engaging educational camp experience. You have just sat down at your desk and opened a large envelope from her with a variety of documents and noticed that you have several emails from her as well. It is your job to sort through the papers and emails and make sense of what you find, entering information into QuickBooks whenever appropriate and answering any other questions in a word-processing document saved as: **EYS_Chapter03 _LastnameFirstinitial**. Remember, you are digging through papers you just dumped out of an envelope and addressing random emails from Arlaine, so it is up to you to determine the correct order in which to complete the tasks.

- Sticky note: New source for cultural competency books—enter Woods Publishing Company as a vendor: 921 Pamela Lake Drive, Pittsburg, KS 66762; (620) 555-2211; Terms—Net 30; Contact—Pam Woods.

- Bill: From Network Links (for website hosting), dated 7/3/2019, for $34.57, due 7/13/2019.

- Canceled check: Written to USPS for stamps on 7/2/2019 for $25.10, number 1003.

- Sticky note dated 7/15/2019: There are some checks that can be used with the printer. Could you please print checks for any bills that I didn't write a check for?

- Note: Would like to track employee anniversaries. How can I do that?

- Scribbled on a scrap of paper: I need a report that shows all of the bills that have been entered into QuickBooks.

- Packing slip and bill: Materials received for a cultural competency seminar; need to enter the bill for $124.32, payable to Chandler Distributors, dated 7/1/2019, terms Net 15. (Arlaine is not tracking inventory in QuickBooks.)

- Carbon copies of checks: Used to pay Network Links (#1004, 7/7/2019, for full amount) and Hernandez Catering (#1005, 7/15/2019, for full amount).

- Note: We have donors who are referred to us by a local service organization. Can we include them in the customer type list?

- Bill: From Child Play, Inc. for supplies for the camp, dated 7/5/2019, for $1,212.65, due 7/15/2019.

- Printed email message from accountant: Please send a report that shows the amount owed to each vendor as of 7/10/2019.

- Bill: From Hernandez Catering for food provided at a fundraising event in California, dated 7/8/2019, payment due on receipt, for $167.21.

4 | Performing Banking Tasks

Banking has two components. There's the actual physical process such as making a trip to the bank to deposit checks, transferring funds via an online account, and utilizing your credit and debit cards. Then there's the QuickBooks component. What you've done in the first component must be matched in QuickBooks. In this chapter, you will work with bank and credit card accounts, from creating them to running reports about them. You will also have an opportunity to explore a little about banking online with QuickBooks.

LEARNING OBJECTIVES

▸ Create a credit card account

▸ Transfer funds and make deposits

▸ Manage debit and credit card transactions

▸ Reconcile accounts

▸ Create banking reports

▸ Use online banking with QuickBooks

📂 Project: Average Guy Designs

Guy has been getting comfortable performing the basic vendor and customer transactions in QuickBooks. Because his business has grown, he has hired you to take over the books so that he can concentrate on the actual design work and maintaining solid customer relationships. You will be responsible for ensuring money is on hand to pay bills, running timely banking reports, and reconciling both the bank and credit card accounts.

In addition, you will look into how online banking with QuickBooks works.

Moving Funds Between Accounts

Guy's business has two bank accounts—one to pay bills (Checking) and one where he keeps extra cash (Savings) and also gets a higher interest rate. These accounts are set up in QuickBooks as asset accounts. He also uses a company credit card in his business. This is set up as a liability account in QuickBooks.

Every business will have a need to transfer money between its bank accounts. QuickBooks has a feature that allows you to record this transfer. If you use online banking, you may even be able to set QuickBooks to perform the transfer for you when you go online (if your financial institution allows it).

Because you are transferring funds between two asset accounts, you want to debit the account that is increasing and credit the account that is decreasing. Look at the following T-accounts to visualize this transaction.

FLASHBACK TO GAAP: MONETARY UNIT

Remember that it is assumed a stable currency is going to be the unit of record.

BEHIND THE SCENES

In this illustration, you are transferring funds from the Checking account to the Savings account.

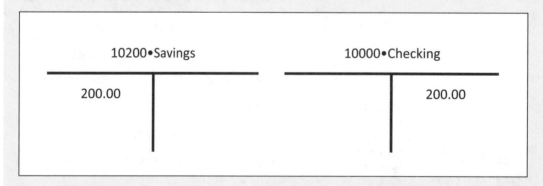

10200•Savings		10000•Checking	
200.00			200.00

Banking→Transfer Funds

In this exercise, you will transfer funds between the Checking and Savings accounts. The password for all files unless otherwise stated is Password1. *Leave the company file open unless otherwise instructed.*

1. Start QuickBooks 2019 and toggle to Pro, if necessary.
2. Choose **File→Open or Restore Company**.
3. Open **DYS_Chapter04 (Company)** or restore **DYS_Chapter04 (Portable)** from your file storage location and save your file as: **DYS_Chapter04 Average Guy Designs**
4. Close all windows except for the Home Page, if necessary.
5. Choose **Banking→Transfer Funds**.
6. Enter this information to complete the funds transfer:
   - Date: **121823**
   - Transfer Funds From: **10000•Checking**
   - Transfer Funds To: **10200•Savings**
   - Transfer Amount: **1000**

   Notice that QuickBooks displays the account balances of the accounts involved in the transfer so you can verify sufficient funds are available. Funds transfer also appears in the Memo field.

BEHIND THE SCENES BRIEF
10200•Savings DR 1,000.00; **10000•Checking CR <1,000.00>**

7. Click **Save & Close** to record the transaction and leave the company file open.

Working with an Account Register

Each balance sheet account (except for Retained Earnings) has its own register, which is a record of all transactions pertaining to the account. A QuickBooks register looks like the check register you may already keep for your personal checking account. The running balance automatically recalculates as you record each new transaction.

QuickBooks responds differently when you double-click items in the Chart of Accounts, depending on the type of account, as explained in the following table.

DOUBLE-CLICKING ACCOUNTS AND QUICKBOOKS RESPONSES	
When you double-click this type of account...	**QuickBooks responds by...**
Any balance sheet account (asset, liability, or equity)	Opening an account register for that account (Exception: The Retained Earnings account, which is a specially created account without a register; you will get a QuickReport when you double-click this account)
Any income statement account (income, expense)	Creating an account QuickReport

This checking account register image is the result of double-clicking the checking account. Double-clicking on a transaction takes you to the source of the transaction.

Edit a transaction or run a QuickReport from the menu.

The header, consisting of two lines, describes each field.

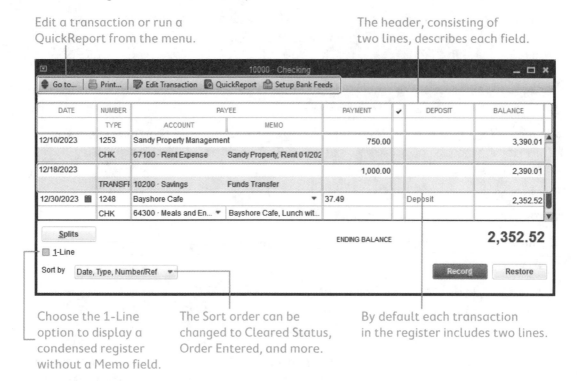

Choose the 1-Line option to display a condensed register without a Memo field.

The Sort order can be changed to Cleared Status, Order Entered, and more.

By default each transaction in the register includes two lines.

The Chart of Accounts

In accounting, a business' accounts are all listed in a Chart of Accounts. This is no different in QuickBooks, where you will see the Chart of Accounts is a list of all of the asset, liability, equity, income, and expense accounts your company utilizes.

A company can add accounts to the Chart of Accounts according to its needs. Careful planning and a discussion with an accountant are needed to make sure that you are tracking your financial data properly, which is very important when it comes to filing taxes and producing reports with meaningful data. For example, you may wish to create one account that tracks specific photography income and another to track income from video editing services.

Note! Remember, there is an exchange of funds from one account to another as you enter transactions that are handled behind the scenes by QuickBooks. This "moving about" is what keeps your books balanced and allows you to run meaningful reports. You use the forms (Create Invoices, Receive Payments, etc.) to perform the transactions, and QuickBooks does the rest!

NAME	⚡	TYPE	BALANCE TOTAL	ATTACH
⬥ 10000 · Checking		Bank	3,352.52	
⬥ 10200 · Savings		Bank	5,882.35	
⬥ 11000 · Accounts Receivable		Accounts Receivable	2,640.00	
⬥ 12000 · Undeposited Funds		Other Current Asset	2,770.00	
⬥ 15000 · Furniture and Equipment		Fixed Asset	0.00	
⬥ 17000 · Accumulated Depreciation		Fixed Asset	0.00	
⬥ 20000 · Accounts Payable		Accounts Payable	411.49	
⬥ 22000 · RiverBank Mastercard		Credit Card	164.50	
⬥ 24000 · Payroll Liabilities		Other Current Liability	0.00	
⬥ 24500 · Advance Customer Payments		Other Current Liability	0.00	
⬥ 30000 · Opening Balance Equity		Equity	12,815.02	
⬥ 30800 · Owners Draw		Equity	0.00	

The Chart of Accounts displays all accounts for a company and shows balances for balance sheet accounts. It does not show balances for income, COGS, and expense accounts. Columns can be sorted by clicking the column headings. The highlighted account (Checking) will be affected if you issue any command.

Searching in the Chart of Accounts

Some companies have a very large number of accounts, and QuickBooks has a search feature at the top of the Chart of Accounts window that can help you search through them to find the one you need. All you need

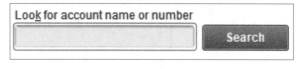

to do is type all or part of the name of the account or account number in the search field.

↗ Company→Chart of Accounts | Lists→Chart of Accounts

DEVELOP YOUR SKILLS 4-2

In this exercise, you will view the Chart of Accounts and checking register to see the transaction you performed and how it affected the two accounts. You will also drill down to see a customer's bill.

1. Click the **Chart of Accounts** task icon in the Company area of the Home Page.

   Sort the list, if necessary, by clicking the Type column heading. Note the balance totals for both checking and savings accounts.

2. Resize the window, if necessary, and then double-click **10000•Checking** to open the associated register.

   Note that the 1,000 you transferred is in the Payment column for 12/18/2023.

3. Close the Register and double-click **10200•Savings Account**.

   Note that the 1,000 is in the Deposit column.

4. Close the Savings Account register and leave the Chart of Accounts open.

Open a Register and Drill Down

5. Locate and then double-click the **10000•Checking** register.

6. Locate and then double-click anywhere within the two lines of the 11/20/2023 Ricky's Electric City **No. 1257 Bill Payment** transaction.

   It may be easier to find the transaction if you make the window larger. QuickBooks will take you to the [Bill Payments(Check) - Checking] window.

7. Close the Bill Payments (Check) and 10000•Checking windows and leave the Chart of Accounts open.

Creating and Editing Accounts

You can add new accounts to the Chart of Accounts as needed. When you add an account, the main type of account must be specified. A previously utilized account should not be deleted if no longer used. It should be made inactive.

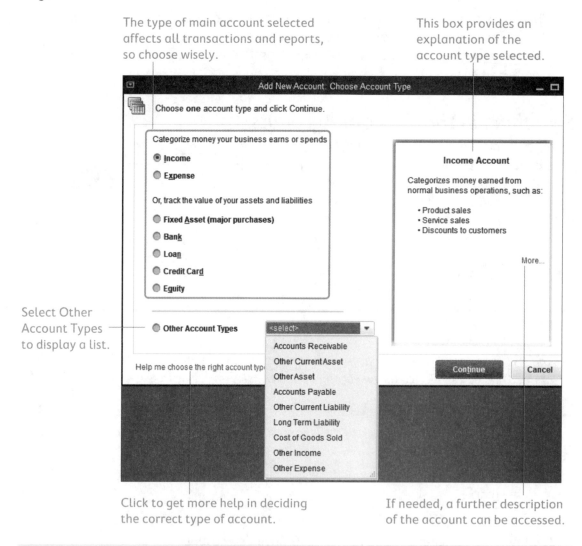

The type of main account selected affects all transactions and reports, so choose wisely.

This box provides an explanation of the account type selected.

Select Other Account Types to display a list.

Click to get more help in deciding the correct type of account.

If needed, a further description of the account can be accessed.

Company→Chart of Accounts: Account→New [or other action]

Note! In this chapter, all you need to understand is that asset account numbers will start with a "1" and liabilities with a "2."

In this exercise, you will edit the savings account number you didn't have on hand when the account was first set up. You will also create a new account for the credit card that Guy just obtained.

1. Choose **Company→Chart of Accounts** if the Chart of Accounts is not open.

2. Single-click the **Savings** account to select it.

3. Choose **Account→Edit Account** from the bottom menu bar.

4. Use this information to complete the edit:

   - Description: **RiverBank Savings Account**
   - Bank Acct. No.: **22222-33333**
   - Routing Number: **599222043**

Note! You can change the Opening Balance, if necessary, and set up a check order reminder, make the account inactive, and set up bank feeds from this window.

5. Click **Save & Close** and leave the Chart of Accounts open.

Create a New Account

You will now create a new credit card account for the new card Guy has received and pay one bill using the new card.

6. Click the **Account** button drop-down arrow ▼ and then click **New**.

7. Complete these steps to create the new credit card account:

   - Select **Credit Card** (and click **Continue**)
   - Number: **21000**
   - Account Name: **RiverBank Visa**
   - Description: **Company Credit Card**
   - Credit Card Acct. No.: **4555222230304545**

   If this card was in use before your QuickBooks start date and had a balance, you would need to put in the Opening Balance from your last statement.

8. Click **Save & Close**; click **No** in the Set Up Bank Feed window.

9. Close the Chart of Accounts window and leave the company file open.

Making Deposits

If you have utilized the Undeposited Funds account when you received funds through the Receive Payments and Enter Sales Receipts windows, you will need to take one more step to move your payments to your bank account. This step is accomplished through the Make Deposits window. The Make Deposits window can also be used when you make a sale and do not need a sales receipt, or when you want to deposit a lump sum that will credit an income account and debit your bank account.

Think of the Undeposited Funds account as a "holding tank" that stores all of the funds you have collected together until you are ready to make a deposit. In this section, you will learn how to empty the Undeposited Funds account.

If you have payments sitting in your Undeposited Funds account and you click the Record Deposits task icon on the Home Page, you will get the Payments to Deposit window. Here you can choose which payments you wish to deposit.

✓	DATE	TIME	TYPE	NO.	PAYMENT METH...	NAME	AMOUNT
	12/20/2023		RCPT	1	Cash	Hakola, Ashley:Wedding	180.00
	12/07/2023		PMT	1547	Check	Huff, Evelyn:Holiday F...	105.00
	12/10/2023		PMT	45RS6671...	Check	Miata Events, Inc.:Expl...	160.00
	12/11/2023		PMT	762	Check	Hakola, Ashley:Wedding	120.00
	12/12/2023		PMT	1299	Check	James Limousine Ser...	175.00
	12/13/2023		PMT	1003	Check	JLR Doggie Playhous...	190.00
	12/14/2023		PMT	152	Check	Learners, Inc.:Marketing	135.00
	12/19/2023		PMT	2548	Check	Lucy's Cupcake Factor...	100.00
	12/22/2023		RCPT	2	Check		200.00
	12/23/2023		PMT	470	Check	Jones, Mary	270.00
	12/27/2023		PMT	1632	Check	Lite Foot Dance Comp...	245.00
	12/29/2023		PMT	872	Check	JLR Doggie Playhous...	180.00
	12/29/2023		PMT	341	Check	Lucy's Cupcake Factory	200.00
	12/30/2023		PMT		MasterCard	Learners, Inc.	50.00
	12/11/2023		PMT		Visa	Learners, Inc.:Marketing	140.00

The Payments to Deposit window displays the type and method of payment. You can filter by payment method and sort by the Date, Payment Method, No., Name, and Amount.

Tip! You can always click OK to close the Payments to Deposit window if you are not ready to deposit the payments and yet still need to work with the Make Deposits window.

Print a detailed report, including deposit slips, from this menu. Select a transaction to run a Journal report.

Change deposit accounts, date, or Memo here.

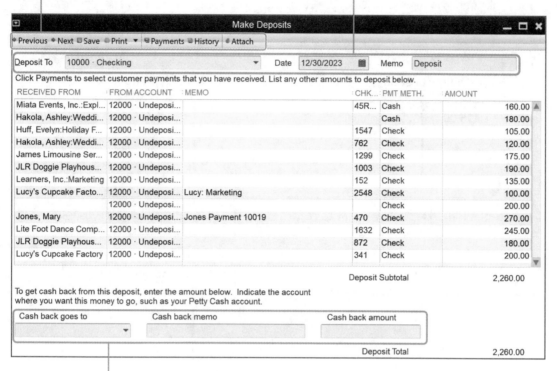

RECEIVED FROM	FROM ACCOUNT	MEMO	CHK...	PMT METH.	AMOUNT
Miata Events, Inc.:Expl...	12000 · Undeposi...		45R...	Cash	160.00
Hakola, Ashley:Weddi...	12000 · Undeposi...			Cash	180.00
Huff, Evelyn:Holiday F...	12000 · Undeposi...		1547	Check	105.00
Hakola, Ashley:Weddi...	12000 · Undeposi...		762	Check	120.00
James Limousine Ser...	12000 · Undeposi...		1299	Check	175.00
JLR Doggie Playhous...	12000 · Undeposi...		1003	Check	190.00
Learners, Inc.:Marketing	12000 · Undeposi...		152	Check	135.00
Lucy's Cupcake Facto...	12000 · Undeposi...	Lucy: Marketing	2548	Check	100.00
	12000 · Undeposi...			Check	200.00
Jones, Mary	12000 · Undeposi...	Jones Payment 10019	470	Check	270.00
Lite Foot Dance Comp...	12000 · Undeposi...		1632	Check	245.00
JLR Doggie Playhous...	12000 · Undeposi...		872	Check	180.00
Lucy's Cupcake Factory	12000 · Undeposi...		341	Check	200.00

Deposit Subtotal   2,260.00

To get cash back from this deposit, enter the amount below. Indicate the account where you want this money to go, such as your Petty Cash account.

Cash back goes to   Cash back memo   Cash back amount

Deposit Total   2,260.00

If you wish to keep cash back from the deposit, for instance to refresh your petty cash account, you can indicate it here.

BEHIND THE SCENES

If you make deposits from your Undeposited Funds account, the following accounting will occur behind the scenes:

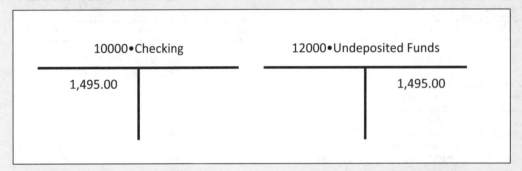

If you use the Make Deposits window to record sales, the accounting involved is as follows:

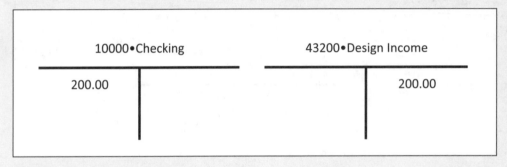

Banking→Make Deposits

DEVELOP YOUR SKILLS 4-4

In this exercise, you will work with the Make Deposits window to deposit funds from the Undeposited Funds account and to make a deposit without a sales form. The Record Deposits task icon will display a number indicating the number of deposits being held in Undeposited Funds.

1. Click the **Record Deposits** task icon in the Banking area of the Home Page.
2. Click the **View Payment Method Type** drop-down arrow ▼ and choose **Cash and Check**.
3. Click the **Select All** button; QuickBooks will place a checkmark to the left of thirteen payments totaling $2,260.00 waiting to be deposited.

Note! The thirteen payments you've selected can be printed on a Deposit Slip, which you can take to the bank. The total amount will be reflected on your monthly bank statement.

4. Click **OK** to accept the payments for deposit and move on to the Make Deposits window.

5. Finish the deposit with this information:
   - Deposit To: **10000•Checking**
   - Date: **123023**

6. Choose the **Print drop-down arrow** ▼→**Deposit Slip** and then click **Preview** to view the Deposit Slip.

   Only Cash and Checks can be printed on the Deposit Slip. You will need to make another deposit for the remaining four payments.

7. Click **Close** and then **Cancel**.

8. Click **Save & New** to make the deposit to your Checking account.

   The Payments to Deposit window will still be open displaying the remaining Credit Card and E-Check payments.

9. Click **Select All** and then click **OK**.

10. Finish the $510.00 deposit with this information:
    - Deposit To: **10000•Checking**
    - Date: **123023**

11. Click **Save & New** to make the deposit to your Checking account and leave the Make Deposits window open for the next step.

> **BEHIND THE SCENES BRIEF**
>
> 10000•Checking DR 2,770.00; **12000•Undeposited Funds CR <2,770.00>**

Undeposited Funds has been cleared out and is no longer "holding" money that has been deposited. This will reflect in any balance sheet reports that are run.

Make a Deposit Without Specifying a Customer

You and Guy worked at a Quick Sketch fundraiser where people could meet with a graphic artist for 15 minutes to describe a need they have for their organization. For $15 they received a sketch and description of a possible solution to their stated need. Average Guy Designs made $5 from each of the quick consultations. Because there were multiple customers whom Guy does not want to track individually, you will make a deposit to Checking, directly crediting Design Income without using a specific item.

12. Complete the deposit with these entries:
    - Deposit to: **10000•Checking**
    - Date: **122323**
    - From Account: **43200•Design Income**
    - Memo: `Quick Sketch Event`
    - Pmt Meth.: **Cash**
    - Amount: **200**

There is no item entered for this transaction, but you do need to fill in the account. Remember that an item is used to direct funds to the underlying account. You cannot leave the From

Account field blank because you must specify the account that will be credited as you will be debiting a bank account with the deposit.

BEHIND THE SCENES BRIEF
10000•Checking DR 200.00; **43200•Design Income CR <200.00>**

13. Click **Save & Close**; your deposit will be recorded and the window will close; leave the company file open.

Managing Credit and Debit Card Transactions

Credit cards give business owners an easy way to track their expenses. QuickBooks allows you to track credit card transactions just as you track checking and savings account transactions. You can set up as many credit card accounts as you need.

Note! If you use your personal credit cards occasionally for business purposes, you should *not* enter them in QuickBooks as business credit cards. Create accounts only for business credit cards.

Credit card transactions are classified as either a charge (when you make a purchase) or a credit (when you make a return). As you will use the same form for both types, you need to choose the correct type when entering transactions.

Type of Account and Normal Balance

A credit card is a liability, so its normal balance is a credit. This means you credit (increase) the account when you make a purchase and debit (decrease) the account when you make a payment.

Dealing with Debit Card Transactions

When you make a purchase or pay a bill with a debit card, funds are taken directly from your checking account, which is different from what occurs for credit card purchases. Use the Write Checks window to handle debit card transactions. If you use the Enter/Pay Bills windows in QuickBooks, you can continue to use them when working with debit card purchases. This means that if you have entered a bill in QuickBooks and then choose to use a debit card to pay it, you must enter that payment through the Pay Bills window. Otherwise, the expenses will be over-stated, and you will leave the bill hanging out in Accounts Payable.

When you enter a debit card transaction in the Write Checks window, indicate it by entering a code such as "DB" in the No. field.

Other Types of Transactions Affecting the Checking Account

In addition to debit card transactions, you may have other ones that also draw funds from the checking account. For instance, ATM cards and a service such as PayPal™ can withdraw funds directly from your bank account. All of these transactions will be entered using the Write Checks window; you just need to create common codes that will be used in the No. field to record each type of transaction. Common codes include DB for debit card, ATM for an ATM card transaction, and PP for a PayPal payment. You do not have to use the codes suggested here; however, you should choose one code for each type of transaction and stick with it!

Paying a Bill with a Credit Card

You have the option to pay a bill with a credit card. You use the Enter Credit Card Charges window to pay the vendor.

Warning! If you use a credit card to pay a bill that you entered through the *Enter Bills* window, you must use the *Pay Bills* window when you pay it. If you were to use the Write Checks window or Enter Credit Card Charges window, then the expense and Accounts Payable will be overstated!

Banking→Enter Credit Card Charges

Banking→Write Checks [for debit card transactions]

Vendors→Pay Bills

BEHIND THE SCENES

A purchase credits the credit card account, as shown here:

64900•Office Supplies		64400•Advertising and Promotion		21000•RiverBank Visa	
57.84		31.25			89.09

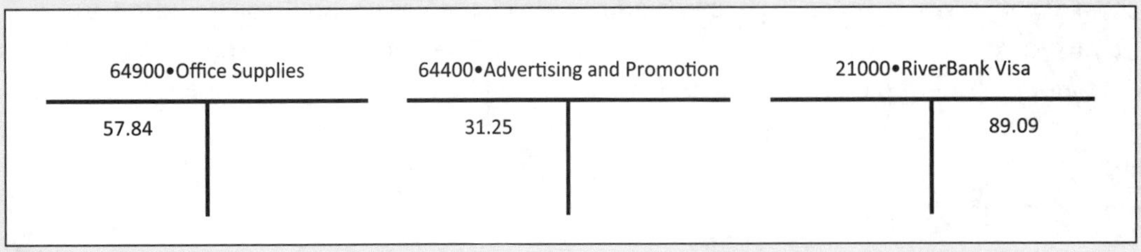

A payment or refund debits the credit card account, as shown here:

64900•Office Supplies		21000•RiverBank Visa	
	10.46	10.46	

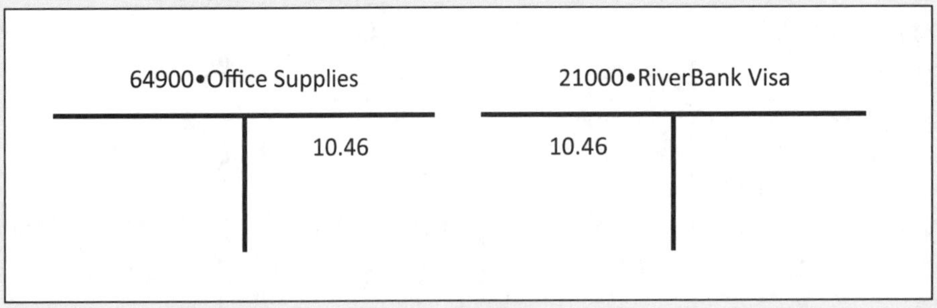

When you use a credit card to pay a bill, the following occurs behind the scenes:

20000•Accounts Payable		21000•RiverBank Visa	
363.27			363.27

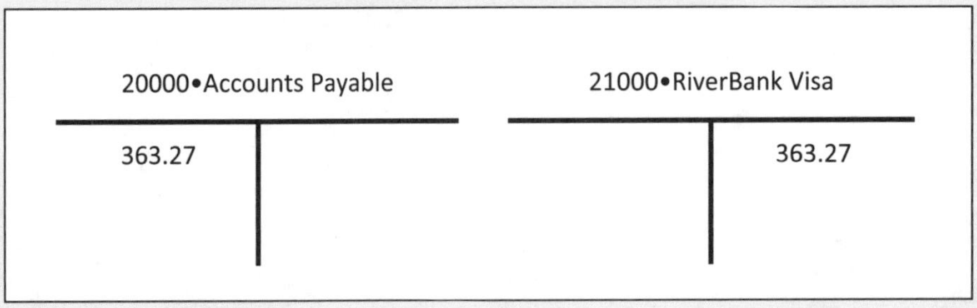

Using a debit card to make the same bill payment as above looks like the following behind the scenes:

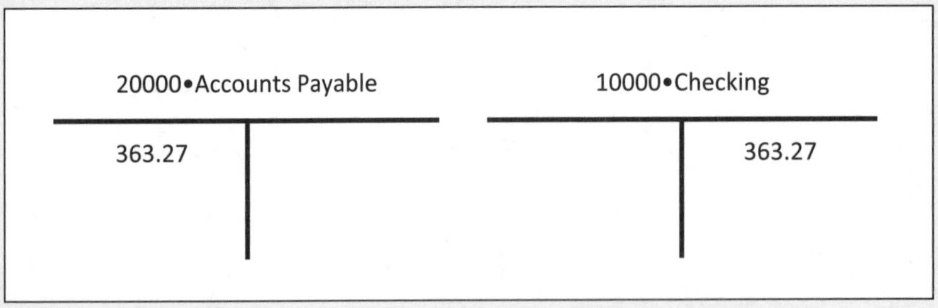

20000•Accounts Payable		10000•Checking	
363.27			363.27

When you use a debit card to purchase office supplies, the following occurs behind the scenes:

64900•Office Supplies		10000•Checking	
363.27			363.27

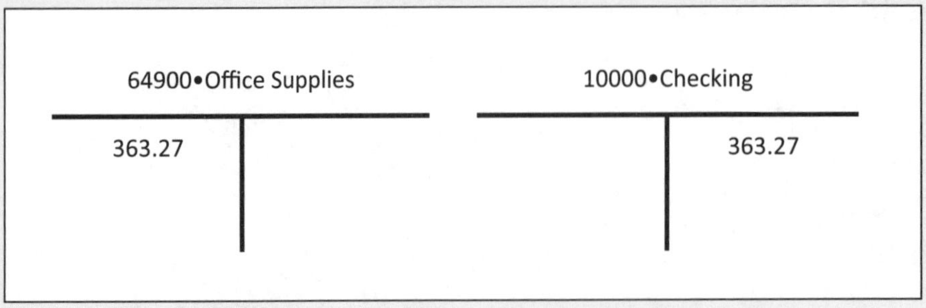

You have purchased some supplies for the office using the company credit card and have also purchased USB drives to give away to clients. In this exercise, you will enter a credit card purchase, set up a new account, enter a return to be credited to a credit card, and pay a bill using a debit card.

1. Click the **Enter Credit Card Charges** 🃏 task icon in the Banking area of the Home Page.

   Because you have two credit cards set up at this time, you will need to choose the appropriate card before entering other information.

2. Use this information to enter the credit card charge information:

   - Credit Card: **RiverBank Visa**
   - Purchased From: **Star Office Supplies**
   - Date: **111823**
   - Ref No.: **01**
   - Amount: **89.09**
   - Memo: **Office supplies and customer USB drive giveaway**
   - Change the Amount next to 64900•Office Supplies: **57.84**

   The 57.84 represents the amount spent on the Office Supplies only. Notice that Office Supplies filled in because the account was the default for the vendor.

3. Memo on Expenses tab: **Office supplies**

Set Up a New Account

There is no account applicable to which you can charge the USB drives, so you are creating one "on the fly."

4. Click the row below *Office Supplies* in the Account column, click the drop-down arrow ▼, and then scroll up to locate and then click on **Add New**.

5. Choose **Expense** and then click **Continue**.

6. Use this information to complete the account:

   - Number: **64400**
   - Account Name: **Advertising and Promotion**
   - Description: **Advertising and promotion including customer giveaways**

7. Click **Save & Close**.

   Notice that the amount was calculated and filled in automatically, and now that this account has been added, you will be able to track these expenses going forward.

BEHIND THE SCENES BRIEF

64900•Office Supplies DR 57.84; 64400•Advertising and Promotion DR 31.25; **21000•RiverBank Visa CR <89.09>**

---

8. Type this in the Memo field: **Customer USB drive giveaway**

9. Click the **Save & New** button.

Record a Credit Card Return

In the next transaction, you will record a credit for a returned calculator purchased from Star Office Supplies.

10. Use this information to complete a credit card refund:

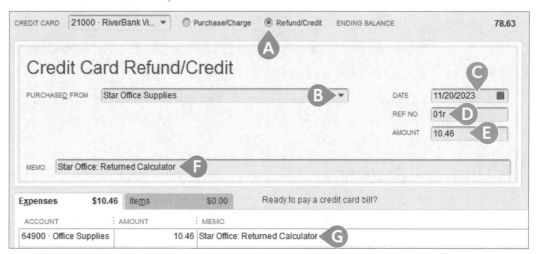

Ⓐ Choose **Refund/Credit**

Ⓑ Tap ⌈Tab⌋, type **st**, and choose **Star Office Supplies**

Ⓒ Date: **112023**

Ⓓ Ref No.: **01r**

Ⓔ Amount: **10.46**

Ⓕ Memo: **Star Office: Returned Calculator**

Ⓖ Memo on Expenses tab: **Star Office: Returned Calculator**

Notice that the account and amount prefill.

BEHIND THE SCENES BRIEF

21000•RiverBank Visa DR 10.46; **64900•Office Supplies CR <10.46>**

---

11. Click **Save & Close** and leave the company file open.

QuickBooks records the transaction and closes the Enter Credit Card Charges window.

Pay a Bill with a Debit Card

You can record a bill paid by debit card in QuickBooks, although you must use the Pay Bills window in order to properly affect Accounts Payable.

12. Click the **Pay Bills** task icon in the Vendors area of the Home Page.

13. Click in the checkbox alongside **Professional Software Distributors**.

14. Use this information to complete the payment at the bottom of the window:

    • Date: **122723**

    • Method: **Check** (choose **Assign Check Number**)

    You will record it as a debit card payment in the next steps.

15. Click **Pay Selected Bills**.

16. Click **Let me assign the check numbers below.**, type **DB** in the Check column, and click **OK**.

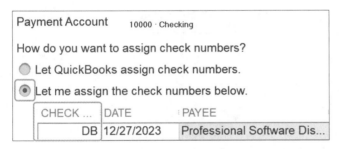

When you pay a bill with a debit card, you are affecting the Checking account, so you will need to assign the transaction the "check number" that you use for all debit card transactions. In the scenario above, you have chosen to use "DB."

17. Click **Done** in the Payment Summary window and leave the company file open.

QuickBooks records the bill payment, debiting Accounts Payable and crediting Checking.

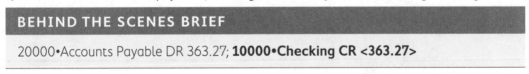

BEHIND THE SCENES BRIEF

20000•Accounts Payable DR 363.27; **10000•Checking CR <363.27>**

Dealing with Bounced Checks

Unfortunately, almost all business owners must deal with customers whose checks are returned for nonsufficient funds (NSF) at some time or another. These are also called bounced checks.

If you've invoiced a customer and used the Receive Payments window, you can easily use the Record Bounced Check feature available in the Receive Payments window. QuickBooks will create a new invoice that will include the fee you want to charge the customer. The original invoice will be marked unpaid. You can then send the customer the new invoice along with either a statement or original invoice.

However, if the bounced check was received on a sales receipt or directly through a deposit, you will need to account for it using an alternate method. Below are the steps necessary to do this:

- Create an *Other Charge* item for the service charge, directing it to the *Other Income* account.
- Record the bank's fee in your bank account register (Bank Service Charges as account).
- Record the check in your bank account register (customer/job as payee; Accounts Receivable as account).
- Enter a statement charge for the customer's fee.
- Send the customer a statement that shows the bounced check and fee.

BEHIND THE SCENES

When you deal with a returned check, you will affect multiple accounts behind the scenes.

11000•Accounts Receivable		10000•Checking	
200.00			200.00
40.00			30.00

60400•Bank Service Charges		48910•Returned Check Charges	
30.00			40.00

 Customers→Receive Payments

DEVELOP YOUR SKILLS 4-6

In this exercise, you will account for a check that was returned to Average Guy Designs for nonsufficient funds.

1. Click the **Receive Payments** task icon in the Customers area of the Home Page.
2. Click the **Previous** button two times until Lucy's Cupcake Factory's check #341 payment is displayed.
3. Click the **Record Bounced Check** button on the Main tab of the Ribbon.

4. Follow these steps to set the fees for the bounced check:

- Bank Fee: **30**
- Date: **122023**

The Expense account is prefilled with 60400•Bank Service Charges. Lucy has decided to charge an additional fee of $10 for the bounced check.

- Customer Fee: **40**

5. Click **Next**.

Bounced Check Summary

When you click Record Bounced Check, here's what will happen in QuickBooks:

1. Following invoices will be marked unpaid:

Invoice 10003	Lucy's Cupcake Factory	Unpaid	200.00

2. These fees will be deducted from your bank account:

Checking	Check 341	200.00
Checking	Service Fee	30.00

3. This invoice will be created for the fee you want to charge your customer:

Invoice	Lucy's Cupcake Factory	40.00

A Bounced Check Summary will be displayed explaining what will happen.

6. Click **Finish**.

The Receive Payments window will again be displayed. You will see that the check has been marked as a Bounced Check, and a new invoice dated 12/27/2023 has been created to account for the bounced check fee.

BEHIND THE SCENES BRIEF

11000•Accounts Receivable DR 240.00; 60400•Bank Service Charges DR 30.00;
10000•Checking CR <230.00>; 48910•Returned Check Charges CR <40.00>

7. Click **Save & Close** and leave the company file open.

Reconciling Accounts

An important task is to ensure that your QuickBooks records match those of your bank. The process of matching transactions to your bank statement, is called reconciliation. There needs to be extra attention paid to details when performing a reconciliation!

When Your Accounts Don't Match

There might be occasions when the reconciliation shows a difference.

Locating Discrepancies

If reconciliation displays a difference, you can use Locate Discrepancies during the reconciliation process. You can also run a Reconciliation Discrepancy report that lists transactions affecting the reconciliation balance. The types of transactions that can affect the balance are:

- Deleted transactions

- A change to a previously cleared amount

- Transactions that were manually un-cleared in the register

- Transactions in which the date was changed to a different statement period

 **Best Practice**

Save each month's recon-ciliation reports as PDFs, as the QuickBooks Pro edition replaces the prior report with the new month's information. An added benefit is that the PDFs can be sent via email if necessary. QuickBooks Premier and Enterprise editions store all reconciliation reports as PDF files for you, and they can be accessed at any time.

Warning! After you have cleared transactions through the reconciliation process, it is important *not* to change them. Changes may alter your starting balance for the next reconciliation. If you find yourself in such a situation, run the Reconciliation Discrepancy report to find the problem(s).

Problem Resolution Process

If you do find yourself in the situation of finishing your reconciliation without balancing, consider the following suggestions:

- Look for a transaction that is exactly the same amount as the difference and ensure whether or not it should be cleared.

- Determine whether you are missing a deposit or a payment by looking at the totals of each on the bank statement and the QuickBooks reconciliation window.

- Compare the number of transactions on the bank statement to the number of cleared transactions in QuickBooks.

- Verify the individual amount of each transaction on the bank statement and compare it to the amounts you have in QuickBooks.

- Determine whether it is a bank error (the bank may have recorded a transaction for the wrong amount).

- If it is a bank error, you can create an adjustment transaction in QuickBooks, notify the bank, and then reverse the adjustment transaction after the bank corrects the error.

- Run a Reconciliation Discrepancy report to see whether any changes were made to previously cleared transactions. If changes were made to previously cleared transactions, undo the last reconciliation and redo it.

FLASHBACK TO GAAP: ASSUMPTION OF A GOING CONCERN

Remember that it is assumed that the business will be in operation indefinitely.

⤴ Banking→Reconcile

⤴ Banking→Reconcile: Locate Discrepancies

⤴ Reports→Banking

DEVELOP YOUR SKILLS 4-7

In this exercise, you will reconcile the Checking account in QuickBooks to the company's September 2023 RiverBank checking account statement.

1. Click the **Reconcile** 🖫 task icon in the Banking area of the Home Page.

   QuickBooks displays the Begin Reconciliation window.

2. Use this information to complete the Begin Reconciliation step:
   - Account: Ensure **10000•Checking** is selected
   - Statement Date: **093023**
   - Ending Balance: **6768.70**
   - Interest Earned: **11.52**
   - Date: **093023**
   - Account: Click the **Account** drop-down arrow ▼ button and choose **Add New**, scrolling, if necessary

3. Use this information to complete the New Interest Income account:
   - Choose **Other Income** if not already selected
   - Number: **70000**
   - Account Name: **Interest Income**
   - Description: **Interest Income from Savings, Money Market, and Checking Accounts**

4. Click **Save & Close** to return to the Begin Reconciliation window.

Begin Reconciliation window completed

5. Click **Continue** to move to the Reconciliation-Checking window.

The Reconciliation-Checking window shows all transactions waiting to be cleared.

Reconcile a Checking Account

Now that you have completed the Begin Reconciliation step, you can begin the actual reconciliation.

6. Click the checkbox alongside **Hide transactions after the statement's end date** to concentrate on this reconciliation period.

Checking Account Statement

Average Guy Designs
110 Sampson Way
Bayshore, CA 91547

Account Number: 11111-44444

Statement Period: Sep. 1 – Sep 30, 2023

Total Deposits:	$1511.52		**Total Payments:**	$175.49
Beginning Balance:	$5432.67		**Ending Balance:**	$6768.70

Transactions:

Date	Transaction Type	Payment	Deposit	Balance
09/18/2023	Check # 1249	125.49		5307.18
09/18/2023	Check # 1250	50.00		5257.18
09/24/2023	Transfer		1,500.00	6757.18
09/24/2023	Interest		11.52	6768.70
Ending Balance:				6768.70

7. Click in the **checkmark** column to the left of each transaction that matches the entry on the bank checking statement displayed above. This will clear it. The interest income appears in the lower-right part of the window.

When you are finished, your Reconciliation-Checking window should match the following illustration.

Checks and Payments					Deposits and Other Credits					
✓ DATE ▲	CHK #	PAYEE	AMOUNT		✓ DATE ▲	CHK #	MEMO	TYPE	AMOUNT	
✓ 09/18/2023	1249	Rankin Family Insura…	125.49		✓ 09/24/2023		Funds Transfer	TRANSFER	1,500.00	
✓ 09/18/2023	1250	GJB Wireless, Inc.	50.00							

Beginning Balance		5,432.67			Modify	Service Charge	0.00
Items you have marked cleared						Interest Earned	11.52
1	Deposits and Other Credits	1,500.00				Ending Balance	6,768.70
2	Checks and Payments	175.49				Cleared Balance	6,768.70
						Difference	0.00

8. Look at the *Difference* at the bottom-right of the window to see whether you have successfully reconciled your account.

The Difference should be zero. If something was missed or there was some other issue, the Difference would display the amount that it is off. The Difference is calculated by determining the difference between the transactions on the bank statement and those that you have marked cleared in QuickBooks, including any interest or other charges that you entered on the Begin Reconciliation window.

9. Click **Reconcile Now** and then click **OK** in the Information window, if necessary.

There might be a pause as QuickBooks records the marked transactions as cleared. The Select Reconciliation Report window is displayed.

10. Choose **Summary** and then click **Display** to view the Summary report.

11. Click **OK** to close the Reconciliation Report window.

Average Guy Designs, Chapter 4
Reconciliation Summary
10000 · Checking, Period Ending 09/30/2023

	Sep 30, 23
Beginning Balance	5,432.67
▼ Cleared Transactions	
Checks and Payments - 2 items	-175.49
Deposits and Credits - 2 items	1,511.52
Total Cleared Transactions	1,336.03
Cleared Balance	6,768.70
Register Balance as of 09/30/2023	6,768.70
▼ New Transactions	
Checks and Payments - 15 ite...	-4,634.66
Deposits and Credits - 3 items	2,970.00
Total New Transactions	-1,664.66
Ending Balance	5,104.04

The Register Balance will be the Beginning Balance for the next reconciliation, and the Ending Balance should match the ending balance in your check register.

12. Close the Reconciliation Summary window and leave the company file open.

Reconciling Credit Cards

You can reconcile your credit cards the same way as you reconcile your bank account by choosing the credit card account. Another method to access the reconciliation task is through the Chart of Accounts.

After you have reconciled the credit card, you have the option to pay any amount due. You can choose to either write a check or enter a bill for the payment. QuickBooks takes the balance due on the credit card and fills it in to either the Enter Bills or the Write Checks window. If you don't plan to pay the entire amount owed, you can change the amount manually. You will reconcile the credit card in the "Tackle the Tasks" section at the end of the chapter.

Fixing Banking Transactions

Inevitably, you will need to deal with errors or modifications to transactions in QuickBooks. It is very important that you do this properly to ensure that everything behind the scenes is correct. Deleted and voided transactions are recorded and become part of the overall records. This helps to create an audit trail that can be traced.

Fixing Errors

The following table outlines two potential errors: The first is related to the Chart of Accounts, and the second occurs when dealing with a debit card transaction incorrectly.

COMMON ERRORS AND FIXES		
Error	**Effect Behind the Scenes**	**The Fix**
The wrong account type was chosen when creating a new account in the Chart of Accounts.	The types of accounts involved will determine what the damage will be behind the scenes. (But there will be damage!)	Edit the account through the Chart of Accounts and choose the correct account type.
A debit card transaction was entered in the Enter Credit Card Charges window.	The wrong account is credited, and you will have an inflated amount displayed in Checking as well as the credit card account.	Delete the credit card transaction and reenter it through a window that affects Checking.

📌 Lists→Chart of Accounts

📌 Banking→Enter Credit Card Charges

DEVELOP YOUR SKILLS 4-8

In this exercise, you will help Guy fix two tasks that were not entered correctly. The business has just received a Discover card that will be used for expenses. By mistake, it was set up as an expense and not as a credit card. First you will fix the error so that it doesn't have huge ramifications behind the scenes!

1. Choose **Company→Chart of Accounts**.

2. Right-click **62300•Discover Card** in the Chart of Accounts window and then choose **Edit Account** from the menu.

3. Use this information to edit the account:

   - Account Type: **Credit Card**
   - Number: **23000**
   - Description: `Company Credit Card`

   You must change the account number when you change the account type.

4. Click **Save & Close** and close the Chart of Accounts window.

Change a Credit Card Transaction

A bill for graphic art supplies was entered as a credit card purchase instead of a debit card purchase. In this exercise, you will fix the transaction so that it is recorded properly by deleting the incorrect credit card charge first. Because the Enter Credit Card Charges window was used, the balance in the credit card account was increased, and the funds have not been removed from the Checking account. Then you will input the transaction properly using Write Checks.

5. Click the **Enter Credit Card Charges** 📧 task icon in the Banking area of the Home Page.

6. Choose **RiverBank Mastercard**.

7. Click the **Previous** arrow ◀ to locate the Graphic Supply Shoppe transaction dated 10/30/2023.

8. Click **Delete** ✖.

9. Click **OK** to confirm the deletion and then close the window.

Enter a Bill Pay Transaction Using a Debit Card

10. Click the **Write Checks** 📝 task icon in the Banking area of the Home Page.

11. Use this information to enter the debit card purchase correctly:

    - Bank Account: Ensure **Checking** is selected
    - No.: **DB**
    - Date: **103023**
    - Pay to the Order Of: **Graphic Supply Shoppe**
    - $ (Amount): **164.50**
    - Memo: `Purchased Ink`
    - Expenses tab: Confirm **61500•Job Materials** is the account selected

    > **BEHIND THE SCENES BRIEF**
    >
    > 22000•RiverBank Mastercard DR 164.50; **61500•Job Materials CR <164.50>**
    > 61500•Job Materials DR 164.50; **10000•Checking CR <164.50>**

12. Click **Save & Close** and leave the company file open.

    You have now ensured the balances in the Checking and Credit Card accounts are correct by deleting the credit card entry and recording the debit card purchase correctly.

Working with Banking and Balance Sheet Reports

Running reports is a method of pulling information out of QuickBooks in a meaningful way. In this section, you will learn which reports to run to depict banking activities, as well as reports that display information about your balance sheet accounts (asset, liability, and equity). Snapshots are a quick way to see the status of payments, the company, and customers. QuickReports are a way of running a more specific report for a specific account.

Banking Reports

QuickBooks comes with preset reports to use to get answers from your data. Banking reports deal with answers to questions such as:

- Can you show all transactions involving a specific payee?
- Which checks have not cleared the bank as of the last bank statement?
- Which payments still need to be deposited?
- Where can I find a list of all transactions that affect my checking account?
- Which changes in transactions may affect my next reconciliation?

QuickReports from the Register

These reports are run right from a register window. From within a Register, once you select a transaction and click the QuickReport button, you will receive a report that shows all transactions for the payee, vendor, or customer for the selected transaction.

Reconciliation Reports

As you saw earlier in this chapter, reconciliation reports show transactions that have cleared as well as those that have yet to clear the bank. QuickBooks allows you to save reconciliation reports in a PDF format.

Alternatives to Printing Reports

While any report can be sent to a printer, there are other options for storing or saving a report:

- **Email:** QuickBooks can convert the report to PDF. This allows viewing of the report exactly as it would print even to those who do not have QuickBooks. You have a choice of sending it as a PDF or an Excel Workbook.
- **Create an Excel Workbook:** QuickBooks can export the report to Microsoft Excel so you can use Excel's powerful spreadsheet features to work with your data.
- **Saving Reports and Forms as PDF**: Save copies for your own records.

  Banking→Use Register: [select a transaction]→QuickReport

  Company→Chart of Accounts: [double-click the account]→[click the transaction]→ QuickReport

  Reports→Banking

In this exercise, you will produce two banking reports and save one of them as a PDF file.

1. Choose **Reports→Banking→Previous Reconciliation**.

2. Use this information to run the report:

   • Account: Ensure **10000•Checking** is displayed

   • Type of Report: **Detail**

   • In this report include: **Transactions Cleared at Time of Reconciliation**

   Notice that you can elect to include cleared transactions at time of reconciliation or cleared transactions plus any changes that might have been made to those transactions.

3. Click the **Display** button to produce the report; resize the report window, if necessary.

Options to save as PDF, print, or open in Adobe

10000 · Checking, Period Ending 09/30/2023

Type	Date	Num	Name	Clr	Amount	Balance
Beginning Balance						5,432.67
Cleared Transactions						
Checks and Payments - 2 items						
Bill Pmt -Check	09/18/2023	1249	Rankin Family Insur...	X	-125.49	-125.49
Bill Pmt -Check	09/18/2023	1250	GJB Wireless, Inc.	X	-50.00	-175.49
Total Checks and Payments					-175.49	-175.49
Deposits and Credits - 2 items						
Transfer	09/24/2023			X	1,500.00	1,500.00
Deposit	09/30/2023			X	11.52	1,511.52
Total Deposits and Credits					1,511.52	1,511.52
Total Cleared Transactions					1,336.03	1,336.03
Cleared Balance					1,336.03	6,768.70
Register Balance as of 09/30/2023					1,336.03	6,768.70
New Transactions						
Checks and Payments - 15 items						
Check	10/03/2023	1251	Star Office Supplies		-36.21	-36.21
Bill Pmt -Check	10/07/2023	1255	Handyman by the Bay		-239.44	-275.65
Bill Pmt -Check	10/07/2023	1256	NoCal Gas & Electric		-82.37	-358.02
Bill Pmt -Check	10/07/2023	1254	GJB Wireless, Inc.		-11.28	-369.30

New unreconciled transactions

Cleared items marked with an x

Cleared amount and balance

4. Close the Reconciliation Detail report window.

Run a Register QuickReport

You will now create a report based on information contained within your Checking account.

5. Click the **Check Register** 🖳 task icon in the Banking area of the Home Page.

6. Click **OK** to choose the **10000•Checking** account.

   The Average Guy Designs Checking register will be displayed.

7. Locate and click on the **Professional Software Distributors 10/09/2023** transaction and then click **QuickReport** from the toolbar at the top of the window.

   The report displays all of the transactions from the checking register for Professional Software Distributors. Notice the various buttons on the toolbar to print, email, export to Excel, and perform other tasks. Leave this report open for the next step.

Produce a PDF Copy of a Report

Now you will save a PDF copy of this report. You will save it in your default file location.

8. Make sure that the Register QuickReport for **Professional Software Distributors** is still the active window and then choose **File→Save as PDF** from the main QuickBooks menu bar.

9. Save the file to your file storage location as: **CH4_D9 Professional Software Distributors**

10. Choose **Window→Close All** and leave the company file open.

Balance Sheet Reports

Many reports can be run as a summary report or a detail report. The Balance Sheet Summary report provides a look at your assets, liabilities, and equity as of a certain date. They should be in balance. This report should be looked at often, especially if the business handles numerous transactions on a daily or weekly basis. The detail version shows at the transaction level and can be a useful troubleshooting tool.

While the default is for a balance sheet report to display all of your asset, liability, and equity accounts (hence the designation the "balance sheet accounts"), you can also customize your report to show only the accounts you wish to display. This report and the profit & loss report (or income statement) are two key financial reports for a business.

> *Note!* The balance sheet when run at the beginning of a fiscal year will display Net Income "rolled" into an Equity account.

Company Snapshot

The Company Snapshot gives you a quick view of your company's bottom line in one convenient place. You can customize it to include "at-a-glance" reports that are most important to your company. The Company Snapshot will show information only within a preset date range within the current year. (If you don't see anything displayed, it is likely because the date for which you are performing the exercise is after the current year available through the snapshot.)

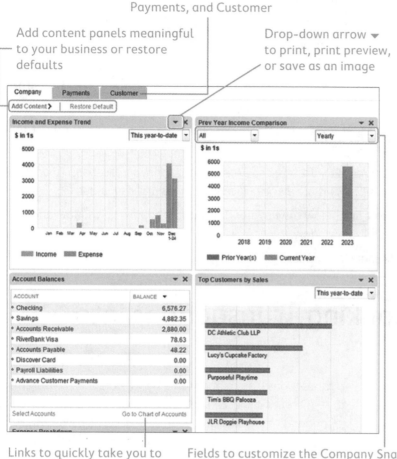

Three tabs: Company, Payments, and Customer

Add content panels meaningful to your business or restore defaults

Drop-down arrow ▼ to print, print preview, or save as an image

Links to quickly take you to another window

Fields to customize the Company Snapshot to display date ranges or specific accounts

 Reports→Company Snapshot

DEVELOP YOUR SKILLS 4-10

In this exercise, you will create both a balance sheet report and a company snapshot for Average Guy Designs. When you create a balance sheet report, it will be based as of a certain date rather than for a period of time (as is the case for a profit & loss report).

1. Choose **Reports→Company & Financial→Balance Sheet Standard**.

2. Tap ⌨Tab, type **12/31/2023**, and then tap ⌨Tab again. Resize the window to see the entire report, if necessary.

   QuickBooks displays a balance sheet report showing the asset, liability, and equity account balances as of December 31, 2023. Notice that Total Assets = Total Liabilities + Equity.

3. Close the Balance Sheet window, choosing not to memorize the report, and leave the company file open.

Display and Customize the Company Snapshot

You will customize the Company Snapshot and then restore the default.

4. Choose **Reports→Company Snapshot**.

   Depending on the date that you perform this exercise, you may or may not have information displayed as all of the transactions entered are for a future date. For this exercise, focus on how to manipulate the snapshots.

5. Add content by clicking **Add Content**, click **Add** for Income Breakdown content, and then click **Done**.

6. Remove the Income and Expense Trend content panel from the snapshot by clicking the ✖ on the panel. Click **OK** to confirm the removal.

   Notice that after you have removed the Income and Expense Trend panel, another panel "snaps" up into the vacated space. You will now restore the default content panels to the snapshot.

7. Click the **Restore Default** link below the Payments tab at the top of the window and then click **Yes** in the Restore Default window.

8. Close ✖ the Company Snapshot window.

Importing Banking Transactions into QuickBooks

There are two methods of bringing in transactions from a bank. One is manual, and the other is to use the automated Bank Feeds feature (Direct Connect). The Bank Feeds feature is a convenient, quick, and more effective way to manage reconciliation and ensure accuracy. With Bank Feeds you can download transactions, view the transactions that have cleared your account, see your current balance, and add new transactions to QuickBooks from your financial institution. This feature can also assist in cash flow management.

You will need to check with your financial institution to determine which services are offered (or if any are offered at all). Although there is no fee to use bank feeds in QuickBooks, your financial institution may charge a fee for the automated service.

Tip! If you choose to do a manual download of transactions, you can do so through Bank Feeds, QuickBooks' online browser, or from any browser, and the downloaded file can be imported into QuickBooks. Not all banks may offer this feature.

QuickBooks provides a listing of financial institutions that participate in bank feeds for banking account access, credit/charge card account access, or payment access. Regardless of which method you use to bring your transactions into QuickBooks, you will first have to activate your banking, credit card, or other account for online service through your financial institution.

Note! Bank feeds exclusivity means that if you work on your company file with others, be aware that only one person at a time can be using bank feeds. The person who will be performing bank feed tasks must acquire exclusive use. This applies if you are working in multiuser mode only.

The Modes of Bank Feeds

You can choose how to work with your banking transactions through bank feeds, as there are two different modes:

- **Express**—In this mode, you work within the Transactions List window in order to match and add transactions; renaming rules are created for you automatically.

- **Classic**—This version is the mode used in QuickBooks 2013 and earlier versions. Here, you work within account registers to match and add transactions, and you work with aliases to match names.

Bank Feeds and Reconciliation

When you use bank feeds you still must reconcile your accounts in the same way as you learned earlier in this chapter. The big advantage to using bank feeds, however, is that the majority (if not all) of your transactions have been matched already, and reconciliation will be quicker. If you do have a discrepancy, then use the same problem-solving process outlined in this chapter to resolve it.

Setting Up Bank Feeds in QuickBooks

The setup process involves four steps that QuickBooks will guide you through. Setting up Credit Card and Checking accounts are similar processes.

During the setup process you will have to link the account to one of your accounts in the Chart of Accounts. Because the account in the image above is for a credit card, the Quick-Books account in this example displays the 23500•Citibank Visa - Credit Card account. Once Bank Feeds is set up, the Bank Feeds Center will show up in the Banking menu.

 Banking→Bank Feeds→Set Up Bank Feed for an Account

Matching and Recording Bank Feeds

After you have set up Bank Feeds in QuickBooks, you will be able to download transactions from your financial institution(s), match them to transactions you have entered into QuickBooks, and properly record new transactions that are not yet entered into QuickBooks (remember you have to get it right behind the scenes!)

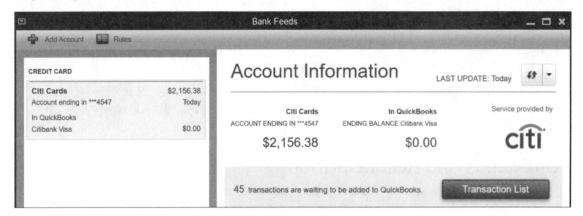

After downloading, the number of transactions is displayed and the Transaction List button brings you to the next step where you will tell QuickBooks how to handle each transaction.

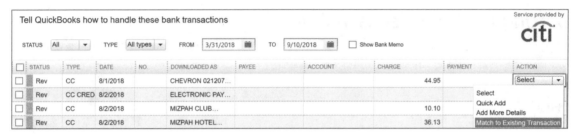

Choosing Match to Existing Transaction will help to reconcile the credit card if you've already paid the credit card bill with Write Checks. You can also choose multiple transactions and then process all of them as a batch.

Note! Recording Deposits and Expenses often requires more than one transaction. You will need to match the individual items in your register to the downloaded information. Avoid creating duplicate entries or selecting the wrong type of account.

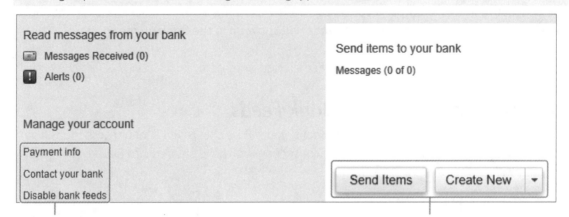

With Direct Connect, you can display current payment information, get contact numbers, or disable bank feeds.

Send a message, make payment, or transfer funds from this area. Pay attention to received messages as they may contain a task for you to complete.

Tip! Making Vendor Payments can also be done by using the QuickBooks online vendor payment service set up through your financial institution, if they support it.

Attaching a File to a Transaction

QuickBooks allows you to add scanned documents or documents stored on your local computer, on your network drive, or from Outlook to transactions. You can add these files to the QuickBooks Doc Center directly and also choose to use the Attach feature from within a form such as an invoice; from bill pay; or from the customer, vendor, or employee centers. Examples of scanned items are invoices, receipts, and packing slips.

If you use the Attach feature in one of the centers or from a form, the documents will be listed in the Doc Center. There is no fee for this feature.

The paper clip appears in the Customer Center and Vendor Center; the Attach File button appears in the forms.

 Customers→Customer Center: Attach | Vendors→Vendor Center: Attach

---

DEVELOP YOUR SKILLS 4-11

In this exercise, you will attach a receipt to a bill.

1. Choose **Vendors**→**Enter Bills** and use the **Previous** ◀ button to locate the bill for Graphic Supply Shoppe dated 12/03/2023 for $302.50.
2. Click **Attach File**, click **Computer**, and then browse to your file storage location and click **Graphic Supply Shoppe Receipt.pdf**.
3. Click **Open**; resize the Attachments window, if necessary.

   The name of the file will appear in the listing. You can select it to detach it, view details, or open it.
4. Click **Done**.

   The Attach File button displays a number, referring to the number of attachments.
5. Click **Save & Close** and leave the company file open if you plan to continue on to Tackle the Tasks, or close your company file if you're done working in QuickBooks.

Tackle the Tasks

Now is your chance to work a little more with Average Guy Designs and apply the skills that you have learned in this chapter to accomplish additional tasks. You will use the same company file you used in the Develop Your Skills exercises throughout this chapter. Enter the following tasks, referring back to the concepts in the chapter as necessary. If you are using the trial software for this course on your computer or in a lab at school, you must toggle to the Pro edition every time you start QuickBooks.

Create Banking and Credit Card Accounts	Use the following information to create two new accounts: 10300•Money Market; RiverBank Money Market; 3245645; 599222043 23500•American Express; Company Credit Card for travel, entertainment, and office supplies; 354650000002
Make a Deposit	On 10/05/2023, Guy traveled to a local business and provided assistance to the owner who was trying to edit a video. He received $250 cash and chose to not enter the customer in QuickBooks. Deposit the funds from this transaction to Checking on the same day with a memo stating Computer Training: edited videos.
Transfer Funds	On 10/05/2023, transfer $1,000 from Checking to Money Market.
Enter Credit Card Transactions	Enter the following American Express credit card transactions: On 10/07/2023, purchased a customer appreciation lunch from Saucy Pizzeria (add as a new vendor); Ref No. 04 for $65.11, using the 64300•Meals and Entertainment account; memos: Customer appreciation day On 10/08/2023, purchased a new wireless mouse; Ref. No. 05; from Ricky's Electric City for $49.52, using 64900•Office Supplies as the account; memos: wireless mouse On 10/09/2023, took a new client out to lunch; Ref. No. 06; at Bayshore Café for $59.12, using 64300•Meals and Entertainment as the account; memos: Kent Reynolds lunch On 10/10/2023, you returned the wireless mouse for $49.52 to Ricky's Electric City; Ref. No.: 05r; memos: Returned wireless mouse
Reconcile a Credit Card	Now it is time to reconcile your 10/31/2023 American Express credit card statement, which is displayed below. After you have reconciled the credit card, choose to enter a bill for payment later (Quick Add American Express as a Vendor), Ref. No.: 06; memos: AMEX 10/23, create a summary reconciliation report, and then pay the bill on 10/31/2023. There are no finance charges. Check to be printed later.
Produce Reports	Display a balance sheet standard report dated October 31, 2023.

American Express

15 Amex Lane
Los Angeles, CA 90017

American Express Statement

Average Guy Designs
110 Sampson Way
Bayshore, CA 91547

Account Number: 354650000002
Statement Period: Oct. 1 – Oct 31, 2023

New Balance:	$124.23	**Account Summary**	
Minimum Payment Due:	$35.00	**Previous Balance:**	$0.00
Payment Due Date:	11/26/2023	**Payments and Credits:**	-$49.52
		New Charges:	+$173.75
		Fees:	$0.00
		Interest Charged:	$0.00
		New Balance:	$124.23
		Minimum Payment Due:	$35.00

Payments and Credits Detail

Beginning Balance:	$0.00	**Ending Balance:**	$124.23

Transactions:

Date		Charge	Credit	Balance
	Beginning Balance			*0.00*
10/05/2023	Saucy Pizzeria	65.11		65.11
10/08/2023	Ricky's Electric City	49.52		114.63
10/09/2023	Bayshore Café	59.12		173.75
10/10/2023	Ricky's Electric City		49.52	124.23
	Periodic Finance Charge	0.00		
Total New Charges:				**$124.23**

Self-Assessment

Check your knowledge of this chapter's key concepts and skills using the Self-Assessment quiz here, in your ebook, or in your eLab course.

1. Payments received on an invoice that are held in Undeposited Funds automatically appear in the Checking register. *True* *False*

2. When you make a deposit to Checking, the amount shows on the credit side of the account. *True* *False*

3. In QuickBooks, Credit Card is a type of bank account. *True* *False*

4. Only bank accounts have registers that detail all account transactions. *True* *False*

5. When you double-click a liability in the Chart of Accounts, a QuickReport is displayed. *True* *False*

6. Bank feeds allow you to save time from having to type in all your transactions, help you to maintain better accuracy in your records, and also assist in cash flow management. *True* *False*

7. Reconciliation is the process of matching your QuickBooks bank accounts to your bank statements. *True* *False*

8. The Chart of Accounts is a list of just your company's bank accounts. *True* *False*

9. A Reconciliation Discrepancy report helps you find the transactions changed since your last reconciliation. *True* *False*

10. Reconciliation reports display only transactions cleared by the bank. *True* *False*

11. What is a recommended first action to take if your cleared QuickBooks transactions and the bank statement don't balance during the reconciliation process?
    A. Look for a transaction that is the same amount as the difference.
    B. Click the Unmark All button so you can start over.
    C. Go through all of the deposit transactions and make sure they are all checked.
    D. Review the payment transactions and make sure they are all the correct amounts.

12. Which window appears when you choose Banking→Make Deposits if there are funds in the Undeposited Funds account?
    A. Undeposited Funds Register
    B. Make Deposits
    C. Deposits in Wait
    D. Payments to Deposit

13. Which account would you find on a Balance Sheet report?
    A. Payroll Liabilities
    B. Utilities Expense
    C. Sales
    D. Cost of Goods Sold

⫟ Reinforce Your Skills

Emily Holly has asked you to take over handling QuickBooks for Electrical Energy on a more permanent basis, and you will take this time to catch up on some banking tasks and run some reports. The password for all files unless otherwise stated is Password1. Leave the company file open unless otherwise instructed. If you are using the trial software on your computer or in a lab at school, remember to toggle to the Pro edition every time you start QuickBooks. If the Future Transactions window appears when entering a transaction, click Yes. If you wish, you can turn off this warning in the Edit Preferences window.

REINFORCE YOUR SKILLS 4-1

Set Up Bank Account, Transfer Funds, and Make a Deposit

In this exercise, you will take care of some banking tasks for Electrical Energy. Because the business checking account does not earn interest, Emily has decided to open a money market account. You will need to set up this account. Leave the company file open unless otherwise stated.

1. Choose **File→Open or Restore Company**.
2. Open **RYS_Chapter04 (Company)** or restore **RYS_Chapter04 (Portable)** from your file storage location and save your file as: **RYS_Chapter04 Electrical Energy**
3. Choose **Lists→Chart of Accounts**.
4. Click the **Account** drop-down arrow ▾ and choose **New**.
5. Choose **Bank** as the account type and then click **Continue**.
6. Use this information to complete the account:
   - Account Number: **10500**
   - Account Name: **East River Money Market**
   - Description: **Company Money Market Account**
   - Bank Acct. No.: **021362-111**
   - Routing Number: **020000002**
7. Click **Save & Close**, choosing **No** in the Set Up Bank Feed window.
8. Close the Chart of Accounts window.

Move Funds Between Accounts

Because the money market account earns interest, you will transfer some funds from the checking account into it.

9. Choose **Banking→Transfer Funds**.
10. Use this information to complete the transfer:
    - Date: **040223**
    - Transfer Funds From: **Checking**
    - Transfer Funds To: **East River Money Market Account**
    - Transfer amount: **8000**
11. Click **Save & Close** to record the transfer and close the window; click **Yes** in the Future Transactions window, if necessary.

Make Deposits

Emily did a presentation for a local organization on the topic of taking precautions when working with electricity. You need to deposit the fee she earned into the checking account along with the funds that are currently in the Undeposited Funds account. You will do this in two separate steps.

12. Choose **Banking→Make Deposits**.

13. In the Payments to Deposit window, choose the **04/24/2023** payment from Linda Chai and then click **OK**.

14. Use this information to complete the deposit:
    - Deposit To: **Checking**
    - Deposit date: **042523** (click **Save & New**)

15. Use this information to start the next deposit:
    - Date: **042623** (leave *Deposit* in the Memo field)
    - From Account: **45200•Consultation Income** (you will need to create a new account, so choose **Add New**)

    Remember, you do not have to enter a customer, but you must enter an income account!

16. Choose **Income** as the account type.

17. Click **Continue** and then use this information to complete the new account:
    - Number: **45200**
    - Account Name: **Consultation Income**
    - Description: **Consultation income including presentations**

18. Click **Save & Close**.

19. Use this information to complete the remainder of the deposit:
    - Memo: **Safety Presentation**
    - Check number: **753**
    - Payment Method: **Check**
    - Amount: **800**

20. Click **Save & Close** to record the transaction.

REINFORCE YOUR SKILLS 4-2

Reconcile a Bank Account

Emily's checking account statement has just arrived. In this exercise, you will reconcile Electrical Energy's Company checking account. Refer to the illustration shown after step 3.

1. Choose **Banking→Reconcile** and select **Checking** as the account.

2. Use the Ending Balance from the statement and this information to begin the reconciliation:
    - Statement Date: **043023**
    - Service Charge: **25**
    - Service Charge date: **042223**
    - Account No.: **60400•Bank Service Charges**

3. In the Reconcile-Checking window, mark only those transactions that have cleared the bank (and are on the bank statement).

Use this bank statement to reconcile the Checking account.

East River Savings Bank
29 Riverside Drive ▶ New York, NY 10003

Checking Account Statement

Electrical Energy
128 Fulton Street
White Plains, NY 10606

Account Number: 0245658
Statement Period: Apr. 1 – Apr 30, 2023

Total Deposits:	$9,953.81		Total Payments:	$10,779.17
Beginning Balance:	$150,000.00		Ending Balance:	$149,174.64

Transactions:

Date	Transaction Type	Payment	Deposit	Balance
04/02/2023	Transfer	8000.00		142,000.00
04/16/2023	Check # 11353	2575.25		139,424.75
04/16/2023	Check # 11354	158.93		139,265.82
04/16/2023	Check # 11355	19.99		139,245.83
04/20/2023	Deposit		3,005.43	142,251.26
04/21/2023	Deposit		3,702.07	145,953.33
04/22/2023	Service Charge	25.00		145,928.33
04/25/2023	Deposit		1,200.00	147,123.33
04/26/2023	Deposit		800.00	147,928.33
04/30/2023	Deposit		1,246.31	149,174.64
Ending Balance:				149,174.64

---

4. Click **Reconcile Now** and then close the Select Reconciliation Report window.

REINFORCE YOUR SKILLS 4-3

Manage Credit Card Transactions

In this exercise, you will set up and use a new Visa company credit card.

1. Choose **Lists→Chart of Accounts**.

2. Choose **Account→New**.

3. Choose **Credit Card**, click **Continue**, and then use this information to create the new credit card account:

- Ensure Account Type says: **Credit Card**
- Number: **21000**

- Account Name: **East River Visa**
- Description: **Company Credit Card**
- Credit Card Acct. No.: **9999222233334444**

4. Click **Save & Close** to enter the new account and close the window, choosing **No** when asked if you want to set up bank feed services.

5. Close the Chart of Accounts window.

Enter a Credit Card Charge

Emily has purchased oil filters for the business vehicles. She is not sure of the exact filter for one of the trucks, so she will purchase two and return one of them later if necessary.

6. Choose **Banking→Enter Credit Card Charges** and ensure that the **East River Visa** is selected.

7. Use this information to complete the charge (East River Visa will be defaulted as the Credit Card):

- Vendor: **Auto Supply Warehouse** (Choose to **Quick Add** the store as a **Vendor**)
- Date: **050223**
- Ref No.: **20**
- Amount: **150**
- Memo: **Auto Supply: Purchased 2 oil filters**
- Account: **60100•Auto and Truck Expense**

8. Copy and paste the memo into the Expenses tab Memo and then click **Save & New** to record the transaction.

Enter a Credit Card Refund/Credit

Now you will process the return for one filter because it wasn't the correct one. The Enter Credit Card Charges window should still be open; if it isn't, open it.

9. Choose **Refund/Credit** at the top of the window.

10. Use the following information to complete the refund:

- Purchased From: **Auto Supply Warehouse**
- Date: **050823**
- Ref No.: **20r**
- Amount: **30**
- Memo: **Returned 1 oil filter, wrong fit**
- Account: Ensure that **60100•Auto and Truck Expense** is the account
- Copy Memo from above and paste it into the Expenses tab Memo

11. Click **Save & Close**.

Produce Banking and Balance Sheet Reports

In this exercise, you will run some banking reports to see the current status of the company's finances. You'll start out with banking reports and then produce a Balance Sheet report.

1. Choose **Reports→Banking→Previous Reconciliation**.
2. Choose the **10000•Checking** account.
3. Choose **Summary** and click **Display**.

   You can save this report as a PDF to keep for the company's records.

4. Close the Reconciliation Summary window.

Run a Deposit Detail Report

Now you will run a report to display all of the bank deposits for April.

5. Choose **Reports→Banking→Deposit Detail**.
6. Change the From Date to **040123** and the To Date to **043023** and then click **Refresh**.

   Notice there is a Refresh button on the toolbar. If you needed to make a change to a transaction, you can leave this report open and choose Refresh to bring in the new data.

Tip! If you tap Tab after changing the date, QuickBooks will automatically refresh the report for you.

7. Close the Deposit Details report window and click **No** when asked to memorize the report.

Display a Balance Sheet Report

8. Choose **Reports→Company & Financial→Balance Sheet Standard**.
9. Type **a** to change the date range to **All**.

   Take a moment to review the report and notice how things are grouped: Assets and Liabilities & Equity. You can clearly see how Checking and Accounts Receivable fall under Assets. Also notice how Assets and Liabilities & Equity are in balance with each other.

10. Choose **Window→Close All** and don't save any memorized reports.
11. Close the company file.

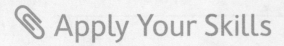
Apply Your Skills

Wet Noses Veterinary Clinic is continuing to do a thriving business. You will be staying on top of the necessary tasks on a day-to-day basis by entering credit card charges, reconciling and creating accounts, paying bills, and running reports. The password for all files unless otherwise stated is Password1. After starting QuickBooks, remember to toggle to Pro as necessary.

APPLY YOUR SKILLS 4-1 QG

Perform Banking Tasks

In this exercise, you will create new accounts for Wet Noses Veterinary Clinic, choosing to not set up online services for either account. Leave the company file open unless otherwise stated.

1. Choose **File→Open or Restore Company**.
2. Open **AYS_A1_Chapter04 (Company)** or restore **AYS_A1_Chapter04 (Portable)** from your file storage location and save your file as: **AYS_A1_Chapter04 Wet Noses Clinic**
3. Create two new accounts for Wet Noses Veterinary Clinic:

   First account
   - Number: **10600**
   - Bank account name: **Money Market**
   - Description: **Company Money Market Account**
   - Account No.: **3336665454**
   - Routing No.: **010000001**

   Second account
   - Number: **21000**
   - Credit card account named: **American Express**
   - Description: **Company Credit Card**
   - Account No.: **7777888899994**

4. Make a Deposit for all six payments from the Undeposited Funds account into your Checking account on: **060923**
5. Transfer **$30,000** from Checking to Money Market on: **061023**
6. Create a Deposit Detail report that displays a detailed list of all Checking account deposits for **040123** through **063023**.
7. Click the **Excel** [Excel ▾] button and export this list to a new worksheet, saving the worksheet to your file storage location as: **CH4_A1 Deposit Detail**
8. Close Excel and then close the company file, choosing not to memorize the report.

Enter Credit Card Transactions

In this exercise, you will enter several credit card charges for purchases made and apply them to the appropriate expense account.

1. Choose **File→Open or Restore Company**.
2. Open **AYS_A2_Chapter04 (Company)** or restore **AYS_A2_Chapter04 (Portable)** from your file storage location and save your file as: **AYS_A2_Chapter04 Wet Noses Clinic**
3. Enter these American Express charges for the month of June, Quick Adding vendors, as necessary:

Date	Vendor	Ref. No.	Amount	Memos
06/01/2023	Bothell Pet Supply Co.	06-01	$115.43	Boarding supplies
06/04/2023	Glen's Handyman Service	06-02	$108.70	12 door hinges – needed for maintenance
06/10/2023	Thrifty Grocery	06-03	$26.73	Bottled water and soda for office
06/14/2023	Karel's Gardening Service	06-04	$60.00	Monthly garden maintenance
06/20/2023	Bothell Pet Supply Co.	06-01r	$38.29	Return-Boarding supplies
06/22/2023	Laura's Cafe	06-05	50.21	Business lunch with potential customer

4. Open the Chart of Accounts and select American Express. Run a QuickReport that displays charges from **06/01/2023** through **06/30/2023** for the **American Express** credit card.
5. Click the **Excel** [Excel ▼] button and export this list to a new worksheet, saving the worksheet to your file storage location as: **CH4_A2 June AMEX Charges**
6. Close Excel and then close the Account QuickReport and Chart of Accounts. Leave the company file open for the next exercise.

Record Bounced Check

In this exercise, you will help Dr. James handle check #6666 from Mary Ann Gulch for $145.65 that was returned for nonsufficient funds. This is called a "Bounced Check" in QuickBooks.

1. Locate the customer payment, check # **6666** from Mary Ann Gulch for $145.65, to record the bounced check.

2. Use this information for the fee in the Manage Bounced Check window:

   - Bank Fee: $**25** on **060623**, using **Bank Service Charges** as the account

   - Customer Fee: **$45**

3. Close any open windows and then run the **Open Invoice** report for **06/30/2023** to display the past-due invoices. You should see two for Mary Ann Gulch.

4. Click the **Excel** Excel ▾ button and export this list to a new worksheet, saving the worksheet to your file storage location as: **CH4_A3 June Open Invoices**

5. Close Excel and then close the company file, choosing not to memorize any reports.

APPLY YOUR SKILLS 4-4 QG

Pay a Bill with a Credit Card

In this exercise, you will use the American Express card to pay a vendor bill. You will need to select the appropriate expense account.

1. Choose **File→Open or Restore Company**.

2. Open **AYS_A4_Chapter04 (Company)** or restore **AYS_A4_Chapter04 (Portable)** from your file storage location, saving your file as: **AYS_A4_Chapter04 Wet Noses Clinic**

3. Use this information to create a bill, selecting the appropriate account, for Billy's Van Service:

   - Vendor: **Billy's Van Service**

   - Date: **060223**

   - Ref. No.: **Van 01**

   - Amount: $**256.49**

   - Memo: **Travel: presentations May 2023**

4. Open the Pay Bills window and choose to pay the bill for Billy's Van Service on 6/12/2023, using the American Express account.

5. Open the Chart of Accounts and select American Express. Run a **QuickReport** that displays charges from **06/01/2023** through **06/30/2023** for the American Express credit card.

6. Click the **Excel** Excel ▾ button and export this list to a new worksheet, saving the worksheet to your file storage location as: **CH4_A4 AMEX QuickReport**

7. Close Excel and then close the company file.

APPLY YOUR SKILLS 4-5 QG

Reconcile a Credit Card Account

In this exercise, you will reconcile the American Express account.

1. Choose **File→Open or Restore Company**.

2. Open **AYS_A5_Chapter04 (Company)** or restore **AYS_A5_Chapter04 (Portable)** from your file storage location, saving your file as: **AYS_A5_Chapter04 Wet Noses Clinic**

3. Reconcile the June American Express account using the following illustration:

American Express
15 Amex Lane
Los Angeles, CA 90017

American Express Statement

Wet Noses Veterinary Clinic
589 Retriever Drive
Bothell, WA 98011

Account Number: 7777888899994
Statement Period: June 1 – June 30, 2023

New Balance:	$579.27	**Account Summary**	
Minimum Payment Due:	$35.00	**Previous Balance:**	$0.00
Payment Due Date:	07/30/2023	**Payments and Credits:**	-$38.29
		New Charges:	+$617.56
		Fees:	$0.00
		Interest Charged:	$0.00
		New Balance:	$579.27
		Minimum Payment Due:	$35.00

Payments and Credits Detail

Beginning Balance:	$0.00	**Ending Balance:**	$579.27

Transactions:

Date		Charge	Credit	Balance
	Beginning Balance			*0.00*
06/01/2023	Bothell Pet Supply Company	115.43		507.35
06/04/2023	Glen's Handyman Service	108.70		108.70
06/10/2023	Thrifty Grocery	26.73		135.43
06/12/2023	Billy's Van Service	256.49		391.92
06/14/2023	Karel's Gardening Service	60.00		567.35
06/20/2023	Bothell Pet Supply Company		38.29	529.36
06/22/2023	Laura's Café	50.21		579.57
	Periodic Finance Charge	0.00		
Total New Charges:				**$579.27**

---

4. Ensure the Summary Reconciliation report is showing and then click the **Excel** `Excel ▼` button and export this list to a new worksheet, saving the worksheet to your file storage location as: **CH4_A5 Summary Reconciliation**

5. After you have completed the reconciliation and run the Summary Reconciliation report, write a check to **American Express** for the entire amount on **07/03/2023**, using **AMEX June 2023** for both memo fields; choose to **Print Later** and then run the **Summary Reconciliation** report.

6. Run the **Balance Sheet Standard** report as of **06/30/2023** that will display the balance for all balance sheet accounts. Total Assets should equal Total Liabilities & Equity!

7. Click the **Excel** `Excel ▼` button and export this list to a new worksheet, saving the worksheet to your file storage location as: **CH4_A5 Balance Sheet**

8. Close Excel and close the company file, choosing not to memorize the report.

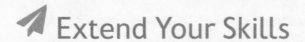

Extend Your Skills

Before You Begin: Open **EYS_Chapter04 (Company)** or restore **EYS_Chapter04 (Portable)** from your file storage location.

You have been hired by Arlaine Cervantes to help her with her organization's books. She is the founder of Niños del Lago, a nonprofit organization that provides impoverished Guatemalan children with an engaging educational camp experience. You have just sat down at your desk and opened a large envelope from her with a variety of documents and noticed that you have several emails from her as well. It is your job to sort through the papers and emails and make sense of what you find, entering information into QuickBooks whenever appropriate and answering any other questions in a word-processing document saved as: **EYS_Chapter04 _LastnameFirstinitial**. Remember, you are digging through papers you just dumped out of an envelope and addressing random emails from Arlaine, so it is up to you to determine the correct order in which to complete the tasks.

- Scribbled on a scrap of paper: I looked at QuickBooks and saw money in an account called "Undeposited Funds." Why isn't it in the Checking account? Can you move it for me? I deposited those funds into the Checking account on 7/11/2019!

- New credit card document on desk: From Jasper State Bank, number 7777 2222 0000 2938, $7,500 credit limit.

- Note: Opened a new Money Market bank account at Jasper State Bank on 7/10/2019. Transferred $1,000 from Savings to fund the new account. Need QuickBooks account set up.

- Bank deposit slip: Check #2323 dated 7/14/2019 for a $2,500 deposit to Checking. Handwritten message on slip reads, "From Hanson Family Trust."

- Credit card receipt: Dated 7/15/2019; for office supplies; $75.11; paid to Supplies Online.

- Note: Would you please create a report that shows all of the activity in the Checking account for July 2019 and save it as a PDF file so I can email it to the accountant?

- Bank deposit slip: Dated 7/30/2019 for $750; handwritten on slip, check #1835 from Lakeside Christian School for remaining balance due.

- Credit card receipt: Dated 7/23/2019; payable to Casey's Service Station; for auto fuel; amount of $35.61. (Hint: This is for travel to a workshop site.)

- Scribbled note from Arlaine: Can you produce a report for me that shows the balances for all of the asset, liability, and equity accounts as of 7/31/2019?

5 | Creating a Company File

NEW BUSINESS
JUST AHEAD

Now that you have had a chance to learn the basics about customers, vendors, and banking with QuickBooks, it is time to go through the process of creating a company file. By taking the knowledge that you gain from this chapter and coupling it with what you will learn in the rest of the book, you will be ready at the end of your QuickBooks studies to create a file for your own company. In this chapter, you will create a new company file as well as set up the Chart of Accounts and new users.

LEARNING OBJECTIVES

▸ Plan and create a company

▸ Edit your QuickBooks preferences and customize a company file

▸ Enter opening balances and historical transactions

▸ Run list reports and find help for QuickBooks

▸ Set up QuickBooks users

▸ Understand closing the books "QuickBooks style"

📁 Project: Average Guy Designs

You have already had a chance to get to know Average Guy Designs. Now we are going to go back in time to two years ago when Guy Marshall first started his company. He was a community college student who just finished his degree in visual communications, started his own graphic design business, and decided to use QuickBooks as the tool to track his business finances. As a part of his degree, Guy took a class that focused on the business of graphic arts, and he learned that there is some important information that he needs to gather before setting up his new QuickBooks company.

AVERAGE GUY DESIGNS CHECKLIST FOR NEW QUICKBOOKS COMPANY			
Company Name	Average Guy Designs	**Need from Accountant**	Chart of Accounts, what should I use for items?
Address	110 Sampson Way Bayshore, CA 91547	**Customers**	Need names and contact information, payment terms, and account numbering system
Office Phone Cell Phone Fax	(650) 555-5555 (650) 555-4455 (650) 555-5252	**Vendors**	Need names, addresses, account numbers, and payment terms for each
Start Date	12/31/2018	**Accounting Basis**	Cash
Start of Fiscal Year	January	**Email**	averageguydesigns@outlook.com
EIN	94-4555555	**Website**	averageguydesigns.wordpress.com
Income Tax Form	1040 (Sole Proprietor)		

Guy has typed out the information he needs to have handy to start his new company file.

Planning and Creating a Company

Before you begin to set up your QuickBooks company, it is important to do some careful planning. You must think about the information you want to get from QuickBooks before you begin. As with many situations, garbage in will equal garbage out!

Choosing Your Start Date

Choosing the start date that is right for you is important. Very ambitious people may think they want to start their QuickBooks file the day they started their company. This is a nice idea, but it isn't very practical for a busy or cost-conscious entrepreneur.

Keep in mind that you must enter all transactions for your company (invoices, checks, bills paid, etc.) from the start date forward. If you choose a date too far in the past, this process will take a long time to complete.

You should strive to start your QuickBooks company file at the beginning of a month, a quarter, or your fiscal year. You may want to discuss this matter with your accountant to help determine the best and most practical starting date for your business. The actual start date should be the last day of the prior period rather than the first day of the current period; for example, we will use 12/31/2018 rather than 1/1/2019.

The Five Ps

Sit down and think about what you want QuickBooks to do for you. It is difficult to go back and add a new field for every customer or change every transaction! A little planning at the beginning can save you a lot of time in the future. Think about the five Ps (Prior Planning Prevents Poor Performance) as you get ready to start your company and take into account the needs of all of the stakeholders involved. What type of information will each stakeholder need to be able to interact efficiently with your business? Potential stakeholders may include your accountant, customers, vendors, employees, stockholders, partners, etc.

How Many Companies Should You Create?

Generally, the best guideline is to set up a separate QuickBooks company file for each tax return you will file.

FLASHBACK TO GAAP: BUSINESS ENTITY

Remember that the business is separate from the owners and from other businesses. Revenues and expenses of the business should be kept separate from the personal expenses of the business owner. Also, revenue and expenses for separate companies must be kept separate from the other companies that may be operated by the same owner.

Creating a New QuickBooks File

There are several ways you can go about creating your new QuickBooks file. Look at the following list to determine which one will work best for your situation:

- Create a company from scratch
- Upgrade from a previous version of QuickBooks
- Convert from a different QuickBooks edition
- Convert a Quicken file
- Convert a file from other accounting software

Choosing a Setup Path

When creating a new company, QuickBooks makes it easy for you to select from a variety of options. Simply click the Start Setup button for the simplest option; use the Advanced Setup method if you wish to fine-tune your company file as you set it up.

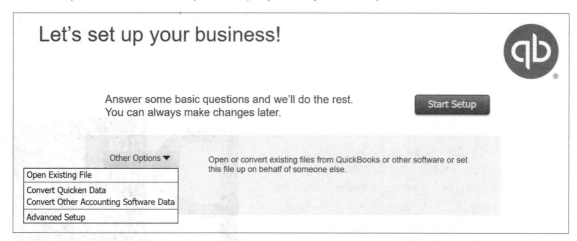

In this window, choose the method for creating a company that works best for you.

Start Setup

The Start Setup option for company setup allows you to provide a minimum amount of information and get started with QuickBooks right away. Once you have entered the Start Setup information and your company file is created, QuickBooks helps you set up the rest of the information needed to run your business.

Advanced Setup/Easy Step Interview

Choosing the Advanced Setup option takes you to the EasyStep Interview window. Here you provide more information when creating your company file.

Using an Existing QuickBooks File as a Template for a New File

If you wish to create your new company file based on an older one, QuickBooks will allow you to keep the lists and preferences from the old file while removing the old, unneeded transactions. Some QuickBooks users prefer to keep a separate company file for each fiscal year of the business, and being able to keep preferences and list data while removing transactions makes this easy.

To complete this task, you must clean up your company data from the old file using the Clean Up Company Wizard. Be sure you have a large window of time available before you start this process, as it can take a while to clean up a large file. QuickBooks will create a backup and archive copy of your file as a part of this process, as well as verify file integrity.

Converting Data to Start a New Company File

An additional option available to you when creating a new company file is to convert an existing file from Quicken or other accounting software.

A Setup Checklist

At the beginning of the chapter, you can see the list that Guy prepared before he started to set up his new company file. A checklist with this information, along with the additional information you will need to have after setup, is provided for you in your student exercise files folder (QuickBooks Company Setup Checklist). The good news is that the majority of the information can be changed after you set up your company. However, the one item that you will want to make sure you have correct for the initial set up is the industry type, as you will not be able to change this later and your entire starter Chart of Accounts is based on it.

A Quick Payroll Primer

Although we don't discuss payroll in this chapter, you will need to know just a tad about it if you choose to create your new company using the Advanced Setup method.

If you wish to include an addition or deduction on an employee's paycheck, you must first set it up as a payroll item. During the EasyStep interview you will have an opportunity to create payroll items. If you will be using QuickBooks for payroll and wish to set it up during the setup process (you can also set this up after the fact if you choose), you will need to have the following information ready:

- Information for each employee: name, address, social security number, and withholding information (from the employee's W-4)

- All "additions" that will be found on a paycheck, such as salaries, hourly wages, and bonuses

- All payroll taxes the employees are required to pay

- All payroll taxes you, as the employer, are required to pay

- Any additional deductions you will be withholding from paychecks, such as investment plan contributions or child support payments

Your Starter Chart of Accounts

During the setup process, QuickBooks will ask you to search for the industry that your company most closely resembles. QuickBooks will use your choice to create a Chart of Accounts close to what you need. (It will take you less time to edit it to fit your unique business than to start from scratch.) QuickBooks will also create profile list entries based on your selection. Choose carefully here, as you cannot go back and change the business type option.

In order to ensure your books are set up properly from the beginning, you should talk to your accountant to make sure that your Chart of Accounts is set up correctly. A quick conversation and small bill now can prevent a large bill in the future.

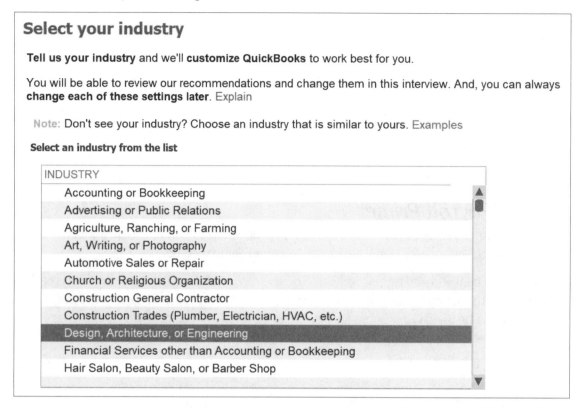

QuickBooks has several predefined company Charts of Accounts for specific industries that will help users in those or similar industries streamline their setup processes.

Warning! Once you select a business type during the setup process, you cannot change it later. You can edit and delete accounts and list entries, though.

Account Beginning Balances

If you have an existing company for which you are setting up QuickBooks, you should enter the balances of all asset and liability accounts during the setup process (although you can also enter them in the registers later). These account beginning balances are termed "opening balances" in QuickBooks. You will learn more about entering and editing these balances later in the chapter.

After you create your first balance sheet account, QuickBooks will create an Opening Balance Equity account, in which the account beginning balances you enter will be placed. Asset beginning balances credit the account, while liability beginning balances debit it. This account is created so you can have a balance sheet that is accurate from the start even if you haven't entered all assets and liabilities for your company.

FIVE MAIN ACCOUNT TYPES

Account type	Description
Accounts Associated with Balance Sheet	
Asset	What the company owns (cars, supplies, inventory, buildings, bank accounts)
Liability	What the company owes (loans, wages, interest, vendor purchases, collected taxes)
Equity	Funds contributed by owners or stockholders plus the retained earnings (or losses)
Accounts Associated with the Profit & Loss Report/Income Statement	
Income	Sales or Revenues (products and services such as consulting, graphic design, web design)
Expense	What the company spends (rent, salaries, purchases such as supplies and display fixtures)

In QuickBooks, you will choose from a variety of account types that are all based on accounting's five main account types. The table below shows the account types available in QuickBooks.

ANATOMY OF A QUICKBOOKS CHART OF ACCOUNTS

Type	Example	Normal Balance	Account Type
Bank	Checking Account	Debit	Asset
Accounts Receivable	Accounts Receivable	Debit	Asset
Other Current Asset	Prepaid Rent	Debit	Asset
Fixed Asset	Machinery	Debit	Asset
Other Asset	Long Term Notes Receivable	Debit	Asset
Accounts Payable	Accounts Payable	Credit	Liability
Credit Card	Silver Falls Bank Visa	Credit	Liability
Other Current Liability	Short Term Loan	Credit	Liability
Long Term Liability	Auto Loan	Credit	Liability
Equity	Opening Balance Equity	Credit	Equity
Income	Sales	Credit	Income
Cost of Goods Sold	Cost of Goods Sold	Debit	Expense
Expense	Telephone Expense	Debit	Expense
Other Income	Interest Income	Credit	Income
Other Expense	Corporate Taxes	Debit	Expense

↱ File→New Company

DEVELOP YOUR SKILLS 5-1

In this exercise, you will begin the first steps of setting up Average Guy Designs using the Advanced Setup process. Leave the company file open unless otherwise instructed.

1. Start QuickBooks 2019 and toggle to Pro, if necessary.
2. Choose **File→New Company**.
3. Click **Other Options** and then choose **Advanced Setup**.

   If you are not using the Pro version of the software, you will not see this option. In order to access the EasyStep Interview, click Detailed Start *in the QuickBooks Desktop Setup window.*

4. Use this information to complete the **Enter Your Company Information** step:
   - Company Name: **Average Guy Designs**
   - Legal Name: **Average Guy Designs**

   The legal name depends on the type of company being set up. It is usually the name associated with the Tax ID used in filing taxes. It is used on payroll tax forms.
   - Tax ID: **94-4555555**
   - Street Address: **110 Sampson Way**
   - City: **Bayshore**
   - State: **CA**
   - Zip: **91547**
   - Phone: **(650) 555-5555**
   - Email: **averageguydesigns@outlook.com**
   - Web Site: **averageguydesigns.wordpress.com**

   This information will appear on forms such as invoices and bills, so ensure that punctuation, capitalization, and spelling are correct.

5. Click **Next**.
6. Use this information to complete the initial setup process, clicking **Next** after each selection:

Step	Choice
Select your industry	**Design, Architecture, or Engineering**
How is your company organized?	**Sole Proprietorship**
Select the first month of your fiscal year	**January**
Set up your administrator password	**Password1** Tap `Tab` and retype **Password1**

Although it says Optional for the password, the next time you sign on, you will be required to enter a password. The administrator has full control over all areas of QuickBooks.

7. In the Create your Company File window, click **Next** again and save the company file to your file storage location as: **Average Guy Designs.QBW**

8. Click **Next** to continue customizing your business and then, clicking **Next** as needed, fill in the following information as indicated:

Step	Choice
What do you sell?	**Services only**
Sales tax	**No**
Estimates	**Yes**
Statements	**Yes**
Progress Invoicing	**Yes**
Manage bills you owe	**Yes**
Do you want to track time in QuickBooks?	**Yes**
Do you have employees?	**No**

All of these preferences can be changed later as your company changes.

Set the Start Date

In the next couple of steps, you will set the date on which you will start tracking the company's finances in QuickBooks.

9. Click **Next** on the Using accounts in QuickBooks window, then choose **Use today's date or the first day of the quarter or month**, type **123118**, and click **Next**.

10. Scroll down and click **Equipment Rental and Interest Income** to include both accounts in the Chart of Accounts and click **Next**.

   The Chart of Accounts list is grouped by type, not by account name. From this window, you can also get answers and explanations on accounts or restore recommendations.

11. Click **Go to Setup** and take a look at the QuickBooks Desktop Setup window and the options it offers.

   We will be working within the individual lists to add data to your QuickBooks file like you will do on an ongoing basis. Just be aware that this setup window is available when you are setting up your own company.

12. Click the **Start Working** button at the bottom of the window and leave your new company file open. Close the New Feature Tour window, if necessary.

Editing Your QuickBooks Preferences

The way you interact with QuickBooks is controlled by the preferences you select. The Preferences window has twenty-three categories of preferences you can set or modify so QuickBooks can work more efficiently for your company.

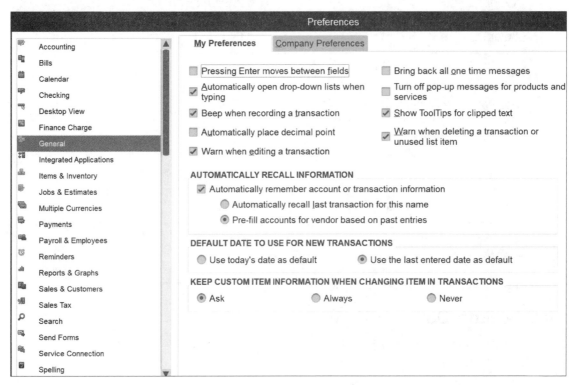

The Preferences window allows you to control how you interact with QuickBooks, and the company administrator can make changes on the Company Preferences tab for how all users interact with it.

Company vs. Personal Preferences

Each category has two tabs on which changes to preferences can be set: the Company Preferences tab and the My Preferences (personal) tab. Company preferences are controlled by the administrator. They determine how the entire company interacts with QuickBooks. Personal preferences are controlled by each individual user. They dictate interactions between QuickBooks and that one user only.

The following illustrations show an example of a company and a personal preference.

Changes made by an administrator affect all users. Here, an administrator turned on the preference to use account numbers in the Chart of Accounts.

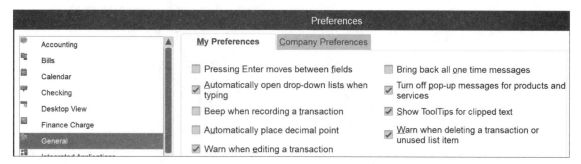

Here, an individual user can change a variety of general settings on the My Preferences tab that will affect only her individual QuickBooks user login. This is a good place to look if QuickBooks is not acting "normal" for you as a preference may have been changed.

Setting a Company Preference: Account Numbers

Many businesses use account numbers for the accounts in their Chart of Accounts. You will be using account numbers as you work with the company file for Average Guy Designs. Account numbers are somewhat standard within the accounting world. "Somewhat" means that each account type begins with the same number, but the accounts listed within the account type are not universally numbered. Examine the following table to understand how account numbers work. Note that account numbers have a minimum of four characters, and you can use five or six. For instance, a Checking account (which is an asset) could be numbered 1000, 10000, or 100000.

ACCOUNT TYPES AND NUMBERING CONVENTIONS		
Account number starts with:	**Type of account**	**Example**
1	Asset	Checking Account
2	Liability	Accounts Payable
3	Equity	Retained Earnings
4	Income	Retail Product Sales
5	Cost of Goods Sold	Purchases – Resale Items
6	Expenses	Utilities Expense
7	Other Income	Interest Income
8	Other Expense	Sales Tax Penalty

Setting a Personal Preference: Show Reminders List

In many of the Preferences categories, an individual user can choose from a variety of options. In the following exercise, you will choose to show the Reminders List when starting your QuickBooks file.

Edit→Preferences

In this exercise, you will turn on the account number preference for the company and turn off Date Warnings. You will then choose for the Reminders List to be displayed when opening QuickBooks.

Whether to turn on the use of account numbers is a company preference, is set by the company administrator, and cannot be changed by other users.

1. Choose **Edit→Preferences**.
2. Click the **Accounting** category and then click the **Company Preferences** tab.
3. Click the **Use account numbers** checkbox and then click to turn off **Date Warnings** for past and future transactions.
4. Click the **Reminders** category and then click **Yes** when the Save Changes window appears.

   Notice there are fourteen Reminders preferences that can be set for the company. Some are grayed out because those features were not turned on during setup.
5. Click the **My Preferences** tab and then click the **Show Reminders List when opening a Company file** checkbox.
6. Click **OK** and then choose **File→Close Company** to close the company file. Click **No** if the Automatic Backup window appears.
7. Click **Open** in the No Company Open window (Average Guy Designs will be the company at the top of the list and selected since it was the last one used), type **Password1**, and then click **OK**.

   The Reminders List should be displayed with no reminders listed.
8. Close the Reminders window.

   Leave the QuickBooks window open and continue with the next topic.

Customizing a Company File

During the setup process, QuickBooks allows you to choose a business type similar to your own. It is up to you to take this generic file and customize it to fit your company.

Modifying the Lists in a New File

You will need to look at several lists after you set up your new QuickBooks company to ensure they are correct. If any of them are incorrect or incomplete, you will need to edit, delete, or add entries to them. These lists include the following:

- Chart of Accounts
- Customers & Jobs List
- Vendor List
- Item List
- Customer & Vendor Profile Lists

- Fixed Asset Item List
- Employees List
- Payroll Items List
- Price Level List

Entries in these lists are populated during the Advanced Setup/EasyStep Interview. If you choose to skip the interview, you will need to populate these lists once the company has been created.

The Chart of Accounts

The Chart of Accounts is composed of all the asset, liability, equity, income, and expense accounts your company utilizes. You use the Chart of Accounts list window to create new accounts, edit existing accounts, and delete unused accounts.

Customizing the Chart of Accounts

The first task you have with your new company file is to fine-tune your Chart of Accounts. If you are using QuickBooks for an existing business, you will want to talk to your accountant and get a copy of your current Chart of Accounts. If you are starting a new business, you may also want to contact your accountant for guidance on how best to set up your Chart of Accounts for your unique company.

Adding Accounts

When you add an account to the Chart of Accounts, make sure to select the correct account type, as this is one of the most prevalent errors accountants find in their clients' QuickBooks files. Keep in mind that your "behind the scenes" action will be incorrect if the wrong account type is selected.

To Edit or Delete—That Is the Question...

The generic Chart of Accounts that QuickBooks provides will have some accounts you probably won't need for your unique business. You can choose to either rename (edit) these accounts or delete them. Renaming an account is appropriate if you are working with the same account type. Deleting is appropriate if you no longer need additional accounts of the same type.

Moving and Sorting Accounts Within the List

You can change the order in which accounts appear within your Chart of Accounts. By default, QuickBooks alphabetizes accounts by type. The Chart of Accounts is structured so that assets are listed first, liabilities second, equity accounts third, income accounts fourth, cost of goods sold accounts fifth, and expense accounts last. This structure must remain intact; you can move accounts around only within their own type.

Moving list items works the same way in the various lists in QuickBooks—by clicking and dragging the diamond to the left of the list entry.

If you move your accounts and later decide you want them alphabetized by type once again, QuickBooks allows you to resort the list. Resorting the list restores the QuickBooks default.

Subaccounts

To keep precise records, you may wish to use QuickBooks subaccounts. For instance, to keep the number of expense accounts within reason, you are likely to utilize only one telephone expense account for all of your telephone lines. To track expenses more closely, though, you may want to have separate accounts for your office phone and cellular phone. Subaccounts are a great way to track these separate expenses while keeping the number of expense accounts down.

When you run profit & loss reports and budgets, you have the option to expand the report (show subaccounts) to show details or collapse the report (show only main accounts) for brevity.

Using Classes in QuickBooks

In this chapter we don't go into using classes in QuickBooks in detail. Classes allow you to track income and expenses for one specific aspect of your company, and they are not tied to any particular customer, job, vendor, or item. For right now, understand that if you choose to use classes for your own business (after you have learned more about them!), the best option is to set them up when you create your new company file.

 Lists→Chart of Accounts

DEVELOP YOUR SKILLS 5-3

In this exercise, you will take the generic Chart of Accounts created for Average Guy Designs and make it fit the needs of the company.

The first task is to add a bank account that Guy needs but that was not provided in the generic Chart of Accounts, Checking.

1. Click the **Chart of Accounts** ▦ task icon in the Company area of the Home Page. **Resize** the window so that you can see the account names and types.

   QuickBooks opens the generic Chart of Accounts created for you. Notice the account numbers that you turned on in the previous exercise.

2. Click the **Account menu** button at the bottom left of the window and then choose **New**.

3. Click in the circle to the left of **Bank** and then click **Continue**.

4. Use the following information for the new account:

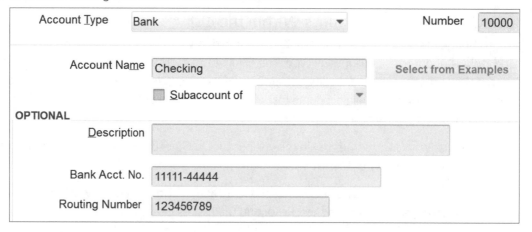

5. Click **Save & Close** and then click **No** in the Set Up Bank Feed window.

   Take a look at your Chart of Accounts window and notice the new Checking account at the top of the list.

Edit an Account

In this exercise, Guy will rename one of the income accounts to better match his business.

6. Scroll down the Chart of Accounts, if necessary, right-click the **Consulting Income** account, and then choose **Edit Account**.

7. Change the Account Name to **Photography Income**, change the Description to **Income from photography jobs**, and then click **Save & Close**.

Delete an Account

8. Scroll to the bottom of the Chart of Accounts window and then right-click the **Ask My Accountant** account.

9. Choose **Delete Account** and then click **OK** in the Delete Account window.

   Because you cannot undo an account deletion, QuickBooks verifies your choice.

Create Subaccounts

Guy wants to track his computer and Internet expenses more carefully, so he has decided to use subaccounts.

10. Single-click **Computer and Internet Expenses** in the Chart of Accounts.

    You technically don't have to click the parent account first, but it can be helpful to visualize where you are making the change by selecting it first.

11. Click the **Account menu** button at the bottom left of the window and then choose **New**.

12. Click in the circle to the left of **Expense** and then click **Continue**.

13. Use the following image to complete the new subaccount:

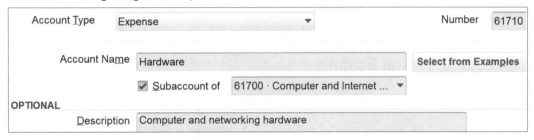

14. Click **Save & New** to save your new account and leave the window open to add another one.

15. Use the following information to create additional subaccounts for Computer and Internet Expenses, clicking **Save & New** after creating the first additional subaccount:

Account Number	Subaccount Name	Description
61720	Software	Computer and device software
61730	Internet Service	Office Internet service

16. Click **Save & Close** to create the last new subaccount; close the Chart of Accounts window.

Working with Opening Balances and Historical Transactions

If you chose a start date for your company that was not the first day you were in business, it is important to enter all of the historical transactions and opening balances in your file.

Entering and Editing Account Opening Balances

You need to make sure that you have the correct opening balances in QuickBooks for all of your accounts. There are five methods by which you can enter opening balances. The type of account that you are dealing with determines which method, or combination of methods, will work the best. The five methods available are:

- EasyStep Interview (for bank accounts only)
- Journal entries
- Forms (for individual transactions)
- Registers
- Lists (lump sums can be entered when creating entries)

Editing a Beginning Balance

If you need to correct a beginning balance that you entered, you will not be able to do it through the EasyStep Interview or the Edit Account window. To accomplish this task, you need to use either the account register or a journal entry. For example, if you incorrectly entered $15,000 as the opening balance for the Savings account when you created it, you will need to open the Savings account register by double-clicking the account in the Chart of Accounts and change the amount in that window.

Entering Historical Transactions for an Account

There are two ways that you can enter historical transactions into your QuickBooks file. Transactions can be entered either individually or in a summary journal entry.

Entering Historical Transactions Individually

If you wish to enter your transactions individually, you must have all the data for each one. This can be very time-consuming if you're already a few months into the year, but you will have all the details for every transaction available in QuickBooks if you do decide to use this method. It is very important that you enter the transactions in the correct order. Check out the following illustration to see the correct order for historical transaction entry.

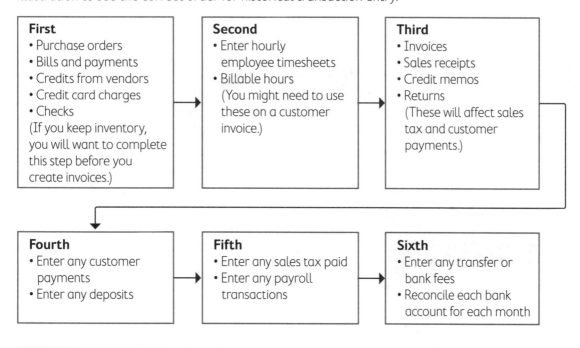

First
- Purchase orders
- Bills and payments
- Credits from vendors
- Credit card charges
- Checks
(If you keep inventory, you will want to complete this step before you create invoices.)

Second
- Enter hourly employee timesheets
- Billable hours
(You might need to use these on a customer invoice.)

Third
- Invoices
- Sales receipts
- Credit memos
- Returns
(These will affect sales tax and customer payments.)

Fourth
- Enter any customer payments
- Enter any deposits

Fifth
- Enter any sales tax paid
- Enter any payroll transactions

Sixth
- Enter any transfer or bank fees
- Reconcile each bank account for each month

Note! Be careful not to duplicate bill payments or customer deposits.

Making a Summary Journal Entry

In a summary journal entry, you will not enter the details of individual transactions; you will enter only the total amounts. If you are not an experienced QuickBooks user, general journal entries should be made only under the guidance of a bookkeeper or accountant, so we will not use them. Rather, you will have an opportunity to edit an opening balance in a register.

 Banking→Use Register

DEVELOP YOUR SKILLS 5-4

In this exercise, you will work with a register to deal with an adjustment to the opening balance for the Checking account because it was not entered when you created the account. The account you will credit in this transaction is 30000•Open Balance Equity.

1. Click the **Check Register** task icon in the Banking area of the Home Page.

   There is only one bank account at this time, so the Checking register will open automatically for you. You may wish to resize the register window so you can see each field better.

2. Use the following information to enter the opening balance for the Checking account, tapping Tab to move from field to field:

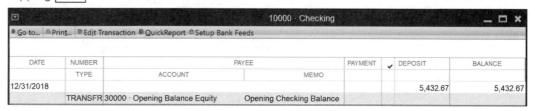

DATE	NUMBER	PAYEE		PAYMENT	✔	DEPOSIT	BALANCE
	TYPE	ACCOUNT	MEMO				
12/31/2018						5,432.67	5,432.67
	TRANSFR	30000 · Opening Balance Equity	Opening Checking Balance				

3. Click the **Record** button at the bottom of the register window.

4. Close the Checking register window.

Finding Help in QuickBooks

When you're starting a new company file, there will be some questions that you might need help with. QuickBooks has a built-in help feature as well as a "coaching" feature that can come to your rescue. Through the Help menu you can get a New Business Checklist guide, Year End Guides, Add Services, and other useful tools. There are two main ways to get help. You can use the Search field on the icon bar to search through the company file, or you can use the Help menu.

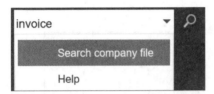

Choosing Search Company File will search through customers, invoices, and other areas of the company file. Typing a topic and then choosing Help will search and open the Have a Question? Window with help on that topic.

You can also choose Help→QuickBooks Desktop Help from the menu to launch the Have a Question? Window.

The "Have a Question?" Window

The "Have a Question?" window is a separate window you can launch to search for help. This window is contextual, which means its contents change depending on the active window. For instance, if you choose to launch it while you have the Chart of Accounts window open, the results will relate to that window. When you choose to get help from QuickBooks a separate Help

Article window will also launch and appear to the right of the Have a Question? window. Review the following figure.

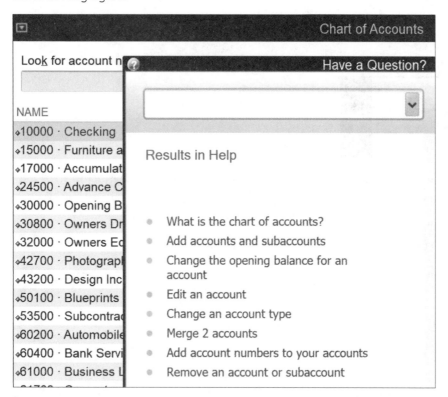

If you launch the Have a Question? window when the Chart of Accounts is the active window, you will find help topics related to it. Don't worry, though, as you can type keywords in the search field related to any aspect of QuickBooks to find help.

Help Articles

Once you see a result in the "Have a Question?" window that you feel is relevant to your needs, click on it. The Help Article window will launch with the information you selected displayed. And remember as we discussed above that this window will launch with the "Have a Question?" window automatically if you issue the help command.

 Help→QuickBooks Desktop Help

DEVELOP YOUR SKILLS 5-5

In this exercise, you will use the contextual help feature in QuickBooks to look for help on invoices and then use the search field to search the company.

1. Choose **Lists→Chart of Accounts**.
2. Choose **Help→QuickBooks Desktop Help**.

   The "Have a Question?" window will display with information about the active window, Chart of Accounts. You can click on a link to read more about the topic for which you searched.

3. Type **Invoice** in the blank search field at the top of the window and then tap ⌷Enter⌷.
4. Click on one of the articles and read through it.

5. Close the Have a Question? window and then click in the **Search Company or Help** field at the top of the icon bar.

    You may need to choose to view your icon bar to the left to see the icon bar (View→Left Icon Bar).

6. Type `invoice`, choose **Search Company File**, and click the **magnifying glass** icon.

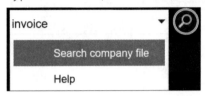

7. Tap ⌨ Enter to use the recent search and then click **Update Search Information** so that it searches for the newest transactions.

    The search will return with results. You can choose any of the links in the various sections.

8. Take some time to click the links and explore the Search window.

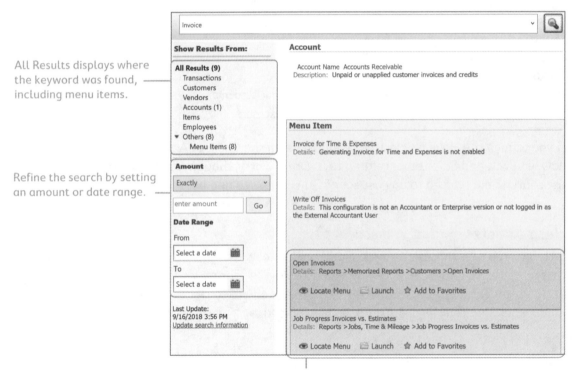

All Results displays where the keyword was found, including menu items.

Refine the search by setting an amount or date range.

Run a report that matches the searched keyword.

9. When you are done, close the Search window and the Chart of Accounts.

Setting Up Users

When your company grows, and you hire additional employees, you may decide that you need to allow certain employees access to your QuickBooks file.

When a company has employees that need access to QuickBooks, you can define different roles by creating users and granting them access to specific areas or functions. The use of passwords is required to ensure protection of the Company data.

Stay signed in! A user can stay logged in for up to 90 days. There are additional things to consider when enabling this option. This feature is not available in a hosted environment that uses roaming profiles. If multiple users are accessing the same company file on the same computer, you still have to explicitly log off. (Talk to your IT professional.)

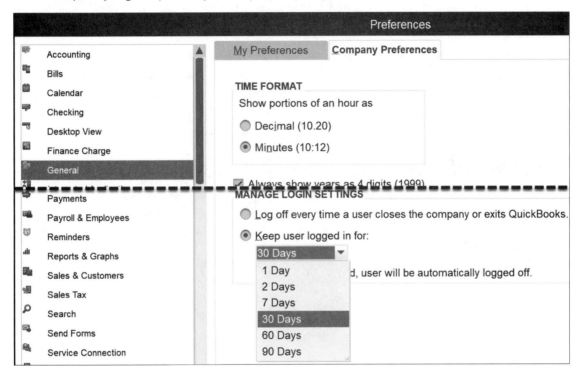

The company administrator can choose how long users can remained signed in through the general preferences category.

Administrators and Users

During the setup process the admin user is created. This is the Administrator account, and it controls access for all users and determines the company's preferences. If you are the sole user of the company file, you can continue to use that account.

Limiting access is sometimes done according to a role the employee plays. For example, you can hire an employee to do accounts payable and receivable, giving that user access only to those areas. You can further restrict access to not allow the printing of checks. It is a good idea to have a plan as to which users or roles have access to which areas of QuickBooks. A written guide in a table format might be a good approach.

The administrator controls all company preferences in the Preferences window. Users can change only their own personal preferences. QuickBooks allows you to set up unlimited users for your company file, although the number that can access the file at any one time depends on your QuickBooks license agreement.

> **Note!** If you set up an External Accountant, that user has access to all areas of QuickBooks except those that contain confidential customer information. An External Accountant can conduct reviews of your file and make changes separate from those of other users. Only an administrator can create an External Accountant user.

There are nine areas for which you can give access rights to a user. Guy has asked your coworker Allison to help out at Average Guy Designs with sales and product ordering, so he will need you to set her up as a user with limited access. In the next exercise, you will set Allison up to have access to all areas of sales and accounts receivable (creating new transactions, printing forms, and running reports) and the ability to create new purchase and accounts payable transactions.

Setting Passwords

It is very important to make sure you have a password that is not easy for others to guess and yet that is easy for you to remember. Once you set your username and password, the Change QuickBooks Password window allows you to change your password whenever you wish and to set or change your secret "challenge question" that will allow you to retrieve a forgotten password. This challenge question should not have an answer with which others are familiar.

Working with QuickBooks in a Multi-User Environment

QuickBooks provides a way for more than one user to access a company file at the same time. In QuickBooks Pro and Premier, up to five users can have simultaneous access to the file. Most tasks that you usually do can be completed in multi-user mode, but there are some that must be performed in single-user mode.

You cannot do the following in multi-user mode:

- Create a new company file
- Set or edit a closing date
- Rebuild, clean up, or verify the file
- Create or work with accountant's copies
- Merge, delete, and sort list information
- Change company preferences
- Export and import data

> Company→Set Up Users and Passwords→Set Up Users

> File→Switch to Single-user Mode or Switch to Multi-user Mode

---

DEVELOP YOUR SKILLS 5-6

In this exercise, you will help Guy set up Allison as a user for the Average Guy Designs company file.

1. Choose **Company→Set Up Users and Passwords→Set Up Users**.
2. Type **Password1** as the Admin password and then click **OK**.

3. Click the **Add User** button in the User List window; then use the following information to add Allison as a user:

- User Name: **Allison**
- Password: **Password1**
- Confirm Password: **Password1**

The first time users log in, they will be prompted to change their passwords. Minimum requirements are seven characters with one uppercase letter and one number. It would be more secure to include a symbol such as $ or % in the password. Usernames are not case-sensitive, but passwords are. The next step will be to select the access for the AR/AP Clerk position.

4. Click **Next** twice.

Each time you click Next as you move through the "Set up user password and access" screens, you can change the access for the user in one of nine areas.

5. Click to choose **Full Access** for the Sales and Accounts Receivable option; click **Next**.

6. Click in the circle to the left of **Selective Access** for Purchases and Accounts Payable.

The Create transactions only option will be automatically selected.

7. Click **Next** and view the permissions information for Checking and Credit Cards. Continue clicking **Next**, viewing the details on each screen for the remainder of the nine areas.

You will see a summary of Allison's user access rights on the last screen.

Access for user: Allison   Page 9 of 9

You have finished setting this user's access rights and password. Below is a summary of this user's access rights. Click the Finish button to complete this task.

AREA	CREATE	PRINT	REPOR
Sales and Accounts Receivable	Y	Y	Y
Purchases and Accounts Payable	Y	N	N
Checking and Credit Cards	N	N	n/a
Time Tracking	N	N	N
Payroll and Employees	N	N	N
Sensitive Accounting Activities	N	N	N
Sensitive Financial Reports	N	N	n/a
Changing or Deleting Transactions	Y	n/a	n/a
Changing Closed Transactions	N	n/a	n/a

---

8. Click **Finish**.

Notice that Allison has been added to the User List.

9. Close the User List.

Closing the Books and Running List Reports

You will not actually close the books yet, but it is important to understand how QuickBooks deals with this task, so it will be covered now. You will, however, find the need to produce list reports early on in your QuickBooks experience. For instance, your accountant may wish to see a list of the accounts you have set up for your business to ensure all is well before you get too far down the road.

Keeping the End in Mind

You are not required to "close the books" in QuickBooks, but you can choose to if you like. When you close the books, QuickBooks:

- Transfers the net income or net loss to Retained Earnings

- Restricts access to transactions prior to the closing date by requiring a password

- Allows you to clean up your data

Only the company file administrator can set a closing date and allow or restrict access to prior-period transactions by a user.

The Report Center

As you have seen, there are many preset reports available for you to use in QuickBooks. They are broken into three main categories: list, summary, and transaction. The Report Center is a tool in QuickBooks that allows you to learn about different types of reports without having to create them by trial and error. It includes sample reports and descriptions of the type of information each report provides.

Contributed Reports

Contributed reports are specialized reports submitted by users and integrated into the Report Center. You can search for specialized reports by your industry type, and you can even rate a report for other users to show how valuable it is to you.

List Reports in QuickBooks

One category of reports that you can access contains list reports. They simply display the information that is found in your various QuickBooks lists in an easy-to-read format.

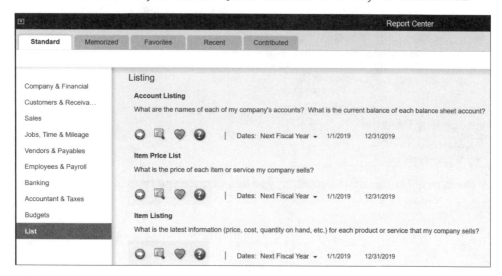

When you view the Report Center in List View, you will see a question that the report will answer below the name of the report. Here you can see the questions that the Account Listing report (it displays your Chart of Accounts) answers.

Viewing Sample Report Images

An additional feature available in the Report Center is the ability for you to view what a report will look like without having to actually produce the report. This feature is available in the Carousel View and Grid View.

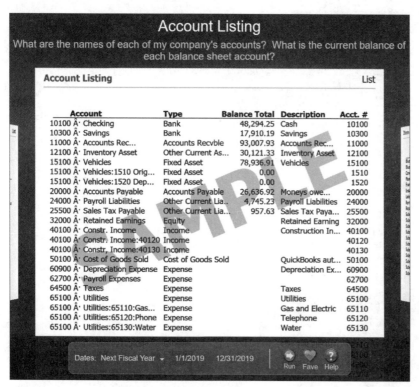

When you view reports in Carousel View, you can see large sample report images so that you can make sure you are creating the correct report.

Email Functionality in Reports

QuickBooks allows you to email reports from any report window. You have a chance to choose whether the recipient will receive the report as an Adobe Acrobat (PDF) or Microsoft Excel file. The report will appear the same as it would as if you printed it from QuickBooks.

When you click the E-mail button on the toolbar, you can choose the type of file that will be attached to your email message.

 Reports→Report Center

DEVELOP YOUR SKILLS 5-7

In this exercise, Guy will create a report for his accountant that displays the accounts in his Chart of Accounts and then view a contributed report that may be helpful in his business.

1. Choose **Reports→Report Center**.
2. Follow these steps to display the report:
   - Click the **List View** button in the top-right portion of the window

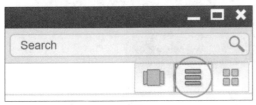

   - Click the **List** category on the left side of the Report Center
   - Scroll down and then click the **Run** button for the Account Listing report

   A report displaying all the accounts in the Chart of Accounts is displayed.

3. Close the Account Listing report.
4. Click the **Contributed** tab in the Report Center.

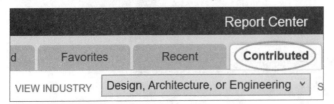

Notice that because Guy chose Design, Architecture, or Engineering as his industry type when creating his company file, it will be displayed in the View Industry field.

5. Scroll through the list of contributed reports, find one that is interesting to you, and then click the **Run** button for it to be displayed.

   You don't have any transactions entered into the company file at this point, so most of the reports will not contain data. The important thing to look at is the "bones" of the report—how it is set up and formatted.

6. Close the window of the contributed report that you are viewing.

7. Close the Report Center window.

8. Leave the company if you are continuing on to "Tackle the Tasks" or close QuickBooks if you are done working in the program.

Tackle the Tasks

Now is your chance to work a little more with Average Guy Designs and apply the skills that you have learned in this chapter to accomplish additional tasks. You will use the same company file you just created to complete the following tasks. If you need to reopen the company file, the password is *Password1*.

Add Accounts	Add the following bank account: 10200•Savings Add the following income account: 48800•Print Layout Services Add the following expense account: 61500•Job Materials
Add Subaccounts	Add the following subaccounts to the Utilities account: 68610•Gas & Electric, 68620•Water
Change Account Opening Balance	Change the Savings account opening balance to $7,382.35, as of 12/31/2018
Search for Help	Use the QuickBooks help feature to learn how to enter an inventory item
Change Preferences	Choose to turn off pop-up messages for products and services (Hint: General/My Preferences) Choose to show the Sales Receipts task icon on the Home Page (Hint: Desktop View/Company Preferences)
Create a List Report	Create a list report that shows all of the Terms available (these list entries were automatically added when you created the company)

Self-Assessment

Check your knowledge of this chapter's key concepts and skills using the Self-Assessment quiz here, in your ebook, or in your eLab course.

1. You should always set your QuickBooks start date to be the first day you start your business.   *True   False*

2. Start Setup is a quick company setup method that asks you for only the basics.   *True   False*

3. The normal balance of an income account is a debit balance.   *True   False*

4. By default, liabilities are always listed first in the Chart of Accounts.   *True   False*

5. Preferences control the way you interact with the QuickBooks program.   *True   False*

6. You should create a separate QuickBooks company file for each tax return you file.   *True   False*

7. The Report Center allows you to view what a report will look like without having to produce it.   *True   False*

8. If you choose the Advanced Setup option, then you will be taken to the EasyStep Interview to create your company file.   *True   False*

9. You can create multiple users and give each user different access rights.   *True   False*

10. Passwords are required in QuickBooks.   *True   False*

11. Subaccounts will always be displayed on a report.   *True   False*

12. Which of these accounts has a credit normal balance?
    A. Auto Loan
    B. Accounts Receivable
    C. Checking
    D. Rent Expense

13. Which of the following can you NOT do when the company file is in multi-user mode?
    A. Enter an invoice
    B. Change company preferences
    C. Enter a new customer
    D. Enter a bill from a vendor

14. Which account number might be used for Sales?
    A. 50230
    B. 19040
    C. 23100
    D. 42300

15. Which of the following accounts is NOT an asset?
    A. Checking
    B. Accounts Payable
    C. Accounts Receivable
    D. Undeposited Funds

Reinforce Your Skills

Solid Ground Construction is a new but expanding business. As the new project coordinator, you will be setting up QuickBooks to keep track of all the company's financial data. This includes setting up the Chart of Accounts and company preferences.

REINFORCE YOUR SKILLS 5-1

Set Up a New QuickBooks Company

In this exercise, you will use the Advanced Start method to create the company file for Solid Ground Construction. Leave the company file open unless otherwise instructed.

1. Launch QuickBooks 2019 and toggle to the Pro edition.
2. Choose **File→New Company**.
3. Click **Other Options** and then choose **Advanced Setup**.

   The EasyStep Interview window is displayed.
4. Use this information to complete the EasyStep Interview:
   - Company Name: **Solid Ground Construction**
   - Legal Name: **Solid Ground Construction**
   - Tax ID (Employer Identification Number or Social Security Number): **99-0987654**
   - Address: **316 Maple Street**
   - City/State/Zip: **Silverton OR 97381**
   - Phone: **(503) 555-3759**
   - Fax: **(503) 555-3758**
   - Email: **CustomerService@email.com**
5. Click **Next** to continue the Interview and then click **Next** after each of the following steps:
   - Select your industry: **Construction General Contractor**
   - Company organization: **Single-Member LLC**
   - Fiscal year: **January**
   - Administrator Password: **Password1**
   - QuickBooks File Name: **Solid Ground Construction**
   - What do you sell? **Services only**
   - Sales tax: **No**
   - Estimates: **Yes**
   - Billing Statements: **Yes**
   - Progress Invoicing: **No**
   - Bill Tracking: **Yes**
   - Time Tracking: **Yes**
   - Employees: **No**

- State Date: Choose Use today's date or the first day of the quarter or month and then type **010119**

- Income & Expense Accounts: **Start with the accounts provided**

6. When the information is entered, click **Go to Setup** to complete the interview.

   The QuickBooks Desktop Set Up window appears.

7. Click **Start Working** and close the New Feature Tour window, if necessary.

REINFORCE YOUR SKILLS 5-2

Change Company Preferences

In this exercise, you will change two preferences for Solid Ground Construction. You will begin by turning on the account number preference so you can assign numbers when you create or edit accounts.

1. Choose **Edit→Preferences**.

2. Choose the **Accounting** category.

3. Click the **Company Preferences** tab.

4. Click in the box to turn on **Use Account Numbers** and then turn off both of the **Date Warnings** preferences.

Display Additional Task Icons on the Home Page

You've decided that you want to create sales receipts in QuickBooks, so you will change the company preferences to reflect this.

5. Choose the **Desktop View** category and then click **Yes** to Save Changes.

6. Click the **Company Preferences** tab.

7. Click the checkbox to the left of **Sales Receipts** in the Customers section of the window.

   Notice the related preferences section shows which features are turned on and off for your company.

8. Click **OK** to change the preference and then click **OK** again to close all the windows.

9. Choose **Company→Home Page**.

   Notice that the Create Sales Receipts task icon has been added to the Customers section, making it easier to create sales receipts.

REINFORCE YOUR SKILLS 5-3

Work with the Chart of Accounts

In this exercise, you will add, edit, and delete accounts as well as add subaccounts in the Chart of Accounts. To begin, you will add a company Checking account.

1. Choose **Lists→Chart of Accounts**.

2. Click the **Account** button and then choose **New**.

3. Choose **Bank** and then click **Continue**.

4. Use the following information to complete the account creation:
   - Number: **10000**
   - Account Name: **Checking**
   - Description: **Company checking account**
   - Bank Acct. No.: **456-456-4444**
   - Routing Number: **333000333**

5. Click **Save & Close** and then close the Set Up Bank Feed window.

6. Click the **Account** button and then choose **New**.

7. Choose **Income** and then click **Continue**.

8. Use the following information to complete the account creation:
   - Number: **42700**
   - Account Name: **Remodel Income**
   - Description: **Remodeling project income**

9. Click **Save & Close**.

REINFORCE YOUR SKILLS 5-4

Work with List Reports

In this exercise, you will create an Account Listing report to review the work that you have completed on the Chart of Accounts.

1. Choose **Reports→List→Account Listing**.

2. **Review** the report to ensure that you entered the two accounts from the previous exercise correctly.

3. Close the Account Listing report and then close your company file.

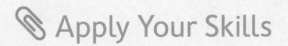

Apply Your Skills

Create a New Company File

In this exercise, you will go back to the beginning and create a QuickBooks company file for Dr. Sadie James, DVM. You should use the Advanced Setup method available in Other Options to set up the company.

1. Use the following information to set up a new company file for Dr. James:
   - Company/Legal Name: **Wet Noses Veterinary Clinic**
   - Tax ID Number: **99-9999999**
   - Address: **589 Retriever Drive, Bothell, WA 98011**
   - Phone: **(425) 555-2939**
   - E-mail address: **Dr.James@email.com**
   - Industry: **Medical, Dental, or Health Service**
   - Company Type: **LLP**
   - Fiscal Year first month: **January**
   - Password: **Password1**

2. Save the file to your file storage location as: **Wet Noses Veterinary Clinic**

3. Use the following information for the remainder of the setup; accept defaults where not stated:
   - You sell services and products
   - Charge sales tax
   - Don't use estimates
   - Use billing statements
   - Use invoices
   - No progress invoicing
   - Track bills
   - Track inventory for products you sell
   - No time tracking
   - Employees: you have 1099 contractors
   - Start Date: **01/01/2019**
   - Select Sub Accounts:

       —**Medical Records Supplies**

       —**Medical Supplies**

4. Choose to **Start Working** and close all windows except for the Home Page.

5. Create the **Account Listing** report to ensure you completed the initial setup properly.

6. Click the **Excel** [Excel ▾] button and export the report to a new worksheet, saving the workbook to your file storage location as: **CH5_A1 Account List Report 1**

7. Close Excel and the Account Listing report; keep the company file open for the next exercise.

Set Company and User Preferences

In this exercise, you will set preferences for Wet Noses as a company and yourself as a user. The categories are provided for you, but you will have to determine if they are company or individual user preferences.

1. Open the **Preferences** window.
2. Display the **Desktop View** category and change the **Company File Color Scheme** to your favorite color.
3. Display the **Accounting** category and choose to turn on **account numbers**.
4. Display the **Reminders** category and choose to have QuickBooks show a list of the **To Do Notes** when you open the company file.
5. Display the **Accounting** category and choose to turn off **date warnings**.
6. Close the **Preferences** window.
7. Create the **Account Listing** report to ensure you set the preferences correctly.
8. Click the **Excel** [Excel ▼] button and export the report to a new worksheet, saving the workbook to your file storage location as: **CH5_A2 Account List Report 2**
9. Close the Excel and Account Listing windows.

Modify the Chart of Accounts

In this exercise, you will modify the Chart of Accounts for the company you just created.

1. Open the **Chart of Accounts**.
2. Add two new **bank** accounts: **10000•Checking** and **11000•Savings**
3. Add a new **income** account: **43000•Boarding Income**
4. Add two new **expense** accounts: **60800•Boarding Food** and **63800•Lab Supplies**
5. Change the name of the 68700•Vaccines and Medicines account to **68700•Pharmaceuticals**
6. Add two **subaccounts** for Pharmaceuticals: **68710•Vaccines** and **68720•Medicines**
7. Delete the **68500•Uniforms** account.
8. Create the **Account Listing** report to ensure you set up the Chart of Accounts correctly.
9. Click the **Excel** [Excel ▼] button and export the report to a new worksheet, saving the workbook to your file storage location as: **CH5_A3 Account List Report 3**
10. Close the Excel and Account Listing windows.

Enter Opening Balances in a Register

In this exercise, you will enter the opening balances for the checking and savings accounts.

1. Open the **10000•Checking** register.
2. Enter the opening balance of **$26,791.80** as a deposit to the account on 01/01/2019, crediting **30000•Opening Balance Equity**. Close the 10000•Checking register window when you are done.
3. Open the **11000•Savings** register.
4. Enter the opening balance of **$57,921.34** as a deposit to the account on 01/01/2019, crediting **30000•Opening Balance Equity**. Close the 11000 · Savings register window when you are done.
5. Create the **Account Listing** report to ensure you entered the opening balances correctly.
6. Click the **Excel** Excel ▾ button and export the report to a new worksheet, saving the workbook to your file storage location as: **CH5_A4 Account List Report 4**
7. Close the Excel and Account Listing report windows; close your company file.

Extend Your Skills

You have been hired by Arlaine Cervantes to help her with her organization's books. She is the founder of Niños del Lago, a nonprofit organization that provides impoverished Guatemalan children with an engaging educational camp experience. You have just sat down at your desk and opened a large envelope from her with a variety of documents as well as noticing that you have several emails from her. It is your job to sort through the papers and emails and make sense of what you find, entering information into QuickBooks whenever appropriate and answering any other questions in a word-processing document saved as: **EYS1_Chapter05 _LastnameFirstinitial**. Remember, you are digging through papers you just dumped out of an envelope and addressing random emails from Arlaine, so it is up to you to determine the correct order in which to complete the tasks.

- An email from her accountant: Set up Chart of Accounts, use Non-Profit as industry type, and add Grant Revenue as an income account.

- A bank statement from Salem First National Bank dated 05/31/2019. Checking account #21375-01, ending balance $5,462.11; Savings account #21375-20, ending balance $18,203.54.

- A handwritten sticky note: Need for three volunteers (Bill, Karel, and Chris) to have access to entering donor revenue. How can I make sure they can do this but don't have access to other areas in QuickBooks?

- A scrap of paper with the following written on it: Fiscal year July–June.

- A scribbled phone message from Arlaine's accountant: Make sure to use account numbers when you set up in QuickBooks.

- The following message on a sticky note: Is there a reminders list to keep me on track???

- Another email from Arlaine's accountant: Make sure to not have the starting date the day you started the organization…would be too much information to enter. How about 5/31/2019 instead since it is the end of the fiscal year?

- A copy of last year's taxes: Form 990, Federal EIN 99-9999999.

- A torn piece of company letterhead:

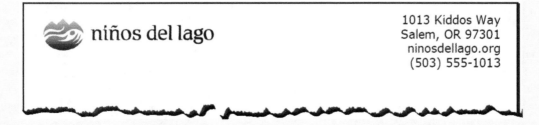

niños del lago

1013 Kiddos Way
Salem, OR 97301
ninosdellago.org
(503) 555-1013

6 | Managing Physical Inventory

In this chapter, you will examine the inventory features available in QuickBooks that help you to track items (goods) that you offer for sale. An example of a company needing to track inventory is a retail store that sells electronics or a salon that sells styling products. When the inventory function is turned on, QuickBooks provides additional features to create inventory items and purchase orders, receive items into inventory, sell inventory items, and run inventory-related reports. Additional accounts are created to track inventory—Inventory Assets and Cost of Goods Sold. You will also learn how to set up and track sales tax, deal with customer refunds, and explore common inventory and sales reports.

LEARNING OBJECTIVES

▸ Create and use items to track inventory
▸ Create purchase orders and receive items
▸ Adjust quantity/value on hand
▸ Sell items and process sales discounts and refunds
▸ Collect, track, and pay sales tax
▸ Utilize reports to manage inventory and sales

📁 Project: Average Guy Designs

Guy Marshall is a graphic designer who owns Average Guy Designs. He started his business two years ago and has successfully landed several corporate accounts. He has been using QuickBooks to account for his service-based business for some time now.

In this chapter, you will help Guy set up inventory items in QuickBooks, as he has decided to sell products from his shop as well as online. After inventory items have been created, he will be able to sell them to his customers, tracking those items sold and the quantities remaining in stock. You will also learn how to set up and receive payments when sales discounts are involved. Finally, you will explore sales reports and inventory reports that will help to manage inventory.

Tracking Inventory in QuickBooks

A useful feature in QuickBooks is inventory tracking. It must be turned on in the Preferences window. When activated, it will add links to the Home Page and options to the menu bar.

 Edit→Preferences

Should I Use QuickBooks to Track My Company's Inventory?

Not all companies are perfectly aligned to use QuickBooks to track their inventory. There are several factors that you should consider before deciding to use QuickBooks to track your company's inventory items:

- **How many types of products do I sell?** QuickBooks Pro and Premier work well for companies that have up to a few hundred items. If you have more items, you may want to consider using QuickBooks' Point-of-Sale edition.

- **Does my inventory include perishable items?** The bookkeeping for perishable items can be a bit tedious due to differences between your on-hand quantities and what you have recorded in QuickBooks.

- **Do I sell unique, one-of-a-kind products?** If you sell items such as antiques, you will have to create a new QuickBooks item for each product you sell.

- **Do I manufacture the products that I sell?** If you purchase raw materials and assemble them into products, QuickBooks Pro is not the most compatible software for your company. You may want to look at purchasing QuickBooks: Premier Manufacturing & Wholesale Edition or QuickBooks Enterprise Solutions: Manufacturing & Wholesale Edition, which address the unique needs of manufacturing businesses.

- **How fast do my inventory items become obsolete?** If this timeframe is quite short, you may find that updating your inventory in QuickBooks is tedious.

- **How do I value my inventory?** QuickBooks Pro uses the average cost method of inventory valuation. If you are using another one of the methods allowed by GAAP, such as LIFO or FIFO, or another method, you may want to look at using a different tool to track your inventory.

FLASHBACK TO GAAP: CONSISTENCY

Remember that the company should use the same accounting principles and methods from year to year.

In this exercise, you will turn on the inventory features of QuickBooks. The password for all files unless otherwise stated is Password1. *Leave the company file open unless otherwise instructed.*

1. Start QuickBooks 2019.

Toggle to QuickBooks Pro

If you are using the trial version of the software provided with this course, your version of QuickBooks is likely showing the Accountant edition. You must toggle to Pro now and every time you start QuickBooks in order for your screen to show the same images as those in the text and for QuickGrader reports to be generated correctly.

2. Choose **File→Toggle to Another Edition**.
3. Click in the circle to the left of *QuickBooks Pro* and then click **Next**.
4. Click **Toggle** and then click **OK**.
5. Choose **File→Open or Restore Company**.
6. Open **DYS_Chapter06 (Company)** or restore **DYS_Chapter06 (Portable)** from your file storage location and save your file as: **DYS_Chapter06 Average Guy Designs**

    Note that you only need to save the file with a different name if you are using a portable company file. If you are working with a company file, you can simply open it from your file storage location and start working.

Set Preferences to Track Inventory

Remember, preferences allow you to customize QuickBooks. There are two customizations that can be made: My Preferences and Company Preferences.

7. Choose **Edit→Preferences**.
8. Follow these steps to turn on the inventory feature:

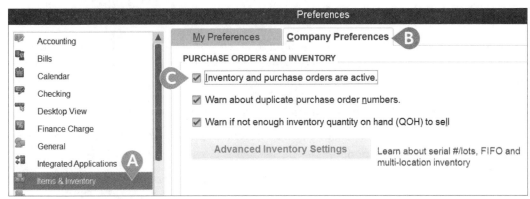

- Ⓐ Click **Items & Inventory**.
- Ⓑ Click the **Company Preferences** tab.
- Ⓒ Click to check the **Inventory and purchase orders are active.** box.

Notice that you will be warned if you use a duplicate purchase order number and if your inventory quantity on hand is not enough.

9. Click **OK** and then **OK** again to allow QuickBooks to close all windows to make this preference change.

Tracking Inventory Sales

You will likely need to create a new account and possibly subaccounts to track the sales of your inventory. In the following exercise, you will be creating a new account and three subaccounts to make sure that you can track your sales effectively.

> **Note!** In some Premier versions of QuickBooks, there is a feature called the Inventory Center. This center looks similar to the Customer and Vendor centers. It provides a convenient place for you to manage your inventory items.

> **Note!** In the Premier and higher versions of QuickBooks, there is a feature that allows you to convert units of measure, where you can work with either single units of measure (e.g., buy or sell a pound) or multiple units of measure (e.g., buy a yard, sell a foot). This is especially useful for companies that distribute or manufacture items.

Show Lowest Subaccount Preference

You might choose to create accounts and subaccounts to better categorize your inventory items. For example, the Clothing account could be a subaccount of Product Sales. However, when viewing transactions, it is often difficult to see the name and number of the subaccount that you used because of the narrow account fields in the windows. You can overcome this problem by choosing to see only the lowest subaccount in these fields. For example, if you need to choose the Clothing subaccount, it would normally be displayed as:

41000•Product Sales:41100•Clothing

By choosing the Show Lowest Subaccount preference, it will simply be displayed as:

41100•Clothing

DEVELOP YOUR SKILLS 6-2

In this exercise, you will first check that your accounts have numbers. Next you will create a new account and subaccounts, which will help you to track inventory income. To see the lowest subaccount names, you will change the company preferences.

1. Choose **Lists→Chart of Accounts**, resizing the window, if necessary.
2. Scroll through the Chart of Accounts to see whether there are any that do not have an account number assigned.

   You will see that all accounts have a number assigned, which is necessary to show the lowest subaccounts only.

Create a New Account

3. Click the **Account** drop-down arrow ▼ at the bottom of the window and choose **New** from the menu.

4. Use this information to create the new account:

- Account Type: **Income** (click **Continue**)
- Number: **41000**
- Account Name: `Product Sales`
- Description: `Sales Income`

5. Click **Save & New**.

Create Subaccounts to Track Inventory Sales

You will now create three subaccounts to further classify your inventory sales income account.

6. Enter this information to create the first subaccount:

- Number: **41100**
- Account Name: `Clothing`
- Subaccount of: Click in the checkbox and choose **41000•Product Sales** from the menu
- Description: `Clothing Sales Income`

7. Click **Save & New**.

8. Use this information to add two additional subaccounts to the income account Product Sales:

Second subaccount:

- Account Number: **41200**
- Account Name: `Accessories`
- Subaccount of: Click in the checkbox and choose **41000•Product Sales** from the menu
- Description: `Accessories Sales Income`

Third subaccount:

- Account Number: **41300**
- Account Name: `Home Decor`
- Subaccount of: Click in the checkbox and choose **41000•Product Sales** from the menu
- Description: `Home Decor Sales Income`

9. Click **Save & Close**.

Because they are subaccounts of Product Sales, they all appear underneath Product Sales. If not, click the Account menu button arrow and choose Hierarchical View.

10. Close the Chart of Accounts window.

Set the Show Lowest Subaccount Preference

11. Choose **Edit→Preferences**.

12. Click the **Accounting** category.

13. Click the **Company Preferences** tab.

14. Click to check the **Show Lowest Subaccount Only** preference.

15. Click **OK**.

Setting Up the Item List

In order to select items that you will be selling from a sales form or purchase order, each one must first be set up as an item in the Item List. Setting up your inventory requires an understanding of when items qualify as inventory items and when they are non-inventory items:

- Inventory parts are tracked and sold by quantity. Examples of inventory parts might be vitamins that a doctor purchases and sells to patients, lamps that an interior decorating company buys and resells, or branded ceramic coffee cups that a bakery might sell.

- Non-inventory parts include items you don't track as inventory, such as nails used by a contractor or thread used by a seamstress, or items you purchase for a particular customer or items you sell but don't first purchase, such as livestock that you breed and sell. These products are necessary for the business, but they are not being stocked for re-sale to customers.

 Lists→Item List: Item→New

Two-Sided Items

When you create an inventory item, it has two sides: one for the purchase information and the other for the sales information. When you purchase items at wholesale to resell to your customers, the purchase price you pay is the cost of goods sold (COGS). Your profit is the difference between your sales price and COGS. All of the information needed to track both sides of the item is detailed in the New Item window.

The purchase information for the items you purchase to be sold

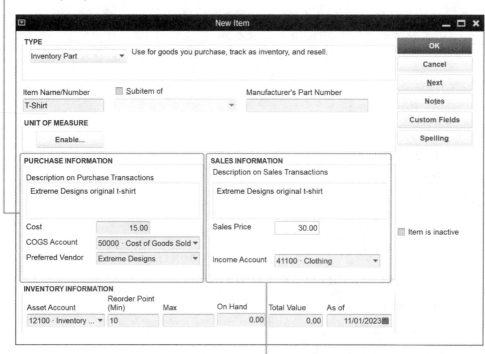

The sales information for tracking the sale of the item, directing it into the correct income account

Add/Edit Multiple List Entries

If you are adding more than a few items at once, QuickBooks has a feature to easily record multiple entries in your lists. This feature is also available for customers and vendors to make your data entry faster. And you can quickly update several entries in your lists by right-clicking and choosing either the Clear Column or Copy Down command.

Tip! You can paste your list from Microsoft Excel.

DEVELOP YOUR SKILLS 6-3

In this exercise, you will help Average Guy Designs create inventory items for the company by entering a single item and then creating additional items using the Add/Edit Multiple List Entries feature.

1. Choose **Company→Home Page**.

   Notice the new task icons that are present now that invoice features are turned on.

2. Click the **Items & Services** task icon in the Company area of the Home Page, resizing the window if necessary.

3. Click the **Item** drop-down arrow ▼ from the bottom of the window and choose **New**.

4. Enter this information to create an inventory item:
   - Type: **Inventory Part**
   - Item Name/Number: **T-Shirt**
   - Description: **Extreme Designs original t-shirt**
   - Cost: **15**
   - Preferred Vendor: **Extreme Designs** (then `Tab` and choose **Quick Add**)
   - Sales Price: **30**
   - Income Account: **41100•Clothing**
   - Reorder Point (Min): **10**

   The quantity On Hand and Total Value will be addressed later when you purchase the t-shirts with a purchase order.

5. Click **OK**, choosing to **Add** "t" to the dictionary in the Spell Check window (and correcting any errors that you may have made), if necessary.

Create Multiple Inventory Items

Next you will create multiple inventory items using the Add/Edit Multiple List Entries window, but first you will customize the columns to include fields currently not displayed.

6. Click the **Item** drop-down arrow ▼ at the bottom of the window and choose **Add/Edit Multiple Items**. If the Time Saving Tip window appears at any time during this exercise, click **OK**.

7. Choose **Inventory Parts** as the List.

8. Click **Customize Columns**.

9. Follow these steps to customize the columns for data entry of the inventory part items:

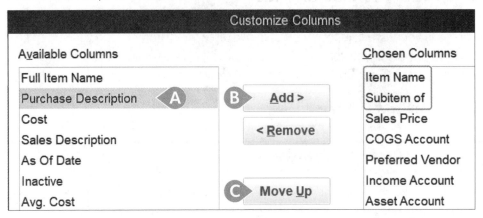

Ⓐ Click the **Purchase Description** column heading.

Ⓑ Click **Add**.

Ⓒ Click **Move Up** until Purchase Description is displayed above *Subitem of* and below *Item Name*.

10. Select the **Sales Description** column heading and **Add** it to the Chosen Columns list. Move it up until it is displayed above *Income Account*.

11. Click **OK** to finish customizing the columns.

12. To add the next inventory part item, click in the row below *T-shirt* and enter this information into the appropriate columns:

Tip! Tapping ⌈Tab⌉ after each entry will move your cursor one field to the right, speeding up data entry. You can also right-click and select from a pick list to copy down, clear a column, and insert or delete lines.

- Item Name: **LS Shirt**
- Purchase & Sales Descriptions: **Extreme Designs original long sleeve shirt**
- Cost: **20**
- Sales Price: **40**
- Preferred Vendor: **Extreme Designs**
- Income Account: **41100•Clothing**
- Reorder Pt (Min): **10**

13. Enter the following inventory items, using **Quick Add** for the new vendors.

Enter this information for a coaster set by Hartwell Designs:

- Item Name: **Coasters**
- Purchase Description: **Coaster Set (4)**
- Cost: **7.93**
- Sales Price: **20**
- Preferred Vendor: **Hartwell Designs**
- Sales Description: **Set of 4 Coasters**
- Income Account: **41300•Home Decor**

- Reorder Pt (Min): **8**

Enter this information for a scarf by Julie's Treasures:

- Item Name: **Scarf**
- Purchase Description: **Handmade Knit Scarf**
- Cost: **10**
- Sales Price: **35**
- Preferred Vendor: **Julie's Treasures**
- Sales Description: **Hand Knit Scarf**
- Income Account: **41200•Accessories**
- Reorder Pt (Min): **12**

Enter this information for small tiles by Hartwell Designs:

- Item Name: **Sm Tiles**
- Purchase Description: **Small hanging tiles with original design**
- Cost: **5.30**
- Sales Price: **18**
- Preferred Vendor: **Hartwell Designs**
- Sales Description: **Small hanging original tiles**
- Income Account: **41300•Home Decor**
- Reorder Pt (Min): **20**

14. Click the **Save Changes** button at the bottom of the window and click **OK** in the Record(s) Saved window.

15. Close the Add/Edit Multiple Entries List.

    View the Item List to confirm that the entries were added.

16. Close the Item List window.

Dealing with Sales Tax in QuickBooks

QuickBooks makes it easy to charge and collect sales tax for items. You can also choose whether to charge tax for customers who resell merchandise to *their* customers. How you set up sales tax in QuickBooks depends entirely on which state(s) you conduct business in. You must know the sales tax laws in your state before you set up sales tax for your company. If your company is selling products and not just services, you/it might need to charge sales tax for those products.

> **Warning!** When dealing with sales tax, learn about the sales tax laws in your jurisdiction. How you display items on invoices, whether items are stated separately or grouped together, can affect the amount of tax due on a transaction. Talk to an accountant, if necessary.

Behind the scenes, the sales tax collected will be directed to a Sales Tax Liability account that QuickBooks automatically creates for you. The funds will be held there until you pay them to the appropriate governing authority.

Sales Tax Items and Groups

To include sales tax on a sales form, you must set up the tax as an item. Often you have to pay the tax collected to multiple tax agencies. QuickBooks allows you to combine multiple sales tax items into a sales tax group. This is necessary, as you can apply only one sales tax item or group to a sales form.

Before you can collect sales tax, you must turn on the preference and create the appropriate sales tax item(s) or group.

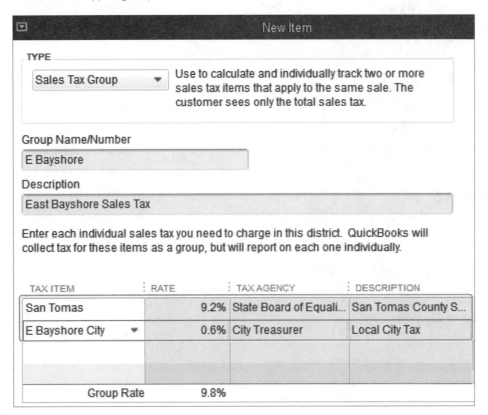

A Sales Tax Group is comprised of two sales tax items payable to two separate tax agencies.

Default Tax Rate

Once you have created your sales tax item(s) and group(s), you should set the default to the most commonly used tax rate in Preferences. This rate will appear when you create a sales form for a customer for whom a tax rate is not specified; you can change it on a sale-by-sale basis.

Dealing with Multiple Sales Tax Rates

Some companies conduct business in multiple jurisdictions. As such, the company must set up different sales tax items and/or groups with the different rates and taxing agencies. You can set one default tax rate for the company or default tax rates for each customer.

Sales Tax Codes

QuickBooks automatically sets up two sales tax codes for you when you turn on the preference, Taxable and Non-taxable. These codes are assigned to customers and items. QuickBooks will apply sales tax to any customer or item where the code is set to Taxable, although this can be changed on an individual basis on the sales forms.

You can even create additional sales tax codes, as needed, through the Sales Tax Code List.

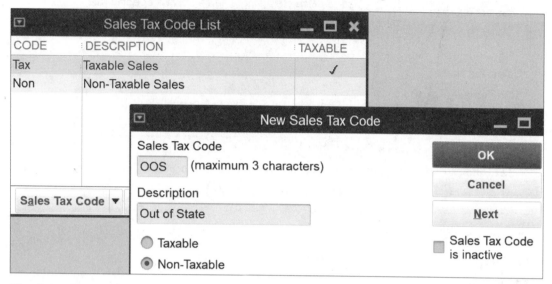

The Sales Tax Code List allows you to create additional codes such as Out of State, allowing you to track sales to customers who do not live in your state and are not required to pay your sales tax.

Edit→Preferences: Sales Tax→Company Preferences tab→Your most common sales tax item

Customers→Customer Center: New Customer & Job→New Customer

DEVELOP YOUR SKILLS 6-4

In this exercise, you will create a sales tax item. Before you can create any sales tax items or groups, the preference must be turned on.

1. Choose **Edit→Preferences**.
2. Click the **Sales Tax** category.
3. Follow these steps to set the sales tax preference and to set up your default sales tax item:

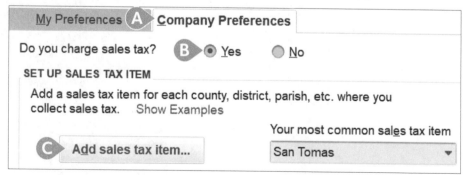

- Ⓐ Click **Company Preferences**.
- Ⓑ Click **Yes** to note you charge sales tax.
- Ⓒ Click **Add Sales Tax Item** (and then tap Tab).

(cont'd.)

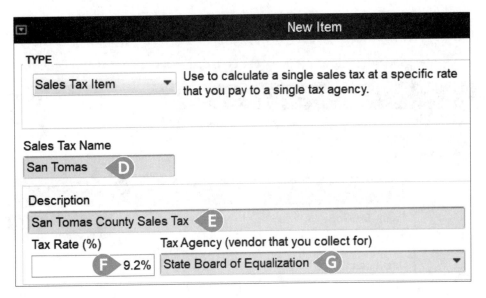

- ⒟ Sales Tax Name: **San Tomas**
- ⒠ Description: **San Tomas County Sales Tax**
- ⒡ Tax Rate: **9.2**
- ⒢ Tax Agency: **State Board of Equalization** (and then **Quick Add** it as a **Vendor**)

4. Click **OK**.

5. Click the drop-down arrow ▼ for **Your most common sales tax item** and then choose **San Tomas**.

6. Click **OK** and then click **OK** again in the Updating Sales Tax window.

   Notice that two Sales Tax Codes are created automatically: Taxable and Non-taxable. These codes are assigned to Customers and Items. QuickBooks will apply tax to any Customer or Item where the code is set to Taxable, although this can be changed on a sales form.

7. Click **OK** in the Warning window.

> *Tip!* You can edit whether a customer is Taxable or Non-Taxable in the Sales Tax Settings tab of the Edit Customer window. You can assign or edit an item's tax code in the Edit Item window. The bottom line is you must know your state's sales tax requirements.

Creating Purchase Orders

Many businesses use purchase orders (POs) for ordering items into inventory. When a PO is created, nothing occurs behind the scenes, as you have done nothing yet to debit or credit an account.

If you purchase items for sale to a specific customer, you can indicate that in the Customer column, allowing you to easily pass on the expense based on the purchase data.

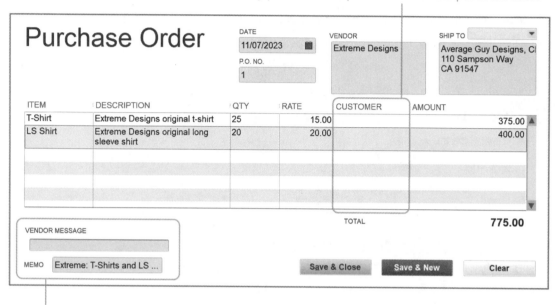

The Vendor Message field will be displayed when the PO is produced for the vendor, whereas the Memo field is for your internal records.

FLASHBACK TO GAAP: COST

Remember that when a company purchases assets, it should record them at cost, not fair market value. For example, if you bought an item worth $750 for $100, it should be recorded at $100.

Non-Posting Accounts

When you create your first PO, QuickBooks creates a non-posting account (an account that *does not* affect your profit & loss report or your balance sheet report) called Purchase Orders. Non-posting accounts appear at the end of your Chart of Accounts. By creating these accounts for you, QuickBooks allows you to create reports based on them.

🏹 Vendors→Create Purchase Orders

DEVELOP YOUR SKILLS 6-5

In this exercise, you will create POs for the inventory Guy will be selling. You will create a PO for an order of t-shirts and long-sleeved shirts from Extreme Designs, and a second PO for an order from Julie's Treasures. You will also look at the Open Purchase Orders report for verification purposes.

1. Choose **Company→Home Page**.
2. Click the **Purchase Orders** task icon in the Vendors area of the Home Page.

3. Enter this information to create a PO:
   - Vendor: **Extreme Designs**
   - Date: **110723**
   - Item: **T-Shirt**
   - Qty: **25**
   - Item: **LS Shirt**
   - Qty: **20**
   - Memo: **Extreme: T-Shirts and LS Shirts 11/2023**

4. Click **Save & New**, closing the Check Spelling on Form window, if necessary.

5. Enter this information to create the second PO:
   - Vendor: **Julie's Treasures**
   - Date: **110723**
   - Item: **Scarf**
   - Qty: **30**
   - Memo: **Julie's: Scarf 11/2023**

6. Click **Save & Close**.

View the Open Purchase Orders Report

Next you will take a look at the Purchase Orders non-posting account QuickBooks created when the first PO was entered and view a QuickReport showing all open POs.

7. Click the **Chart of Accounts** 🖩 task icon in the Company area of the Home Page.

8. Scroll to the bottom of the list and notice the nonposting 90100•Purchase Orders account.

9. Double-click the **Purchase Orders** account.

10. Type **a** to set the date range to **All**.

    QuickBooks creates a QuickReport showing open POs.

11. Choose **Window→Close All**.

Receiving Items

When you receive the items on a PO, you need to enter them into inventory. This transaction can be handled in either one or two steps, depending on how your vendor delivers the accompanying bill.

Two Methods of Receiving Items

If a vendor sends the inventory items and the bill together, you can record them as one transaction. If you receive the items first and the bill later, you will enter them in two separate steps.

When you receive inventory, choose this drop-down arrow ▼ and select Receive Inventory with Bill or without Bill.

If you received the inventory items without the bill, then when the bill arrives, click the Enter Bills Against Inventory task icon.

Including Expenses on a Bill for Items

You may incur additional shipping and handling charges when you order inventory items. These charges should not be entered on the Items tab, where the inventory is entered, but rather as an expense on the Expenses tab.

Expenses	$25.00	Items		$250.00
ACCOUNT		AMOUNT	MEMO	
67500 · Shipping Expense		25.00		

Expenditures listed on the Expenses tab will show up on a Profit & Loss report as an expense, whereas those on the Items tab will show up on the Balance Sheet as an asset.

Discount Payment Terms

Your vendors may offer you discount payment terms as incentive to pay your bills earlier. You can set default payment terms for a vendor; however, you may change the terms on an individual invoice as needed.

> **Note!** You will use the payment terms of 1% 10 Net 30 when entering a bill in this section. This means that if you pay the bill within 10 days of receipt, you will receive a 1 percent discount. But if you don't pay within the first 10 days, the full bill is due in 30 days.

BEHIND THE SCENES

Regardless of the path you take, the behind-the-scenes action is the same: Inventory Asset will be debited, and Accounts Payable will be credited.

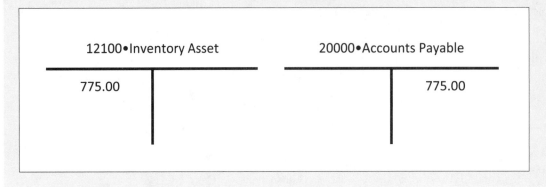

12100•Inventory Asset	20000•Accounts Payable
775.00	775.00

Vendors→Receive Items and Enter Bill

Vendors→Receive Items

Vendors→Enter Bill for Received Items

Lists→Customer & Vendor Profile Lists→Terms List

DEVELOP YOUR SKILLS 6-6

In this exercise, you will receive the shirts and later receive the bill for them. Following the receipt of the bill for the shirts, you will receive the scarves and the bill for them together.

1. Choose **Company→Home Page**.
2. Click the **Receive Inventory** 📇 task icon drop-down arrow ▼ in the Vendors area of the Home Page and then choose **Receive Inventory without Bill**.

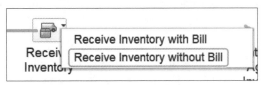

3. Type **extr** and then tap ⌷Tab⌷.

   QuickBooks fills in Extreme Designs, and the Open PO's Exist window appears.
4. Click **Yes** in the Open PO's Exist window to receive inventory against your purchase order.
5. Click to place a checkmark in the first column for **PO number 1** dated 11/07/2023 and then click **OK**.

   QuickBooks displays the Create Item Receipts window with the information from the PO filled in. Notice that the items appear on the Items tab at the bottom of the window, not on the Expenses tab!
6. Tap ⌷+⌷ on the keyboard to change the date to: **11/08/2023**
7. Click **Save & Close** to record the item receipt.

Receive the Bill

8. Click the **Enter Bills Against Inventory** 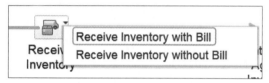 task icon in the Vendors area of the Home Page.

The shirts were entered into inventory when you received them. Now the bill for the items has arrived, and you need to enter it.

9. Enter this information to choose the correct Item Receipt:

- Vendor: **Extreme Designs**

- Click anywhere in the line to select the Item Receipt dated 11/08/2023 (click **OK**)

QuickBooks will display the Enter Bills window, with the order information filled in and the invoice items on the Items tab.

10. In the Memo field type: `Extreme: T-Shirt and LS 11/2023`

11. Click **Save & Close** to record the new bill; click **Yes** to record your changes.

> **BEHIND THE SCENES BRIEF**
>
> 12100•Inventory Asset DR 775.00; **20000•Accounts Payable CR <775.00>**

Receive Inventory Items with a Bill and Add an Expense to the Bill

The scarves and the bill for them arrived at the same time. The bill also included a shipping fee of $25 that must be accounted for on the bill.

12. Click the **Receive Inventory** task icon drop-down arrow ▼ in the Vendor area of the Home Page and then choose **Receive Inventory with Bill**.

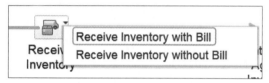

13. Type **j** and then tap [Tab].

QuickBooks fills in Julie's Treasures as the vendor, and the Open PO's Exist window appears.

14. Click **Yes** in the Open PO's Exist window to receive inventory against the open PO.

15. Click to place a checkmark in the first column for **PO number 2**.

16. Click **OK** to move to the Enter Bills window; click **OK** in the Warning window, if necessary.

The Julie's Treasures order was short 5 pieces, so you need to record receipt of only 25.

17. Follow these steps to complete the bill:

- Date: **111023**

- Ref. No.: **Julie's, 11/2023**

- Amount Due: **275**

- Terms: **1% 10 Net 30**

  You will receive a 1 percent discount if you pay the bill by the Discount Date.

- Memo: **Julie's, Inventory Scarves, 11/2023**

- Qty: change *30* to **25**

  Leave the bill open for the next step.

Enter an Expense on the Bill for Inventory Items

You will now enter the $25 shipping charge as an expense on the bill and set up the new account for Shipping Expense.

18. Follow these steps to enter the shipping expense:

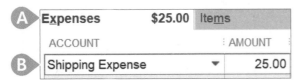

Ⓐ Click to display the **Expenses** tab.

Ⓑ Type **Shipping Expense** and tap Tab.

19. Click **Set Up** and then **Continue** to enter the new expense account using this information:

- Account Number: **67500**

- Description: **Shipping Expense**

20. Click **Save & Close**.

> **BEHIND THE SCENES BRIEF**
>
> 12100•Inventory Asset DR 250.00; 67500•Shipping Expense DR 25.00; **20000•Accounts Payable CR <275.00>**

21. Click **Save & Close** in the Enter Bills window.

22. Click **No** to reject changing the current terms for Julie's Treasures.

Selling Inventory Items

After you have ordered and received your items, it is time to start selling them! In this section, you will use the Create Invoices window, batch process invoices, and apply discount payment terms to a sales transaction.

Selling Inventory for Cash and On Account

You can sell inventory items either of these two ways:

- The Create Invoices window (on account—it affects Accounts Receivable behind the scenes)

- The Enter Sales Receipts window (for immediate payment—it does *not* affect Accounts Receivable)

Batch Invoicing

The batch invoicing feature allows you to fill out an invoice just once for the customers in the "batch" and then create invoices for all of them. This is extremely efficient if your company charges a standard monthly fee for many customers. In order to complete this task, you should first create a billing group of the customers for whom you wish to batch invoice (although you can add customers one at a time as well).

> **Note!** Make sure that the terms, sales tax code, and preferred delivery method are set up in the customer's record for any customer you wish to include in the batch. You also must have an email address entered for the customers you plan to batch invoice.

Batch Invoices Summary

After you have created a batch of invoices for customers, you will see the Batch Invoices Summary window. Here you can choose to either print or email the invoices (based on the preferred send method for each customer).

Batch Invoice Summary

Your invoices are created. They're marked for print or email based on each customer's **Preferred Send Method.** How do I enter or change the Send Method?

0	marked for print	Print
2	marked for email	Email
0	unmarked (you can send these later)	

Send a Batch of Forms

You can send more than just invoices from QuickBooks. In the Preferences window, you can set the default message for twelve types of forms and reports.

When you are ready to send all of the forms and reports that you have indicated you wish to send, QuickBooks uses Microsoft Outlook as the default to send emails after you have chosen to send forms.

> **Note!** Enhanced Webmail allows you to send secure webmail (Gmail, Hotmail, Live, and Outlook) from QuickBooks. In the Preferences window, choose Send Forms and select how to send email in the My Preferences tab.

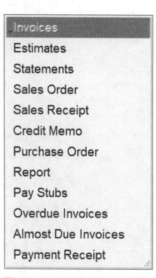

Invoices
Estimates
Statements
Sales Order
Sales Receipt
Credit Memo
Purchase Order
Report
Pay Stubs
Overdue Invoices
Almost Due Invoices
Payment Receipt

The types of forms and reports that you can choose to send from QuickBooks

BEHIND THE SCENES

The accounting that occurs for product sales is different from what occurs when you sell services. Take a look behind the scenes.

When an inventory item is sold, it "moves" the value of the item from the Inventory Asset account to the Cost of Goods Sold account.

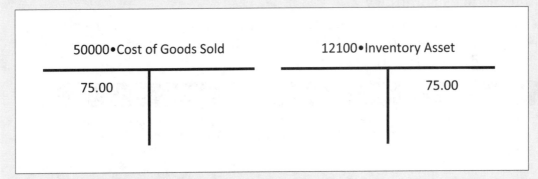

50000•Cost of Goods Sold	12100•Inventory Asset
75.00	75.00

Don't forget Sales tax... The rest of what happens behind the scenes looks similar to what happens when service items are sold. Notice that the credits (Clothing + Design Income + Sales Tax Payable) equal the debits (Accounts Receivable).

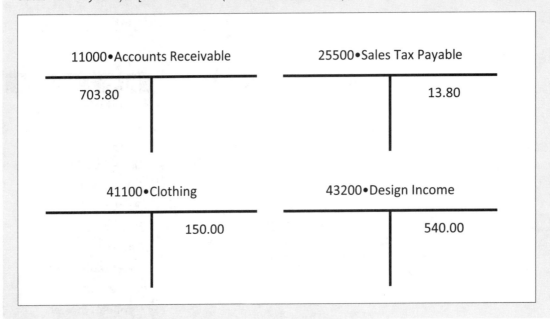

11000•Accounts Receivable	25500•Sales Tax Payable
703.80	13.80

41100•Clothing	43200•Design Income
150.00	540.00

Note! If you have the Premier or Enterprise edition of QuickBooks, there is a sales orders feature available that allows you to manage customer orders for both products and services. After a sales order has been created, you can print a pick list that will assist you in fulfilling the order from inventory. If the order is for a service, you can schedule the service. There are many important benefits to explore if using this feature.

Customers→Create Invoices

Customers→Create Batch Invoices

File→Send Forms

DEVELOP YOUR SKILLS 6-7

In this exercise, you will first help Average Guy Designs to create an invoice for a customer with discount payment terms. Then you will create a batch of invoices for website maintenance services.

Hernando from Lite Foot Dance Company has asked Guy to do design work to produce business cards, letterhead, flyers, and a website mock-up. Also, he likes Extreme Designs' t-shirts and has purchased five of them for his staff. The first step is to create a new job for the customer.

1. Choose **Customers→Customer Center**.
2. Single-click **Lite Foot Dance Company** on the Customers & Jobs List.
3. Click the **New Customer & Job** button on the toolbar above and then choose **Add Job**.
4. Type **Marketing** as the Job Name and then click **OK**.

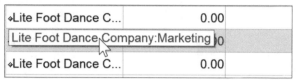

If you hover your mouse pointer over a list entry, it will display a pop-up that shows the full name.

Create an Invoice with Discount Payment Terms

Now that the job has been created, you will create an invoice with discount payment terms that will be emailed. The job you just created should still be selected in the Customers & Jobs List.

5. Click the **New Transactions** button on the toolbar and then choose **Invoices**.

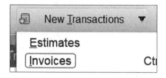

The Create Invoices window will appear with the Customer:Job entered.

6. Complete the invoice for Lite Foot Dance Company: Marketing with this information:
   - Template: **Intuit Product Invoice**
   - Date: **111623**
   - Ship To: **Ship To 1**
   - Terms: **2% 10 Net 30**
   - Via: **US Mail**

   First item:
   - Qty: **12**
   - Item Code: **Graphic Design**
   - Price Each: **45**

   Click OK if the Price Levels window appears.

   Second item:
   - Qty: **5**
   - Item Code: **T-Shirt**

For the remainder of the invoice:

- Customer Message: **It's been a pleasure working with you!**

7. On the Ribbon, click the checkbox for **Email Later** and ensure that Print Later is not selected.

Invoice

DATE	11/16/2023		BILL TO	Lite Foot Dance Company	SHIP TO	Ship To 1
INVOICE #	10024			Hernando Diaz		Lite Foot Dance Company
				541 Humboldt Ave.		Hernando Diaz
				Bayshore, CA 91547		541 Humboldt Ave.
						Bayshore, CA 91547

P.O. NUMBER	TERMS	REP	SHIP	VIA	F.O.B.
	2% 10 Net 30		11/16/2023	US Mail	

QUAN...	ITEM CODE	DESCRIPTION	PRICE ...	AMOUNT	TAX
12	Graphic Design	Graphic Design	45.00	540.00	Non
5	T-Shirt	Extreme Designs original t-shirt	30.00	150.00	Tax

Your customer can't pay this invoice online
Turn on

	TAX	San Tomas	(9.2%)	13.80
		TOTAL		703.80
		PAYMENTS APPLIED		0.00
		BALANCE DUE		**703.80**

CUSTOMER MESSAGE
It's been a pleasure working with you!

Your completed invoice should look like this image. Notice the sales tax has been applied to the inventory item but not the service item.

8. Click **Save & Close**.

   An Information Missing or Invalid window will launch.

9. Type **HDiaz@email.com** and then click **OK**.

10. Click **Yes** in the Information Changed window and then click **No** to continue working if the Outlook Profile window opens.

> ### BEHIND THE SCENES BRIEF
>
> 50000•Cost of Goods Sold DR 75.00; **12100•Inventory Asset CR <75.00>**
>
> 11000•Accounts Receivable DR 703.80; **41100•Clothing CR <150.00>**; **43200•Design Income CR <540.00>**; **25500•Sales Tax Payable CR <13.80>**

11. Leave the Customer Center open.

Set Up Customers for Batch Invoicing

Guy is now offering a monthly fee for website maintenance, so you will create a batch of invoices for the first two customers who subscribe to the monthly maintenance service fee. These customers pay a flat fee for the month. First, you will need to ensure that the two customers are set up correctly.

12. Double-click **Tim's BBQ Palooza** to open it for editing.

13. Enter or verify that this information is in the appropriate fields to ensure Tim's account is set up properly for batch invoicing:

    - Main Email: **timBBQ@email.com**

    - Payment Terms: **Net 30**

- Preferred Delivery Method: **E-mail**
- Tax Code: **Tax**
- Tax Item: **San Tomas**

14. Click **OK**.

15. Double-click **Masters Manufacturing** to open it for editing.

16. Enter this information or verify it is in the appropriate fields to ensure Masters Manufacturing's account is set up properly for batch invoicing:

- Main Email: **mastersm@email.com**
- Payment terms: **Net 15**
- Preferred Delivery Method: **E-mail**
- Tax Code: **Tax**
- Tax Item: **San Tomas**

17. Click **OK**.

18. Close the Customer Center.

Create a New Billing Group

19. Choose **Customers→Create Batch Invoices**; click **OK** in the "Is your customer info set up correctly?" window.

    The Batch Invoice window will appear.

20. Click the **Billing Group** drop-down arrow ▼ on the right side of the window.

21. Choose **Add New**.

22. Enter **Monthly Website Maintenance** as the Group Name and then click **Save**.

23. Select two companies to be in the Billing Group as follows, resizing the Name field and scrolling, if necessary:

NAME ▲	BALANCE TOTAL	TERMS	
Marketing	703.80	Net 30	
Lucy's Cupcake Factory	325.00	Net 15	
Marketing	325.00		
Masters Manufacturing **(A)**	320.00	Net 15	**(C)** Add >
Outside Signage	320.00	Net 15	
Miata Events, Inc.	140.00	Net 15	< Remove
Explore the Coast Miata...	0.00	Net 15	
Marketing	140.00		
Purposeful Playtime	345.00	Net 15	
Open House	345.00	Net 15	
Tim's BBQ Palooza **(B)**	400.00	Net 30	
Menu Design	400.00	Net 30	

Ⓐ Scroll down and then click to select **Masters Manufacturing**.

Ⓑ Press Ctrl and then click **Tim's BBQ Palooza**.

After clicking Tim's BBQ Palooza, both customers should be highlighted in green so that you can add both of them to the group at the same time.

Ⓒ Click **Add**.

24. Click the **Save Group** button located below the Customers in This Group list and then click **Next** on the bottom-left portion of the window.

Create a Batch of Invoices

25. Enter this information to add a new item and set it for the batch invoice:

- Date: **111623**
- Template: **Intuit Service Invoice**
- Item: **Web** (then `Tab`)
- In the Item Not Found window, click **Yes** to add it

New item:

- Type: **Service**
- Description: **Website Design Work**
- Tax Code: **Non**
- Account: **43200•Design Income**
- Click **OK** (if necessary, choose **Add** to add *Website* to the Spelling dictionary)

Batch invoice:

- Amount: **125.00**
- Customer Message: **Thank you for your business.**
- Click **Next**

26. Review the list of invoices that you are preparing to create.

Invoice Date: 11/16/2023

SELECT	CUSTOMER	TERMS	SEND METHOD	AMOUNT	TAX CODE	TAX RATE	TAX	TOTAL	STATUS
✓	Masters Manuf...	Net 15	Email	125.00	Tax	9.2%	0.00	125.00	OK
✓	Tim's BBQ Pal...	Net 30	Email	125.00	Tax	9.2%	0.00	125.00	OK

The screen will show all invoices to be created. You could choose not to create an invoice for a member of the group by deselecting it.

27. Click **Create Invoices**.

The Batch Invoice Summary window displays.

> **BEHIND THE SCENES BRIEF**
>
> 11000•Accounts Receivable DR 250.00; **43200•Design Income CR <250.00>**

28. Click **Close** to close the Batch Invoice Summary window because you will choose to send all of the invoices you have created in this exercise in the following steps.

Choose to Send Forms from QuickBooks

Now you will send the invoice for Lite Foot Dance Company that you marked to be sent by email as well as the two invoices you created as a batch. Because QuickBooks now sends emails utilizing Outlook, we will just look at how to initiate the action but will not actually send them as the computer you are working on may not have Outlook installed or set up.

29. Choose **File→Send Forms**.

The Select Forms to Send window will be displayed.

30. Take a look at the three invoices selected to be emailed.

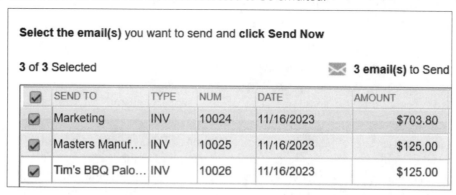

Select the email(s) you want to send and **click Send Now**

3 of 3 Selected   ✉ **3 email(s)** to Send

	SEND TO	TYPE	NUM	DATE	AMOUNT
☑	Marketing	INV	10024	11/16/2023	$703.80
☑	Masters Manuf...	INV	10025	11/16/2023	$125.00
☑	Tim's BBQ Palo...	INV	10026	11/16/2023	$125.00

If you were working with your own company and had Outlook installed, this is when you would click Send Now.

31. Click **Close** in the Send Forms window.

Receiving Discounted and Electronic Payments

The procedure for receiving a discounted customer payment is almost identical to receiving a "regular" payment, except that you must identify the account to be debited for the discount amount.

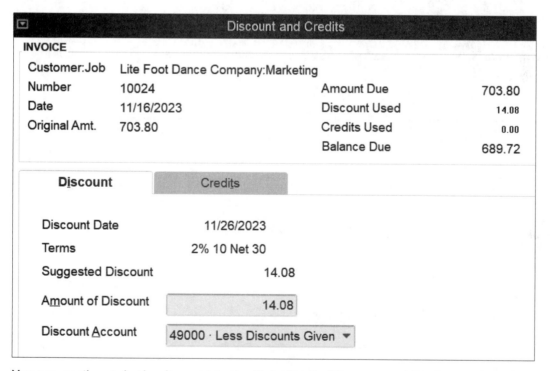

Discount and Credits

INVOICE

Customer:Job	Lite Foot Dance Company:Marketing			
Number	10024	Amount Due	703.80
Date	11/16/2023	Discount Used	14.08
Original Amt.	703.80	Credits Used	0.00
		Balance Due	689.72

Discount   Credits

Discount Date	11/26/2023
Terms	2% 10 Net 30
Suggested Discount	14.08
Amount of Discount	14.08
Discount Account	49000 · Less Discounts Given ▾

You can easily apply the discount in the QuickBooks Discount and Credits window. Quick-Books calculates the discount based on the payment terms.

Working with Electronic Customer Payments/Wire Transfers

In some instances, you may receive payments from your customers electronically. When the bank notifies you that you have received an electronic payment, you enter the receipt in the Receive Payments window, noting E-Check as the payment type. You will then be able to run reports, filtering by payment type, if you need to track electronic customer payments.

Note! For a fee, you can subscribe to QuickBooks Payments. This service has a Pay Now button that you can include on invoices so customers can instantly make payments. The service also allows you to accept credit card payments and bank transfers. In addition, your books will be automatically updated when the money is deposited in your bank account. There are monthly plan and transaction fees for this service.

The Shipping Manager

You can ship a package right from QuickBooks from both the Create Invoices and Enter Sales Receipt windows using FedEx, UPS, and now the United States Postal Service (through Stamps .com). You can use either your existing account(s) for any of these services, or you can sign up right from QuickBooks. QuickBooks will process the shipment and create a shipping label for you with the customer information that you have stored in QuickBooks. In addition, you can track your shipments from within QuickBooks.

BEHIND THE SCENES

When you receive a discounted payment, you need to credit the customer's Accounts Receivable account for the full amount even though you are not receiving the full amount in cash. The additional debit will be recorded in an income account called 49000•Less Discounts Given.

12000•Undeposited Funds		11000•Accounts Receivable		49000•Less Discounts Given	
689.72			703.80	14.08	

Note! The Less Discounts Given is a contra account; its normal balance is the opposite of others in its account type.

↗ Customers→Receive Payments

↗ Customers→Create Invoices: Send/Ship

In this exercise, you will record a discounted payment and process an electronic payment for Average Guy Designs. Lite Foot Dance Company has made its payment within 10 days of the invoice, therefore qualifying for a discounted payment.

1. Click the **Receive Payments** task icon in the Customers area of the Home Page.
2. Enter this information to record the discounted payment:
   - Received From: **Lite Foot Dance Company: Marketing**
   - Payment Amount: **689.72**
   - Date: **111823**
   - Reference #: **2Q78X901**
   - Payment Method: **e-Check**

   Notice the Underpayment section on the bottom-left portion of this window. Whenever you enter a payment amount that is less than the total amount due, you will see this section. You can then choose how to handle the underpayment. You will leave this as an underpayment and apply the discount for early payment to the invoice to take care of the underpayment in this case.

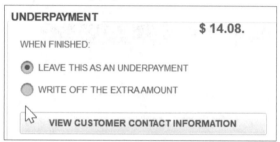

3. On the ribbon at the top of the window, choose **Discounts And Credits**.
4. In the Discount Account field, type: **Less Discounts Given** (then Tab)
5. Click **Set Up**.
6. Enter this Income account information:
   - Number: **49000**
   - Description: **Account to track discounts**
7. Click **Save & Close**.
8. Click **Done** to return to the Receive Payments window.

BEHIND THE SCENES BRIEF

12000•Undeposited Funds DR 689.72; 49000•Less Discounts Given DR 14.08; **11000•Accounts Receivable CR <703.80>**

9. Click **Save & Close** to complete the payment receipt.

Deposit an Electronic Payment

Now you will record the deposit of the electronic payment into your bank account.

10. Click the **Record Deposits** task icon in the Banking area of the Home Page.

    The Payments to Deposit window will appear. Note the 1 on the task icon, indicating one deposit is ready to be recorded.

11. Click the **e-Check** you just entered to select it and then click **OK**.

12. Ensure the deposit is going to the Checking account.

13. Enter **111923** as the Date.

14. Click **Save & Close** to record the deposit to Checking from Undeposited Funds where it was held prior to actually being deposited.

Working with Refunds

There are many times when you may need to issue a refund to a customer, and a variety of reasons for doing so, such as:

- For merchandise that has been returned

- For an order that was canceled

- To reimburse for an overpayment

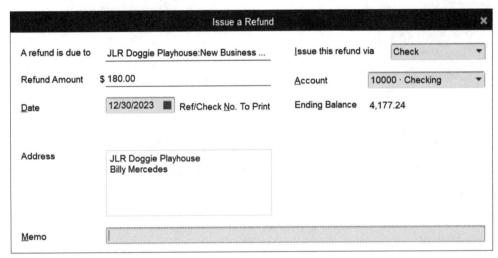

When you choose to issue a refund, the Issue a Refund window will appear. In this window, you can enter the information for the refund check.

Creating a Credit Memo

To account for returned merchandise, you will create a credit memo. After a credit memo has been created, you can choose to apply the credit to an invoice (so the customer can apply it toward a future purchase), or you can choose to issue a refund check or a return of funds to a credit card.

One-Click Credit Memo

If you need to refund a customer for a purchase that was made on an invoice, you can use a feature in QuickBooks that allows you to convert an invoice to a credit memo with one click. This can save you time as you will not have to retype the information for the new transaction.

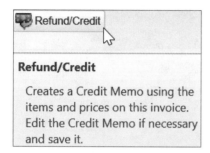

Convert an invoice to a credit memo by clicking the Refund/Credit button on the Create Invoice window Ribbon.

Applying a Credit as a Part of a Payment

After a credit has been issued to a customer, you can apply it against invoices for future purchases. This is done through the Create Invoices or Receive Payments windows.

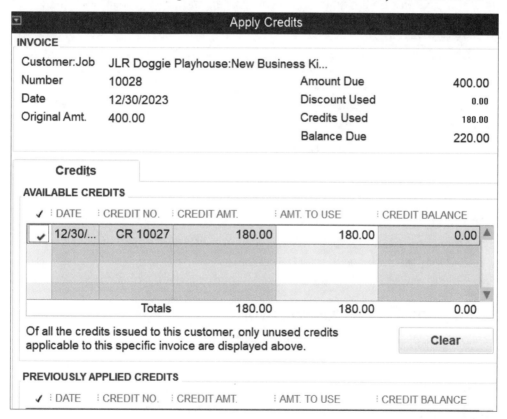

The Apply Credits window allows you to apply existing customer credits against an invoice.

Entering a Credit from a Vendor

If you are on the receiving end of a credit memo, you will need to enter it in your QuickBooks file as well. This is easily done through the Enter Bills window. After you have recorded the credit, use it when you pay bills to this vendor in the future.

In this exercise, you will create a credit memo and then apply the credit toward a future invoice. In this example, you have told Billy Mercedes that you will refund invoice 10013 as he has decided to go with you for a comprehensive branding plan.

1. Choose **Customers→Customer Center**.
2. Single-click **JLR Doggie Playhouse** in the Customers & Jobs list.
3. Double-click the **Invoice #10013** displayed on the Transactions tab to open it.

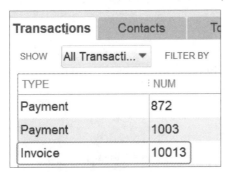

4. Click the **Refund/Credit** button on the Ribbon to convert the Invoice to a Credit Memo.

QuickBooks will automatically open the Credit Memo window with the information from the invoice displayed.

5. To create the credit memo for Billy, enter this information:
    *   Date: **113023**
    *   Credit No.: **CR 10027**
    *   Tax: **San Tomas**

Leave the Create Credit Memos/Refunds window open. You will issue the refund from it in the next step. It may seem strange to enter a sales tax item when no tax is involved, but it is required in order to make sure non-taxable sales are reported correctly for each jurisdiction.

Apply a Credit and Create a New Invoice

You will now choose to apply the credit to a new invoice, rather than issue a refund, and then create the new invoice.

6. Click the **Use credit to apply to invoice** button on the Ribbon.

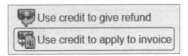

7. Click **OK** in the Warning window; click **Save & Close** to record the credit memo.

BEHIND THE SCENES BRIEF

43200•Design Income DR 180.00; **11000•Accounts Receivable CR <180.00>**

---

8. Click **Save & New** in the Create Invoices window.

9. In the Create Invoices window, enter this information to create an invoice for the branding:
   - Customer: Job: **JLR Doggie Playhouse: New Business Kickoff Campaign**
   - Date: **113023**
   - Invoice #: **10028**
   - Item: **Branding**
   - Quantity: **1**
   - Customer Message: **Thank you for your business.**

10. Click the **Apply Credits** button on the Ribbon.

11. Click **Yes** in the Recording Transaction window.

    The Apply Credits window will launch. Take a look at how the credit has been applied to the invoice, and the balance due is now $220.

12. Click **Done** in the Apply Credits window; click **Save & Close** in the Create Invoices window. Close the Customer Center window.

Producing Inventory Reports

QuickBooks features many preset reports to help you efficiently manage inventory and sales.

Periodically, it is important to physically count your inventory items and to make sure that what is "on the books" is actually what you have in stock. Many businesses do this type of procedure annually and adjust their books accordingly. QuickBooks provides a great report that can aid in this process—the Physical Inventory Worksheet. It shows the name, description, preferred vendor, and on-hand quantity of each item you have in inventory. It also provides a column with blank lines, where you can record what you actually have during a physical inventory count.

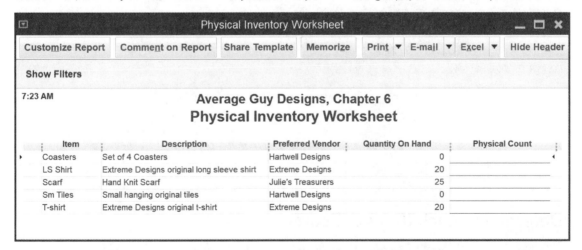

The Physical Inventory Worksheet aids you in conducting a count of your inventory items to ensure the quantity on hand in QuickBooks matches the actual amount you physically have.

The following table lists many reports useful when you work with inventory items:

INVENTORY REPORTS AND THEIR PURPOSES	
Inventory Report Name	**What it will tell you...**
Inventory Valuation Summary	The value of your inventory by item
Inventory Valuation Detail	The details of the transactions that affect the value of inventory
Inventory Stock Status by Item	The inventory items you need to reorder and the current number in stock of each item
Inventory Stock Status by Vendor	Similar to the Inventory Stock Status by Item but arranged by vendor
Physical Inventory Worksheet	A printable worksheet used to count physical inventory or to compare physical quantity to the number QuickBooks has recorded

 QuickBooks now allows you to include inactive items in inventory reports to help you make sure that your inventory valuation reports and general ledgers match.

Tracking Sales

The Sales area of the Report Center features reports and graphs that help you to understand your company's sales. You can choose reports that show Sales by Customer, Sales by Item, and Sales by Rep. You can also view sales information by job if you have jobs set up for your company. The Sales Graph visually displays your sales by item, customer, and rep.

> **Note!** Graphs are a great tool for data visualization. If QuickBooks doesn't provide a preset graph that works for you, you can export your data to Excel and create your graphs there.

↗ Reports→Report Center: Inventory | Reports→Inventory

↗ Reports→Report Center: Sales | Reports→Sales

DEVELOP YOUR SKILLS 6-10

In this exercise, you will run a report that will show the dollar value (based on purchase price) of the company's inventory.

1. Choose **Reports→Inventory→Inventory Valuation Summary**.
2. Tap **a** to set **All** as the date range for the report.

   The report will show the number of items you have in inventory as well as their asset value (cost) and retail value.

3. Close the Inventory Valuation Summary window, choosing not to memorize it.

Determine Which Items to Reorder

This report will help Guy to determine when he needs to order additional items.

4. Choose **Reports→Inventory→Inventory Stock Status by Item**.

5. Tap **a** to set the date range to **All**.

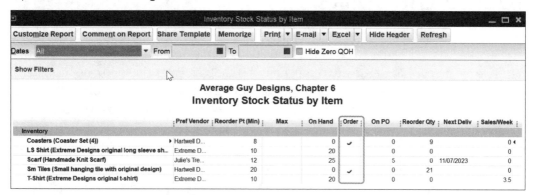

Notice that a checkmark appears in the Order column when it is time to place an order.

6. Close the Inventory Stock Status by Item window, choosing not to memorize it.

Create a Sales Graph

Finally, you will create a graph that will show you all of the sales by month and the sales by customer for the fiscal year to date.

7. Choose **Reports→Sales→Sales Graph**.

8. Click the **Dates** button on the toolbar, type **a**, and then click **OK**.

9. Click the **By Customer** button on the toolbar.

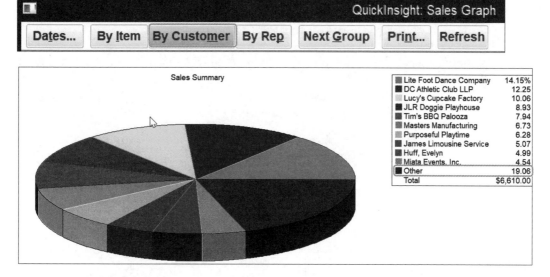

Notice the sales graph in the lower area of the window by customer. There are so many customers for the company that you will have to use QuickZoom to drill down to those classified as "Other."

10. Point to *Other* in the legend of the graph and double-click to QuickZoom, displaying the detail of the Other grouping in a second graph.

11. Close the Sales Graph windows.

Tackle the Tasks

Now is your chance to work a little more with Average Guy Designs and apply the skills that you have learned in this chapter to accomplish additional tasks. You will use the same file you used in the Develop Your Skills exercises throughout this chapter. Enter the following tasks, referring back to the concepts in the chapter as necessary. If you are using the trial software for this course on your computer or in a lab at school, you must toggle to the Pro edition every time you start QuickBooks.

Create Inventory Item	Item Name: Earrings; Description: Designer Earrings; Cost: 19.50; Sales Price.: 40.00; COGS: 50000•Cost of Goods Sold; Pref. Vendor: Holly's Bead Art; Income Acct: 41200•Accessories; Asset Acct.: 12100•Inventory Asset; Reorder: 15; Qty on Hand: 0
Create PO	Create a PO on 11/14/2023 to purchase 25 of the earrings you just entered as an inventory item.
Receive Items	Receive the earrings with the bill on 11/20/2023. Add a $15 shipping charge to the bill.
Sell Items	Sell three pairs of earrings to Chris Nelson (new customer) for his employees on 11/22/2023, terms 2% 10 Net 30. Terms are only for this invoice.
Receive Payment	Receive an e-check, 758946, from Chris Nelson for the earrings on 11/27/2023. Chris has taken advantage of the early payment discount. Deposit the payment to Checking on the same day.
Run Reports	Create a report that shows the inventory on hand and its value as of 11/30/2023. Create a report that shows the total sales for November 2023.

Self-Assessment

Check your knowledge of this chapter's key concepts and skills using the Self-Assessment quiz here, in your ebook, or in your eLab course.

1. Accounts Payable is debited when you create a PO.   *True*   *False*

2. Non-posting accounts appear at the bottom of your Chart of Accounts.   *True*   *False*

3. QuickBooks Pro uses the Last-In, First-Out (LIFO) method of inventory valuation.   *True*   *False*

4. The Show Lowest Subaccount preference helps you overcome the problem of narrow account fields in QuickBooks.   *True*   *False*

5. The Inventory Valuation Detail report tells you which items you need to reorder.   *True*   *False*

6. You must set up sales tax as an item to be able to include it on a sales form.   *True*   *False*

7. In some editions of QuickBooks, sales orders can be used to schedule services to be performed.   *True*   *False*

8. QuickBooks allows you to ship a package within the Create Invoices and Enter Sales Receipt windows using various services.   *True*   *False*

9. You can receive payments from your customers electronically.   *True*   *False*

10. The Sales Graph can display the total sales by item or by vendor.   *True*   *False*

11. In which case might QuickBooks NOT be a good tool for tracking inventory for a company?
    A. The company sells one-of-a-kind antiques.
    B. The company sells approximately 75 items.
    C. The company uses the average cost method for inventory valuation.
    D. The company's items are purchased at wholesale and sold at retail cost.

12. Which report would you run to determine the value of your inventory by item?
    A. Inventory Stock Status by Item
    B. Sales by Item Summary
    C. Inventory Valuation Detail
    D. Inventory Valuation Summary

13. What would the discount be for early payment on an invoice for $100 with terms of 2% 10 Net 30?
    A. $10
    B. $2
    C. $4
    D. $20

14. Which type of account is Purchase Orders?
    A. Inventory Asset
    B. COGS
    C. Inventory Expense
    D. Non-Posting

Reinforce Your Skills

Electrical Energy, Inc., has expanded to a second location in Putnam County, New York. It has also begun to sell products commonly requested by its customers. The password for all files unless otherwise stated is Password1. *Leave the company file open unless otherwise instructed. If you are using the trial software on your computer or in a lab at school, remember to toggle to the Pro edition every time you start QuickBooks.*

REINFORCE YOUR SKILLS 6-1

Set Up Inventory and Sales Tax Items

In this exercise, you will need to set up a new Sales Tax Item for Putnam County, and you will move through the entire process of purchasing, receiving, and selling these products. The first steps are to turn on the sales tax preference and set up a sales tax item.

1. Choose **File→Open or Restore Company**.
2. Open **RYS_Chapter06 (Company)** or restore **RYS_Chapter06 (Portable)** from your file storage location and save your file as: **RYS_Chapter06 Electrical Energy**
3. Choose **Edit→Preferences**.
4. Display the **Company Preferences** tab of the Sales Tax category.
5. Add a new sales tax item using this information:
   - Sales Tax Name: **Putnam County**
   - Description: **Sales Tax**
   - Tax Rate: **8.375%**
   - Tax Agency: **NYS Department of Taxation and Finance**
6. Click **OK** to add the new sales tax item.
7. Ensure *Westchester County* is the most common sales tax item.
8. Click **OK** to close the Preferences.

Turn On Inventory Preferences

Emily Holly wants to start offering switch plates, lighting, and other popular items for sale to her customers. You will now set up QuickBooks to deal with inventory along with the new income and expenses involved.

9. Choose **Edit→Preferences**.
10. Click the **Items & Inventory** category and then click the **Company Preferences** tab.
11. Click the checkbox to turn on **Inventory and Purchase Orders Are Active**.
12. Click **OK** to close the Preferences window; click **OK** to close the Warning window, allowing QuickBooks to close all open windows.

Create a New Income Account

The next step is to set up a separate income account for the product sales.

13. Choose **Lists→Chart of Accounts**.
14. Click the **Account** drop-down arrow ▼ and then choose **New**.

15. Choose **Income** as the account type and then click **Continue**.

16. Enter this information to set up the income account:

    • Number: **45000**

    • Account Name: **Product Sales**

    • Description: **Income from Product Sales**

17. Click **Save & Close** and then close the Chart of Accounts window.

Create a New Inventory Item

Now you will set up a taxable inventory item that Electrical Energy will be able to sell using one of the sales forms.

18. Choose **Lists→Item List**, click the **Item** drop-down arrow ▾, and then choose **New**.

19. Choose **Inventory Part** as the item type.

20. Enter this information to create a new inventory item:

    • Item Name: **LED Track Lighting**

    • Description: **LED Track Lighting – light bronze finish**

    • Cost: **52**

    • Sales Price: **99.99**

    • Preferred Vendor: **Tri-County Electrical Supply** (**Quick Add** the **Vendor**)

    Next you will create the income subaccount to track sales of light fixtures.

    • Income Account: **Lighting** (then ⌷Tab⌷ and click **Set Up**)

    • Number: **45001**

    • Subaccount of: Click in the **checkbox** and choose **45000•Product Sales** from the menu

    • Description: **Lighting Sales Income**

21. Click **Save & Close**.

22. Enter a Reorder Point (Min) of: **6**

23. Click **OK**, close the Item List, and leave the company file open.

REINFORCE YOUR SKILLS 6-2

Create POs and Receive Items

In this exercise, you will help Electrical Energy to order and receive inventory items. You will begin by creating a PO for LED Lighting.

1. Choose **Vendors→Create Purchase Orders**.

2. Enter the following information into the PO:

    • Vendor: **Tri-County Electrical Supply**

    • Date: **041023**

    • PO No.: **1001**

    Fill in the vendor address under the vendor name:

    • **8 Commerce Street** ⌷Enter⌷ **Yorktown Heights, NY 10598**

    • Item: **LED Track Lighting**

- Qty: **12**
- Memo: `Tri-County: LED Track Lighting`

3. Click **Save & Close**.

4. Click **Yes** to make the address for the vendor permanent in the Information Changed window. Add *Tri* to the dictionary in the Check Spelling on Form window.

Receive the Items

The light fixtures have arrived without the bill, so Emily needs to receive them into QuickBooks.

5. Choose **Vendors→Receive Items**.

6. Choose **Tri-County Electrical Supply** as the vendor and then click **Yes** to receive against an open PO.

7. Click the checkmark column to select the PO dated **04/10/2023** and then click **OK**.

8. Change the date of the Item Receipt to **041223** and then click **Save & Close**.

Receive the Bill

The bill for the light fixtures has just arrived, so it is time to enter it into QuickBooks.

9. Choose **Vendors→Enter Bill for Received Items** and then choose **Tri-County Electrical Supply** as the vendor.

10. Click on the Item Receipt dated **04/12/2023** to select it and then click **OK**.

11. Enter this information to complete the bill:
   - Date: **041423**
   - Ref. No.: `Inv TCE0616`
   - Terms: **Net 15**
   - Memo: `Tri-County: LED Track Lighting 04/2023`

12. Click **Save & Close**, clicking **Yes** to agree to change the transaction.

13. Click **Yes** to permanently change the information for Tri-County Electrical Supply and leave the company file open.

REINFORCE YOUR SKILLS 6-3

Sell Inventory Items

When the products have been entered into inventory, it is time to start selling! In this exercise, you will record inventory sales.

1. Choose **Customers→Enter Sales Receipts**.

2. Enter `Miller, Sally` as the Customer: Job and Quick Add her as a customer.

3. Enter this information for the sales receipt:
   - Payment Method: **Check**
   - Date: **042023**
   - Check No.: **53095**
   - Item: **LED Track Lighting**
   - Qty: **2**

- Customer Message: **Thank you for your business.**
- Memo: **Miller: LED (2)**

4. Click **Save & New** to record the sale.

Record Sales from an On the Job Sale

One of the electricians sold lighting fixtures to a customer while on the job in Westchester County. You will now help to enter the sales.

5. Use a Sales Receipt with no customer name and the default tax of Westchester to record the sale:
   - Payment Method: **Cash**
   - Date: **042223**
   - Item: **LED Track Lighting**
   - Qty: **2**
   - Memo: **On the Job Sale**

6. Click **Save & Close** to record the sale and leave the company file open.

REINFORCE YOUR SKILLS 6-4

Process Payments

In this exercise, you will deposit all of the payments received into the company Checking account.

1. Choose **Banking→Make Deposits**.

   The Payments to Deposit window will appear.

2. Click the **Select All** button and then click **OK**.

3. Change the date of the deposit to **042523**, ensure that *Checking* is the account displayed, and then click **Save & Close**, leaving the company file open.

   All of the payments waiting in the Undeposited Funds account have now been deposited into the company Checking account.

REINFORCE YOUR SKILLS 6-5

Produce a Report

In this exercise, you will create an inventory report that details the quantity and value of inventory on hand and use QuickZoom to make a change to an underlying form.

1. Choose **Reports→Inventory→Inventory Valuation Detail**.

2. Type **a** to set the date range to **All**.

3. Using **QuickZoom**, go to the bill for the LED Track Lighting.

4. Change the terms of the bill to **Net 30**.

5. Save the bill with the changes, choosing to have the new terms appear next time and become a permanent change to the vendor record.

6. Click **Yes** to refresh the report.

7. Close the report, choosing not to memorize it, and then close the company file.

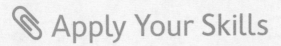# Apply Your Skills

Wet Noses Veterinary Clinic has started buying and selling inventory. You will manage the sales tax, purchase and receive inventory items, and sell products to customers. As needed, you will issue credit memos and discount purchases based on payment terms. The password for all files unless otherwise stated is Password1. *After starting QuickBooks, remember to toggle to Pro as necessary.*

APPLY YOUR SKILLS 6-1 QG

Set Up Sales Tax and an Item List

In this exercise, you will set up sales tax and items to begin selling to customers.

1. Choose **File→Open or Restore Company**.
2. Open **AYS_A1_Chapter06 (Company)** or restore **AYS_A1_Chapter06 (Portable)** from your file storage location and save your file as: **AYS_A1_Chapter06 Wet Noses Clinic**
3. Open the **Preferences** window and set the preference to collect sales tax.
4. Set up a new sales tax item (**King County Sales Tax** for **10%**, payable to **King County Treasurer**) and then set it as the most common sales tax item.
5. Choose to make all existing customers taxable but NOT all existing non-inventory and inventory parts.
6. Open the **Preferences** window and then turn on the **Inventory and Purchase Order** feature.
7. Open the **Chart of Accounts** and then create a new income account numbered **45000** called **Inventory Sales**.
8. Create these inventory part items:

   First item:

   - Item Name: **Toothbrush**
   - Purchase/Sales Description: **Dog toothbrush and paste kit**
   - Cost: **6.49**
   - Preferred Vendor: **Seattle Vet Supply**
   - Sales Price: **14.99**
   - Income Account: **45000•Inventory Sales**
   - Reorder Point: **15**

   Second item:

   - Item Name: **Chew Toy**
   - Purchase/Sales Description: **The great indestructible ball!**
   - Cost: **3.71**
   - Preferred Vendor: **Bothell Pet Supply Co.**
   - Sales Price: **8.99**
   - Income Account: **45000•Inventory Sales**
   - Reorder Point: **20**

Third item:

- Item Name: **Cat Collar**
- Purchase/Sales Description: **Designer cat collar**
- Cost: **8.00**
- Preferred Vendor: **Take a Walk**
- Sales Price: **19.99**
- Income Account: **45000•Inventory Sales**
- Reorder Point: **10**

9. Run the **Item Listing** report for detailed information about each item.

10. Click the **Excel** Excel ▾ button and export this list to a new worksheet, saving the worksheet to your file storage location as: **CH6_A1 New Item Listing**

11. Close Excel and the company file.

APPLY YOUR SKILLS 6-2 QG

Purchase and Receive Inventory Items

In this exercise, you will purchase and receive new inventory items in order to have them in stock.

1. Choose **File→Open or Restore Company**.

2. Open **AYS_A2_Chapter06 (Company)** or restore **AYS_A2_Chapter06 (Portable)** from your file storage location and save your file as: **AYS_A2_Chapter06 Wet Noses Clinic**

3. Create POs for these three items:
   - 25 toothbrushes from Seattle Vet Supply on 07/01/2023
   - 40 chew toys from Bothell Pet Supply Co. on 07/02/2023
   - 15 cat collars from Take a Walk on 07/02/2023

4. You received all 25 toothbrushes from Seattle Vet Supply on 07/07/2023, along with the bill. Receive the items and enter the bill, making sure to receive against the PO you created.

5. You received 33 of the chew toys from Bothell Pet Supply Co. The rest are on back order, so you did not receive the bill yet. Receive these 33 items into inventory on 07/08/2023.

6. You received all 15 of the cat collars from Take a Walk on 07/12/2023, along with the bill. Included on the bill was a shipping charge of $12.95. Receive the items into inventory and enter the bill and create a 66500•Postage and Delivery account for the shipping charge.

7. On 07/14/2023 you received a bill for the chew toys you received on 07/08/2023, along with a shipping charge of $13.50. You then receive the seven chew toys that were on back order, along with a bill for the items with no shipping charge, on 07/25/2023.

8. Run the **Inventory Stock Status by Item** report for All dates to determine how many inventory items are currently in stock.

9. Click the **Excel** Excel ▾ button and export this report to a new worksheet, saving the worksheet to your file storage location as: **CH6_A2 Current Inventory Status**

10. Close the company file.

Sell Inventory

In this exercise, you will process sales of inventory items.

1. Choose **File→Open or Restore Company**.

2. Open **AYS_A3_Chapter06 (Company)** or restore **AYS_A3_Chapter06 (Portable)** from your file storage location and save your file as: **AYS_A3_Chapter06 Wet Noses Clinic**

3. Sell two of the new designer cat collars to Jill Ann Tank on 07/14/2023. She pays with cash.

4. Sell seven toothbrushes and seven chew toys to King County Sheriff K-9 Unit on 07/15/2023. The Terms should be 2% 10 Net 30 and should not be made permanent.

5. Create an invoice for Stacy LiMarzi's cat, Reagan, dated 07/19/2023. The invoice should include a New Patient Exam, a FIV/FeLV test, a dose of Revolution-Cat/Small Dog for a cat, and a cat collar. Only the collar is taxable.

6. Run the **Sales by Customer Summary** report to show the sales amount for each customer for the month from 07/01/2023 to 07/31/2023.

7. Click the **Excel** Excel ▾ button and export this report to a new worksheet, saving the worksheet to your file storage location as: **CH6_A3 Sales by Customer Summary**

8. On 07/21/2023, King County Sheriff K-9 Unit has paid the invoice from 07/15/2023 in the amount of $180.96 with check 7796. Because the payment was received within 10 days, a 2 percent discount of $3.69 will be applied and should be reflected in the 47320•Less Discounts Given income account.

9. Stacy LiMarzi has paid the entire amount of the invoice for her cat Reagan with check 448 on 07/22/2023.

10. Run the **Sales by Item Summary** report that shows which items sold the most during the month of July 2023.

11. Click the **Excel** Excel ▾ button and export this report to a new worksheet, saving the worksheet to your file storage location as: **CH6_A3 Sales by Item Summary**

12. Close the company file.

Issue Credits and Refunds and Manage Returned Inventory

In this exercise, you will issue a credit memo, process a refund check, and review inventory on hand.

1. Choose **File→Open or Restore Company**.

2. Open **AYS_A4_Chapter06 (Company)** or restore **AYS_A4_Chapter06 (Portable)** from your file storage location and save your file as: **AYS_A4_Chapter06 Wet Noses Clinic**

3. Sampson, a City of Seattle K-9 Unit dog, did not receive the nail trim he was charged for. Create a Credit Memo numbered RF1 on 07/14/2023 and give a refund to the K-9 Unit as a check that will be printed later. Nail trims are a service and therefore not a taxable item.

4. Run the **Item Listing** report to view Quantity on Hand for each item on the Item List.

5. On 7/19/2023 Jill Ann Tank returned the cat collar she purchased. Process a refund check that will be printed later.

6. Run the **Inventory Stock Status by Item** report for All dates to display total inventory on hand by item.

7. Click the **Excel** Excel ▾ button and export this list to a new worksheet, saving the worksheet to your file storage location as: **CH6_A4 After Return Inventory Status**

   Notice the returned cat collar has changed the On Hand amount from 12 to 13 as the item was added back into inventory.

8. Close the company file.

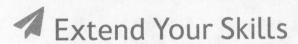
Extend Your Skills

Before You Begin: Open **EYS_Chapter06 (Company)** or restore **EYS_Chapter06 (Portable)** from your file storage location.

You have been hired by Arlaine Cervantes to help her with her organization's books. She is the founder of Niños del Lago, a nonprofit organization that provides impoverished Guatemalan children with an engaging educational camp experience. You have just sat down at your desk and opened a large envelope from her with a variety of documents and noticed that you have several emails from her as well. It is your job to sort through the papers and emails and make sense of what you find, entering information into QuickBooks whenever appropriate and answering any other questions in a word-processing document saved as: **EYS_Chapter06_LastnameFirstinitial**. Remember, you are digging through papers you just dumped out of an envelope and addressing random emails from Arlaine, so it is up to you to determine the correct order in which to complete the tasks.

- Sticky note from Arlaine: We are going to start selling items made by Guatemalan women. I would like to see if we can set them up in QuickBooks. Our accountant told me that we should use the "average cost" method to keep track of our inventory. Will we be able to track this in QuickBooks? (Explain your answer.)

- Packing slip and bill from GWAA dated 8/14/2019. You have received the rest of the scarves and cosmetic bags, and a $45 shipping charge was included on the bill.

- Note from Arlaine: A box containing traditional Guatemalan scarves was damaged in shipment to our sales rep in the U.S., and three scarves are no longer in sellable condition. Please figure out a way to take them out of inventory in QuickBooks.

- Scribbled on a scrap of paper: If we can track inventory in QuickBooks, please set up "Traditional Guatemalan Scarf" as an inventory item; the cost from Guatemalan Women's Art Alliance (GWAA) is $7.00, and the resale price is $20.00. Also, please set up two more inventory items to track "Cosmetic Bag" and "Handbag". The cost from GWAA for the cosmetic bag is $8.00 with a resale price of $18.00, and the cost for the handbag is $15.00 with a resale price is $35.00. As of 8/1/2019, order the following inventory: 50 scarves, 40 cosmetic bags, and 25 handbags.

- Handwritten invoice: 10 scarves and 5 handbags sold to Average Guy Designs, dated 8/16/2019, due 2% 10 Net 30.

- Packing slip from GWAA: Dated 8/5/2019 for receipt of 45 scarves, 30 cosmetic bags, and 25 handbags; the rest are on backorder.

- Photocopy of a check: Check 2007 from Average Guy Designs dated 8/23/2019 written for the total amount due and with a memo stating the company took advantage of the 2 percent discount.

- Scribbled note from Arlaine: Can you produce a report for me that shows the value of the inventory we currently have in stock? How about the number of each item?

7 Working with Balance Sheet Accounts and Budgets

I n this chapter, you will work with additional accounts that are reported on a company's balance sheet in QuickBooks: Other Current Assets, Fixed Assets, Current Liabilities, Long Term Liabilities, and Equity. These other balance sheet accounts allow you to track the various assets owned by your business, liabilities owed by your business, loans that span more than one year, prepaid expenses, and owner/ shareholder investments in a company. Finally, you will learn how to use the budgeting feature in QuickBooks.

LEARNING OBJECTIVES

▶ Create and use current asset accounts and transfer funds between accounts

▶ Track petty cash

▶ Create and use fixed asset accounts and items

▶ Record depreciation of assets

▶ Pay current liabilities and set up a long term liability

▶ Create and manage equity accounts

▶ Set up and use QuickBooks budgets

📂 Project: Average Guy Designs

Average Guy Designs has been approached by the landlord who offered a discount on the monthly rent amount if the company will pay six months of rent up front. Guy has decided to take advantage of this offer and will use QuickBooks to track this rent prepayment.

To grow his business, Guy has decided to take out a loan to purchase a Vespa scooter for sales calls and deliveries. The Vespa will be set up as a fixed asset, and a Long Term Liability account needs to be set up to track the loan.

One company task that comes due periodically is paying the sales tax collected from sales of inventory. This tax will be paid from the current liability account, Sales Tax Payable. You will also explore how to work with budgets in QuickBooks.

Working with Other Current Assets

Companies use other current assets to help them match their expenses to income within the same reporting period. This is a particularly important aspect when you use the accrual basis of accounting, which means that expenses are recorded when accrued, not when cash is paid. This means that even if you pay a six-month insurance policy or six months of rent up front, you must expense it during the month that it covers.

Balance Sheet Accounts

Remember, the balance sheet accounts are the asset, liability, and equity accounts. You have already learned about many balance sheet accounts: bank, credit card, current liabilities (sales tax payable), Accounts Receivable, and Accounts Payable. Now you will focus on the remaining balance sheet accounts. Refer to the following table to learn more about these other accounts:

ADDITIONAL TYPES OF BALANCE SHEET ACCOUNTS		
Account Type	**Description**	**Examples**
Other Current Asset	Assets you plan to either use or convert to cash within one year	• Prepaid Insurance • Security Deposit
Fixed Asset	Assets you do not plan to convert to cash within one year; they are usually depreciable	• Vehicle • Equipment
Other Current Liability	Funds your business owes and plans to pay within a year	• Sales Tax Payable • Payroll Liabilities
Long-Term Liability	Liabilities (loans) you do not plan to pay off within the next year	• Mortgage • Auto Loan
Equity	The owner's equity in the company, whether it is a sole proprietor, a partner, or shareholders	• Owner's Equity • Retained Earnings

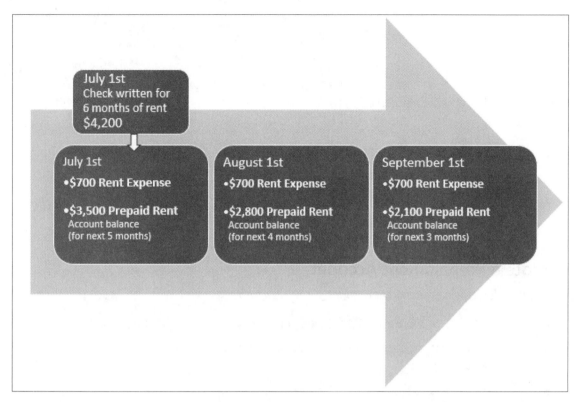

Notice how the Prepaid Rent account "holds" funds that you have prepaid so you can expense them in the month they are actually used. Continue this cycle until the Prepaid Rent account has been depleted.

In this exercise, you will help set up QuickBooks to track the prepayment of rent for the company and then you will write a check to pay the rent for six months, July through December. The password for all files unless otherwise stated is Password1. *Leave the company file open unless otherwise instructed.*

1. Start QuickBooks 2019 and toggle to Pro, if necessary.
2. Choose **File→Open or Restore Company**.
3. Open **DYS_Chapter07 (Company)** or restore **DYS_Chapter07 (Portable)** from your file storage location and save your file as: **DYS_Chapter07 Average Guy Designs**

Create a Prepaid Rent Account

Now you will create a prepaid rent account.

4. Click the **Chart of Accounts** 🖩 task icon in the Company area of the Home Page.
5. Click the **Account** drop-down arrow ▼ at the bottom of the window and then choose **New**.
6. Follow these steps to create the new account:

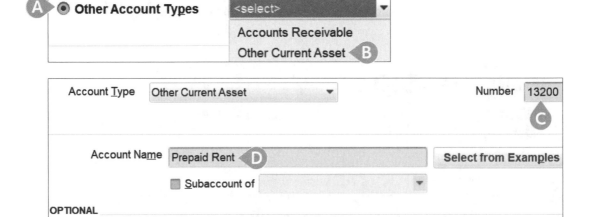

- Ⓐ Click to choose **Other Account Types**.
- Ⓑ Select **Other Current Asset** and then click **Continue**.
- Ⓒ Enter the Account Number: **13200**
- Ⓓ Enter the Account Name: **Prepaid Rent**
- Ⓔ Enter the Description: **Prepaid Rent holding account**
7. Click **Save & Close** and then close the Chart of Accounts window.

Fund the Prepaid Rent Account

Before paying the rent for six months, you will first need to transfer funds from Savings to Checking to cover the expense.

8. Choose **Banking→Transfer Funds**.

9. Enter this information to complete the transfer:
   - Date: **070123**
   - Transfer Funds From: **10200•Savings**
   - Transfer Funds To: **10000•Checking**
   - Transfer Amount: **5000**
   - Memo: **Funds Transfer to prepay 6 mo rent**

10. Click **Save & Close** and close the Chart of Accounts.

Write a Check to Prepay the Rent

You will now write the check for the rent payment, expensing the current month and placing the rest in the prepaid rent account.

11. Click the **Write Checks** ✎ task icon in the Banking area of the Home Page.

12. Use this information to write the rent check:
   - Click checkbox on the Ribbon at the top of the window to choose **Print Later**
   - Date: **070123**
   - Pay to the Order of: **Sandy Property Management**
   - Amount: **4200**
   - Memo: **Sandy: Rent for July-Dec 2023**

   There are two line items that must be entered under Expenses to split the total amount of the check. The first line is the July rent that you will expense for the month, and the second line is the prepaid rent account that will hold the remainder.

Expenses	$4,200.00	Items	$0.(
ACCOUNT		AMOUNT	
67100 · Rent Expense		700.00	
13200 · Prepaid Rent		3,500.00	

   - Account: **67100•Rent Expense**
   - Amount: **700**
   - Account: **13200•Prepaid Rent**
   - Amount: **3500**

   > **BEHIND THE SCENES BRIEF**
   >
   > 67100•Rent Expense DR 700.00;13200•Prepaid Rent DR 3,500.00; **10000•Checking CR <4,200.00>**

13. Click **Save & Close** and leave the company file open.

Paying Down the Other Current Asset Account

After you place funds in an Other Current Asset account, you will expense them when they are used. It is important to match expenses to income during the period in which they are utilized. Another term for this movement of funds from the asset to the expense account for an intangible asset is *amortization*. Amortization is simply the process of a balance decreasing over time. For instance, if you have a mortgage on a company property, prorating the cost over 30 years is amortization. You can accomplish this transfer in the register window of the asset.

BEHIND THE SCENES

Each month the amount for the current month's rent should be expensed.

67100•Rent Expense		13200•Prepaid Rent	
700.00			700.00

Memorizing Transactions

There are many transactions (such as the expensing of other current assets) that you have to repeat over and over again. You can choose to have QuickBooks memorize these transactions to increase your efficiency. When QuickBooks memorizes a transaction, you can choose:

- To be reminded about the transaction
- Not to be reminded and simply have it listed on the Memorized Transaction List
- To have QuickBooks automatically enter it based on a set schedule

By default, QuickBooks will choose for you to be reminded of the memorized transaction. You must make sure to choose one of the other options if you want the transaction to be listed or to occur automatically.

Recurring Transactions

When you are creating a new memorized transaction that you want QuickBooks to enter automatically for you, you can group it with other transactions you have memorized.

Whenever you open QuickBooks, if you have memorized transactions, the Enter Memorized Transactions window appears with a list of those scheduled to be entered. This detailed list includes automatic transactions and helps you to stay on top of which transactions are slated to be recorded.

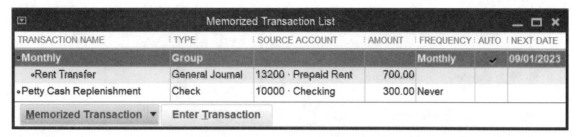

TRANSACTION NAME	TYPE	SOURCE ACCOUNT	AMOUNT	FREQUENCY	AUTO	NEXT DATE
◦Monthly	Group			Monthly	✓	09/01/2023
◦Rent Transfer	General Journal	13200 · Prepaid Rent	700.00			
◦Petty Cash Replenishment	Check	10000 · Checking	300.00	Never		

The Memorized Transaction List keeps track of all your memorized transactions for you. Access it via the Lists option on the menu bar.

Using Memorized Transactions for Common Transactions

You can use the Memorized Transaction List for transactions that you complete on a regular basis. For instance, if you send an invoice to the same customer monthly, you can set up the invoice and memorize it. Then when you need to enter it, you just double-click it in the Memorized Transaction List.

Lists→Memorized Transaction List

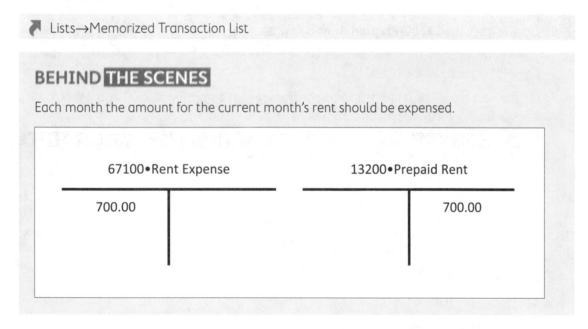

BEHIND THE SCENES

Each month the amount for the current month's rent should be expensed.

67100•Rent Expense		13200•Prepaid Rent	
700.00			700.00

DEVELOP YOUR SKILLS 7-2

In this exercise, you will record the first transfer of funds from Prepaid Rent to Rent Expense. After the transfer is set up, you will memorize it to occur automatically. Before you set up your first recurring monthly transaction in your Memorized Transaction List, you will create a group called "Monthly" for this list entry. You can then add new monthly transactions as they are created.

1. Choose **Lists→Memorized Transaction List**.
2. Click the **Memorized Transaction** drop-down arrow ▼ at the bottom of the window and then choose **New Group**.

3. Use this information to create the new group:

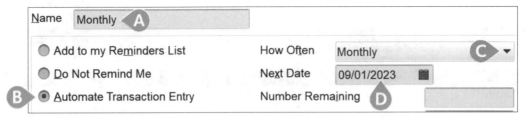

Ⓐ Name: **Monthly**

Ⓑ Click **Automate Transaction Entry**

Ⓒ How Often: **Monthly**

You will create the transaction to move $700 from Prepaid Rent to Rent Expense for August, which you will then memorize. Therefore, the first automatic transaction will begin in September.

Ⓓ Next Date: **090123**

4. Click **OK** to record the new memorized group and then close the Memorized Transaction List.

Record Next Month's Rent Expense

5. Choose **Lists→Chart of Accounts**, resizing the window, if necessary.

6. Double-click the **13200•Prepaid Rent** account.

The register for the asset will open. Notice that QuickBooks has registered an increase in the Prepaid Rent account for $3,500.

7. On the next blank line, enter this information to record a transfer of $700 from Prepaid Rent to the Rent expense account for August:

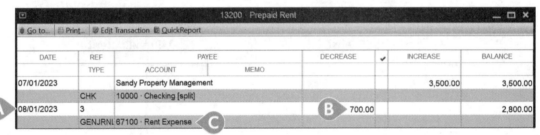

Ⓐ Date: **080123**

Ⓑ Decrease: **700**

Ⓒ Account: **67100•Rent Expense**

> ### BEHIND THE SCENES BRIEF
>
> 67100•Rent Expense DR 700.00; **13200•Prepaid Rent CR <700.00>**

8. Click **Record** at the bottom-right portion of the register window.

Memorize the Transaction

To avoid having to sit down at the computer at the first of each month and record this transfer, you will memorize it and choose for QuickBooks to include it in the Enter Memorized Transactions list.

9. Click anywhere within the two lines of the transaction you just recorded.

10. Choose **Edit→Memorize General Journal**.

    This transaction is considered a General Journal Entry because it is a basic transfer between accounts.

11. Use this information to memorize the transaction in the Monthly group:
    - Name: **Rent Transfer**
    - Click **Add to Group**
    - Group Name: **Monthly**

12. Click **OK** to memorize the transaction.

13. Close the Prepaid Rent account register and the Chart of Accounts window.

14. Choose **Lists→Memorized Transaction List**, resizing the window, if necessary.

    Take a look at the Memorized Transaction List and notice the new group and rent transfer entries. If you do not continue to take advantage of prepaid rent, you will need to delete this memorized transaction when the last transfer has been completed.

15. Close the Memorized Transaction List window and leave the company file open.

Tracking Petty Cash

Most businesses keep cash around for small expenditures. This is known as petty cash. In QuickBooks, you set up Petty Cash as a bank account in your Chart of Accounts. You fund it by transferring money from another account or by keeping cash back when you make a deposit.

End of Month Entry Option

Many businesses track petty cash expenditures at the end of the month with one journal entry. This text will show you how to track expenditures individually; however, you should be aware that they can also be handled in a different manner.

DATE 09/30/2023		ENTRY NO. 4	
ACCOUNT	DEBIT	CREDIT	MEMO
67500 · Shipping Expense	18.49		stamps
64900 · Office Supplies	74.23		printer toner
64300 · Meals and Entertain...	42.78		meal with client
10000 · Checking		135.50	replenish petty cash

Here is an example of what a monthly journal entry to replenish Petty Cash would look like. You will notice that in this method you don't actually credit Petty Cash, but rather Checking. Petty Cash would be affected only if the amount contained in the fund is changed, or if you close the petty cash account.

Recording Methods

QuickBooks offers two methods to record petty cash expenditures:

- **Write Checks Method:** You can choose Petty Cash as the account and use the Write Checks window to record your petty cash expenses.

- **The Register Method:** You can enter petty cash expenditures directly into the Petty Cash register.

Tip! The register method allows you to enter your petty cash expenditures more quickly, as you can tab through it faster.

BEHIND THE SCENES

When you use the checking account to fund the petty cash account, you debit Petty Cash and credit Checking.

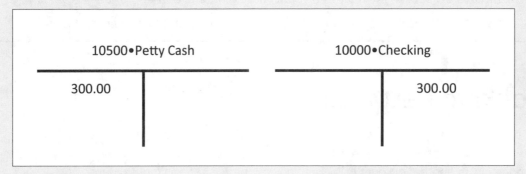

When you use petty cash for a purchase, you debit the expense account (in this example Shipping Expense) and credit Petty Cash.

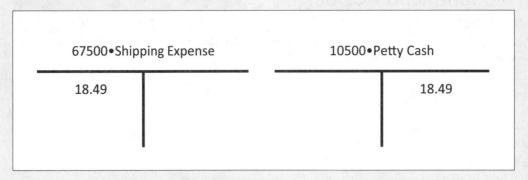

DEVELOP YOUR SKILLS 7-3

In this exercise, you will create, fund, and use a petty cash account; memorize a transaction; and use the petty cash account.

1. Choose **Lists→Chart of Accounts**.

   Note that, currently, there is no account set up to track petty cash.

2. Click the **Account** drop-down arrow ▼ and then choose **New**.

3. Choose **Bank** as the account type and then click **Continue**.

4. Use this information to create the new account:

- Number: **10500**
- Account Name: **Petty Cash**

5. Click **Save & Close**; click **No** in the Set Up Bank Feed window.

6. Close the Chart of Accounts window.

Fund the Petty Cash Account and Memorize the Transaction

Next you will transfer $300 from the Checking account to the Petty Cash account.

7. Click the **Write Checks** 🖉 task icon in the Banking area of the Home Page.

8. Ensure that *Checking* is the account and then use this information to complete the check and fund petty cash:
   - Date: **090123**
   - Pay to the Order of: **Cashier** (**Quick Add** it as a **Vendor**)
   - Amount: **300**
   - Memo: **Add funds to Petty Cash account**
   - Account: **10500•Petty Cash**

> **BEHIND THE SCENES BRIEF**
>
> 10500•Petty Cash DR 300.00; **10000•Checking CR <300.00>**

9. Click **Save & Close**.

Pay for Shipping Using the Petty Cash Register

You will now pay to ship a framed photograph to a customer, pay with petty cash, and record the transaction in the Petty Cash register.

10. Click the **Chart of Accounts** 🔢 task icon in the Company area of the Home Page.

11. Double-click the **Petty Cash** account in the Chart of Accounts window.

12. Use this information to record the charge to petty cash:

DATE	NUMBER	PAYEE		PAYMENT	✔	DEPOSIT	BALANCE
	TYPE	ACCOUNT	MEMO				
09/01/2023		Cashier				300.00	300.00
	CHK	10000 · Checking [split]					
09/10/2023		USPS		18.49			281.51
	CHK	67500 · Shipping Expense					

Ⓐ Date: **091023**

Ⓑ Delete the check number in the Number field

Ⓒ Payee: **USPS** (**Quick Add** it as a **Vendor**)

Ⓓ Amount: **18.49**

Ⓔ Account: **67500•Shipping Expense**

> **BEHIND THE SCENES BRIEF**
>
> 67500•Shipping Expense DR 18.49; **10500•Petty Cash CR <18.49>**

13. Click **Record** and then close the Petty Cash register window.

14. Close the Chart of Accounts window.

Writing Off Uncollectable Receivables

Virtually every business has to write off money owed as bad debt at some point or another and remove it from Accounts Receivable. QuickBooks does allow you to do this via one of two methods: treating it as a discount or using a credit memo. Regardless of the method selected, you will need to create an expense account to which you will direct the bad debt.

An example of when you may choose to write off receivables is when you learn that a customer's company has gone out of business. You believe it is unlikely that you will be able to collect for the amount due and decide that it is time to write off the amount owed by this customer as a bad debt.

 **Best Practice**

Your sales tax liability will not be affected if you choose to treat bad debt as a discount, whereas it will be reduced if you use the credit memo method. It is for this reason that the credit memo is recommended when sales tax is involved.

FLASHBACK TO GAAP: MATERIALITY

Remember that when an item is reported, its significance should be considered.

Treating Bad Debt as a Discount

To treat bad debt as a discount (not recommended for a debt that has sales tax associated with it), you would enter it as a discount in the Receive Payments window. Make sure, though, that you use the proper expense account for the bad debt (e.g., Bad Debt Expense).

> **Note!** If you receive a partial payment from a customer, you can also choose to "Write off the extra amount" in the Receive Payments window if you do not expect to ever receive the remaining balance.

If you were to choose to use the discount method to write off the amount of Purposeful Playtime's Open House invoice, you would launch the Discount and Credits window from the Receive Payments window and choose 60300•Bad Debt Expense as the account.

Using a Credit Memo to Write Off a Bad Debt

If you create a credit memo in order to write off a bad debt, you will use an Other Charge item to "route" the bad debt to the appropriate expense account (which will be debited). Accounts Receivable will be credited. You can include both taxable and nontaxable bad debts on a single credit memo. Using this method, the credit memo is applied to the original invoice.

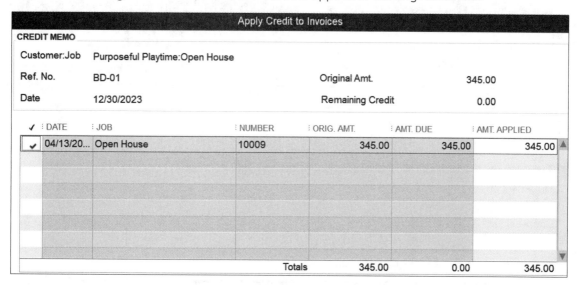

The Apply Credit to Invoices window appears immediately after you create a Credit Memo. In this example, Credit Memo BD-01 is applied to Invoice #10009 by checking the checkbox, writing off the bad debt.

Treating Bad Debt as an Allowance

Another way that companies deal with bad debt is by treating it as an allowance. In this method, which follows the GAAP matching principle, a business can estimate what the bad debts will be as either a percentage of sales or percentage of receivables. This amount is written off by debiting Bad Debt Expense and crediting an Allowance for Doubtful Accounts account, which is a contra account as it is an asset with a credit normal balance. When an account is actually determined to be uncollectable, the funds are removed from Accounts Receivable (it is credited) and the Allowance for Doubtful Accounts account is debited. There are potentially three sets of accounting entries you would encounter when using this method, as shown in the Behind the Scenes example below.

BEHIND THE SCENES

In this example, we will look at how to handle bad debts using the allowance method.

First, an adjusting entry would be made to record the bad debt expense. In this example, it was estimated that there would be approximately $1,000 of bad debt for the fiscal period.

Next, when a debt is determined to be uncollectable, it is removed from Accounts Receivable by debiting the allowance contra account. In this example, the uncollectable debt is for $200.

The final accounting takes place only if the debt was collected after being written off. It is a two-step process where you have to first reverse the previous entry and then record receipt of the payment.

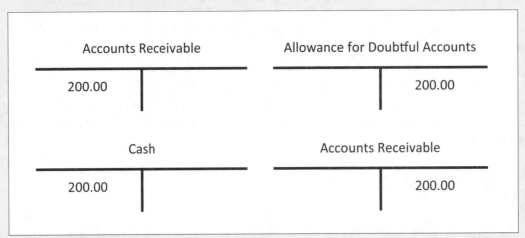

You will now complete an exercise using the direct write-off method by addressing a specific uncollectable debt and using a credit memo to handle it in QuickBooks.

In the following exercise, you will account for bad debit using the credit memo method. The accounting that QuickBooks takes care of for you is displayed below.

BEHIND THE SCENES

When you write off a bad debt, you need to credit the Accounts Receivable account and the customer subregister (which automatically occurs when you choose the customer) and debit the expense account you created to track bad debts, in this case Bad Debt Expense.

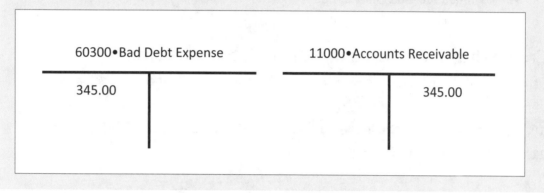

60300•Bad Debt Expense		11000•Accounts Receivable	
345.00			345.00

🔺 Customers→Receive Payments

🔺 Customers→Create Credit Memos/Refunds

DEVELOP YOUR SKILLS 7-4

In this exercise, you will use the credit memo method to write off the amount owed by Purposeful Playtime. The first step is to create an expense account for the payment.

1. Click the **Chart of Accounts** 🖩 task icon in the Company area of the Home Page.
2. Click the **Account** drop-down arrow ▼ and then choose **New**.
3. Choose **Expense** as the account type and then click **Continue**.
4. Use this information to create the new account:
   - Number: **60300**
   - Account Name: **Bad Debt Expense**
   - Description: **Expense account to write off uncollectible receivables**
5. Click **Save & Close** and then close the Chart of Accounts window.

Set Up the Bad Debt Item

The next step in writing off a bad debt using a credit memo is to create the item.

6. Click the **Items & Services** 🖩 task icon in the Company area of the Home Page.
7. Click the **Item** drop-down arrow ▼ and then choose **New**.
8. Use this information to create the new item:
   - Type: **Other Charge**
   - Item Name/Number: **Bad Debt**

- Description: **Bad Debt Write-off**

  The amount is left blank here so you can fill in the correct amount for each transaction on the credit memo.

- Tax Code: **Non**

  The Tax Code is set to Non, but you can change this on the credit memo for each receivable written off when necessary.

- Account: **60300•Bad Debt Expense**

9. Click **OK** and then close the Item List window.

Create the Credit Memo and Apply It to an Invoice

Finally, you will create the credit memo to write off the bad debt and choose to which invoice(s) it should be applied.

10. Click the **Refunds & Credits** task icon in the Customers area of the Home Page.

11. Use this information to complete the credit memo:

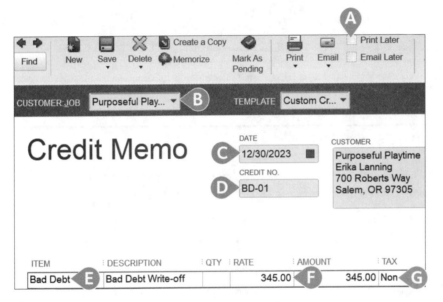

Ⓐ Click to remove checkmark from **Print Later**

Ⓑ Customer:Job: **Purposeful Playtime:Open House**

Ⓒ Date: **123023**

Ⓓ Credit No.: **BD-01**

Ⓔ Item: **Bad Debt** and then click **OK** in the Warning window

Ⓕ Rate: **345**

Ⓖ Tax: **Non**

You will leave the transaction Non-taxable, as the original invoice did not include tax.

12. Click **Save & Close**.

An Available Credit window appears from which you can decide what to do with the resulting credit.

13. Choose **Apply to an Invoice** and then click **OK**.

> This credit memo or refund has a remaining balance which
> you may use.
>
> What would you like to do with this credit?
>
> ○ Retain as an available credit
> ○ Give a refund
> ⦿ Apply to an invoice

The Apply Credits to Invoice window appears, listing all open invoices for the customer. Be sure QuickBooks has checked the correct invoice to apply the credit to, in this case the Open House job.

14. Click **Done** in the Apply Credits to Invoice window.

The total amount owed by Purposeful Playtime has now been transferred to the Bad Debt Expense account.

BEHIND THE SCENES BRIEF

60300•Bad Debt Expense DR 345.00; **11000•Accounts Receivable CR <345.00>**

Working with Fixed Assets

A fixed asset is one that you don't plan to use up or turn into cash within the next year. A business uses fixed assets in a productive capacity to promote the main operations of the company. Fixed assets are depreciable, which means that you don't expense the assets when you purchase them but rather over the useful life of the asset.

The main types of fixed assets that you will find in QuickBooks are Land, Buildings, Leasehold Improvements, Furniture & Equipment, and Vehicles.

> **Note!** While land is a fixed asset for a company, it is not depreciable.

Setting Up Fixed Assets in QuickBooks

There are many correct ways to set up your fixed assets in QuickBooks. You should ask your accountant which method is preferred for your company. One method involves creating a fixed asset account for each major type of fixed asset and then an account to track accumulated depreciation for all fixed assets.

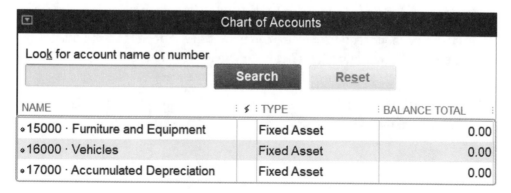

Depreciation

Depreciation provides a business with a way to match income to expenses. A fixed asset is used to produce income over a period of time, and depreciation allows you to record the appropriate expense for each accounting period. Many small businesses record depreciation transactions just once a year, but they can be entered monthly or quarterly if the business produces financial statements for those periods.

FLASHBACK TO GAAP: MATCHING

Remember that expenses need to be matched with revenues.

Accumulated Depreciation

Each accounting period, a business records a depreciation expense for the fixed asset(s). These depreciation expenses "accumulate" in an account called Accumulated Depreciation, which is also a fixed asset account. Accumulated Depreciation is a *contra account*, which means it offsets the balance of the related fixed asset accounts by entering a negative amount so that the book value is displayed rather than the original cost on the balance sheet report.

Note! You need to consult with your accountant before entering depreciation, and often she will enter it for you at the end of the accounting period.

Fixed Asset Items

Fixed asset items provide a convenient way to track your fixed assets. After creating your fixed asset account and subaccounts, you should set up the fixed asset items. These items help you to consolidate all of the important information about each fixed asset in a convenient place. In addition, your accountant can transfer the information from your Fixed Asset Item List to the Fixed Asset Manager, if they use that feature of QuickBooks.

NAME	FAM...	PURCHASE DATE	PURCHASE DESCRIPTION	ACCOUNT	COST	ATTACH
Fixed Asset Item List						
• Vespa Scooter		10/28/2023	2017 Used Vespa Electric Scooter	16000 · Vehicles	4,500.00	

Item ▼   Activities ▼   Reports ▼   Attach   ☐ Include inactive

Creating Fixed Asset Items

There are two ways that a new fixed asset item can be set up:

- Create the new item when entering the purchase transaction.

- Open the Fixed Asset Item List and create a new item.

When you enter fixed assets upon creation of a new company, you will debit the fixed asset account and credit Opening Balance Equity; this account is created by QuickBooks when the first balance sheet account is created so you have an accurate balance sheet from the beginning.

If a loan is associated with the fixed asset, the loan amount will be entered in a Long Term Liabilities account and the difference in an equity or bank account.

> **Note!** When you set up a fixed asset item, you indicate the account into which it has been entered. This does not enter it into the account or affect what happens behind the scenes. You must also complete the appropriate transactions to purchase the assets, pay for those assets, and set up the depreciation to make sure it is tracked properly.

Accountant Tool: Fixed Asset Manager

If your accountant uses the Premier Accountant version of QuickBooks, fixed asset information can be pulled from your Fixed Asset Item list into the Fixed Asset Manager. This tool will help determine how to depreciate the fixed assets as well as the amount that needs to be posted back to the company file as an adjusting entry.

FLASHBACK TO GAAP: COST

Remember that when a company purchases assets, it should record them at cost, not fair market value. For example, if you bought an item worth $750 for $100, it should be recorded at $100.

 Company→Chart of Accounts: Accounts→New→Fixed Asset

 Lists→Fixed Asset Item List

DEVELOP YOUR SKILLS 7-5

In this exercise, you will create a new fixed asset item for the Vespa, purchase the Vespa, and record the vehicle's depreciation. To begin, create a new fixed asset account for Vehicles.

1. Click the **Chart of Accounts** 🔲 task icon in the Company area of the Home Page.
2. Click the **Account** drop-down arrow ▾ and then choose **New**.
3. Choose **Fixed Asset** as the account type and then click **Continue**.
4. Use this information to create the new account:
   - Number: **16000**
   - Account Name: **Vehicles**
   - Description: **Vehicles with a useful life exceeding one year**
5. Click **Save & Close**.

Create a Fixed Asset Item

6. Choose **Lists→Fixed Asset Item List**.
7. Click the **Item** drop-down arrow ▾ and then choose **New**.

8. Use this information to create the new item:

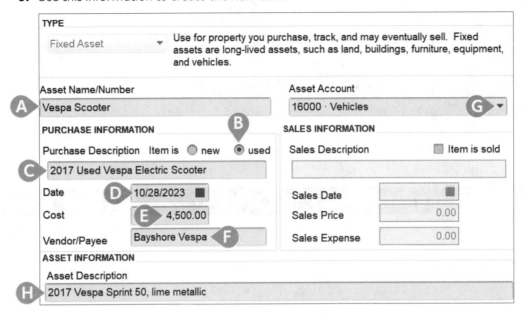

A. Asset Name/Number: **Vespa Scooter**

B. Item is: **used**

C. Purchase Description: **2017 Used Vespa Electric Scooter**

D. Date: **102823**

E. Cost: **4500**

F. Vendor: **Bayshore Vespa**

G. Asset Account: **16000•Vehicles**

H. Asset Description: **2017 Vespa Sprint 50, lime metallic**

9. Click **OK**, choosing to **Add** *Vespa* to the dictionary if necessary.

10. Close the Fixed Asset Item List and then close the Chart of Accounts window.

You did not affect anything behind the scenes in this exercise. You just set up the item that will be tracked and the account that will be used to track it.

Purchase a Fixed Asset

Now it is time to record the transaction to purchase the Vespa.

11. Click the **Enter Bills** task icon in the Vendors area of the Home Page.

12. Use this information to enter the bill:

- Vendor: **Bayshore Vespa** (**Quick Add** it as a **Vendor**)
- Date: **102823**
- Ref No.: **Vespa 10/2023**
- Amount Due: **4500**
- Memo: **Bayshore Vespa: 2017 Sprint 50 10/2023**
- Account: **16000•Vehicles**

13. Click **Save & Close**.

14. Click the **Pay Bills** task icon in the Vendors area of the Home Page.

15. Ensure **Show All Bills** is selected and then click the checkbox to select the **Bayshore Vespa** bill.

16. Use this information to complete the bill payment:
    - Date: **102523**
    - Payment Method: **Check** (select **To Be Printed**)
    - Account: **10000•Checking**

17. Click **Pay Selected Bills** and then click **Done** in the Payment Summary window.

Dealing with Current Liabilities

Current liabilities are funds that your company owes and expects to pay within a year. You have been collecting sales tax for your inventory sales. Now it is time to learn how to pay the collected tax (a current liability) to the appropriate tax agencies.

Sales Tax Payable

When you bill a customer and collect sales tax, QuickBooks holds the funds in a current liability account. These taxes are never actually the property of your business, so you have been using a liabilities payable account as a place to "store" the taxes until it is time to pay them.

When you are ready to pay your sales tax, it is *imperative* that you do so through the Pay Sales Tax window. This is to ensure that the proper liability account is affected behind the scenes when the payment is processed.

> **Warning!** When you are ready to pay sales tax, you must use the proper procedure, or you will not "empty" the Sales Tax Payable account behind the scenes.

The Sales Tax Liability Report

You can choose to run a Sales Tax Liability report to see what funds you are holding in your Sales Tax Payable account. This report will give you the values you need to file your sales tax return: total sales, taxable sales, nontaxable sales, and the amount of tax collected.

The Manage Sales Tax Window

The Manage Sales Tax window helps you manage all of your sales tax activities and reports easily by providing links to all of the tasks you will be performing when working with sales tax, from setting it up to paying it.

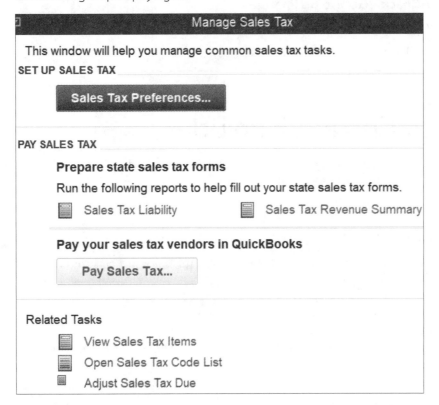

Sales Tax Adjustments

There are many situations that could result in an incorrect amount in the Pay Sales Tax window or on the Sales Tax Liability report. You may have charged a customer a tax rate for the wrong jurisdiction or tax may have been charged for a nontaxable item. There could also be rounding errors, penalties, or credits/discounts that you need to take into account.

You can make an adjustment to the tax owed through the Pay Sales Tax window or by choosing Adjust Sales Tax Due from the Vendors menu. Make sure that you don't use Sales Tax Payable as the "pay from account." Instead, you should use the following types of accounts:

- **For a rounding error:** You can set up a special account or use the Miscellaneous Expense. Some businesses opt to create a special income account for a negative error or a special expense account for a positive error.

- **For a credit or to apply a discount:** Use an income account such as Other Income.

- **For interest due, fines, or penalties:** Use an expense account such as Interest Expense or Non-deductible Penalties.

If you make an adjustment to the Sales Tax Liability account, you will need to choose the adjustment the next time you pay sales tax in order to get the correct amount to pay.

Changing a Tax Jurisdiction

If a customer is charged sales tax for the wrong jurisdiction, you need to go back to the original transaction and choose the correct sales tax item or group. If you charged tax on a nontaxable item (or vice versa), you need to adjust the invoice or sales receipt where the sale was made. This may require you to issue a credit to the customer who overpaid or reissue the invoice/receipt (or a statement) to a customer who underpaid.

BEHIND THE SCENES

When you pay sales tax, behind the scenes you will see the funds leave the Sales Tax Payable account as a debit.

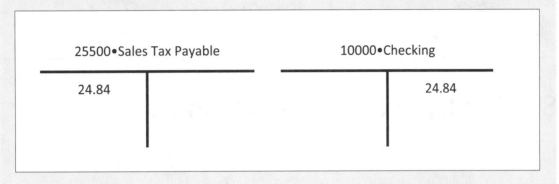

25500•Sales Tax Payable		10000•Checking	
24.84			24.84

➦ Vendors→Sales Tax→Manage Sales Tax *or* Pay Sales Tax *or* Sales Tax Liability

➦ Reports→Vendors & Payables→Sales Tax Liability

DEVELOP YOUR SKILLS 7-6

In this exercise, you will pay the sales tax collected in December 2023. The first step is to run a report to determine how much sales tax is owed and to whom.

1. Click the **Manage Sales Tax** 📄 task icon in the Vendors area of the Home Page.
2. Click the **Sales Tax Liability** link in the middle of the Manage Sales Tax window.
3. Enter this information to run the report:
   - From: **120123**
   - To: **123123**
   - Click **Refresh** on the report toolbar (resize the window to view the data)

   The information you need to pay and file your taxes is in the last column, Sales Tax Payable as of Dec 31, 2023, which is $24.84.
4. Close the Sales Tax Liability report, choosing not to memorize it.

Pay the Sales Tax

From the report you just ran, you know that Average Guy Designs owes $24.84 as of 12/31/2023 to the State Board of Equalization.

5. Click the **Pay Sales Tax...** button in the Manage Sales Tax window.
6. Use this information to pay the taxes due:
   - Pay From Account: **10000•Checking**
   - Check Date: **123123**

- Show sales tax due through: **123123**
- Click checkbox for **To Be Printed** at the bottom of the window
- Click the **Pay All Tax** button and note that the button name changes after it has been clicked; click **OK**.

The liability check has now been entered into the queue of checks to be printed.

BEHIND THE SCENES BRIEF
25500•Sales Tax Payable DR 24.84; **10000•Checking CR <24.84>**

7. Close the Manage Sales Tax window.

Setting Up a Long Term Liability

Most companies have to take out a loan for a fixed asset using a Long Term Liability account to track a loan that is scheduled to take longer than a year to pay off. In this section, you will create a Long Term Liability account to track a new computer system loan.

The QuickBooks Loan Manager

QuickBooks provides a tool for you to track your loans, similar to the Fixed Asset Item List that allows you to track your fixed assets. The Loan Manager allows you to set up loans based on information that you have entered in a Long Term Liability or Other Current Liability account. The Loan Manager tracks the principle and interest payments without having to set up separate amortization schedules. You can also use the Loan Manager to compare different loan scenarios.

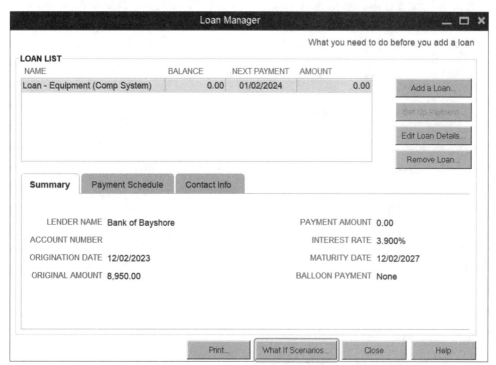

The Loan Manager provides you with a place to track your long term liabilities. You can even click the What If Scenarios button to explore possible loan situations before you make a decision.

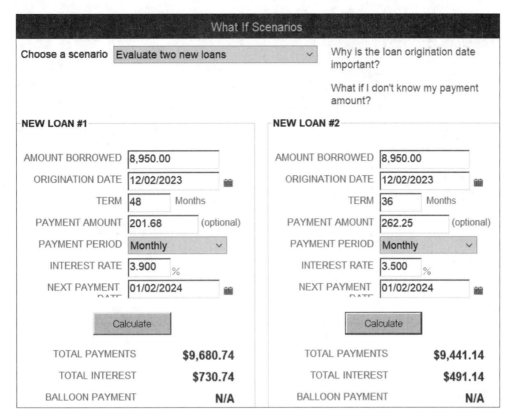

The Loan Manager also provides a "what if" tool that allows you to see whether you can afford a loan and to compare multiple loan options.

There are a number of items you should prepare before you set up a loan in the Loan Manager:

- **Set Up Your Accounts:** Make sure to set up any liability (e.g., 26000•Loan – Equipment (Comp System)), expense (e.g., 63400•Interest Expense), and escrow (only if required) accounts that will be affected by the loan.

- **Set up the Vendor, if not already in your Vendor List.**

- **Check Previous Transactions:** If you are working with an existing (rather than new) loan, you will also need to confirm that all of the transactions related to it are entered into QuickBooks before setting up the loan in the Loan Manager.

- **Gather Loan Documents:** Make sure you have all of your original loan documents handy before you begin to set up the loan. It is important that you enter the opening balance and other information properly.

Once all transactions are up to date and the loan has been entered into the Loan Manager, you will be able to record future loan payments in the Set Up Payment window.

BEHIND THE SCENES

When you pay for the computer system with your new loan and down payment, the offsetting account will be the fixed asset account.

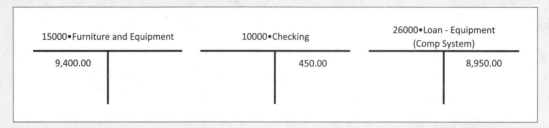

15000•Furniture and Equipment		10000•Checking		26000•Loan - Equipment (Comp System)	
9,400.00			450.00		8,950.00

Making a payment affects three accounts (unless you have a 0 percent interest loan): the loan account, the bank account, and the interest expense account.

63400•Interest Expense		26000•Loan - Equipment (Comp System)		10000•Checking	
29.09		172.59			201.68

 Banking→Loan Manager

DEVELOP YOUR SKILLS 7-7

In this exercise, you will set up a fixed asset account for a new computer system, pay a down payment, set up the loan account for the system, fund the loan, and set up the loan in the Loan Manager. First, you will create the new liability account and vendor.

1. Click the **Chart of Accounts** task icon in the Company area of the Home Page.
2. Click the **Account** drop-down arrow ▾ and then choose **New**.
3. Follow these steps to create the new Long Term Liability account:
   - Choose **Other Account Types**
   - Account type: **Long Term Liability** (click **Continue**)
   - Number: **26000**
   - Account Name: **Loan – Equipment (Comp System)**
   - Description: **Long-term loan for new computer system**
4. Click **Save & Close** to record the new account and then close the Chart of Accounts window.
5. Click **Vendors→Vendor Center** and then click the **New Vendor** button on the toolbar of the Vendor Center and choose **New Vendor**.

6. Enter this information to complete the vendor record:

   - Vendor Name: **MicroCentral Hardware**
   - Company Name: **MicroCentral Hardware**
   - Full Name: **Ms. Hayden English**
   - Job Title: **Accounts Receivable Manager**
   - Main Phone: **(650) 555-0147**
   - Address Details Billed From: **425 Green St.** [Enter] **Palo Alto, CA 94303**

7. Click **OK** to enter the new vendor and leave the Vendor Center open.

Create a Fixed Asset Item

8. Choose **Lists→Fixed Asset Item List**.

9. Click the **Item** drop-down arrow ▼ and then choose **New**.

10. Use this information to create the new item:

    - Asset Name/Number: **Computer System**
    - Item is: **new**
    - Date: **120123**
    - Purchase Description: **Computer hardware and networking equipment**
    - Cost: **9400**
    - Vendor: **MicroCentral Hardware**

    Although this vendor is on your Vendor List, the name will not autofill here.

    - Asset Account: **15000•Furniture and Equipment**
    - Asset Description: **Computer system for offices**

11. Click **OK** and then close the Fixed Asset Item List window.

Write a Check for the Down Payment

You will now prepare a check for funds that the company paid as a deposit on the new computer system.

12. Choose **Banking→Write Checks**.

13. Ensure **Print Later** is checked on the Ribbon and then follow these steps to create the check for the down payment:

    - Bank Account: **10000•Checking**
    - Pay to the Order of: **MicroCentral Hardware**
    - Date: **120123**
    - Amount: **450**
    - Memo: **MicroCentral: Computer System Down Payment 12/2023**
    - Account: **15000•Furniture and Equipment**

    > **BEHIND THE SCENES BRIEF**
    >
    > 15000•Furniture and Equipment DR 450.00; **10000•Checking CR <450.00>**

14. Click **Save & Close** to record the transaction.

Fund the Long Term Liability Account

Average Guy Designs has received the computer system, and the First Bank of Bayshore has issued the funds on your behalf to MicroCentral Hardware for the outstanding balance. You will record the starting balance for the loan for the computer system.

15. Click **Lists→Chart of Accounts** and then double-click the **26000•Loan — Equipment (Comp System)** account, resizing the window to view the data, if necessary.

The register window for the liability account will appear.

16. Use this information to record the funding of the loan:

- Date: **120223**
- Increase: **8950**
- Account: **15000•Furniture and Equipment**
- Memo: `Loan for purchase of computer system`

> **BEHIND THE SCENES BRIEF**
>
> 15000•Furniture and Equipment DR 8,950.00; **26000•Loan — Equipment (Computer System) CR <8,950.00>**

17. Click **Record**.

18. Close the register window.

The 15000•Furniture and Equipment account will be increased by $9400, the total cost of the computer system ($450 from the down payment and $8,950 from the loan).

19. Close the Chart of Accounts window.

Enter a Loan in the Loan Manager

You will enter a four-year loan from the bank. Before you can enter the loan in the Loan Manager, you must first enter the bank as a vendor on the Vendor List.

20. Click the **New Vendor** button on the toolbar of the Vendor Center and then choose **New Vendor**.

21. Enter **Bank of Bayshore** as the Vendor Name; click **OK** to save the new vendor.

You can always go back and enter the rest of a vendor's information later. When working in your own company, you should enter all of the information before continuing.

22. Close the Vendor Center.

23. Choose **Banking→Loan Manager**.

If you receive a Feature Update window, you will be required to reboot your computer to use the Loan Manager feature. You can continue using other features of QuickBooks if you don't reboot.

24. Click the **Add a Loan...** button.

25. Use this information to enter the account information for the loan:

- Account Name: **Loan — Equipment (Comp System)**
- Lender: **Bank of Bayshore**
- Origination Date: **120223**

- Original Amount: **8950**
- Term: **48** (choose **Months**)

26. Click **Next** and use this information to enter the payment information:

- Due Date of Next Payment: **010224**
- Payment Amount: **201.68**

See your accountant, use a loan calculator, or complete a What If Scenario prior to this step to determine affordability of monthly payments (principal + interest) based on criteria such as origination date, loan amount, interest rate, and term. It can also be used to evaluate two loans to determine the best option.

27. Click **Next** and use this information to enter the interest information:

Ⓐ Interest Rate: **3.9**

Ⓑ Payment Account: **Checking**

Ⓒ Interest Expense Account: **Interest Expense**

The loan is now set up in the Loan Manager, ready for you to track.

28. Click **Finish** and then close the Loan Manager window.

Working with Equity Accounts

Equity accounts reflect the net worth of a company. In Appendix A, "Need to Know Accounting," notice that the accounting equation teaches that the sum of the equity accounts is equal to assets (what you own) less liabilities (what you owe):

Equity = Assets – Liabilities

An equity account has a credit normal balance. It represents how viable your company is, as it shows how much you would have left if you sold all of your assets and then paid off the liabilities.

Owner's Equity / Capital Stock

In a sole proprietorship, the equity is what the owner has invested in the company. In a corporation, the equity is what the shareholders have invested in the company (capital stock). An owner's investment occurs when an owner deposits funds or other assets into the company or shareholders purchase stock. An owner's withdrawal of funds from the company is known as a draw; if it is a corporation, you will see shareholder distributions.

Retained Earnings

At the end of the fiscal year, a business will show either a net income or a net loss. When the books are closed, this amount is transferred into the Retained Earnings account to clear out all income and expense accounts for the next year. When the fiscal year ends, QuickBooks automatically makes this transfer.

Opening Balance Equity

QuickBooks creates the Opening Balance Equity account when you first create your company. As you enter opening balances into the accounts, QuickBooks uses Opening Balance Equity as the offset account so you can have a working balance sheet right from the beginning. You may need to enter a transfer between accounts if there is a balance in the Opening Balance Equity account after all of your new accounts are entered into QuickBooks. In addition, there are other times when QuickBooks may use the Opening Balance Equity account and an adjustment must be made. For instance, when you set QuickBooks up to track inventory and enter a beginning number of inventory items on hand, you debit 12100•Inventory Asset, and 30000•Opening Balance Equity is credited behind the scenes. You should talk to your accountant about how to deal with equity transactions for your unique company.

FLASHBACK TO GAAP: BUSINESS ENTITY

Remember that the first assumption of GAAP is that the business is separate from the owners and from other businesses. Business revenues and expenses should be kept separate from the business owner's personal expenses.

 Banking→Make Deposits [and use Owner's Equity in the From Account field]

Banking→Write Checks: Bank Account→Owner's Draw

DEVELOP YOUR SKILLS 7-8

In this exercise, you will enter a transaction for Guy, the owner, to add working capital to the business.

1. Choose **Banking→Make Deposits**.
2. Use this information to add Guy's investment to the checking account as equity:
   - Deposit To: **10000•Checking**
   - Date: **120223**
   - From Account: **32000•Owner's Equity**
   - Memo: **Owner's investment for working capital**
   - Pmt Meth: **Cash**
   - Amount: **2000**
3. Click **Save & Close** and then click **OK** in the Retained Earnings window.

Budgeting and Predicting in QuickBooks

QuickBooks includes a budgeting feature that allows you to create account-based budgets for Balance Sheet or Profit & Loss accounts. Budgets can be created based on a previous year's budget or from scratch—or, if you have been using QuickBooks for a year, the actual figures from the previous year.

Budget Reports

After you have created a budget, you will run a report to view the information. QuickBooks provides several reports that will allow you to use the information in your budget(s).

BUDGET REPORTS AND THEIR PURPOSES	
Budget Report Name	**What it will tell you...**
Budget Overview	Company's projected income and expenses for each month
Budget vs. Actual	Actual income and expenses compared to budgeted amounts for the company as a whole
Profit & Loss Budget Performance	Actual income and expenses compared to budgeted amounts for the current month and year
Budget vs. Actual Graph	Income and expenses as over or under budget

Predicting the Future Cash Flow

In addition to budgets, QuickBooks also supplies you with a Cash Flow Projector feature that assists you with making predictions about the future. It allows you to conduct "what-if" analyses as well as look at future cash flow or revenue. Projections can be based on actual figures from the last year or from scratch.

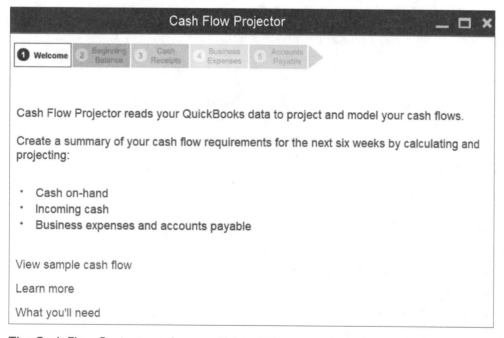

The Cash Flow Projector takes you through five steps in order to give you a cash flow report that will show you your "liquidity" over the next six weeks.

➚ Company→Planning & Budgeting→Set Up Budgets

➚ Reports→Budgets→Budget Overview

➚ Company→Planning & Budgeting→Cash Flow Projector

DEVELOP YOUR SKILLS 7-9

In this exercise, you will create a budget for 2024.

1. Choose **Company→Planning & Budgeting→Set Up Budgets**.
2. Set **2024** as the year and **Profit and Loss** as the type; click **Next**.
3. Ensure that **No Additional Criteria** is selected; click **Next**.

   Your budget will be based on all Customers:Jobs, so you do not need to provide additional criteria at this time.

4. Ensure **Create Budget from Scratch** is selected and then click **Finish**.

   A blank budget will be displayed with all of your income and expense accounts included. In order to populate the budget, you will enter a monthly amount in the January column for each account and then copy the amount across. The amounts entered will be "averages" in this example, but when you are creating your own company's budget, you can also choose to enter a different amount for each month.

5. Enter the following information for the income and COGS accounts in the budget, clicking **Copy Across** after each entry:

Warning! If you press ⏎Enter⏎, you will leave the Set Up Budgets screen. To bring it back, choose Company→Planning & Budgeting→Set Up Budgets.

- Begin by clicking in the **JAN24** column in the **41100•Clothing** row and typing **500**. (remember to click **Copy Across** after each entry).

ACCOUNT	ANNUAL T...	JAN24
41000 · Product Sales		
41100 · Clothing	500.00	500.00
41200 · Accessories	300.00	300.00
41300 · Home Decor	250.00	250.00
42700 · Photography Income	700.00	700.00
43200 · Design Income	5,000.00	5,000.00
48800 · Print Layout Income	1,500.00	1,500.00
48900 · Video Editing Income	2,500.00	2,500.00
48910 · Returned Check Charges		
49000 · Less Discounts Given		
50000 · Cost of Goods Sold	500.00	500.00
50100 · Blueprints and Reproduction		
53500 · Subcontracted Services		

6. Click **Save** to update the budget with what you have entered so far.

7. Enter each of the Jan 2024 expense amounts as displayed below, making sure to click **Copy Across** after each one:

Automobile Expense	**50**	Advertising/Promotion	**300**
Bad Debt Expense	**20**	Office Supplies	**200**
Bank Service Charges	**25**	Payroll Expense	**4000**
Business Licenses and Permits	**20**	Professional Fees	**250**
Job Materials	**100**	Rent Expense	**700**
Computer and Internet	**100**	Repairs and Maintenance	**100**
Continuing Education	**50**	Shipping Expense	**100**
Depreciation Expense	**125**	Office Phone	**40**
Dues and Subscriptions	**25**	Fax Line	**40**
Insurance Expense	**200**	Cell Phone	**100**
Interest Expense	**50**	Gas & Electric	**80**
Meals and Entertainment	**400**	Water	**75**

8. Click **OK** when you are finished entering all budget amounts.

Produce a Budget Report

Now that the budget for 2024 has been produced, Guy would like to see a report showing an overview of it.

9. Choose **Reports→Budgets→Budget Overview**.

   A Budget Report "wizard" will walk you through selections that will help you create the report you desire.

10. Click **Next** two times and then click **Finish**.

    The budget for 2024 will be displayed by month.

11. Scroll down and note whether there is a Net Income or Net Loss projected for each month.

    You will see that there is a $3,100 net income budgeted per month.

12. Close the budget report window.

Tackle the Tasks

Now you will apply the skills that you have learned in this chapter using the same company file you used in the Develop Your Skills exercises throughout this chapter. Enter the following tasks, referring back to the concepts in the chapter as necessary. If you are using the trial software for this course on your computer or in a lab at school, you must toggle to the Pro edition every time you start QuickBooks.

Create and Fund a Prepaid Insurance Account	Average Guy Designs has decided to prepay the insurance for the next six months. Create 13300•Prepaid Insurance as an Other Current Asset account. Write a check to be printed to Rankin Family Insurance on 01/01/2024 for $1,050, expensing $175 in January to 63300•Insurance Expense, placing the rest in the Prepaid Insurance account.
Record and Memorize a Transfer of Funds	Record a transfer of $175 from 13300•Prepaid Insurance to 63300•Insurance Expense on 02/01/2024. Memorize the transaction in the Monthly group.
Make a Petty Cash Expenditure	Use 10500•Petty Cash to purchase a birthday cake on 02/21/2024 for Allison's birthday. The total amount is $33.75, payable to Jordan Bakery, expensed to 64300•Meals and Entertainment.
Create a New Fixed Asset Item	Guy purchased new furniture for his office on 02/14/2024 for $2,639 from Pa's Custom Furniture. Create a new Fixed Asset item called Office Furniture and use 15000•Furniture and Equipment as the Asset Account.
Create a Long Term Liability	Create a Long Term Liability account for the new furniture called 28300•Loan – Furniture (Office). On 02/14/2024 enter the total amount of the furniture as an increase in the new liability account you just created, using 15000•Furniture and Equipment as the Account.
Use the Loan Manager	Use the What If Scenario tool to calculate the monthly payment for the Loan of $2,639 for the furniture, using the Loan Origination date of 02/14/2024. The interest rate is 7.25% and the loan is for 24 months. The next payment date is 03/14/2024. Click Calculate to show the payment amount of $118.45.
	Enter the furniture loan in the Loan Manager. The loan is issued by Bank of Bayshore. The Payment Account is Checking, and the Interest Expense account is Interest Expense. Note: Due to the dates in the future, you will see the loan in the list with a zero balance for the amount and the payment schedule won't display.
Create a Budget Report	Create a Budget vs. Actual report for the FY2024 budget.

Self-Assessment

Check your knowledge of this chapter's key concepts and skills using the Self-Assessment quiz here, in your ebook, or in your eLab course.

1. When you memorize a transaction, QuickBooks always automatically enters the transaction for you. *True False*

2. Petty Cash is set up as an expense account in your Chart of Accounts. *True False*

3. You can fund your Petty Cash account by holding cash back from a deposit. *True False*

4. Depreciation allows a business to match income to expenses. *True False*

5. Accumulated Depreciation is an example of a contra account. *True False*

6. A Long Term Liability is a loan that will be paid off in less than a year. *True False*

7. A company's net income is transferred into the Retained Earnings account at the end of the year. *True False*

8. An Other Current Asset is often amortized. *True False*

9. You can enter petty cash expenditures just as you enter checks. *True False*

10. Budgets that you create in QuickBooks must be account based. *True False*

11. Which of the following is NOT a method used to account for petty cash?
    A. Register method
    B. End-of-month journal entry method
    C. Chart of Accounts method
    D. Write checks method

12. Which of the following is an Other Current Asset account?
    A. Checking
    B. Land
    C. Money Market
    D. Prepaid Rent

13. Which type of accounts do you depreciate?
    A. Long Term Liabilities
    B. Fixed Assets
    C. Equity Accounts
    D. Other Current Assets

14. Which account does QuickBooks create for you so you have a working balance sheet account from the start?
    A. Retained Earnings
    B. Opening Balance Equity
    C. Owner's Equity
    D. Accounts Receivable

📌 Reinforce Your Skills

Electrical Energy is a growing company, and Emily will begin prepaying and automating some transactions and using a petty cash account in QuickBooks. To support the growth of the business, Emily will buy a new service van by taking out a loan. The password for all files unless otherwise stated is *Password1*. Leave the company file open unless otherwise instructed. If QuickBooks is closed and you are using the trial software on your computer or in the lab at school, you must toggle to the Pro edition after starting QuickBooks.

REINFORCE YOUR SKILLS 7-1

Use a Prepaid Rent Account

In this exercise, you will set up and use a Prepaid Rent account. The first step is to set up an Other Current Asset account.

1. Choose **File→Open or Restore Company**.
2. Open **RYS_Chapter07 (Company)** or restore **RYS_Chapter07 (Portable)** from your file storage location and save your file as: **RYS_Chapter07 Electrical Energy**
3. Choose **Lists→Chart of Accounts**.
4. Click the **Account** drop-down arrow ▼ and then choose **New**.
5. Create a new Other Current Asset account called: **13000•Prepaid Rent**

   Leave the Chart of Accounts open.

Write the Rent Check

The next step is to write the check for the rent.

6. Choose **Banking→Write Checks**.
7. Use this information to complete the check to be printed later:
   - Date: **100123**
   - Pay to the Order of: **Capitol Property Services**
   - Amount: **6900**
   - Memo: **Capitol: Rent Oct 2023-Mar 2024**

   Next you will expense the first month's rent and place the remainder in the Prepaid Rent account.
   - Account: **67000•Rent Expense**
   - Amount: **1150**
   - Account: **13000•Prepaid Rent**
   - Amount: **5750**
8. Save the check and close the Write Checks window.

Memorize a Funds Transfer

Now you will make the first transfer from Prepaid Rent to Rent Expense. The Chart of Accounts should still be open. If it isn't, choose Lists→Chart of Accounts.

9. Double-click the **Prepaid Rent** account to open the register.
10. Record a transfer of **$1,150** to Rent Expense on **11/01/2023**.

11. Click within the transaction and choose **Edit→Memorize General Journal**.

12. Create a memorized transaction called **Rent Transfer** that is a monthly automated transaction entry. The next transfer will be on **12/01/2023** and there are **4** remaining. Close the Memorize Transaction window.

13. Click **Record** and then close the Prepaid Rent register window.

REINFORCE YOUR SKILLS 7-2

Track Petty Cash

In this exercise, you will replenish Petty Cash and then make a purchase using it.

1. Choose **Banking→Write Checks** and then choose **10000•Checking**.

2. Use this information to complete the check:
   - No.: **11358**
   - Date: **102823**
   - Pay to the Order Of: **Cashier** (**Quick Add** it as a **Vendor**)
   - Amount: **300**

3. In the Account section, type **Petty Cash**, tap ⬚Tab⬚, and choose **Set Up**.

4. Set up the Petty Cash account as a **Bank** account numbered **10200**, click **Save & Close**, and then **Save & Close** the check.

Make a Purchase with Petty Cash

Now that the Petty Cash account is set up, you will use it to purchase postage stamps.

5. Double-click the **10200•Petty Cash** account from the Chart of Accounts window to open the register.

6. Use this information to complete the transaction:
   - Date: **103023**
   - Payee: **USPS** (**Quick Add** it as a **Vendor**)
   - Payment: **46.00**
   - Account: **66500•Postage and Delivery**
   - Memo: **stamps**

7. Record the transaction and then close the Petty Cash register.

REINFORCE YOUR SKILLS 7-3

Create a New Fixed Asset Item

Emily purchased a new van for traveling to customer locations, with great storage capabilities. In this exercise, you will set up this purchase as a fixed asset item in the QuickBooks company file.

1. Choose **List→Fixed Asset Item List**.

2. Create a new **Fixed Asset Item** for the vehicle using the following information:
   - Asset Name: **Service Van**
   - Item is: **Used**

- Purchase Description: **Used Service Van**
- Date: **110123**
- Cost: **14560**
- Vendor: **Carmel Auto Sales**
- Asset Account: **15200•Vehicles** (choose **Set Up** and create the account)
- Asset Description: **Service van with storage shelving.**

3. Save the new Fixed Asset Item; close the Fixed Asset Item List.

REINFORCE YOUR SKILLS 7-4

Pay Sales Tax and Track a Long Term Liability

Emily needs to pay the sales tax collected for sales as well as set up a loan for a portion of the cost of the new service van. In this exercise, you will pay sales tax, set up the Long Term Liability account, and record the purchase transaction.

1. Choose **Vendors→Sales Tax→Pay Sales Tax**.
2. Use this information to pay the sales tax:
   - Pay From Account: **10000•Checking**
   - Check Date: **123123**
   - Show sales tax due through: **123123**
   - Click to add a checkmark for **To Be Printed**
   - Click **Pay All Tax** and then click **OK** to send the liability checks to the queue to be printed.

Create the Long Term Liability Account

3. Click the **Account** drop-down arrow ▾ in the Chart of Accounts window and then choose **New**.
4. Choose to create a new **Long Term Liability** account (which is an Other Account Type) and then click **Continue**.
5. Enter this information to create the account:
   - Number: **28000**
   - Account Name: **Loan - Vehicle**
6. Click **Save & Close**.

Enter the Down Payment Transaction

You will now enter the two transactions to account for the full purchase price of the service van. The first is the down payment.

7. Choose **Banking→Write Checks**.
8. Use this information to create the check, which is to be printed later:
   - Bank Account: **10000•Checking**
   - Date: **120123**
   - Payee: **Carmel Auto Sales** (**Quick Add** it as a **Vendor**)

- Amount: **2000**
- Memo: **Carmel: Service Van down payment 12/2023**
- Account: **15200•Vehicles**

9. Click **Save & Close**.

Enter the Loan Transaction

The loan has been funded by the bank, so now you need to account for it in QuickBooks.

10. In the Chart of Accounts window, double-click the **28000•Loan-Vehicle** Long Term Liability account to open the register.

11. Use this information to enter the loan transaction:
    - Date: **120123**
    - Increase: **12560**
    - Account: **15200•Vehicles**

12. Click **Record**, close the Loan-Vehicle and Chart of Accounts windows, and then close the company file.

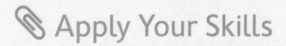
Apply Your Skills

Wet Noses Veterinary Clinic is ready to work with Fixed Asset, Current Liability, Long Term Liability, and Equity Accounts. In addition to prepaying expenses, buying equipment, and drawing from the owner's equity, the clinic will also have to account for bad debt. The password for all files unless otherwise stated is Password1. After starting QuickBooks, remember to toggle to Pro as necessary.

APPLY YOUR SKILLS 7-1 QG

Set Up Prepaid Expenses

Wet Noses Veterinary Clinic will pay a website hosting fee for one year in advance. In this exercise, you will set up an Other Current Asset account to track the prepaid web hosting expense, transfer funds to the expense account, and set up a monthly automatic transfer for the remainder of the year.

1. Choose **File→Open or Restore Company**.
2. Open **AYS_A1_Chapter07 (Company)** or restore **AYS_A1_Chapter07 (Portable)** from your file storage location and save your file as: **AYS_A1_Chapter07 Wet Noses Clinic**
3. Create a **Prepaid Web Hosting** Other Current Asset account, number **12200**.
4. Write a check to **Zoom Web Services** for a year's worth of monthly web hosting on **07/22/2023**, to be printed later, for **$1,068.00**. Expense the month of July's **Computer and Internet Expense** and send the remainder to the **Prepaid Web Hosting** account.
5. Record a transaction in the **Prepaid Web Hosting** register to decrease the prepaid account for Computer and Internet Expenses of $89 for the month of August on **08/22/2023**.
6. Memorize the transaction as **Web Host Transfer**, to be automated monthly beginning in September for the remaining 10 months.
7. Run a **QuickReport** on the **Prepaid Web Hosting** account to show the transaction detail for this account.
8. Click the **Excel** | Excel ▾ | button and export this report to a new worksheet, saving the worksheet to your file storage location as: **CH7_A1 Prepaid Web QuickReport**
9. Close the company file.

APPLY YOUR SKILLS 7-2 QG

Track and Use Petty Cash and Take an Owner's Draw

In this exercise, you will create a petty cash account and use it to pay for an expense.

1. Choose **File→Open or Restore Company**.
2. Open **AYS_A2_Chapter07 (Company)** or restore **AYS_A2_Chapter07 (Portable)** from your file storage location and save your file as: **AYS_A2_Chapter07 Wet Noses Clinic**
3. Create a **Petty Cash** account numbered **10700** and write a check to Cashier, to be printed later, for **$200** from the Checking account on **07/08/2023** to fund the account.

4. Purchase an appetizer platter for **$44.95** from Laura's Café for an office party on **07/12/2023**. Use **Petty Cash** to pay for it.

5. Create a transaction for Sadie James, Partner, as a Partner's Draw for Partner 1 of $2,000 on 07/15/2023 from her equity in the business, choosing to print the check later.

6. Run the **Balance Sheet Standard** report to show a snapshot of the business for All dates.

7. Click the **Excel** `Excel ▾` button and export this report to a new worksheet, saving the worksheet to your file storage location as: **CH7_A2 Balance Sheet Standard**

8. Close Excel and the company file.

APPLY YOUR SKILLS 7-3

Account for Bad Debt

You have learned that a customer has moved out of town and you do not expect to receive payment for her outstanding invoices. In this exercise, you will write off the amount as bad debt using a credit memo.

1. Choose **File→Open or Restore Company**.

2. Open **AYS_A3_Chapter07 (Company)** or restore **AYS_A3_Chapter07 (Portable)** from your file storage location and save your file as: **AYS_A3_Chapter07 Wet Noses Clinic**

3. Create a **Bad Debt Expense** expense account, number **60500**.

4. Create a new **Other Charge** item called **Bad Debt**, setting it up as Non-Taxable and routing it to the Bad Debt Expense account you just created. Leave the amount as zero.

5. Generate a **Credit Memo/Refund** for **Natalie Sheehan: Dog-Sandy** on **07/13/2023**. Use **BD1** as the credit number for the **Bad Debt** item in the amount of **547.60**, non-taxable.

   There were two invoices outstanding: #27 for $399.50 and #117 for $148.10. All of the items on the invoices were non-taxable. The credit memo will not be printed.

6. Apply the amount of the credit to both invoices.

7. Keep the company file open for the next exercise.

APPLY YOUR SKILLS 7-4 (QG)

Buy a New Fixed Asset and Work with Liabilities

In this exercise, you will enter a new ultrasound machine into the Fixed Asset Item List. Then you will pay the sales tax due and use the Loan Manager to track the loan that you took out for the ultrasound machine.

1. Use the following information to create a new fixed asset item:
   - Asset Name: **Ultrasound Machine**
   - Purchase Description: **New Health Power Ultrasound Machine**
   - Date: **07/21/2023**
   - Cost: **$2,050**
   - Vendor: **Seattle Vet Supply**

- Asset Account: **15000•Furniture and Equipment**
- Asset Description: **High Performance +7.5 MHz Vet Ultrasound**

2. Run the **Sales Tax Liability** report for July 2023. Close the report once you have noted the total amount due.

3. **Pay Sales Tax** on **07/31/2023**, through **07/31/2023**, ensuring that **Checking** is the payment account. Choose for the check to be printed and to pay all tax due.

4. Create a new Long Term Liability account numbered **26000**, called **Loan-Ultrasound**, and then fund the loan by entering an increase to the Ultrasound Loan account for **$2,050** on **07/22/2023**, debiting the **15000•Furniture and Equipment** fixed asset account.

5. Use a **What If Scenario** to calculate the monthly payment amount of a loan for **$2,050** for **36** months at **7.8%** interest.

6. Create a new loan in the **Loan Manager** using the following information:

Account Name	**Loan-Ultrasound**	Payment Amount	**$64.05**
Lender	**Bank of Bothell**	Payment Period	**Monthly**
Origination Date	**07/21/2023**	Interest Rate	**7.8%**
Original Amount	**$2,050**	Payment Account	**Checking**
Term	**36** months	Interest Expense Account	**Interest Expense**
Due Date of Next Payment	**08/21/2023**	Fees/Charges Expense Account	**Bank Service Charge**

7. Run the **Account Listing** report.

8. Click the **Excel** Excel ▼ button and export this report to a new worksheet, saving the worksheet to your file storage location as: **CH7_A4 Account Listing**

9. Close **Excel** and then close your company file.

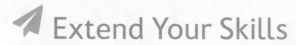 Extend Your Skills

Before You Begin: Open **EYS_Chapter07 (Company)** or restore **EYS_Chapter07 (Portable)** from your file storage location.

You have been hired by Arlaine Cervantes to help her with her organization's books. She is the founder of Niños del Lago, a nonprofit organization that provides impoverished Guatemalan children with an engaging educational camp experience. You have just sat down at your desk and opened a large envelope from her with a variety of documents and noticed that you have several emails from her as well. It is your job to sort through the papers and emails and make sense of what you find, entering information into QuickBooks whenever appropriate and answering any other questions in a word-processing document saved as: **EYS_Chapter07 _LastnameFirstinitial**. Remember, you are digging through papers you just dumped out of an envelope and addressing random emails from Arlaine, so it is up to you to determine the correct order in which to complete the tasks.

- Receipt from USPS: Dated 8/15/2019, $46.00 for 100 first-class stamps, paid for with petty cash.

- Deposit slip: Check #578 for $5,000 from the House Foundation, deposited in the Checking account on 8/12/2019; $200 was kept back for petty cash.

- Bill from landlord of U.S. office for six months of rent at a discount: Arlaine wrote a note on the bill stating she wants to take advantage of a discounted rent by prepaying it for six months. The amount per month is $500, payable to Keely Amaral Properties, LLC. Pay the rent for August 2019 on 8/5/2019 and then set it up for the remaining months of rent to automatically transfer the on the fifth of each month for the remainder of the six-month term.

- Note from the accountant: Need to set up account for loan for new computer equipment for U.S. office. Total financed is $3,029. Loan was funded on 8/10/2019. Please set up the equipment as a fixed asset item as well, using Furniture & Equipment as the account. Description of equipment is two new Sony desktop computers, two 21-inch dual monitors, and a new laser printer. The vendor is Lancaster Computer Sales. It was financed by Cherry City Finance.

- Scribbled note from Arlaine: I would like to set up a budget for our new fiscal year (July 2019– June 2020) based on the amounts spent and received in July and August. Is that something you could do in QuickBooks for me? If so, please create the budget for me and save it for me as a PDF file so I can send it by email.

8 | Using QuickBooks for Payroll

P ayroll is a sensitive subject as it affects people's livelihoods. As an employer, you should be well-informed of all payroll options and well-equipped to efficiently manage payroll for your business. In this chapter, you will first manage the Employees List and input payroll information from an outside service. Then you will examine how QuickBooks deals with payroll by creating paychecks, tracking payroll liabilities, and processing payroll forms by using a sample company file that includes a free payroll subscription.

LEARNING OBJECTIVES

▸ Manage the Employees List

▸ Input information from an outside payroll service into QuickBooks

▸ Set up QuickBooks to run payroll

▸ Create paychecks

▸ Track and pay payroll liabilities

▸ Fix payroll errors

▸ Process payroll forms and reports

📁 Project: Average Guy Designs

Average Guy Designs has been doing so well that Guy needs to hire three employees. You know that Guy has been using an outside service to run the company's payroll, so you will enter the new employees into the Employees List and then enter the information from the payroll service for them. You will also evaluate payroll options available through QuickBooks instead of an outside service and complete a payroll cycle with a sample company file to see how it works.

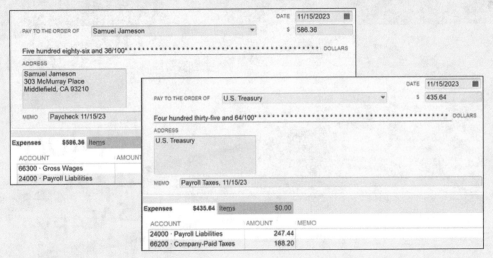

When you use an outside service for payroll, you will write checks to employees and vendors or agencies based on the information provided to you by the service.

Warning! This book teaches how to use QuickBooks to run payroll for a company using a basic service with a sample company file as well as fictitious information from an outside payroll service. Contact your local tax agency to determine which tax laws apply to you and to whom you should submit taxes. Do NOT use the specific percentages, vendors, or amounts shown, even if from your local jurisdiction, because tax laws change all the time! It is your responsibility to stay informed, either on your own or through a paid service (such as those offered by Intuit).

Working with Employees in QuickBooks

The QuickBooks definition of an employee is someone to whom you issue a W-2 at the end of the year. Subcontractors are *not* to be entered into the Employees List but should be entered as vendors. You will use the Employee Center to track employees.

Managing the Employees List

You will edit, delete, and create new employees the same way you did for customers and vendors. New employees can also be set up as part of the QuickBooks Payroll Setup Interview.

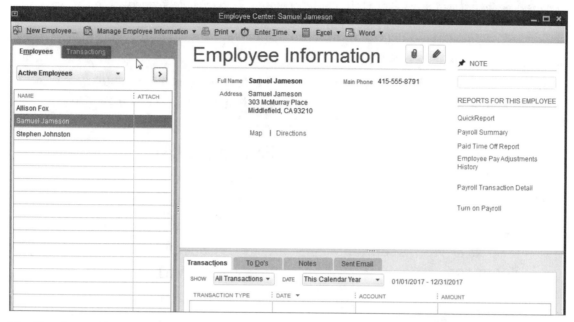

The Employee Center

Setting Up a New Employee

Employee information required for payroll setup include name, address, Social Security number, birth date, and federal and state exemption information. Also needed are the salaries, hourly wages, bonuses, and additional deductions to be withheld, such as investment plan contributions or child support payments for your employees.

In addition, to run payroll you must enter tax information for each employee. If you don't have your employees' W-4 forms handy, you can always add the information later—as long as it is entered before you first run payroll. (This is not optional!)

It is important to have all of your employees' W-4 and I-9 forms filed neatly with all personnel records (or that your outside payroll service has all of them completed). Workers' compensation companies thoroughly review company payroll records. Even though you do not treat independent contractors as employees in QuickBooks, it is important that you have an I-9 form on file for each subcontractor as well.

Setting Employee Defaults

Before setting up your employees, you should set the employee defaults if you are using Quick-Books for payroll. When setting employee defaults, you choose the options that apply to the majority of employees you will create; for example, pay schedule, health insurance, and union dues. These preferences are applied to each new employee you create, and you can change them as needed.

 Employees→Employee Center: New Employee

In this exercise, you will set up three employees for Average Guy Designs. The password for all files unless otherwise stated is Password1. *Leave the company file open unless otherwise instructed.*

1. Start QuickBooks 2019 and toggle to Pro, if necessary.
2. Choose **File→Open or Restore Company**.
3. Open **DYS_Chapter08 (Company)** or restore **DYS_Chapter08 (Portable)** from your file storage location and save your file as: **DYS_Chapter08 Average Guy Designs**

Set Up a New Employee Using the Employees List

4. Click the **Employees** button in the Employees area of the Home Page.
5. Click the **New Employee** button on the Employee Center toolbar.
6. Enter this information to set up the personal information for an employee:
   - Legal Name: **Mr. Stephen Johnston**
   - Social Security No.: **999-22-3333**
   - Gender: **Male**
   - Date of Birth: **111276**
   - Marital Status: **Single**
   - US Citizen: **Yes**
   - Ethnicity: **White**
   - Disabled: **No**
   - I-9 on-file: **Yes**
   - U.S. Veteran: **Yes**
   - Status: **Reserve**
7. Click the **Address & Contact** tab to enter this information for Stephen Johnston:
   - Address: **7534 Golden Pony Road**
   - City: **Bayshore**
   - State: **CA**
   - Zip: **94326**
   - Main Phone: **(415) 555-0530**
8. Click **OK** and then click **Leave As Is** in the New Employee: Payroll Info (other) window.

Add Additional Employees

You will now help Gary add two more employees—Sam Jameson and Allison Fox!

9. Use this information to add two more employees.

   First additional employee:
   - Legal Name: **Mr. Samuel Jameson**
   - Social Security No.: **999-88-7777**
   - Gender: **Male**
   - Date of Birth: **013078**
   - Marital Status: **Married**
   - US Citizen: **Yes**
   - Ethnicity: **White**
   - Disabled: **No**
   - I-9 on-file: **Yes**
   - U.S. Veteran: **Yes**
   - Status: **Reserve**
   - Address: **303 McMurray Place**
   - City: **Middlefield**
   - State: **CA**
   - Zip: **93210**
   - Main Phone: **(415) 555-8791**

Second additional employee:

- Legal Name: **Ms. Allison Fox**
- Social Security No.: **999-77-5555**
- Gender: **Female**
- Date of Birth: **040572**
- Marital Status: **Domestic Partner**
- US Citizen: **Yes**
- Ethnicity: **American Indian**

- Disabled: **No**
- I-9 on-file: **Yes**
- U.S. Veteran: **No**
- Address: **130 Technology Way**
- City: **Bayshore**
- State: **CA**
- Zip: **94326**
- Main Phone: **(415) 555-7733**

10. Close the Employee Center.

Working with an Outside Payroll Service

Many companies choose to go with an outside payroll service. If this is the case, you still must enter the information into QuickBooks so you can create meaningful financial statements. The level of information you track in QuickBooks does not have to be as detailed when you use an outside service because much of the information is tracked for you.

Information to Track

You need not worry about setting up QuickBooks for payroll or using the payroll features of the software because you are not tracking specific withholdings and deductions. Your intent when working with an outside service is to track expenses, cash flow, and balances being held in liability accounts so your balance sheet, profit & loss, and cash flow reports are accurate.

Warning! Do not turn on the QuickBooks payroll features if you track payroll from an outside source.

Track Employees

Enter your employees into the Employees List in QuickBooks. You will not need to enter information on the Payroll Info tab, though, as that will be tracked by the service.

Track Expenses

To account for the payroll expenses for your company, you set up an expense account, such as Payroll Expenses, and appropriate subaccounts for each type of payroll expense. Examples of subaccounts are Gross Wages, Company-Paid Benefits, and Company-Paid Taxes.

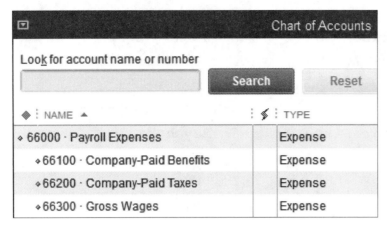

Notice the subaccounts that are set up for Payroll Expenses and used to track information from an outside payroll service.

Track Liabilities

You will still be holding deductions and withdrawals from employees that have to be paid to the appropriate agency in the future. To do so requires that you set up an Other Current Liability account, such as Payroll Liabilities, to track this information.

Enter Information from the Outside Service into QuickBooks

When you receive a report from the payroll service that shows the payroll activity for your company, you will need to enter it into QuickBooks. You will see payments going to employees and out to the agencies for which you are currently holding funds in the Payroll Liabilities account.

Enter Employee Paychecks

Employee paychecks are entered in the Write Checks window. You enter gross wages on the first line of the Expenses tab. All deductions are entered on the second line as a negative amount and will flow to the Payroll Liabilities account.

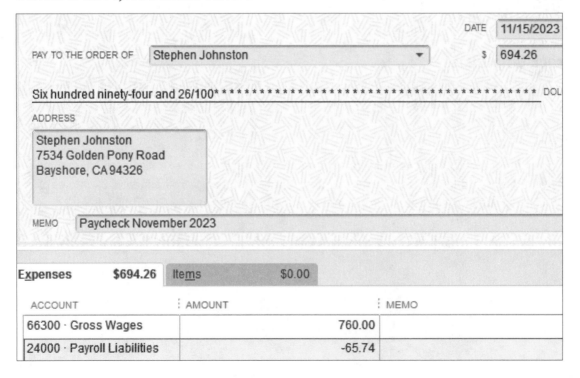

Enter Tax and Benefit Payments

When using an outside payroll service, you also use the Write Checks window to enter payments when you pay the payroll liabilities. On the Expense tab, you enter the employee-paid taxes and deductions being held in Payroll Liabilities. Company-paid taxes and benefits are entered on separate lines using the appropriate Payroll Expenses subaccounts.

> **Warning!** What we are talking about here applies *only* when a company is using an outside payroll service! *Never* use the Write Checks window for payroll transactions if you are completing payroll using QuickBooks' Payroll feature!

BEHIND THE SCENES

When you issue paychecks from an outside service, you credit Checking and Payroll Liabilities, while debiting the Gross Wages subaccount of Salary Expense.

66300•Gross Wages		24000•Payroll Liabilities		10000•Checking	
2,460.00			272.04		2,187.96

When it is time to pay the payroll liabilities, you debit that account as well as the expense account that tracks company-paid taxes. Checking is credited for the total amount. Below, only the federal taxes are being paid (hence the different amount from the example above).

66200•Company-Paid Taxes		24000•Payroll Liabilities		10000•Checking	
188.20		247.44			435.64

🔧 Edit→Preferences: Payroll & Employees→Company Preferences tab

🔧 Banking→Write Checks

🔧 File→Print Forms→Checks

DEVELOP YOUR SKILLS 8-2

In this exercise, you will enter information from an outside payroll service for the first half of November 2023 (employees are paid on the 15th and last day of each month). To begin, you will turn off payroll in QuickBooks.

1. Choose **Edit→Preferences**.
2. Click the **Payroll & Employees** category.
3. Click the **Company Preferences** tab.
4. Choose **No Payroll** to turn off the QuickBooks payroll features and click **OK**; then click **OK** in the Warning window.

Set Up Expense and Liability Accounts

5. Choose **Lists→Chart of Accounts** and then scroll down to verify that 24000•Payroll Liabilities and 66000•Payroll Expenses are set up.

   You will now create the expense subaccounts to track payroll expenses.

6. Click the **Account** drop-down arrow ▼ and then choose **New**.

7. Use this information to create the new account:

   • Type: **Expense** (click **Continue**)

   • Number: **66100**

   • Account Name: **Company-Paid Benefits**

   • Subaccount Of: Click in the checkbox and then click the drop-down arrow ▼ and choose **66000•Payroll Expenses**

8. Click **Save & New**.

9. Now create two more Payroll Expenses subaccounts with this information, choosing **Save & Close** when finished:

   • **66200•Company-Paid Taxes**

   • **66300•Gross Wages**

10. In the Chart of Accounts window, choose **Account** ▼**→Hierarchical View** and then click **Yes** in the Hierarchical View window to see the subaccounts indented under the main account.

11. Close the Chart of Accounts window.

Create Paychecks Using Data from an Outside Service

You will now enter data received from an outside payroll service into QuickBooks. Here is the statement received from the payroll service:

AVERAGE GUY DESIGNS NOVEMBER 2023 MONTHLY PAYROLL						
Employee	Gross Wages	Employee Fed Taxes W/H	Employee State Taxes W/H	Net Pay	Company Fed Taxes Owed	Company Benefits Owed
Allison Fox	$1,000.00	$82.66	$10.00	$907.34	$76.50	$203.50
Samuel Jameson	$700.00	$106.64	$7.00	$586.36	$53.56	$0.00
Stephen Johnston	$760.00	$58.14	$7.60	$694.26	58.14	$0.00
Totals, 11/15/2023	$2,460.00	$247.44	$24.60	$2,187.96	$188.20	$203.50

Note! In this example, all employee federal taxes, withholding and FICA, are combined.

12. Choose **Company→Home Page** and then click the **Write Checks** 🖎 task icon in the Banking area of the Home Page.

13. Use this information to create the first paycheck for Allison:

   • On the Main tab, click the checkbox for **Print Later**

- Bank Account: **10000•Checking**
- Date: **111523**
- Pay to the Order of: **Allison Fox**
- Click **Not Now** in the Warning window, whenever necessary, to indicate that you will not turn on Payroll.
- $ (Amount): **907.34**
- Memo: **Paycheck 11/15/2023**

14. Use this information to complete the paycheck:

Expenses	$907.34	Items
ACCOUNT		**AMOUNT**
Ⓐ 66300 · Gross Wages		1,000.00
Ⓑ 24000 · Payroll Liabilities		-92.66

  Ⓐ Account and Amount (first row): **66300•Gross Wages** and **1000**

  Ⓑ Account and Amount (second row): **24000•Payroll Liabilities** and **-92.66**

Whenever necessary, click Cancel *in the QuickBooks message regarding paying payroll liabilities.*

15. Click **Save & New**.

16. Use this information to record Samuel's paycheck:
- Bank Account: **10000•Checking**
- Date: **111523**
- Pay to the Order of: **Samuel Jameson**
- $ (Amount): **586.36**
- Memo: **Paycheck 11/15/2023**
- Account and Amount (first row): **66300•Gross Wages** and **700**
- Account and Amount (second row): **24000•Payroll Liabilities** and **-113.64**

17. Click **Save & New**.

18. Using the information in the preceding steps and the data in the monthly payroll statement, create a November 15, 2023, paycheck for **Stephen Johnston**.

19. Click **Save & New** and leave the Write Checks window open.

BEHIND THE SCENES BRIEF

66300•Gross Wages DR 2,460.00; **24000•Payroll Liabilities CR <272.04>, 10000•Checking CR <2,187.96>**

Warning! Remember, you use the Write Checks window to create paychecks only if you use an outside payroll service. *Never* use it if you are running payroll through QuickBooks!

Pay Payroll Liabilities

Now you will use the monthly payroll statement to create a payroll liability check and a benefits check for November 15, 2023. The state taxes are due quarterly, so you will not remit them at this time.

20. Use this information to create a liability check to the U.S. Treasury for all federal taxes owed (this includes the amount held in Payroll Liabilities as well as the amount owed by the company):

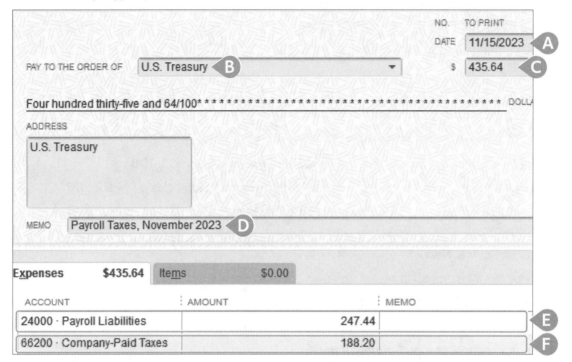

ⓐ Date: **111523**

ⓑ Pay to the Order of: **U.S. Treasury** (**Quick Add** it as a **Vendor**)

ⓒ $ (Amount): **435.64**

ⓓ Memo: **Payroll Taxes, November 2023**

ⓔ Account and Amount (first row): **24000•Payroll Liabilities** and **247.44**

ⓕ Account and Amount (second row): **66200•Company-Paid Taxes** and **188.20**

> **BEHIND THE SCENES BRIEF**
>
> 24000•Payroll Liabilities DR 247.44, 66200•Company-Paid Taxes DR 188.20;
> **10000•Checking CR <435.64>**

21. Click **Save & New**.

22. Use this information to record the benefits payment:

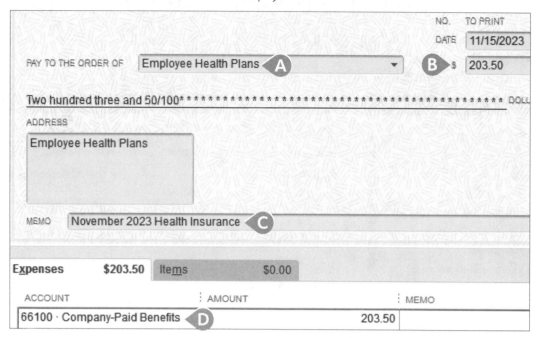

(A) Pay to the Order of: **Employee Health Plans** (**Quick Add** it as a **Vendor**)

(B) $ (Amount): **203.50**

(C) Memo: **November 2023 Health Insurance**

(D) Account: **66100•Company-Paid Benefits**

23. Click **Save & Close**.

BEHIND THE SCENES BRIEF

66100•Company-Paid Benefits DR 203.50; **10000•Checking CR <203.50>**

Print Paychecks and Liability Checks

The final step is to print the paycheck and liability checks. Because you have additional checks in the queue, you will print them as well.

24. Click the **Print Checks** 🖶 task icon in the Banking area of the Home Page.

25. Click **OK** to choose to print the checks in the queue, including the paychecks and liability checks you just created; the first check # should be 1259.

26. Verify the information is correct in the Print Checks window and then choose to either print the checks to PDF or physically print them. (Ask your instructor what you are required to do.)

27. If you printed the checks, click **OK** in the Print Confirmation window.

28. Choose **File→Close Company**.

Setting Up QuickBooks to Run Payroll

Now that you have learned about working with the Employee Center and how to enter payroll from an outside service, you will look at the payroll options in QuickBooks and learn how to set up payroll items properly.

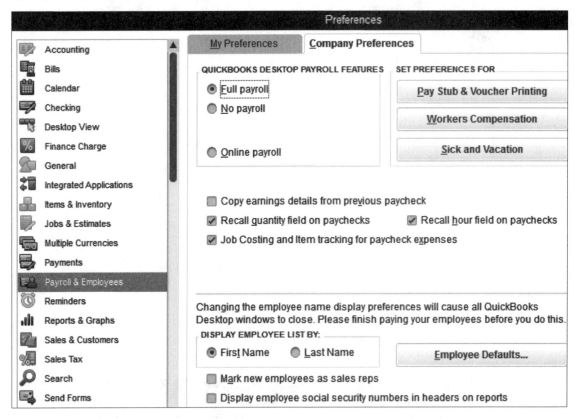

Notice all the preferences the company administrator can set for payroll.

Payroll Recordkeeping in QuickBooks

To produce the required federal, state, and local payroll forms and reports, QuickBooks keeps a separate set of records for payroll. This separate set of records tracks payroll liabilities, paychecks (and the items listed on them), and taxes. Due to this method of payroll recordkeeping, only those transactions entered via QuickBooks' payroll features will affect payroll reporting.

Evaluating Payroll Options

QuickBooks payroll offers multiple options: Manual, Basic, Enhanced, and Full Service. In addition, there are separate services for accountants, online edition users, and those who need to process household and nanny payroll. There are also mobile payroll apps that allow you to keep up with your payroll tasks on the go. Each option has its pros and cons, and all but the Manual option have an associated fee for the service. Intuit does not recommend the Manual option, as it requires you to stay on top of all tax law changes and there is a higher likelihood of errors and resulting penalties when you have to enter everything yourself.

Note! Intuit produces a separate line of products for the Canadian market that addresses multiple currencies and Canadian payroll regulations. Find more information at: quickbooks.ca

To learn more about the payroll options available through QuickBooks, visit the Intuit website at: quickbooks.intuit.com. QuickBooks can change its payroll options at any time, so it is advised that you check out the website to ensure you are dealing with the most current information.

QuickBooks is not ideal for all companies' payroll needs. If multiple states require you run payroll for an individual employee, or you withhold a certain percentage of wages on paychecks, using QuickBooks for payroll may not be the best solution for you.

Common Mistakes When Using QuickBooks for Payroll

Two common mistakes people make when using QuickBooks for payroll are:

- Making a payroll liabilities adjustment with a journal entry
- Paying the liabilities with a "regular check" rather than a liability check similar to what you used when paying sales tax

In both cases, the Chart of Accounts is affected, but the separate payroll records that Quick-Books keeps is not. If you have used a regular check for payroll liabilities, you will need to make an adjustment in the Liability Adjustment window, from where you can choose for QuickBooks to not affect the Chart of Accounts.

Another common error is for people to set up their payroll items incorrectly. If you choose to use subaccounts and remap your payroll accounts manually, be careful to map the payroll items correctly!

Entering Historical Amounts

If you are beginning to use the QuickBooks payroll feature for existing employees who have received at least one paycheck from you (and it is not the first day of January), you must enter the payroll history amounts. This will ensure that QuickBooks properly calculates taxes with thresholds. It also ensures that you will be able to produce accurate W-2s at the end of the year.

QuickBooks offers step-by-step help to assist you in entering the required payroll history. Before you begin setting up historical amounts, make sure you have:

- Prior-period paychecks
- Prior liability payments

Step-by-step help for this task is accessible through the QuickBooks Payroll Setup Interview. After you have entered the information, you will have the opportunity to reconcile and verify your data to ensure it is correct.

FLASHBACK TO GAAP: TIME PERIOD

Remember that the activities of the business can be divided into time periods.

 Edit→Preferences: Payroll & Employees: Company Preferences tab

In this exercise, you will view how to set the payroll preference for a company. The first step is to open a QuickBooks sample file that includes a payroll service. The password for all files unless otherwise stated is Password1.

> **Note!** You will be using a sample data file provided by Intuit, with dates set in 2017, 2018, and 2019. Net amounts and tax amounts may vary depending on the QuickBooks release installed on your computer. If prompted, you can choose Update Now; however, you will not be able to open your company file in an older version of QuickBooks if you do.

1. Choose **File→Open or Restore Company**.
2. Open **DYS_Chapter08-PR (Company)** or restore **DYS_Chapter08-PR (Portable)** from your file storage location and save your file as: **DYS_Chapter08-PR**
3. Click **OK** in the QuickBooks Desktop Information window.

View the Payroll Preference

If you are setting up QuickBooks to run payroll for the first time in your company file, you must set the preference. In this case, you will verify that it is set correctly.

4. Choose **Edit→Preferences**.
5. Click the **Payroll & Employees** category and then the **Company Preferences** tab.
6. Notice that Full Payroll is turned on for this company file.
7. Click **Cancel** to close the Preferences window.

Payroll Deductions

You have learned about two of the three main tasks associated with setting up QuickBooks to run payroll—setting up payroll items and employees. Now you will need to let QuickBooks know which taxes and deductions to collect and to whom they need to be paid. You can use the QuickBooks Payroll Setup Interview to walk through the taxes you have set up to make sure they are correct. In addition, you can view the Payroll Item Listing report to verify that the taxes and deductions are being routed to the right expense and liability accounts, as well as the actual Payroll Item List to make sure the vendors to whom you pay them are correct.

You must have your Federal Employer Identification Number (FEIN or EIN for Employer Identification Number) listed in your company file for payroll to be processed correctly. If you did not enter this correctly when you created your company file, you can make that change at any time.

The Payroll Setup Interview

To set up payroll in QuickBooks, you are provided with a Payroll Setup Interview that will walk you through the steps to make sure you set up taxes, compensation, and benefits correctly. After the interview leads you through the steps to set up your payroll items, it will help you to set up your employees and enter historical amounts so you can begin doing your company's payroll in QuickBooks.

Payroll Items

Anything you wish to include on a paycheck—such as wages, taxes, employee loans, and 401(k) withholdings—must first be set up as a payroll item. Most payroll mistakes are made because payroll items were not set up properly.

ITEM NAME	TYPE	A...	LIMIT	TAX TRACKING	PAYABLE TO	ACCOUNT ID
Sick - Hourly	Hourly Wage			Compensation		
Vacation - Hourly	Hourly Wage			Compensation		
Bonus (one-time cash award)	Addition	0.00		Compensation		
Employee Advance	Addition	0.00		None		
Mileage Reimbursement	Addition	0.00		None		
125 -Health Insurance (pre-tax)	Deduction	0.00		Premium Only/1...	Sec125 Administrator	Acct# 870547
401(k) Emp.	Deduction	0.00		401(k)	401K Administrator	45632010
Charity Donation	Deduction	0.00		None	Ninos del Lago	AGD
Insurance Emp -Other (taxable)	Deduction	0.00		Other	Natural Health Insura...	87-5541
Owner's Labor Deduction	Deduction	0.00		None		
Wage Garnishment	Deduction	0.00		None	County Financial Serv...	00-7904153
Workers Compensation	Company C...			None		
Advance Earned Income Credit	Federal Tax			Advance EIC Pa...	My Local Bank	94-4555555
Federal Unemployment	Federal Tax	0.6%	7,000.00	FUTA	My Local Bank	94-4555555
Federal Withholding	Federal Tax			Federal	My Local Bank	94-4555555
Medicare Company	Federal Tax	1.4...		Comp. Medicare	My Local Bank	94-4555555
Medicare Employee	Federal Tax	1.4...		Medicare	My Local Bank	94-4555555
Social Security Company	Federal Tax	6.2%	127,200....	Comp. SS Tax	My Local Bank	94-4555555
Social Security Employee	Federal Tax	6.2%	-127,200...	SS Tax	My Local Bank	94-4555555

Payroll Item ▼   Activities ▼   Reports ▼   ☐ Include inactive

The Payroll Item List displays all payroll items, from compensation to taxes and other deductions. Keep in mind that the payroll item limits change often and that the figures in this image are simply an example and are not to be used for your own company.

> **Tip!** If you need to add payroll items later, you can always return to the QuickBooks Payroll Setup Interview or access the Payroll Item List from the menu bar.

Making Payroll Data More Meaningful

When you turn on the payroll preference in QuickBooks, the payroll expense and liability accounts are created for you. QuickBooks then routes payroll items set up through the Quick-Books Payroll Setup to these accounts. To provide more meaningful information in your reports and make troubleshooting more user-friendly, you may want to set up subaccounts for the payroll accounts QuickBooks creates for you. When you create these subaccounts, you must remap each payroll item to the correct one through the Payroll Item List.

Verifying Correct Payroll Item Setup

To verify that payroll items are set up correctly and mapped to the correct accounts, run a Payroll Item Listing report (which you will run later in this chapter). If you see either Payroll

Liability-Other or Payroll Expense-Other displayed on a balance sheet or P&L, you know that you have a payroll item mapped to a parent account rather than to a subaccount.

Average Guy Designs. Chapter 8-PR
Payroll Item Listing

Payroll Item	Type	Amount	Limit	Expense Account	Liability Account	Tax Tracking
Owner's Time Unbillable	Hourly Wage			3000 · Gary Marshall Ca...		Compensation
Sick - Hourly	Hourly Wage			6500 · Wages - Non Pro...		Compensation
Vacation - Hourly	Hourly Wage			6500 · Wages - Non Pro...		Compensation
Bonus (one-time cash award)	Addition	0.00		6500 · Wages - Non Pro...		Compensation
Employee Advance	Addition	0.00		1310 · Employee Advan...		None
Mileage Reimbursement	Addition	0.00		6130 · Car/Truck Expen...		None
125 -Health Insurance (pre-tax)	Deduction	0.00			2100 · Payroll Liabilities:2110 · SEC125 M...	Premium Only/125
401(k) Emp.	Deduction	0.00			2100 · Payroll Liabilities:2120 · 401K Pay...	401(k)
Charity Donation	Deduction	0.00			2100 · Payroll Liabilities	None
Insurance Emp -Other (taxable)	Deduction	0.00			6500 · Wages - Non Project Related:6516...	Other
Owner's Labor Deduction	Deduction	0.00			3000 · Gary Marshall Capital:3130 · Gary...	None
Wage Garnishment	Deduction	0.00			2100 · Payroll Liabilities	None
Workers Compensation	Company Cont...			6500 · Wages - Non Pro...	2100 · Payroll Liabilities	None
Advance Earned Income Credit	Federal Tax				2100 · Payroll Liabilities:2130 · Payroll Ta...	Advance EIC Paym...
Federal Unemployment	Federal Tax	0.6%	7,000.00	6500 · Wages - Non Pro...	2100 · Payroll Liabilities:2130 · Payroll Ta...	FUTA
Federal Withholding	Federal Tax				2100 · Payroll Liabilities:2130 · Payroll Ta...	Federal
Medicare Company	Federal Tax	1.45%		6500 · Wages - Non Pro...	2100 · Payroll Liabilities:2130 · Payroll Ta...	Comp. Medicare
Medicare Employee	Federal Tax	1.45%			2100 · Payroll Liabilities:2130 · Payroll Ta...	Medicare
Social Security Company	Federal Tax	6.2%	127,200.00	6500 · Wages - Non Pro...	2100 · Payroll Liabilities:2130 · Payroll Ta	Comp. SS Tax

Notice that the Payroll Item Listing report shows you what happens behind the scenes with expense and liability accounts when you use a payroll item.

Workers' Compensation Insurance

QuickBooks can process workers' compensation insurance in much the same way that it processes payroll taxes. To track this payroll expense, the preference must be turned on.

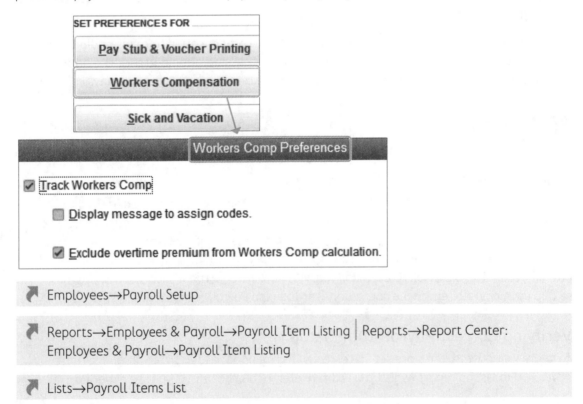

Employees→Payroll Setup

Reports→Employees & Payroll→Payroll Item Listing | Reports→Report Center: Employees & Payroll→Payroll Item Listing

Lists→Payroll Items List

In this exercise, you will make sure the FEIN is entered properly and the company is set up correctly to account for payroll taxes and deductions.

1. Choose **Company→My Company**, resizing the window, if necessary.

2. Verify that **94-4555555** is the FEIN entered for Average Guy Designs and then close the My Company window.

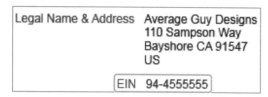

Verify Correct Payroll Tax Setup

You will now use the QuickBooks Payroll Setup Interview as a tool to make sure the payroll taxes are set up properly. If there is an obvious error, QuickBooks will alert you and ask you to make a change.

3. Choose **Employees→Payroll Setup** from the menu bar.

4. Click in the box to the left of **Taxes** and then click **Continue**.

   You will see a list of federal taxes that have been set up for you. Notice that both Medicare and Social Security have two separate entries; they are paid by both company and employee.

5. Click **Continue**.

   On this next screen, you will see the state taxes that QuickBooks has set up for you. Remember that this text is meant to be a training tool only. You must contact your accountant or local tax agency to know how to set up taxes for your jurisdiction!

6. Click **Continue**.

   A Scheduled Payments window appears, showing an error in the State Payroll Taxes account number format.

7. Enter **999–9999–9** in the CA Employment Development Dept Employer Acct No field and click **Next**.

8. Enter **999-9999-9** on the next screen as the CA Employment Development Dept Employer Acct No. and then click **Finish**.

   On this summary screen, you see how and when you pay your scheduled tax payments.

9. Click **Finish Later** at the bottom left of the QuickBooks Payroll Setup window and then click **OK** in the Finish Later window.

   Even after your payroll is set up, you can use the QuickBooks Payroll Setup feature to examine the information you have entered for it.

Create a Payroll Item Listing Report to Verify Accounts

It is important for your payroll items to link to the proper accounts in your Chart of Accounts. You will now review a report that shows how the items are linked so you can ensure you are doing payroll properly.

10. Choose **Reports→Employees & Payroll→Payroll Item Listing**.

    The Payroll Item Listing report will be displayed.

11. Note the Expense Account and Liability Account columns.

    The expense accounts indicate the payroll expenses for your company, from salaries and benefits to employer taxes you are required to pay. The liability accounts are where you "hold" the funds until you pay them to the proper taxing authority. QuickBooks keeps a separate set of records for payroll behind the scenes, so when you choose to pay your payroll liabilities with a special Liability Check window, it will "empty" these accounts properly.

12. Close the Payroll Item Listing window.

Verify Vendors and Edit a Payroll Item

The final step you will take to verify that your payroll taxes are set up properly is to make sure you are paying the taxes to the proper vendors.

13. Choose **Lists→Payroll Item List**, resizing the window as necessary so you can see all columns clearly.

    Look in the Payable To column, which shows to whom you must pay each tax you are holding in your liability accounts. Notice that there is no vendor listed for Insurance Emp-Other (taxable) in this column. You will add this information now.

14. Double-click **Insurance Emp-Other (taxable)** to open it for editing.

    An Edit Payroll Item window displays. You will be clicking Next to move through the screens to modify this item.

15. Click **Next** to keep this item name, as it is correct.

16. Use this information to select the vendor to whom you will pay the insurance premiums:

Ⓐ Agency Name: **Natural Health Insurance Co.**

Ⓑ ID Number: **87-5541**

The Liability account is correct, so you do not need to edit it.

17. Click **Next**.

18. Type **o** in the Tax Tracking Type screen to choose **Other**; click **Next**.

19. Click **Next** in the following screens: Taxes, Calculate Based on Quantity, and Gross vs. Net.

20. Click **Finish** in the Default Rate and Limit window.

   You will enter the deduction amount when you set up each new employee, rather than entering a default here.

Create a Payroll Item

You will now create a new payroll item to track court-mandated child support deductions as well as payments to a charity the company has adopted, Niños del Lago. The Payroll Item List should still be displayed from the previous step, but, if not, Choose Lists→Payroll Item List.

21. Choose **Payroll Item ▾→New**.

22. Click **Next** to choose EZ Setup.

23. Click to select **Other Deductions** and then click **Next**.

24. Click in the boxes to the left of **Wage Garnishment** and **Donation to Charity**; click **Next**.

25. Use this information to set up the payment schedule for the charity donations:

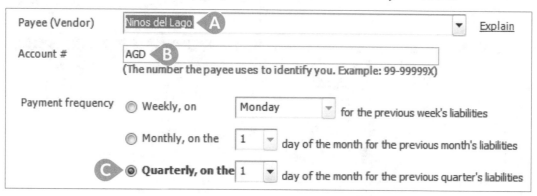

   (A) Payee (Vendor): `Ninos del Lago`

   (B) Account #: **AGD**

   (C) Payment frequency: **Quarterly, on the 1 day of the month...**

26. Click **Next** and then use this information to set up the payment schedule for the child support deductions:

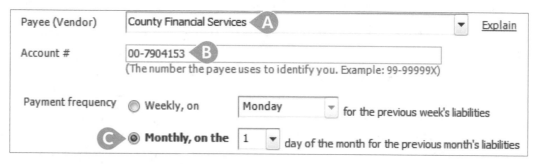

   (A) Payee (Vendor): **County Financial Services**

   (B) Account #: **00-7904153**

   (C) Payment frequency: **Monthly, on the 1 day of the month...**

27. Click **Next** and then click **Finish**.

   You will now see the Payroll Item List displayed with your two new payroll items added to it. If you wish, you can rename the items from this list.

28. Close the Payroll Item List.

Creating Paychecks

After you have chosen your payroll method, made sure your payroll items are set up properly, and set up your employees and payroll tax information, you can begin to create paychecks for your employees. When you first choose to pay employees, you will see an Enter Hours window displayed. After you have entered the paycheck information for each employee, you will see all the data displayed in the Review and Create Paychecks window.

The Pay Liabilities tab helps ensure you pay all funds in your payroll liability accounts on time.

The File Forms tab guides you through the creation of W-2s and other payroll forms.

The Pay Employees tab lets you process payroll.

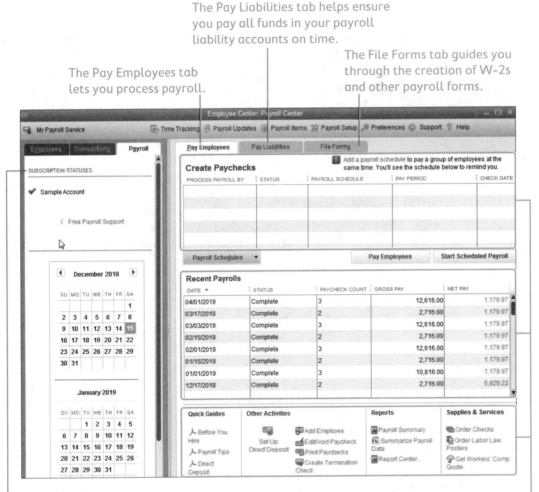

We're using the QuickBooks sample file. If you use a QuickBooks payroll service, your subscription status will appear here.

For each tab, the top portion shows current information, while the middle shows historical data. The lower portion includes links to guides, activities, and reports.

The Payroll Center, an element of the Employee Center, becomes active once you turn on the QuickBooks payroll feature.

You will have the opportunity to enter information for each employee in a Review or Change Paycheck window, moving from one employee to another using the Next and Previous buttons.

Working with Payroll Schedules

When you use QuickBooks for payroll, you have the option to set up payroll schedules so payroll runs more efficiently. Payroll schedules allow you to set how often you pay employees, the date on which the paycheck is due, and the date on which you will run payroll, all the while considering holidays and weekends to ensure you pay employees on time. Another benefit of using scheduled payroll is that you can choose to pay employees by group or by batch.

Payroll schedules are created from the Payroll Center after the payroll setup is complete. Using scheduled payroll does not limit you from creating a paycheck for an employee "off schedule."

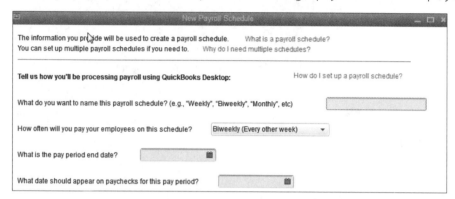

In the New Payroll Schedule window, you can set vital information that will apply to the payroll schedule being created for a group of employees.

Passing On Billable Time to Customers

If an employee has time spent on a job, those billable payroll expenses can be passed on to customers. When you create a paycheck for an employee who has billable hours, make sure to choose the correct customer or job to which to pass on the expense.

Assigning Sick or Vacation Hours

To document an employee's use of "banked" paid time off, you will assign the time to payroll items that specifically track the banked time.

BEHIND THE SCENES

When you create paychecks, you will pay employees, pay taxes, and withhold taxes from employee paychecks. In this example, we will look at Jonathan Graham's paycheck, which you will create in the next exercise. You will issue a net paycheck for $1,755.66, with $744.34 of employee deductions going to the Payroll Liability subaccounts (only the parent accounts of Payroll Liabilities and Wages are shown in this example). The gross pay is $2,500.00.

6500•Wages		2100•Payroll Liabilities		1110•Company Checking	
2,500.00			744.34		1,755.66

DEVELOP YOUR SKILLS 8-5

In this exercise, you will run payroll for two employees for the period ending 06/15/2019.

1. Choose **Company→Home Page**.
2. Click the **Pay Employees** 🖼 task icon in the Employees area of the Home Page.

   The Employee Center: Payroll Center window opens.
3. Click the **Pay Employees** button in the middle of the Pay Employees tab.

   The Enter Payroll Information window displays with the Check Date field selected.
4. Use this information to select which employees to pay, when to pay them, and what and how many hours to pay them for:

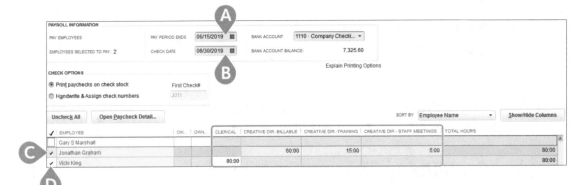

- Ⓐ Pay Period Ends: **061519** (click **Yes** in the Pay Period Change window)
- Ⓑ Check Date: **063019**
- Ⓒ Employee: Click to the left of **Jonathan Graham** to select that record and enter these hours (you may need to resize the window to see the column names):
  - Creative Dir.-Billable: **60**
  - Creative Dir.-Training: **15**
  - Creative Dir.-Staff Meetings: **5**
- Ⓓ Employee: Click to the left of **Vicki King** to select that record and enter **80** for clerical hours.

5. Click **Continue**.

   The Review and Create Paychecks window appears. When you enter the hours for each employee, QuickBooks calculates payroll taxes automatically. This will happen for your own company, as well, if you have subscribed to a QuickBooks payroll service. You can choose to do paychecks manually, but that will require you to enter each amount manually and to stay on top of all tax law changes. It results in a much greater chance for error.

6. Click **Create Paychecks**.

The Confirmation and Next Steps window appears. This window shows you the "flow" for payroll and allows you to print paychecks and pay stubs.

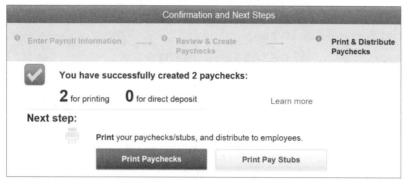

In the following Behind the Scenes Brief section, the numbers reflect both paychecks. You are also viewing the parent accounts in this case, not the various subaccounts.

BEHIND THE SCENES BRIEF

6500•Wages DR 3,460.00; **2100•Payroll Liabilities CR <915.47>**; **1110•Checking CR <2,544.53>**

Print Paychecks and Pay Stubs

After you have created paychecks, you need to print them. You will print the paychecks from the Confirmation and Next Steps window and then print the pay stubs using the menu bar command that is always available.

7. Click the **Print Paychecks** button in the Confirmation and Next Steps window.

The Select Paychecks to Print window displays. At this point, you would place preprinted checks into the printer. For this exercise there are no preprinted checks, so you will print to a PDF file.

8. Change the First Check Number to **5388** and then click **OK** to choose to print both paychecks.

The Select Paychecks to Print dialog box displays. When you are dealing with your own company, look at the checks you place in the printer to verify that the first check number is correct.

9. Choose the appropriate Printer Name that allows you to print/save to a PDF file and click **Print**.

10. Navigate to your file storage location and click **Save**.

11. Click **OK** to verify that all checks printed correctly and then close the Confirmation and Next Steps window.

Yes, you could have printed the pay stubs from that window, but it is important for you to know how to print paychecks and pay stubs from the menu bar as well!

12. Choose **File→Print Forms→Pay Stubs**.

13. Change the Checks Dated dates to: **063019** thru **063019**

Now only the pay stubs for the paychecks you just created display.

14. Click **Preview** to view what the employee pay stubs will look like. Close the Print Preview window when you are finished.

15. Close the Select Pay Stubs and the Employee Center: Payroll Center windows.

Tracking and Paying Payroll Liabilities

When you run payroll, you must collect taxes and other deductions and hold them in a Payroll Liabilities account until you are required to pay them.

QuickBooks has preset reports that you can run to determine how much you need to pay from what you hold in Payroll Liabilities. Remember that you hold taxes along with other deductions in the payroll liabilities account.

Tip! If your bank sends your federal payroll taxes electronically, clear the Print Later checkbox and enter EFTPS (Electronic Federal Tax Payment Service) in the check number field.

Average Guy Designs. Chapter 8-PR
Payroll Liability Balances
June 2019

	BALANCE
▼Payroll Liabilities	
Federal Withholding	289.00
Medicare Employee	73.70
Social Security Employee	315.89
Federal Unemployment	0.00
Medicare Company	73.70
Social Security Company	315.89
CA - Withholding	119.66
CA - Disability Employee	67.22
CA - Unemployment Company	86.52
Medicare Employee Addl Tax	0.00
CA - Employment Training Tax	0.00
125 -Health Insurance (pre-tax)	50.00
Total Payroll Liabilities	**1,391.58**

The Pay Payroll Liabilities Window

Just as you used the Pay Sales Tax window to pay your sales tax liabilities, you will use a special Pay Liabilities window to pay your payroll taxes and deductions. Never use Write Checks for your payroll taxes if you are using QuickBooks Payroll because QuickBooks will not properly debit the liability accounts.

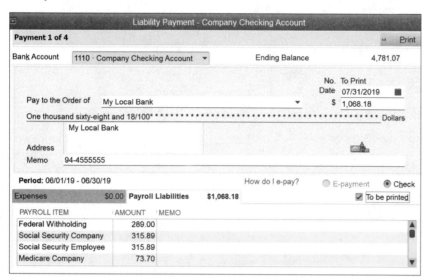

When you choose to pay payroll liabilities, they are entered in a Liability Payment window on a Payroll Liabilities tab.

BEHIND THE SCENES

When you pay your payroll liabilities, you decrease the amount in your checking (by crediting) and payroll liabilities (by debiting) accounts. In this example, you can see the result of the four liability payments ($1,068.18 + 186.88 + 50.00 + 86.52 = $1,391.58) you will make in the next exercise for 07/31/2019. Only the parent account, Payroll Liabilities, is used in this example.

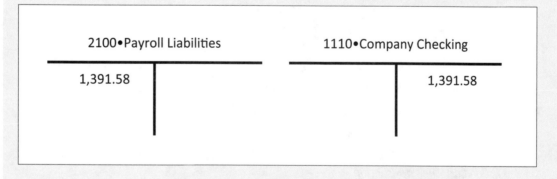

Reports→Employees & Payroll→Payroll Liability Balances

Employees→Payroll Tax and Liabilities→Pay Scheduled Liabilities

DEVELOP YOUR SKILLS 8-6

In this exercise, you will pay the payroll liabilities that have been collected. To see exactly how much you need to pay to the various payroll vendors, you will run a report that shows all taxes and deductions being held in the payroll liabilities account.

1. Choose **Reports→Employees & Payroll→Payroll Liability Balances**.

2. Set the date range for the report:
   - From: **060119**
   - To: **063019**

3. Click the **Refresh** button.

   Note the balance shown on the report.

4. Close the Payroll Liability Balances report; choose to not memorize the report.

Proceed with Paying

You are now ready to pay the payroll liabilities due in July 2019. You will pay them by using a liability check. Remember that if you are paying liabilities for your own company, you need to pay them based on the schedule that applies to your business.

5. Click the **Pay Liabilities** 🏛 task icon in the Employees area of the Home Page.

   The Employee Center: Payroll Center will launch with the Pay Liabilities tab displayed.

6. Follow these steps to pay the liabilities due in July:

	DUE DATE	STATUS	PAYMENT	METHOD	PERIOD	AMOUNT DUE
Pay Taxes & Other Liabilities						
✓	07/15/19	> 6 Months	Federal 941/944/943	Check	Jun 2019	1,068.18
✓	07/15/19	> 6 Months	CA Withholding and Disability Insura	Check	Jun 2019	186.88
✓	07/20/19	> 6 Months	125 -Health Insurance (pre-tax)	Check	Q2 2019	50.00
✓	07/31/19	> 6 Months	CA UI and Employment Training Tax	Check	Q2 2019	86.52

Total Selected Items: 1,391.58 **B** View/Pay

   A Click to select all four liabilities due.

   B Click **View/Pay**.

   The Liability Payment – Checking window (not the Write Checks window) appears with the check information for the first payroll vendor filled in.

7. Change the date on the check to **07/31/2019** and then click **Save & Next**.

   Because this is a sample company file, QuickBooks loads 12/15/2018 as the date each time you create a new transaction. In your own company file, the displayed date would be the last date you used in another transaction.

   The second liability payment information displays in the window.

8. Change the date on the second payroll liability check to **07/31/2019** and then click **Save & Next**.

9. Change the date on the third liability check to **07/31/2019**; click **Save & Next**.

10. Change the date on the fourth liability check to **07/31/2019**; click **Save & Close**.

   A Payment Summary window displays. Notice that you can print the checks from this window. If you choose to print them later, they will be placed in the queue of checks waiting to be printed, which you can access from the menu bar.

   In this Behind the Scenes Brief section, you are viewing the parent account for Payroll Liabilities, not the various subaccounts.

BEHIND THE SCENES BRIEF
2100•Payroll Liabilities DR 1,391.58; **1110•Checking CR <1,391.58>**

11. Close the Payment Summary and Employee Center: Payroll Center windows.

Correcting Payroll Errors

When correcting payroll errors, ensure that you do so properly. Remember that QuickBooks keeps a separate "set of books" for payroll, so you must make changes via the payroll features.

The Edit/Void Paychecks window allows you to choose which paycheck to edit/void and provides guidance. In the following figure, note the important message at the top of the window regarding voiding paychecks as well as the message at the bottom that refers to the selected paycheck (Vicki King's).

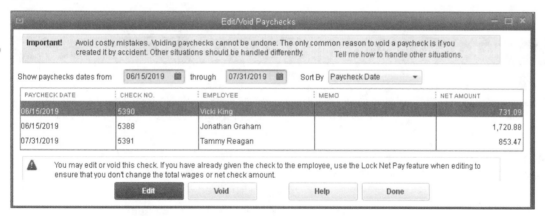

Fixing a Paycheck

It is only on rare occasions that you should void a paycheck. Two such times that it would be warranted are when you accidentally created a paycheck or when you have to correct a paycheck from a prior year.

Correcting a Paycheck Error from a Prior Year

If you need to change the date of a paycheck from one year to another, you must void the paycheck and reissue it. Voiding a paycheck is done in basically the same way as voiding any transaction in QuickBooks. Just remember that when you re-create the paycheck, you must do so through the proper method. That is, you cannot just create a new check in the Write Checks window.

Lock Net Pay Feature

If you need to make changes to a paycheck and want to make sure that you don't change the amount of the check (which is dealt with differently), you can use the Lock Net Pay feature that ensures you don't change the amount of the paycheck or the total wages. When this feature is activated, you will be able to make only changes that do not affect the amount of the check, such as the class to which it is assigned, vacation or sick time accrual, or select/deselect to use a direct deposit.

Unscheduled Payroll Checks

There may be times when you need to issue a paycheck to an employee when it is not at the end of a pay period. For instance, you may have underpaid an employee and do not want that employee to have to wait until the next payday to receive the compensation, or you may need to issue a final paycheck. These situations can easily be dealt with in QuickBooks from the Payroll Center window by choosing either to conduct an unscheduled payroll or to create a termination check.

Notice the additional options available in the Other Activities area on the Pay Employees tab of the Payroll Center.

COMMON PAYROLL ERRORS AND THEIR FIXES	
The Error	**The Fix**
An issued paycheck was lost or damaged.	Reprint and reissue the check with the next check number; document the lost check by creating and then voiding a check.
The pay period dates on a paycheck are wrong but within the same calendar year.	Edit the pay period dates in the Review Paycheck window and create a memo in the check register.
An employee was overpaid.	Correct the overpayment on the next payroll (rather than reissuing the paycheck).
An employee was underpaid.	Issue an unscheduled payroll check or correct the underpayment on the next payroll.
A paycheck item is incorrect and the error does not affect the due amount.	Edit the paycheck information while in Lock Net Pay mode.

Note! Depending on the type of payroll service you subscribe to, there may be limitations on how you will be able to correct certain payroll errors.

Making Corrections to a Payroll Liability Payment

Paying a payroll liability with a regular check rather than a liability check will create issues for you behind the scenes. To set things right, you need to void the regular check and then process the payment through the Pay Payroll Liabilities feature in QuickBooks.

DEVELOP YOUR SKILLS 8-7

In this exercise, you will replace a lost paycheck for Vicki King.

1. Click the **Check Register** 🖳 task icon in the Banking area of the Home Page.

2. Click **OK** to choose **1110•Company Checking Account** as the account to use and then resize the window.

3. Scroll, if necessary, and double-click anywhere within **Vicki King's paycheck, 5389** transaction.

   The Paycheck – Company Checking Account window displays.

4. Write down the check number (5389) and net amount ($756.20) for future reference.

5. Use this information to reprint the check:

   - Click the checkbox to select **Print Later**.
   - Click **Print** (the icon, not the drop-down arrow ▾).
   - Click **Yes** in the Recording Transaction window.
   - Click **OK** in the Print Paycheck window displaying the next check number (5390).

6. Ensure that the correct printer is selected (or choose to print to PDF) and then click **Print**; if you chose to print to PDF, navigate to your file storage location and click **Save**.

7. Click **OK** in the Print Checks Confirmation window.

   This is the check you will give Vicki.

8. Click **Save & Close** in the Paycheck – Checking window.

   Leave the 1110•Company Checking Account register window open; you will need to use it again to create and then void the lost check.

9. Choose **Banking→Write Checks**.

10. Ensure that the check will not be printed later(this option is located on the ribbon at the top of the window).

11. Use this information to create a check matching the one that was lost:

    - Check No.: **5389**
    - Date: **073119**
    - Payee: **Vicki King Employee** (click **Not Now** in the Warning window)
    - $ (Amount): **756.20**
    - Memo: **Lost paycheck, reissued as #5390**
    - Account: **6560•Payroll Expenses**

12. Click **Save & Close**; close the Set Check Reminder window, if necessary.

    The 1110•Company Checking Account register window should be displayed.

13. Locate the check you just created (5389) in the 1110•Company Checking Account window, scrolling if necessary.

14. Right-click anywhere within the two lines of the check 5389 transaction and choose **Void Check**.

    You will see VOID: *preceding the memo you entered into the check, and the dollar amount will be zero.*

15. Click **Record**; click **Yes** to record the transaction.

16. Click **No, Just Void the Check**, close the Set Check Reminder window (if necessary), and then close the Checking register window.

Working with 1099s and Processing Payroll Forms and Reports

The forms you can produce through QuickBooks depend on the payroll option selected. Let's look at a few basic payroll forms used in the United States and how QuickBooks supports each of them. If you live in Canada, check out quickbooks.ca to learn about payroll solutions and Intuit products available for the Canadian market.

W-2s and W-3s

W-2s are provided to each employee. They summarize earnings and deductions for the year. A W-3 form is what you prepare and submit to the government. It summarizes the W-2 information you provided to employees.

If you subscribe to one of the Enhanced payroll services, you can print W-2s and W-3s on blank paper right from QuickBooks. If you subscribe to the Full Service, QuickBooks will provide the completed forms for you.

940 and 941

Form 941 is the Employer's Quarterly Federal Tax Return. QuickBooks will fill in the appropriate amounts. You can edit the amounts if the IRS rules instruct you to do so.

Form 940 is the Employer's Annual Federal Unemployment (FUTA) Tax Return. QuickBooks stores forms for only one year at a time. You will need to subscribe to a payroll service to download the correct year's form. QuickBooks will fill in the appropriate amounts, which you can edit if necessary.

1099-MISC and 1096

When you have vendors to whom you subcontract work, you will report their earnings on a 1099-MISC form that is provided to them. The 1096 form is something you prepare for the federal government. It summarizes the 1099 information you provided to subcontractors.

You can print 1099-MISC forms for your subcontractors right from QuickBooks. If you subscribe to the Full Service, Intuit will prepare the 1099-MISC forms for you.

Before you can run 1099-MISC forms, you must turn on the preference and properly set up your 1099 vendors. A wizard will walk you through 1099 and 1096 form preparation and filing.

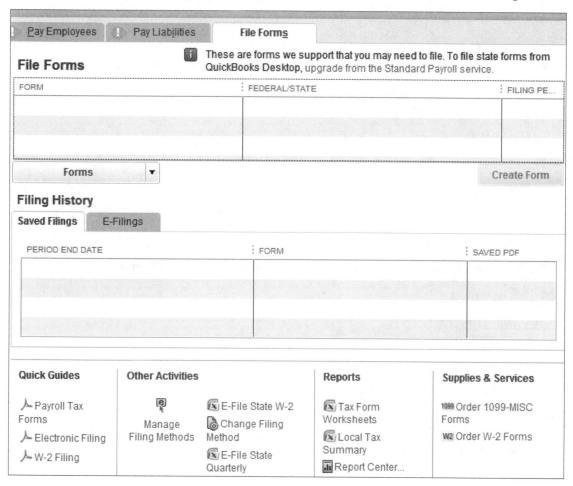

When you choose to process payroll forms, the File Forms tab of the Employee Center: Payroll Center is displayed.

Other Payroll Reports

In addition to the reports you have already seen that deal with payroll, QuickBooks provides a variety of additional reports, including some that can be run in Excel. All of these reports can be found in the Employees & Payroll category in the Report Center.

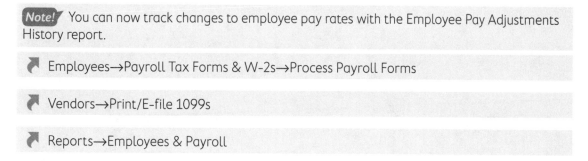

Note! You can now track changes to employee pay rates with the Employee Pay Adjustments History report.

🔋 Employees→Payroll Tax Forms & W-2s→Process Payroll Forms

🔋 Vendors→Print/E-file 1099s

🔋 Reports→Employees & Payroll

DEVELOP YOUR SKILLS 8-8

In this exercise, you will produce three payroll reports available when you use QuickBooks for payroll.

1. Choose **Reports→Employees & Payroll→Payroll Transactions by Payee**.
2. Set the report dates:
   - From: **060119**
   - To: **073119**
3. Click **Refresh** on the report toolbar.

   A report displays, showing all completed payroll transactions.
4. Close the Payroll Transactions by Payee window, choosing to not memorize it.

Produce an Employee Earnings Summary

5. Choose **Reports→Employees & Payroll→Employee Earnings Summary**.
6. Set the report dates:
   - From: **010119**
   - To: **073119**
7. Click **Refresh**.

   A report showing all amounts by payroll item for the time period displays.
8. Close the Employee Earnings Summary window, choosing to not memorize it.

Produce an Employee Withholding Report

9. Choose **Reports→Employees & Payroll→Employee Withholding**.

   A report displays to show all your employees and their tax withholding information.
10. Close the Employee Withholding window, choosing to not memorize it, and leave the company file open.

Tackle the Tasks

Now is your chance to work a little more with Average Guy Designs and apply the skills that you have learned in this chapter to accomplish additional tasks. You will use the same company file you used in the Develop Your Skills exercises throughout this chapter. Enter the following tasks, referring back to the concepts in the chapter as necessary. If you are using the trial software for this course on your computer or in a lab at school, you must toggle to the Pro edition every time you start QuickBooks.

Add an Employee	Add the following new employee.
	Tammy Reagan; SS# 333-22-1111; Female; DOB 06/17/1969; 14896 Highridge Estates, Bayshore, CA 91547; (415) 555-4004; Marital Status: Divorced; U.S. Citizen: Yes; Ethnicity: White; Disabled: No; I-9 Form: On file; U.S. Veteran: No
	On the Payroll Info tab: Pay frequency: Semimonthly; Earnings Items: Clerical; Rate $20/hour; Holiday Pay Rate $30; Deductions: 126-Health insurance $50/paycheck; click the Taxes button and then enter Federal Filing Status: Single with one allowance; State: CA; State Worked: CA; State Subject to Withholding: CA, single with one allowance
Pay Employee	Use the Pay Employees button in the Employee Center:Payroll Center window to create a paycheck for Tammy for the pay period ending 07/31/2019. Date the paycheck 07/31/2019 for 56 hours of clerical work.
Print a Paycheck and Pay Stub	Print the paycheck you just created for Tammy using check #5391; print a pay stub to go with it.
Pay Liabilities	Pay the two payroll liabilities due on 08/15/2019 from Tammy's check on 07/31/2019.
Run a Report	Create a report showing all of your employees and their withholding information.

Self-Assessment

Check your knowledge of this chapter's key concepts and skills using the Self-Assessment quiz here, in your ebook, or in your eLab course.

1. Most payroll mistakes are due to payroll items being set up incorrectly.   True   False

2. You should enter your subcontractors in the Employees List.   True   False

3. Only those transactions entered via QuickBooks' payroll features affect payroll reporting.   True   False

4. You should set up employee defaults before you set up your employees.   True   False

5. Workers' compensation can be tracked within QuickBooks Payroll.   True   False

6. Payroll schedules allow you to set how often you pay employees.   True   False

7. To pay the payroll liabilities while running full payroll in QuickBooks, you can open a Write Checks window to make the payment.   True   False

8. When you use an outside payroll service, you should set up QuickBooks to track full payroll.   True   False

9. In QuickBooks, an employee is someone to whom you issue a W-2 or a 1099-MISC.   True   False

10. If you discover that an employee was overpaid after you have issued the paycheck to the employee, void the paycheck and create a new one with the correct amount.   True   False

11. Which of these is NOT a payroll item?
    A. Federal withholding
    B. Hours worked
    C. Vacation hourly
    D. Health insurance

12. When you create paychecks, which account is credited?
    A. Gross Wages
    B. Payroll Expenses
    C. Payroll Liabilities
    D. Savings

13. In which account do you hold the taxes you withhold from your employees?
    A. Sales Tax Payable
    B. Payroll Liabilities
    C. Checking
    D. Payroll Assets

14. Which payroll form do you provide to subcontractors at the end of the year?
    A. W-2
    B. 940
    C. 1099-MISC
    D. 1096

Reinforce Your Skills

Angela Stevens has just relocated her company, Quality-Built Construction, from California to Silverton, Oregon, and has hired a new employee. You will enter a new employee, create a paycheck, and pay payroll liabilities. You will be working with a QuickBooks sample company file in these exercises as it will allow you to run full payroll without having to purchase a payroll subscription. The password for all files unless otherwise stated is Password1. Leave the company file open unless otherwise instructed. If you are using the trial software on your computer or in a lab at school, remember to toggle to the Pro edition every time you start QuickBooks.

REINFORCE YOUR SKILLS 8-1

Turn on Payroll and Enter a New Employee

In this exercise, you will add a new employee that was just hired.

1. Choose **File→Open or Restore Company**.
2. Open **RYS_Chapter08 (Company)** or restore **RYS_Chapter08 (Portable)** from your file storage location and save your file as: **RYS_Chapter08 Quality-Built Construction**
3. Click **OK** to acknowledge you are opening a QuickBooks Desktop sample file.
4. Choose **Edit→Preferences** from the menu bar.
5. Click the **Payroll & Employees** category and then the **Company Preferences** tab.
6. Confirm that the Full Payroll function is turned on and click **OK**.

Enter a New Employee

7. Choose **Employees→Employee Center**.

   The Employee Center will be displayed with seven current employees.

8. Click the **New Employee** button and use this information to set up a new employee:
   - Name: **Ms. Aiyana Harrison**
   - SSN: **999-88-6666**
   - Gender: **Female**
   - Date of Birth: **04/13/1986**
   - Marital Status: **Single**
   - U.S. Citizen: **Yes**
   - Ethnicity: **Black**
   - Disabled: **No**
   - I-9 Form: **On File**
   - U.S. Veteran: **Yes**
   - Status: **Reserve**
   - Address: **503 Birch Hill Road, Woodcrest, CA 92504**
   - Main Phone: **(951) 555-2134**

- On the Payroll Info tab in the Earnings box, Item Name: **9891-Office** (delete the other items added by default)
- Hourly Rate: `20.00`
- Filing Status and Allowances: `Single, 0`
- State worked and State Subject to Withholding: **CA**

9. Click **OK** four times , click **Leave As Is**, and then close the Employee Center window.

Create Paychecks for Employees

In this exercise, you will create a paycheck for Aiyana Harrison (only) for the period of 12/16/2019–12/31/2019. You have discovered that you don't have sufficient funds in the Payroll Checking account, so first you will transfer funds.

1. Choose **Banking→Transfer Funds** and set the date to **12/31/2019**.
2. Choose to transfer funds from **1110•Company Checking** to **1130•Payroll Checking**.
3. Enter **5000** as the transfer amount and click **Save & Close**.
4. Choose **Employees→Payroll Center**.
5. Click the **Pay Employees** button toward the center of the Payroll Center.

    No scheduled payrolls have been set up for this company, so there is no Unscheduled Payroll button. Instead, you see a Pay Employees button.

6. Set the Check Date and the Pay Period Ends date both to: **12/31/2019**
7. If the Pay Period Change Window opens, click **No**.
8. Select **Print Paychecks on Check Stock** under Check Options.
9. Enter **80** hours in the Office column and then ensure there is a check to the left of **Aiyana Harrison** to choose to pay her.

Create and Print Paychecks

You will now review the information entered for Aiyana and then create the paycheck.

10. Click **Continue**.

    The Review and Create Paychecks window displays.

11. Click **Create Paychecks**.

    The Confirmation and Next Steps window appears, showing a summary of how many paychecks were created as well as providing you with a shortcut to printing paychecks and pay stubs.

12. Click **Print Paychecks** and then type **497** as the first check number.

13. Click **OK** in the Select Paychecks to Print window and then choose to print to paper or PDF file, as desired, and click **OK** in the Print Checks Confirmation window.

14. Click the **Print Pay Stubs** button.

15. Set the date range (if necessary):
    - From: **123119**
    - To: **123119**

16. Click **Preview** to view how the pay stubs will print and then close the Print Preview window.

17. Close the Select Pay Stubs and Confirmation and Next Steps windows.

18. Close the Payroll Center.

REINFORCE YOUR SKILLS 8-3

Pay the Payroll Liabilities

In this exercise, you will pay the payroll liabilities due in January 2020.

1. Choose **Employees→Payroll Taxes and Liabilities→Pay Scheduled Liabilities**.

2. Click to the left of all liability payments due in January to place checkmarks.

3. Click the **View/Pay** button in the Pay Scheduled Liabilities area of the Payroll Center.

   A Liability Payment – Checking Account window for the first payment appears.

4. Change the date to **01/31/20** and enter **U.S. Treasury** as the vendor; click **Save & Next** to view the next payment.

5. Change all the dates to: **01/31/20**

6. Click **Save & Next** to record each liability check; click **Save & Close** when finished.

7. Close the Payment Summary window and then close the company file.

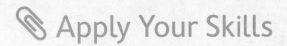

Apply Your Skills

Wet Noses Veterinary Clinic is expanding and must hire a new employee to keep up with demand. The clinic continues to use an outside payroll service and will pay employees and payroll liabilities, as well as review reports to help analyze the business spending. The password for all files unless otherwise stated is Password1. After starting QuickBooks, remember to toggle to Pro as necessary.

APPLY YOUR SKILLS 8-1 QG

Set Up QuickBooks to Track Payroll from an Outside Service

Dr. James has been using an outside payroll service. In this exercise, you will help her verify that the correct accounts are set up to properly track expenses and liabilities. Then you will enter a new employee. You will need to have accounts set up in your Chart of Accounts to track your payroll expenses and liabilities.

Note! The QuickBooks payroll features should not be turned on when entering payroll from an outside source.

1. Choose **File→Open or Restore Company**.
2. Open **AYS_A1_Chapter08 (Company)** or restore **AYS_A1_Chapter08 (Portable)** from your file storage location and save your file as: **AYS_A1_Chapter08 Wet Noses Clinic**
3. Open the **Chart of Accounts** and verify that Payroll Liabilities is set up as an Other Current Liability.
4. Scroll down and verify that Payroll Expenses is set up as an Expense account.

   Dr. James has learned that she should set up subaccounts for the Payroll Expenses account, so you will help her do this now.
5. Set up three subaccounts for Payroll Expenses: **66010•Gross Wages**, **66020•Company-Paid Taxes**, and **66030•Company-Paid Benefits**

Enter a New Employee

When entering a new employee and using an outside payroll service, you do not need to set up tax information.

6. Create a new employee for Wet Noses using this information:
   - Name: **Mr. Viho Locklear**
   - SSN: **000-33-5555**
   - Gender: **Male**
   - Date of Birth: **04/24/1983**
   - Address: **2611 Lake Road, Kirkland, WA 98034**
   - Main Phone: **(425) 555-1066**

7. Run an **Employee Contact List** report to show the details for each employee.

8. When the report is displayed, you notice that you forgot to enter phone numbers for three employees. Using QuickZoom, add the following phone numbers to the employee records and then return to the report:

   - Bently Batson: **(206) 555-8789**
   - Carrie Jones: **(425) 555-2052**
   - Samantha Reese: **(425) 555-1742**

9. Click the **Excel** | Excel ▾ | button and export this report to a new worksheet, saving the worksheet to your file storage location as: **CH8_A1 Employee Contact List**

10. Close the Excel window and close the company file.

APPLY YOUR SKILLS 8-2 QG

Create Paychecks Based on Information from an Outside Payroll Service

Dr. James received a statement from the payroll service showing the amount to pay each employee and the amount that has been deducted. In this exercise, you will help her create the paychecks for the employees.

WET NOSES VETERINARY CLINIC JUNE 2023 PAYROLL					
Employee	Gross Wages	Employee Federal Taxes Withheld	Net Pay	Company Federal Taxes Owed	Company Benefits Owed
Bently Batson	$1,500.00	$234.62	$1,265.38	$114.75	$450.00
Carrie Jones	$2,166.00	$395.72	$1,770.28	$165.70	$450.00
Samantha Reese	$2,166.00	$324.21	$1,841.79	$165.70	$450.00
Viho Locklear	$1,000.00	$119.48	$880.52	$76.50	$225.00
Totals	$6,832.00	$1,074.03	$5,757.97	$522.65	$1,575.00

1. Choose **File→Open or Restore Company**.

2. Open **AYS_A2_Chapter08 (Company)** or restore **AYS_A2_Chapter08 (Portable)** from your file storage location and save your file as: **AYS_A2_Chapter08 Wet Noses Clinic**

3. Create paychecks for the employees listed above dated **06/30/2023** using the Write Checks window.

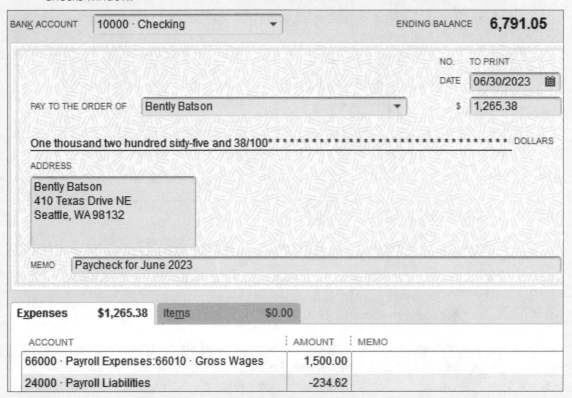

BANK ACCOUNT 10000 · Checking ▼ ENDING BALANCE **6,791.05**

NO. TO PRINT
DATE 06/30/2023 📅

PAY TO THE ORDER OF Bently Batson ▼ $ 1,265.38

One thousand two hundred sixty-five and 38/100********************************* DOLLARS

ADDRESS

Bently Batson
410 Texas Drive NE
Seattle, WA 98132

MEMO Paycheck for June 2023

Expenses **$1,265.38** Items $0.00

ACCOUNT	AMOUNT	MEMO
66000 · Payroll Expenses:66010 · Gross Wages	1,500.00	
24000 · Payroll Liabilities	-234.62	

Warning! Remember, use the Write Checks window to create paychecks only if you use an outside payroll service. *Never* use it if you are running payroll through QuickBooks!

4. Run a **QuickReport** on the **Payroll Liabilities** account to show the transaction detail for this account from **06/30/2023** to **06/30/2023**.

5. Click the **Excel** Excel ▼ button and export this report to a new worksheet, saving the worksheet as: **CH8_A2 Payroll Liabilities**

6. Close the QuickReport and Chart of Accounts windows; keep the company file open for the next exercise.

APPLY YOUR SKILLS 8-3 QG

Pay the Payroll Liabilities and Print Checks

In this exercise, you will use the information in the table shown in Apply Your Skills 8-2 to create a payroll liability checks for June 2023. You will first need to transfer funds to cover the checks you are about to write.

1. Make a $5,000 transfer from **10600•Money Market** to **10000•Checking** on 7/1/2023.

2. Open the **Write Checks** window and set the date to: **07/01/2023**

3. Create a liability check to the **U.S. Treasury** (**Quick Add** it as a **Vendor**) for all federal taxes owed.

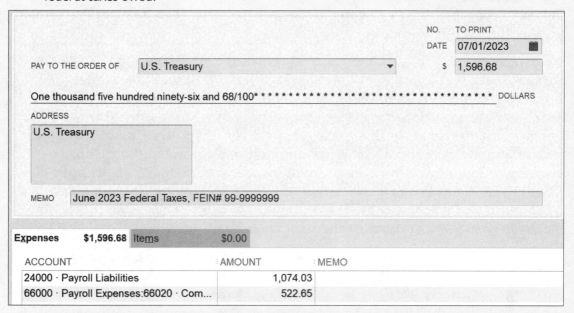

			NO.	TO PRINT
			DATE	07/01/2023
PAY TO THE ORDER OF	U.S. Treasury	▼	$	1,596.68

One thousand five hundred ninety-six and 68/100* DOLLARS

ADDRESS

U.S. Treasury

MEMO   June 2023 Federal Taxes, FEIN# 99-9999999

Expenses $1,596.68   Items $0.00

ACCOUNT	AMOUNT	MEMO
24000 · Payroll Liabilities	1,074.03	
66000 · Payroll Expenses:66020 · Com...	522.65	

4. Create a second check dated **07/01/2023** for **$1,575** made payable to **Kellerman Insurance** for the company-paid medical benefits owed, entering **June 2023 Medical/Dental Insurance for Employees** as the Memo and **66030•Company-Paid Benefits** as the Account.

5. Choose to print all checks in the queue waiting to be printed, using **1441** as the first check number.

6. Run a **Check Detail** report from the Banking section of the Report Center for checks dated from **07/01/2023** to **07/01/2023**.

7. Click the **Excel** Excel ▼ button and export this report to a new worksheet, saving the worksheet to your file storage location as: **CH8_A3 Check Detail**

8. Run a **QuickReport** for the Checking account; click **Customize Report** and choose the **Filters** tab and filter by **Name**, choosing **All Employees**, to see how much has been paid in payroll.

9. Click the **Excel** Excel ▼ button and export this report to a new worksheet, saving the worksheet to your file storage location as: **CH8_A3 Employee Payroll**

10. Close the company file.

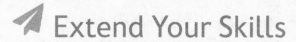# Extend Your Skills

Before You Begin: Open **EYS_Chapter08 (Company)** or restore **EYS_Chapter08 (Portable)** from your file storage location.

You have been hired by Arlaine Cervantes to help her with her organization's books. She is the founder of Niños del Lago, a nonprofit organization that provides impoverished Guatemalan children with an engaging educational camp experience. You have just sat down at your desk and opened a large envelope from her with a variety of documents and noticed that you have several emails from her as well. It is your job to sort through the papers and emails and make sense of what you find, entering information into QuickBooks whenever appropriate and answering any other questions in a word-processing document saved as **EYS1_Chapter08 _LastnameFirstinitial**. Remember, you are digging through papers you just dumped out of an envelope and addressing random emails from Arlaine, so it is up to you to determine the correct order in which to complete the tasks.

- Sticky note from Arlaine: Hired two part-time employees to work at the U.S. office to raise funds and sell inventory on 8/15/2019. Will use an outside payroll service. How will we enter the payroll information into QuickBooks? (Explain your answer.)

- Completed W-4 and I-9: Chelsea Sathrum; 8213 NW College Ct., Salem, OR, 97304; 503-555-2003; SS# 999-22-3333; Female; DOB 05/21/1988.

- Sticky note from Arlaine: Please prepare a check to pay all federal payroll liabilities that are owed. The amount in Payroll Liabilities that is owed to the U.S. Treasury is $66.55, but don't forget to pay the company's share!

- Note from accountant: Enter the accounts and subaccounts necessary to track an outside payroll service in QuickBooks.

- Statement from payroll service, dated 8/31/2019:

Employee	Gross Wages	Employee Federal & State Taxes Withheld	Net Pay	Company Federal Taxes Owed	Company Unemployment Owed
José Martinez	$450.00	$78.00	$372.00	$34.42	$16.28
Chelsea Sathrum	$420.00	$48.71	$371.29	$32.13	$15.35

- Completed W-4 and I-9: Jose Martinez; 16932 SE Freedom Way, Salem, OR 97306; SS# 999-22-1111; Male; DOB 07/04/1987.

- Scribbled note from Arlaine: Can you produce a report for me that shows how much has been paid in payroll for each employee?

9 | Job Costing, Creating Estimates, and Time Tracking

uickBooks lets you create estimates for your jobs or for your customers if you don't have jobs assigned to them. Once you're awarded a job based on an estimate, QuickBooks makes it easy to convert the estimate to an invoice, so you don't have to reenter the information. Job costing is an important aspect for many businesses. In this chapter, you will use jobs in QuickBooks to track profitability by those jobs. You will also use progress invoicing and deal with customer deposits. You will also explore the time-tracking feature, which allows you to track time spent by employees on each job, resulting in more accurate payroll expenses for job costing. Finally, we will take a look at one of the QuickBooks apps that aids you in time tracking and employee scheduling, TSheets.

LEARNING OBJECTIVES

▸ Create an estimate for a job or customer and convert it to a progress invoice

▸ Apply the time tracking feature and create a paycheck based on tracked time

▸ Enter customer deposits on account

▸ Assign finance charges to overdue accounts

▸ Run appropriate job-related reports for estimates and time tracking

Project: Average Guy Designs

Guy Marshall will be bidding for a job for the City of Bayshore to completely redo its branding, including new logo, stationery, report covers, brochures, and other business documents.

For this job, you will first create an estimate to be submitted with the proposal. When the job is awarded, you will convert the estimate to an invoice and bill the city as portions of the job are completed using QuickBooks' progress invoicing feature. You will receive payment from the city and handle customer deposits for unearned income.

In addition, time tracking will be used for those employees who worked on another job, and a paycheck will be created using the time data. Finance charges will be assessed for customers. You will then run job reports for analyzing this and other jobs, estimates, and time tracking data for the company. Finally, Guy will explore the possibility of using TSheets to track his employee time more precisely.

Job Costing

To keep track of the income and expenses involved in this and all jobs that Average Guy Designs does, individual jobs are created for each customer. When applied via sales and purchase forms, job costing provides a method for determining profitability of each job and will help in creating future plans.

Job information is stored with the customer data in the Customers & Jobs List, which is a component of the Customer Center. If you have multiple projects for an individual customer, you can create separate jobs for that customer. If you will perform just one job for a customer, you can track that information in the customer's record on the Job Info tab. As you create your estimates and invoices or incur any expenses for that job, you enter them for the job and not the customer directly.

For Average Guy Designs, all customers have a job associated with them, so you must always choose a job on a form, not just the customer.

Time tracking is a feature that allows a company to track employee time and create paychecks and invoices based on the data collected. You can also charge employees' time to jobs.

Job Profitability

For companies that deal with jobs, especially businesses such as construction companies, it is important to be able to look at the profitability of each job. To conduct job costing in QuickBooks, you need to take three basic steps:

1. Set up your data in the Customers & Jobs List.
2. Enter all job revenues and expenses.
3. Use QuickBooks reports to analyze job data.

The first two steps are covered if you set up your customers and jobs correctly and then enter them properly on sales and purchase forms. We will look at the QuickBooks job costing reports later in this chapter.

Creating an Estimate for a Job

QuickBooks creates a non-posting account when you create an estimate, which allows you to track outstanding estimates (the same as it does for purchase orders and sales orders). This account is displayed at the bottom of your Chart of Accounts. The non-posting account is created because estimates, like purchase orders, do not affect anything behind the scenes and, therefore, do not affect actual QuickBooks accounts.

You can create estimates for customers or each job you do for a customer. You can also create multiple estimates for a customer or a job. If a customer does not have jobs created for it, there will be a Job Info tab in the Edit Customer window. However, if even one job has been created for a customer, that Job Info tab is no longer available, and you will work with the individual jobs that have been created for the customer. Estimates must be turned on in the Company Preferences window.

FLASHBACK TO GAAP: MATCHING

Remember that expenses need to be matched with revenues. A sink bought for a bathroom remodel should be a job cost for that remodel. This principle allows for a better evaluation of the profitability and performance.

Creating a Change Order

A change order occurs after an estimate has been entered. If a customer wants a change to an estimate and if you are using the Contractor version or the Accountant's version of QuickBooks Desktop, when you make any change to an estimate it will ask you if you want to add it as a change order to the estimate. The changes will be listed under the original estimate. If you are using a different version, you can make changes to estimates, but they will not be called out as change orders. The change order feature will detail the amount of each change, exactly what changed, and the net change to the amount of the estimate. It will also document the change order for you in the description field of the estimate window.

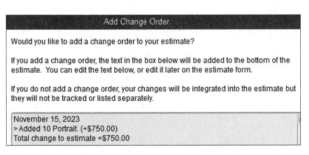
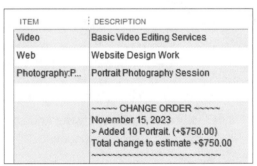

Add Change Order window and estimate with change order added (not available in all versions of QuickBooks)

➹ Customers→Customer Center: [choose customer]→New Customers & Jobs button→ Add Job

➹ Edit→Preferences: Jobs & Estimates→Company Preferences tab

➹ Customers→Create Estimates

➹ Customers→Create Invoices [then choose the desired customer and estimate]

In this exercise, you will turn on the preference for progress invoicing and create an estimate for a new customer. The password for all files unless otherwise stated is Password1. *Leave the company file open unless otherwise instructed.*

1. Start QuickBooks 2019 and toggle to Pro, if necessary.
2. Open **DYS_Chapter09 (Company)** or restore **DYS_Chapter09 (Portable)** from your file storage location and save your file as: **DYS_Chapter09 Average Guy Designs**

    It may take a few moments for the portable company file to open.

Turn On Progress Invoicing

3. Choose **Edit→Preferences**.
4. Choose the **Jobs & Estimates** category and then display the **Company Preferences** tab.
5. Choose **Yes** under *Do you do Progress Invoicing?*, click **OK**, and then click **OK** in the Warning window.

    QuickBooks needs to close and reopen the file to incorporate this preference.

Create a New Customer

The City of Bayshore is not yet set up as a customer, so you will create a new customer and job for the City of Bayshore.

6. Choose **Customers→Customer Center** and then press Ctrl + N to open a New Customer window.
7. Use this information to create the new customer:
    • Customer Name: **City of Bayshore**
    • Company Name: **City of Bayshore**
    • Full Name: **Mr. James Richards**
    • Main Phone: **(415) 555-2496**
    • Address: **1706 Duck Pond Lane** Enter **Bayshore, CA 91547**
8. Click Copy >> , click **OK** in the Add Shipping Address Information window, and then click **OK** in the New Customer window.

    You will see your new customer selected on the Customer & Jobs list.

Create a New Job for the Customer

9. Click the **New Customer & Job** button and then choose **Add Job**.
10. Type **Branding** in the Job Name field.
11. Click the **Job Info** tab and use this information to complete the New Job form, clicking **OK** when finished:
    • Job Description: **Create new city-wide branding campaign**
    • Job Type: **Government** (**Quick Add** it as a **Job Type**)
    • Job Status: **Pending**

Create an Estimate for a Job

The newly created job now appears indented under City of Bayshore in the Customers & Jobs List. It is selected, and now you're ready to create a new transaction for that job.

12. Click the **New Transactions** button and then choose **Estimates**.

The Create Estimates window opens with the Branding project job already filled in.

13. Use this information to complete the estimate:

A Date: **110623**

B Enter these rows by first choosing the item and then entering the quantities and costs. You will be changing the cost for Branding, so click **OK** on the Price Levels window, if necessary.

The Description will populate, and the Total will calculate automatically. Service items are defaulted to Nontaxable.

C Customer Message: **We look forward to working with you.** (Quick Add it as a new customer message.)

D Memo: **City of Bayshore: Branding**

14. Click **Save & Close** and click **Add** in the Check Spelling on Form window to add *Bayshore* to the dictionary, if prompted.

The estimate is created. Remember that nothing happens behind the scenes here! If the Job doesn't come through, you can select Mark as Inactive in the estimate.

15. Close the Customer Center.

Create a Progress Invoice

If you have a job that will span weeks or months, Progress Invoicing allows you to submit invoices based on parts of the work completed (stages or phases) as you go through the job. You start by creating an estimate for the entire job and then create an invoice and choose one of these three options:

- Create an invoice for the entire estimate (100%).

- Create an invoice for a percentage of the entire estimate.

- Create an invoice for selected items or for different percentages of each item.

You can create an invoice by opening the existing estimate or using the Create Invoices window and selecting the customer.

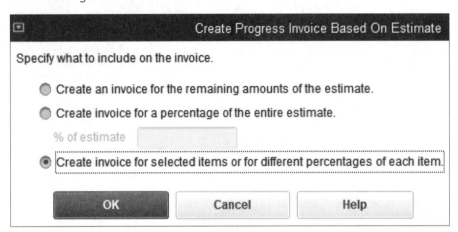

There will be several new columns included on the invoice template depending on which option is selected: Est Amt, Prior Amt, and Total %. Every time you create a subsequent invoice for that Customer (or Customer:Job), it will reflect the prior amount(s) and/or percentages. It is an easy way to bill your customer as you work through the job and for your customer to see what's already been done.

After you've selected one of the three options and have chosen how much to include on the invoice, QuickBooks will display the Progress Invoice template.

BEHIND THE SCENES

You will be creating a progress invoice based on the estimate for 50 percent of the branding work that has been completed. Take a look at the following T-accounts to see what is happening behind the scenes in this transaction:

11000•Accounts Receivable	43200•Design Income
1,000.00	1,000.00

↗ Customers→Create Invoices [then choose the desired customer and estimate]

↗ Customers→Create Estimates: [find estimate]→Create Invoice button

---

DEVELOP YOUR SKILLS 9-2

Guy has been awarded the City of Bayshore Branding Job and has already started working on it. In this exercise, you will edit the Customer:Job record to change the status to In progress and then use the job estimate created earlier to create the progress invoice. The first step is to open the Edit Job window for the City Branding Project and change the status of the job on the Job Info tab.

1. Choose **Customers→Customer Center**.
2. Double-click the **Branding** job for the City of Bayshore to open it for editing.
3. Click the **Job Info** tab and then use this information to edit the job:
   - Job Status: **In progress**
   - Projected End Date: **122223**
   - Start Date: **110823**
4. Click **OK** to save the Job and then close the Customer Center window.

Create the Invoice

Now you will create a progress invoice based on the estimate. Average Guy Designs has completed 50 percent of the branding portion of the job.

5. Choose **Company→Home Page** and click the **Create Invoices** 📄 task icon in the Customers area of the Home Page.
6. Choose the **City of Bayshore:Branding** Job as the Customer:Job.

   The Available Estimates window appears, displaying all the available estimates for the job.

7. Click the **11/06/2023** estimate for $5,820.00 in the Available Estimates window and then click **OK**.

   The Create Progress Invoice Based On Estimate window appears with three choices.

8. Click the circle to the left of **Create invoice for selected items or for different percentages of each item** and then click **OK**.

   The Specify Invoice Amounts for Items on Estimate window appears.

9. Use this information to create the invoice for 50 percent of the Branding portion of the job:

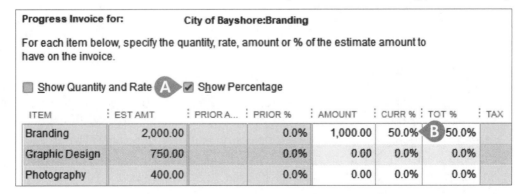

Ⓐ Click in the **Show Percentage** checkbox.

Ⓑ Change the percentage in the CURR % column for Branding to: **50.0%**

10. Click **OK** and then **OK** in the Zero Amount Items window.

The Create Invoices window displays using the Progress Invoice template. Fifty percent of the Branding charge is filled in for you. You can change the Company Preferences to not print items with zero amounts, but do not delete the items on the invoice with zero amounts.

11. Use this information to complete the invoice:

   • Date: **111323**

   • Invoice #: **10030**

   • Memo: `City Bayshore: Branding 11/13`

   > **BEHIND THE SCENES BRIEF**
   >
   > 11000•Accounts Receivable DR 1,000.00; **43200•Design Income CR <1,000.00>**

12. Click **Save & Close**.

   The progress invoice is recorded. The next time you choose to create an invoice based off the estimate for the Branding job, the 50 percent that you just invoiced for will show as a prior amount.

Unearned Income

There will be some cases in which you require a deposit on a job or a customer prepayment. Funds received as a deposit or sold as a gift certificate are considered unearned income because no work has been performed and no product has been sold. You may also hear this called unearned revenue or deferred revenue. You shouldn't credit unearned income to an income account. The proper way to deal with it is to hold it in a liability account such as Customer Deposits or Unearned Revenues. After you have delivered the goods or performed the service, you can then decrease the liability account and credit, or increase, an income account.

Customer Deposits

Customer deposits and gift certificates are tracked the same way in QuickBooks. And they both require you to go through the three steps of setting up, collecting, and recording. We will deal specifically with customer deposits, but you can apply the same principles if you need to account for gift certificates.

It will take three steps for this process:

1. **Set Up to Track Customer Deposits:** The first step in dealing with unearned income is to set up an Other Current Liability account and two items (an Other Charge and a Payment type). The Other Current Liability account is necessary because, by accepting a customer deposit or a payment for a gift certificate, you essentially are accepting both as a liability. The deposit will then be turned into a payment and the gift certificate will eventually be redeemed for goods or services. By setting up a liability account, you will be able to show that you are holding the funds in a separate account until the income becomes "earned." You need the two new items so they can be used on an Invoice.

2. **Receiving a Customer Deposit:** You will then use an invoice to record the receipt of the deposit, selecting the new items and directing the funds to a liability account. In essence, you are "liable" for doing something in return for the funds you are receiving. You will not record the income until the service is performed, the product is delivered, or the gift certificate is redeemed. This will not affect an income account or Accounts Receivable because the balance owing on the invoice will be zero.

3. **Turning a Deposit into a Payment:** After you have delivered on your promise and have traded goods or services for the deposit or gift certificate, you will use an invoice to record the income. The invoice will increase an income account and then reduce the liability account when the income becomes "earned" and you are no longer liable to perform or deliver.

Passing on Expenses to Customers

If you recall, when you enter a bill or make a purchase using cash or a credit card, you may be acquiring equipment or supplies whose costs you want to pass on to a customer. QuickBooks allows you to easily indicate which expenses are to be billed to a customer by providing a "Billable?" column in the Enter Bills window. When you make an item billable to a specific customer, the next time you invoice that customer you will be asked if you'd like to add the outstanding billable time and costs to the invoice.

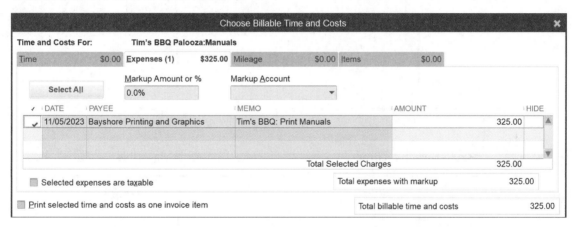

The Choose Billable Time and Costs window allows you to select what time, expenses, mileage, and/or items you wish to pass on to a customer and include on their invoice.

BEHIND THE SCENES

When you receive the customer deposit or issue a gift certificate, you will increase both Undeposited Funds (by debiting it) and Customer Deposits (by crediting it).

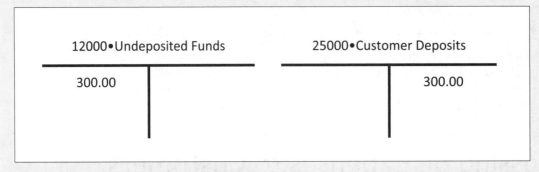

When the gift certificate is redeemed or the goods/services are delivered, you will remove the funds from the Customer Deposits liability account and realize the earned income. In the exercise you are about to complete, the cost of the service was more than the deposit amount, so the remainder will go into Accounts Receivable.

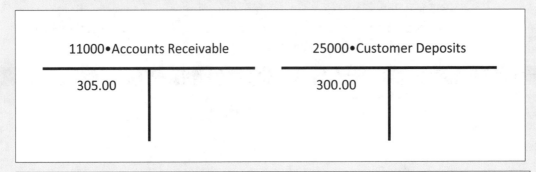

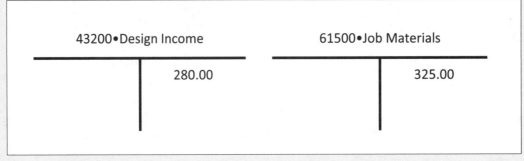

Lists→Chart of Accounts: Account→New: Other Account Types→Other Current Liability account │ Company→Chart of Accounts: Account→New: Other Account Types→Other Current Liability

Lists→Item List: Item→New: Other Charge *or* Payment

In this exercise, you will prepare to track customer deposits, receive a deposit for a customer, and turn the deposit into a payment. Before you can deal with unearned income, you must set up the proper account and items.

1. Click the **Chart of Accounts** ▦ task icon in the Company area of the Home Page.
2. Click the **Account** drop-down arrow and then choose **New**.
3. Use this information to complete the account:
   - Click to choose **Other Account Types**
   - Choose **Other Current Liability** (click **Continue**)
   - Number: **25000**
   - Account Name: **Customer Deposits**
4. Click **Save & Close** and close the Chart of Accounts.

   Now you will create the services for the two items needed to track the deposit.
5. Click the **Items & Services** ▤ task icon in the Company area of the Home Page.
6. Click the **Item** drop-down arrow, choose **New**, and then use this information to complete the first item:
   - Type: **Other Charge**
   - Item Name/Number: **Cust Dep**
   - Description: **Customer Deposit**
   - Tax Code: **Non**
   - Account: **25000•Customer Deposits**

   The Amount field is left as 0.00; you will fill that in at the time of sale.
7. Click **Next** and then use this information to create the second new item:
   - Type: **Payment**
   - Item Name/Number: **Cust Dep Pmt**
   - Description: **Customer Deposit Payment**
8. Click **OK** and then close the Item List window.

Collect a Customer Deposit

Tim Laughlin just called and asked Average Guy Designs to do a graphic design job that includes a large amount of printing. Guy asked for a deposit to be made before the work begins. You will record this deposit, creating a new job for this customer first.

9. Choose **Customers→Customer Center**.
10. Scroll down, right-click **Tim's BBQ Palooza**, and choose **Add Job**.
11. Type **Manuals** as the Job Name and click **OK**.

    The Customer Center will still be open with the new job selected.
12. Click the **New Transactions** button and choose **Invoices**.

13. Use this information to complete the invoice:

- Date: **110323**
- Invoice #: **10031**
- Terms: **Due on receipt**

First item:

- Item: **Cust Dep**
- Description: **Customer Deposit for printed material: manual**
- Rate: **300** (tap [Tab] for the Amount field to fill in)

Second item:

- Item: **Cust Dep Pmt**
- Description: **Customer Deposit Payment: manual**
- Rate: **–300** (tap [Tab] for the Amount field to fill in)

  The total due for the invoice should be 0.00 because the net effect to Accounts Receivable is 0.00. In other words, the customer doesn't owe anything as a result of the transaction. Behind the scenes, though, you collected the $300 deposit that debited Undeposited Funds and credited Customer Deposits as the Cust Dep item was tied to the Other Liability Account: 25000•Customer Deposits.

14. Click the checkbox for **Email Later** to clear it and then click **Save & Close**.

15. Click **No** in the Information Changed window and close the Customer Center.

You changed the terms to due upon receipt *for this one transaction but want the default terms you have set for the customer to remain the same.*

> **BEHIND THE SCENES BRIEF**
>
> 12000•Undeposited Funds DR 300.00; **25000•Customer Deposits CR <300.00>**

Pass an Expense to a Customer

Because Tim's BBQ Palooza job to print manuals is a large job, you used an outside printer who can handle the volume. Next you will pay for the printing using a credit card and pass the expense on to Tim's BBQ Palooza.

16. Click the **Enter Credit Card Charges** task icon in the Banking area of the Home Page.

17. Choose **21000•RiverBank Visa** as the credit card account.

18. Use this information to complete the charge that will be passed on to your customer:

- Purchased From: **Bayshore Printing and Graphics** (press [Enter] and then **Quick Add** it as a **Vendor**)
- Date: **110523**
- Ref No.: **Bay 01**
- Amount: **325**
- Memo: **Tim's BBQ: Print Manuals**
- Expenses tab, Account: **61500•Job Materials**
- Copy the memo to the Expenses tab Memo field

- Customer:Job: **Tim's BBQ Palooza: Manuals**
- Ensure the **Billable** checkbox is checked and then click **Save & Close**

Turn a Deposit into a Payment

The final step when working with customer deposits is to turn the deposit into a payment. You will also add the billable amount for Bayshore Printing and Graphics to Tim's BBQ Palooza's invoice.

19. Choose **Customers→Create Invoices**.

20. Choose **Tim's BBQ Palooza:Manuals** as the Customer:Job.

    The Billable Time/Costs window will appear, informing you that this customer has outstanding billable time and costs.

21. Ensure the option for **Select the outstanding billable time and costs to add to this invoice?** is selected and click **OK**.

    Notice that you can put off billing for this cost to a later date and also save this selection as a preference.

22. Click the **Expenses** tab and click the checkbox column to the left of the **11/05/2023** date for the billable charge. (The Expenses tab displays a number indicating how many items are listed on it.)

    There are four tabs that could contain billable costs or charges: Time, Expenses, Mileage, and Items. In this case, there is only one expense charge. Notice that you can enter a Markup by Amount or %. You can also print all selected time and costs as one invoice item so the breakdown doesn't show on the invoice.

23. Click **OK**.

    The 325.00 will appear on the first line of the invoice. The Item and Quantity remain blank.

24. Click in the **Date** field and type **110623** and then use this information to complete the Item section on line two:
    - Item: **Graphic Design**
    - Quantity: **7**
    - Rate: **40** (click **OK** in the Price Level/Billing window, if necessary)

    Third item:
    - Item: **Cust Dep**
    - Rate: **−300**
    - Customer Message: **Thank you for your business.**
    - Memo: **Tim's BBQ: Print Manual, applied 300 deposit**

    It is up to you to type the amount of the deposit that will be applied to the invoice. In this case, the invoice is greater than the deposit, so the customer still owes $305, and Accounts Receivable will be debited for this net amount still owed on the invoice. If the deposit was for more than the total invoice amount, you would enter the amount from the Customer Deposit that covered the invoice; the rest would remain in the liability account. Total bill: $605 less $300 deposit = $305

25. Click the **Email Later** checkbox to clear it and then click **Save & Close**, adding *BBQ* to the dictionary in the Check Spelling on Form window.

    The invoice is recorded. There are no longer funds on deposit in the liability account for this customer.

26. Choose **Company→Chart of Accounts** and then double-click **25000•Customer Deposits** to see how the money increased and then decreased from that account. Now you have a record of the deposit.

27. Close the register and the Chart of Accounts window.

BEHIND THE SCENES BRIEF

25000•Customer Deposits DR 300.00; 11000•Accounts Receivable DR 305.00;
43200•Design Income CR <280.00>; 61500•Job Materials CR <325.00>

Assessing Finance Charges and Producing Statements

If you are invoicing customers, you will inevitably find that not all of your customers pay their invoices on time. You may wish to assess finance charges, or, in some states, you may need to call them "Late Fee" or "Service Charge" for these late-paying customers.

Warning! Finance charge (lending) laws will vary! Research your jurisdiction to know whether you can assess finance charges on overdue balances. Do *not* use the specifics provided in this book; rather, find out the laws that apply to your location and apply them appropriately.

QuickBooks allows you to set several finance charge preferences in the Finance Charge category on the Company Preferences tab.

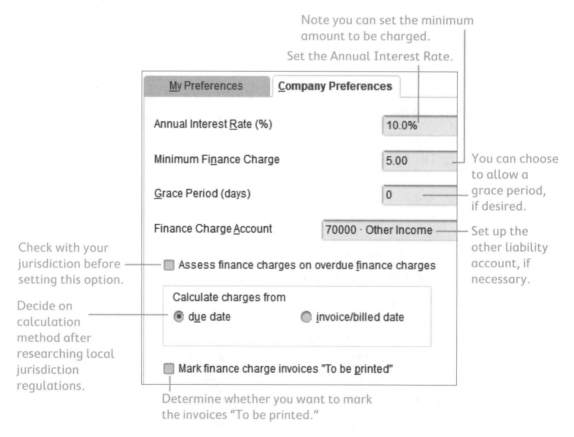

The finance charge account is an Other Income account as the income received is not the result of your normal business practices (unless you are a bank).

Note! If assessing a finance charge, a statement with payment terms should be clearly noted on the invoice. Include such wording as "Accounts not paid within terms are subject to a ___% monthly finance charge and a $___ late fee. Grace period 5 days." (Provided for example only, so do your research for your own company.)

↰ Edit→Preferences: Finance Charge→Company Preferences

↰ Customers→Assess Finance Charges

↰ Customers→Enter Statement Charges

↰ Customers→Create Statements

DEVELOP YOUR SKILLS 9-4

In this exercise, you will set the company preferences to incur a finance charge with a minimum charge for any customers with an overdue balance.

1. Choose **Edit→Preferences** and click the **Finance Charge** category. Then click the **Company Preferences** tab.
2. Use this information to complete the charges:
   - Annual Interest Rate (%): **10%**
   - Minimum Finance Charge: **5.00**
   - Finance Charge Account: **70000 Other Income** (tap ⌷Tab⌷ and then click **Set Up**)
3. Add a new account using this information:
   - Account Type and Name: **Other Income**
   - Description: **Finance Charges**
4. Click **Save & Close** and click **OK** to set the preferences.

The Assess Finance Charges Window

The Assess Finance Charges window does more than provide you with a means to determine which customers are overdue and should be charged a finance charge. It also calculates the charge due (based on the preferences set) and gives you a quick way to view the preferences and customize the finance charge invoice template.

Choosing the assessment date will display all past-due invoices.

You can change the form or leave the default Finance Charge form.

Customize the Finance Charge template here (for example, by adding a logo).

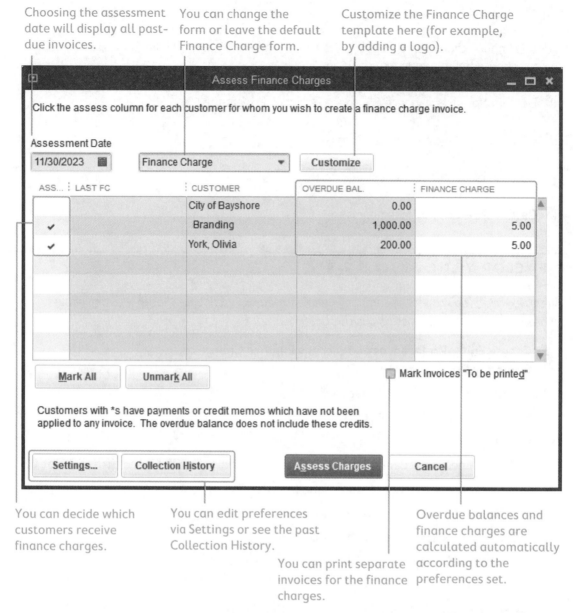

Assess Finance Charges

Click the assess column for each customer for whom you wish to create a finance charge invoice.

Assessment Date
11/30/2023   Finance Charge ▼   Customize

ASS...	LAST FC	CUSTOMER	OVERDUE BAL.	FINANCE CHARGE
		City of Bayshore	0.00	
✔		Branding	1,000.00	5.00
✔		York, Olivia	200.00	5.00

Mark All   Unmark All   ☐ Mark Invoices "To be printed"

Customers with *s have payments or credit memos which have not been applied to any invoice. The overdue balance does not include these credits.

Settings...   Collection History   **Assess Charges**   Cancel

You can decide which customers receive finance charges.

You can edit preferences via Settings or see the past Collection History.

You can print separate invoices for the finance charges.

Overdue balances and finance charges are calculated automatically according to the preferences set.

The Assess Finance Charges form gives you many options. Because payment terms were not set for City of Bayshore, QuickBooks set the due date for 10 days. Olivia York has payment settings of Due on Receipt.

The Assess Finance Charges window can also serve as a way to see customers that need friendly collections calls or may need to have their balances written off as bad debt.

BEHIND THE SCENES

When you assess finance charges, QuickBooks will debit Accounts Receivable and the appropriate accounts receivable customer subregister (you can see the example for Olivia York below), as well as indicate the account credited by the charge (in this case, 70000•Other Income).

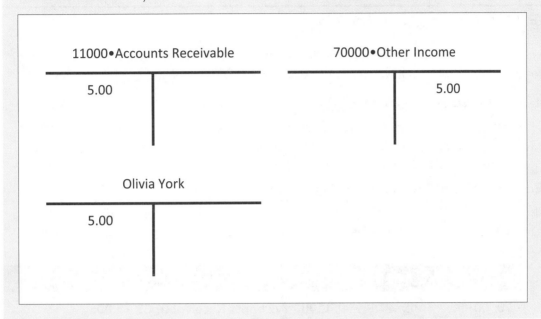

11000•Accounts Receivable

5.00

70000•Other Income

5.00

Olivia York

5.00

DEVELOP YOUR SKILLS 9-5

In this exercise, you will choose to assess finance charges on all overdue invoices and send statements to affected customers.

1. Click the **Finance Charges** task icon in the Customers area of the Home Page.

   The Assess Finance Charges window will be displayed.

2. Type **113023** as the Assessment Date and tap ⌨Tab.

   All customers with open invoices that are past due as of November 30 display, along with the calculated finance charge.

3. Click **Assess Charges** in the Assess Finance Charges window for all Customers listed.

   The finance charges are now reflected in Accounts Receivable for each customer assessed.

BEHIND THE SCENES BRIEF

11000•Accounts Receivable DR 10.00 (each customer's subregister is also debited for the finance charge amount); **70000•Other Income CR <10.00>**

Remove a Finance Charge

After finance charges have been applied, you may decide not to charge a specific customer a finance fee especially if it's a good customer or one whom you might expect to get a volume of work from. You can use the Statement Charges window to do this. You can still decide to charge a finance fee in the future for this customer.

DEVELOP YOUR SKILLS 9-6

In this exercise, you will delete the finance charge assessed to the City of Bayshore because you are expecting a lot of additional business from them. You will do this through the customer's register.

1. Click the **Statement Charges** task icon in the Customers area of the Home Page.

   When you choose to enter a statement charge, you will view the Accounts Receivable register for a customer. It is important that you choose the correct customer. If there were multiple charges, you would click the drop-down arrow for the Customer:Job field and choose the job.

2. Choose **City of Bayshore:Branding** as the **Customer:Job**.

3. Right-click anywhere within the two lines of the **City of Bayshore:Branding FC 1** finance charge transaction, choose **Delete Invoice**, and then click **OK** in the Delete Transaction window.

BEHIND THE SCENES BRIEF
70000•Other Income DR 5.00; **11000•Accounts Receivable CR <5.00>**

4. Close the City of Bayshore:Branding - Accounts Receivable window.

Creating Statements for Customers

There are many instances when you may wish to send your customer a statement rather than an invoice. You may have one customer for which you do multiple jobs within a billing period and you wish to bill them with an itemized statement. Another example would be to create a statement to bill a customer for a finance charge. Statements can be produced for an individual customer or in a batch for multiple customers.

> **Tip!** You can send an invoice reflecting assessed finance charges to your customers. Just ensure there is a checkmark ✓ in the "To be printed" checkbox in the Preferences window.

Statements can be printed individually for each customer as needed or can be run as a batch and then you select which statements to print. There are a number of options to set to determine which statements you want to print and how they will print.

> ✔ **Best Practice**
>
> The more common way to alert customers to finance charges that they owe is to produce a statement that reflects the finance charge, outstanding invoices, and aging information.

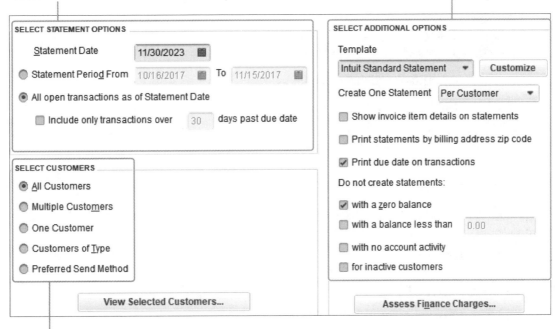

Select which dates or transactions to print.

Set additional options and choose or customize a template.

Select the desired customer(s).

The Create Statements window

DEVELOP YOUR SKILLS 9-7

In this exercise, you will create statements for all customers with a balance, including those with finance charges.

1. Click the **Statements** task icon in the Customers area of the Home Page.

2. Use this information to produce a batch of statements for all customers with a balance:

   • Statement Date: **113023**

   • Click the **All Open Transactions as of Statement Date** radio button.

   • Choose **All Customers**, if necessary.

   • Click the **With a Zero Balance** checkbox.

3. Click **Preview** and then use the **Next Page** button to advance through the four statements.

   You can now see what each statement will look like printed.

4. Click the **Close** button at the top of the Print Preview window.

   At this point, you would choose to print or email the statements by clicking the appropriate button at the bottom of the window. You will see the finance charge on the last statement for Olivia York.

5. Click **Close** in the Create Statements window. Close the company file.

   You will be using a sample company for the rest of the chapter exercises so you can perform the payroll tasks associated with time tracking.

Time Tracking and Mileage Features

The Time Tracking feature allows you to create weekly timesheets so you can break down the hours by customer/job or to record single activities for a customer/job. In addition to these payroll benefits, time tracking also allows you to:

- Invoice customers for number of hours worked

- Automatically fill in the hours worked on paychecks

- Track time for subcontractors by automatically filling in time data on bills and checks

- Track payroll costs by job, class, or type of work performed

- Track billable versus non-billable time

After you have used time data, you can run reports such as the Time by Job Summary to view how many hours were put into each job. Time tracking also allows you to allocate the appropriate payroll costs to a job, making your job costing reports more accurate and meaningful.

Methods of Entering Time

When you enter a single activity, it is recorded on that employee's weekly timesheet. A single activity can be entered by typing in the amount of time or by using the timer feature to actually track the exact amount of time on a task. If you choose to use the timer feature, it can be used only for timed activities on the current day.

There are two methods by which you can enter time data in QuickBooks:

- **As a single activity when it occurs:** You can either type the amount of time in the single activity window or use the built-in timer to record the exact amount of time.

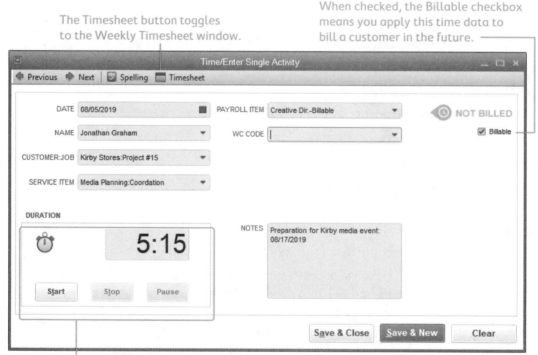

The Timesheet button toggles to the Weekly Timesheet window.

When checked, the Billable checkbox means you apply this time data to bill a customer in the future.

Type the duration of a task or click Start to record the actual time.

- **On a weekly timesheet:** The weekly timesheet allows you to enter time data for multiple customer/jobs, service items, and payroll items for a single employee. You can use this information to create paychecks when you process payroll. You can use the "Billable" column on a Timesheet to determine whether the time is billable. If a checkmark is in this field, the customer can be billed for the time. If an invoice icon appears, then the time has already been invoiced.

Fields Available in Both Time Data Entry Windows

Regardless of whether you choose to enter time as single activities or on a weekly timesheet, each window provides the following fields:

- **Customer:Job:** Information entered in this field allows you to bill a customer for the time and to keep track of information required for accurate job costing.

- **Service Item:** Information entered in this field allows you to track services performed.

- **Payroll Item:** Information entered in this field allows you to create paychecks from your time data.

- **Billable:** If you choose this field, the information is made available for you to bill the customer for the time.

- **Notes:** Information entered in this field is displayed in the description field on reports and invoices.

Batch Timesheets

Some businesses may find that they have employees or vendors who work the same hours for a job, for instance, if you are a construction company with crews who work together on the same jobs each day. These businesses can create one timesheet for multiple payroll names (employees for whom you have chosen to use time data to create paychecks) or multiple non-payroll names (such as vendors or employees).

> **Tip!** If you choose to work with batch timesheets, all workers for whom you are creating a timesheet must have the following criteria in common: job, number of hours worked per day, payroll item(s), and service item(s).

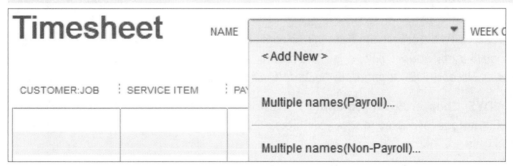

When you choose a name for a weekly timesheet, at the top of the list are options to choose multiple payroll or multiple non-payroll names in order to create a batch timesheet.

Tracking Mileage

The mileage tracking feature in QuickBooks allows you to track billable mileage for your business vehicle. Its purpose is not for reimbursing employees. The mileage data can be billed to customers for the expense or for tax reporting purposes. QuickBooks will calculate the mileage expense based on the approved rate on the specific day. You will need to ensure that you have the latest IRS mileage reimbursement rates entered. To track mileage for a particular vehicle, you need to enter the vehicle into the Vehicle List first.

To view your mileage information after you have started tracking it, QuickBooks provides mileage reports from which you can choose to display your data. You can also choose to pass on the mileage expense to your customers and create reports to view the amount that has been billed.

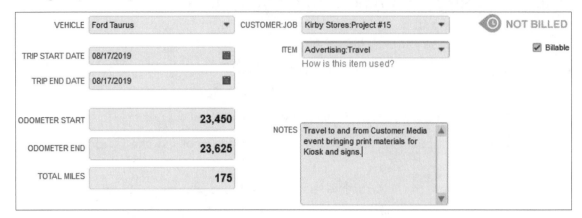

Billable Vehicle Mileage will be pulled into an invoice for this customer.

🔖 Employees→Enter Time→Use Weekly Timesheet *or* Time/Edit Single Activity

🔖 Company→Enter Vehicle Mileage

🔖 Lists→Customer & Vendor Profile Lists→Vehicle List: Vehicle→New

🔖 Lists→Item List: Item→New

🔖 Reports→Jobs, Time & Mileage | Reports→Report Center: Jobs, Time & Mileage

DEVELOP YOUR SKILLS 9-8

In this exercise, you will track time to be used to create paychecks for a company and will first record time spent on two jobs. You will be opening a sample file in order to be able to work in a file with active payroll. The date will automatically be set to December 15, 2018. The Password is Password1.

1. Open **DYS_Chapter09-PR (Company)** or restore **DYS_Chapter09-PR (Portable)** from your file storage location and save your file as: **DYS_Chapter09PR Average Guy Designs**

2. Click **OK** to acknowledge that you are using a sample company file.

3. Click the **Enter Time** 📇 task icon in the Employees area of the Home Page and then choose **Time/Enter Single Activity**.

4. Use this information to enter the employee's billable time:
   - Date: **080519**
   - Name: **Jonathan Graham (Employee)**
   - Customer Job: **Kirby Stores:Project #15**

5. Service Item: **Media Planning: Coordination** (Payroll Item should default to *Creative Dir.–Billable*)

   - Duration: **5:15**
   - Billable: Ensure that it's checked
   - Notes: **Preparation for Kirby media event: 8/17/19**

6. Click **Save & Close**.

> *Note!* If you enter the duration with a colon, as in this example, it calculates the time in minutes and seconds. Alternatively, if you use a decimal instead of a colon, it will calculate it as a fraction of a minute.

Enter Time Using a Weekly Timesheet

You will now enter the rest of Jonathan's time for the week.

7. Click the **Enter Time** 🖼 task icon in the Employees area of the Home Page and then choose **Use Weekly Timesheet**.

8. In the Name field, type **jo** and tap ⎯Tab⎯ to fill in *Jonathan Graham (Employee)*. You will see a prior timesheet.

9. Use these steps to set the time frame for the timesheet:

   - Click the **calendar** 📅 icon to the right of the Week Of date range.
   - Use the right arrow button to the right of December 2018 to advance to **August 2019**.
   - Click the **5** (Monday).

   QuickBooks sets the week of Aug 5 to Aug 11, 2019, as the date range for the timesheet. Notice that the time data you just entered as a single activity appears on the weekly timesheet for the week of 08/05/2019. There is another entry for 3 hours on Tuesday the 6th.

10. Use this information to complete the remainder of the time data for the week:

Customer Job	Service Item	M	Tu	W	TH	F
Peacock Research Project #14	Film Production:Editing	3:00	6:00	8:00		
Kirby Stores:Project #15	Event Planning:Meetings				1:30	1:00
Kirby Stores:Project #15	Event Planning:Research				4:00	
Kirby Stores:Project #15	Event Planning:Lay Out					7:00

> *Note!* Be careful! If you hit ⎯Enter⎯, it will save what you've entered and display a new, blank time sheet. If this happens to you, repeat steps 7 and 8.

11. The Payroll Item *Creative Dir.-Billable* will fill in automatically for each line; ensure **Billable** is checked for all items.

    Your entries should match those in the following illustration. Total hours should be 38:45 on the Total row at bottom of screen.

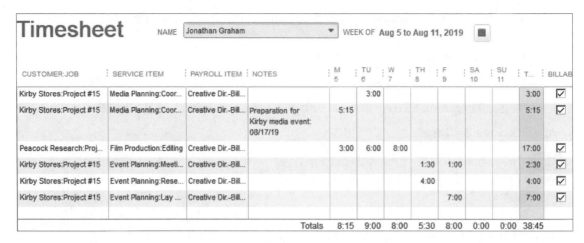

Timesheet NAME Jonathan Graham ▼ WEEK OF Aug 5 to Aug 11, 2019 ■

CUSTOMER:JOB	SERVICE ITEM	PAYROLL ITEM	NOTES	M 5	TU 6	W 7	TH 8	F 9	SA 10	SU 11	T...	BILLAB
Kirby Stores:Project #15	Media Planning:Coor...	Creative Dir.-Bill...			3:00						3:00	☑
Kirby Stores:Project #15	Media Planning:Coor...	Creative Dir.-Bill...	Preparation for Kirby media event: 08/17/19	5:15							5:15	☑
Peacock Research:Proj...	Film Production:Editing	Creative Dir.-Bill...		3:00	6:00	8:00					17:00	☑
Kirby Stores:Project #15	Event Planning:Meeti...	Creative Dir.-Bill...					1:30	1:00			2:30	☑
Kirby Stores:Project #15	Event Planning:Rese...	Creative Dir.-Bill...					4:00				4:00	☑
Kirby Stores:Project #15	Event Planning:Lay ...	Creative Dir.-Bill...						7:00			7:00	☑
			Totals	8:15	9:00	8:00	5:30	8:00	0:00	0:00	38:45	

12. Click **Save & Close**.

Using Time Tracking Hours for Paychecks and Invoices

You can use time data for employees to create their paychecks and for vendors to create their bills by entering the time using the single or weekly timesheets. Using Time Tracking for either employees or vendors will also allow you to invoice your customers for any billable time.

Allocating time spent by salaried employees or vendors on a job should help in producing more accurate job cost reports. By marking the time as Billable on the timesheets, the hours will automatically be imported when creating the paychecks or bills.

When you create an invoice, you can choose to pass billable time to customers, just as you did with an expense earlier in this chapter. You will be prompted that there is billable time, including billable mileage if you are tracking that as well. Regardless of which type of cost you are passing on to the customer, the process is virtually the same—and you can even choose to specify a markup amount for the hours.

↱ Employees→Pay Employees

↱ Customers→Create Invoices

DEVELOP YOUR SKILLS 9-9

In this exercise, you will create a paycheck for Jonathan based on the time data that was entered and then invoice one of the customers.

1. Click the **Pay Employees** 📇 task icon in the Employees area of the Home Page.

2. Click the **Pay Employees** button in the middle of the Employee Center: Payroll Center window.

The Enter Payroll Information window displays. Look at the Creative Dir-Billable column for Jonathan Graham (you may have to resize the columns to read the headers) and notice that the amount is in blue, which indicates it is for the amount of billable time that you have entered.

3. Change the Check Date to: **082019**

4. Click in the **checkmark** ✓ column to the left of *Jonathan Graham*.

5. Click **Jonathan**'s name and review the Preview Paycheck window:

Earnings reflects total hours imported
from the weekly timesheet for each job.

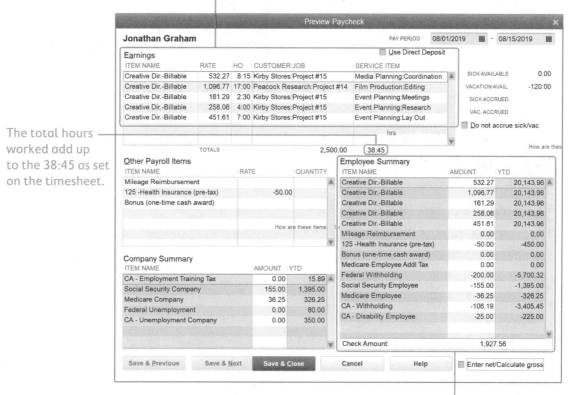

The total hours
worked add up
to the 38:45 as set
on the timesheet.

Employee Summary data will be
used to create the paycheck.
Notice the total of $1,927.56.

The net Check Amount may differ from that in the illustration due to updates to the payroll tax table.

6. Click **Save & Close** and then click **Continue** to move to the Review and Create Paychecks window.

This window lists the paychecks to be created. You can choose Finish Later if necessary.

7. Click **Create Paychecks** and then close the Confirmation and Next Steps window. The Payroll Center now reflects the paycheck status of To Print for Payroll 08/20/2019. Close the Payroll Center.

The following Behind the Scenes Brief section shows the parent accounts, not the various subaccounts.

BEHIND THE SCENES BRIEF

6500•Wages DR 2,499.99; **2100•Payroll Liabilities CR <572.43>; 1110•Company Checking CR <1,927.56>**

Create an Invoice from Time Data

You will now create an invoice for Kirby Stores that includes the time costs for the work completed.

8. Click the **Create Invoices** 📄 task icon in the Customers area of the Home Page.

If you are using a Premier version of the software, the Home Page task icon will be called Invoices, and once you click it you will need to choose Invoice for Time & Expense. You will then need to click OK in the Choose Multiple Customers to Invoice for Time and Expenses window.

9. Click the **Customer:Job** field drop-down arrow and choose **Kirby Stores:Project #15**.

The Billable Time/Costs window appears.

10. Click **OK** in the Billable Time/Costs window to choose the default of selecting the outstanding billable time and costs to add to this invoice.

The Time tab of the Choose Billable Time and Costs window displays.

11. Click the **Select All** button and then click **OK**.

The Create Invoices window displays with the total hours for each item.

12. Change the Invoice Date to: **081619**

13. Enter these rates on the appropriate Item line in the **Rate** column tapping the down arrow ⬇ after each entry:

- Media Planning Coordination: **65**
- Event Planning Meetings: **55**
- Event Planning Research: **65**
- Event Planning Layout: **75**

These rates needed to be entered because they were not entered on the items in the item list. This enables you to set the rate as needed.

14. Click the **Memo** field and type: `Kirby Proj. 15 Billable Hrs.`

15. Click **Save & Close** and then close the Check Spelling on Form window, if necessary.

BEHIND THE SCENES BRIEF

1210•Accounts Receivable DR 1,458.75; **4200•Event Income CR <1,458.75>**

---

16. Click the **Receive Payments** 💳 task icon in the Customers area of the Home Page.

17. Use this information to complete the payment receipt:

- Received From: **Kirby Stores:Project#15**
- Payment Amount: **1458.75**
- Date: **082219**
- Payment: **Check**
- Check # **2468**
- Memo: `Kirby:Proj#15 billable hrs.`

18. Click **Save & Close**.

The Record Deposits notification just changed to 1.

> **BEHIND THE SCENES BRIEF**
>
> 1500•Undeposited Funds DR 1,458.75; **1210•Accounts Receivable CR <1,458.75>**

Jobs, Time & Mileage Tracking Reports

QuickBooks' job costing, estimating, and time tracking features include many preset reports that you can run to learn more about your business. Not all of the Jobs, Time & Mileage reports are in all versions of QuickBooks. There are other reports available if you use a Premier version of QuickBooks that is specialized for your type of company. Like other reports, these standard reports can be customized.

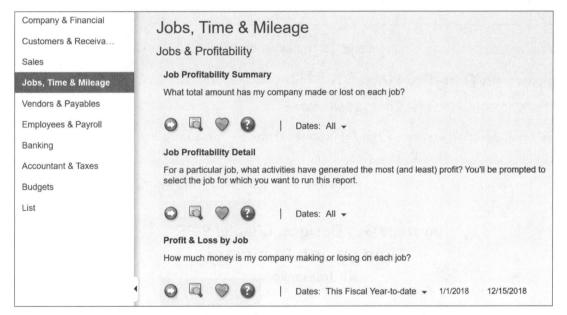

When you choose the Jobs, Time & Mileage category in the Report Center, you can view all of the reports available in your version of QuickBooks. Here are just three that are available in all versions.

Reports→Jobs, Time & Mileage | Reports→Reports Center→Jobs, Time & Mileage

In this exercise, you will produce a variety of Job-related reports for Average Guy Designs.

1. Choose **Reports→Jobs, Time & Mileage→Job Progress Invoices vs. Estimates**.

   The Job Progress Invoices vs. Estimates report displays.

Average Guy Designs. Chapter 9-PR
Job Progress Invoices vs. Estimates
All Transactions

Type	Date	Num	Estimate Active	Estimate Total	Progress Invoice	% Progress	
Nguyen Database Corp.							
Project #02							
Estimate	02/01/2018	0710...	✓	13,820.00	5,000.00	36.18% ◀	
Bowden Agency							
Project #03							
Estimate	03/30/2018	71002	✓	10,500.00	5,500.00	52.38%	

2. Close the Job Progress Invoices vs. Estimates window.

Report on Time Tracking

The next report will show the time spent on each job.

3. Choose **Reports→Jobs, Time & Mileage→Time by Job Summary**.

4. Type **a** to set the date range to All.

   The Time by Job Summary report displays for all dates. Notice the time for which you invoiced Kirby Stores for the Project #15 job, as shown in this illustration.

Average Guy Designs. Chapter 9-PR
Time by Job Summary
All Transactions

	Aug 22, 19
▼ **Kirby Stores:Project #15**	
Event Planning:Contract Review	8:00
Event Planning:Coordination	24:00
Event Planning:Event Review	16:00
Event Planning:Lay Out	23:00
Event Planning:Meetings	18:30
Event Planning:Research	44:00
Media Planning:Coordation	8:15
Print Production:Coordination	36:00
Print Production:Editing	42:00
Total Kirby Stores:Project #15	219:45

5. Close the Time by Job Summary window, choosing not to memorize the report.

Report on Job Costing

The third report will show the profitability of each job.

6. Choose **Reports→Jobs, Time & Mileage→Job Profitability Summary**.

   The Job Profitability Summary report displays with the default date range of all dates. Note the profitability so far for the Kirby Stores.

Average Guy Designs. Chapter 9-PR
Job Profitability Summary
All Transactions

	Act. Cost	Act. Revenue	($) Diff.
▸ **Hamby Product Company** ▸	30,596.53 ◂	95,167.20	64,570.67
▾ **Kirby Stores**			
Project #15	9,248.52	18,120.15	8,871.63
Project #09	6,724.31	28,430.50	21,706.19
Total Kirby Stores	15,972.83	46,550.65	30,577.82

7. Close the Job Profitability Summary window.

Time Tracking with TSheets

You may find that the time tracking that is standard in QuickBooks Desktop doesn't meet your company's needs. Well, you are in luck as there is an "app for that" that Intuit now owns that works seamlessly with QuickBooks, TSheets. There is an additional fee to utilize TSheets, but you may find that the cost is worth it due to the benefits it offers. Let's look at some of those benefits.

Precision & Reduced Payroll Processing Time

Gone are the days of rounding up on timesheets with TSheets. Employees can clock in and out right from their mobile devices and receive reminders regarding breaks, overtime, and clocking in and out. They can choose to clock in for specific jobs as well, which makes it easier for you to invoice clients for the time spent on their jobs.

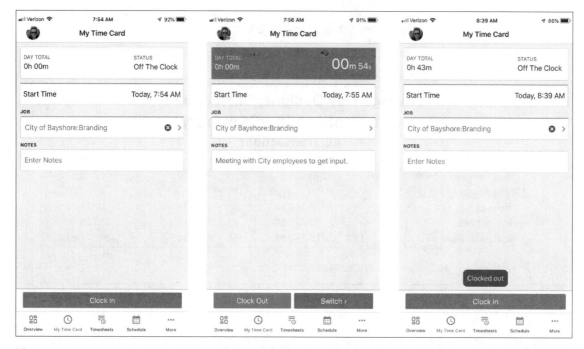

Here you can see what the TSheets Time Card feature looks like on an iPhone when an employee is preparing to clock in, has clocked in and added a note as to what the time is for, and has clocked out. Note the precision of time tracked—this employee could have easily rounded up to an hour!

Payroll specialists may be scared over the fact that payroll processing will become more efficient, but it can free them up to do less rote work and more innovative projects! With the days of handwritten time cards in the past, electronic timesheet approvals will leave you with more time available for activities that can boost both the bottom line and morale.

QuickBooks Integration

With just one click you can take all the data in TSheets and export it to QuickBooks. You will be able to use the same customers, jobs, classes, items, etc., that you use in QuickBooks, making it very easy to sync the two together.

Scheduling and GPS

This app also provides scheduling capabilities so that you can see who's working where and on what job easily. You will also be able to track employee time on the job by GPS, providing another benefit to your clients and your employees (it helps solve the "he said-she said" question that may pop up from time to time regarding whether an employee was at a particular job site).

TSheets is just an example of one of the many apps available to QuickBooks users. As a person who is learning QuickBooks, it may be worth your while to spend some time learning TSheets and other popular apps that integrate with QuickBooks, as it could make you more valuable to your employer or may help to make your own business more efficient. To learn about all the apps that work with QuickBooks, simply visit apps.com.

Tackle the Tasks

Now is your chance to work a little more with Average Guy Designs and apply the skills that you have learned in this chapter to accomplish additional tasks. You will continue to use the company file you used in the last Develop Your Skills exercises. Enter these tasks, referring to the concepts in the chapter as necessary. If you are using the trial software for this course on your computer or in a lab at school, you must toggle to the Pro edition every time you start QuickBooks.

Create an Estimate for a New Job	Create a new job for Chancey and Co. called Marketing Video, as you will be bidding on the opportunity to create a new marketing video.
	Create an estimate for Chancey and Co.:Marketing Video job on 08/23/2019 for Film Production: 2 hours of contract review, 20 hours of research, 10 hours of meetings, 30 hours of coordination, 25 hours on location, and 40 hours of editing. The hourly rate for all is $45/hour. Enter a memo: Chancey Marketing Video proposal.
Create a Progress Invoice Based on an Estimate	You have been awarded the Marketing Video job for Chancey and Co., so edit the job to show this. The dates for the start and projected end of the job will be 09/01/2019 and 12/01/2019, respectively. The job type is Production Services and its description is New Product Marketing.
	Create a progress invoice dated 09/25/2019 for 50 percent of the entire estimate. Set the terms for the invoice as Net 15 (do not make the change permanent). Choose to not apply the available credits to the invoice.
	Run a QuickReport to see the transactions.
Receive a Customer Deposit	Bowden Agency would like you to do some print production work for them and to print a large number of items for which you will collect a deposit up front.
	Receive a deposit from Bowden Agency using a new job, Project #17, on 09/17/2019 for $500 for the printing. The account (2200•Client Deposits) and Payment Item (Payment) already exist.
	You will have to set up Cust Dep (Other Charge item, charge to the Client Deposit account), Description: Customer Deposit;
	Invoice memos:
	Cust Dep: Customer Deposit for Printing
	Payment: Payment of Deposit

(cont'd.)

Apply a Customer Deposit as a Payment	Create a bill for Business Supply Center on 09/26/2019 for Printing and Reproduction for $500, billable to Bowden Agency:Project #17.
	Create an invoice for the completed Bowden Agency: Project #17 and be sure to Select the outstanding billable time and costs to add to this invoice.
	Set the date to 09/28/2019 and add these items to the invoice: Print Production: coordination for 10 hours, 40 hours of editing both at an hourly rate of $50.
	Apply the $500 customer deposit to the invoice with terms of Net 10 (do not make the change in terms permanent).
	Run a Profit & Loss by Job report for dates 09/01/2019–9/30/2019 to see the $2,500 net income from this job.
Create an Invoice from Billable Time	Create an invoice for Peacock Research Project #14 for the 3 billable film editing time entries in August only. Date the invoice 09/30/2019. (Hint: The total amount you are passing on is $1,445.)

Self-Assessment

Check your knowledge of this chapter's key concepts and skills using the Self-Assessment quiz here, in your ebook, or in your eLab course.

1. You can create estimates only for jobs, not for customers.   *True   False*

2. If you choose to create a progress invoice, it must be for a percentage of all items. You cannot create one for selected items from the estimate.   *True   False*

3. You can enter time data as either a single activity or on a weekly timesheet.   *True   False*

4. When you pass on billable time to a customer, you select the cost for the time on the Expenses tab of the Choose Billable Time and Costs window.   *True   False*

5. QuickBooks allows users to track outstanding estimates by utilizing a non-posting account.   *True   False*

6. Unearned income refers to the funds you are holding in the Undeposited Funds account.   *True   False*

7. When you receive funds for a gift certificate, you hold them in an Other Current Liability account.   *True   False*

8. In QuickBooks, you can use the mileage tracking feature to track mileage to be reimbursed to employees for the use of their own cars.   *True   False*

9. You should use the specific finance charge settings outlined in this book for your own company.   *True   False*

10. The most common way to bill customers for finance charges is to create and send separate invoices.   *True   False*

11. Which report would you produce to determine which job is most profitable?
    A. Job Profitability Detail
    B. Job Estimates vs. Actuals Summary
    C. Time by Job Summary
    D. Job Profitability Summary

12. Which of these is NOT a step you need to take to conduct job costing in QuickBooks?
    A. Enter all job revenues and expenses
    B. Create an estimate for the job
    C. Use QuickBooks reports to analyze job data
    D. Set up your data in the Customers & Jobs List

(cont'd.)

13. To enter mileage for a vehicle in QuickBooks, you first need to:

    A. Enter the current IRS mileage rate.

    B. Add the vehicle in the Other Names list.

    C. Create a new non-inventory item in the Item List.

    D. None of these options

14. Which of these is NOT something you need to set up to track customer deposits in QuickBooks?

    A. An inventory-part item

    B. An Other Current Liability account

    C. An other charge item

    D. A payment item

Reinforce Your Skills

Angela Stevens has just hired you as a senior bookkeeper for Quality-Built Construction. You will be entering estimates, creating progress invoices, and performing other tasks such as receiving customer deposits and entering time tracking data to ensure proper billing and job costing. You will be working with a QuickBooks sample file to avoid having to purchase a payroll subscription. The password for all files is Password1. Leave the company file open unless otherwise instructed. If you are using the trial software on your computer or in a lab at school, remember to toggle to the Pro edition every time you start QuickBooks.

REINFORCE YOUR SKILLS 9-1

Create a Job and an Estimate for a Customer

In this exercise, you will enter a new customer and a job for the customer, who has asked you for an estimate for a kitchen remodel. Preferences must be set before you can create estimates and conduct progress invoicing.

1. Start QuickBooks 2019.
2. Open **RYS_Chapter09 (Company)** or restore **RYS_Chapter09 (Portable)** from your file storage location and save your file as: **RYS_Chapter09 Quality-Built Construction**
3. Choose **Edit→Preferences**.
4. Click the **Jobs & Estimates** category and then click the **Company Preferences** tab.
5. Ensure that both the Create Estimates and Progress Invoicing features are turned on and then click **OK**.

Create a Customer and a Job

Next you will enter a new customer and job.

6. Choose **Customers→Customer Center**.
7. Click the **New Customer & Job** button and choose **New Customer**.
8. Type **Bates, Tania** as the Customer Name and click **OK**.

    Bates, Tania *should be selected.*

9. Click the **New Customer & Job** button and choose **Add Job**.
10. Type **Remodel Kitchen** as the Job Name.
11. Click the **Job Info** tab and then use this information to enter the job information:
    - Job Description: **Complete kitchen remodel**
    - Job Type: **Remodel**
    - Job Status: **Pending**
12. Click **OK** to save the new job.

    The new job appears on the Customers & Jobs List; it is selected.

Create an Estimate for a Job

Now that you have a job set up for the kitchen remodel, you will create an estimate for it. The Remodel Kitchen job should still be selected.

13. Click the **New Transactions** button and then choose **Estimates**.

14. Type **010720** as the Date.

15. Type **20-0001** as the Estimate No.

16. Enter this information starting on the first Item row, typing the quantity and estimate cost displayed.

ITEM	DESCRIPTION	QTY	ESTIMATE	TOTAL	MAR...	REVENUE	TAX
01 Plans & Permits .:01.4 Remodel Plans	Plans for home remodel	1	1,200.00	1,200.00		1,200.00	Non
02 Site Work:02.10 Demo	Demolition	8	55.00	440.00		440.00	Non
07 Wall Framing	Wall Framing	5	60.00	300.00		300.00	Non
13 Windows & Trim	Windows & Trim	6	65.00	390.00		390.00	Non
14 Plumbing	Plumbing	5	75.00	375.00		375.00	Non
16 Electrical & Lighting	Electrical & Lighting	8	65.00	520.00		520.00	Non
18 Interior Walls	Interior Walls	8	55.00	440.00		440.00	Non
20 Millwork & Trim	Millwork & Trim	12	50.00	600.00		600.00	Non
23 Floor Coverings	Floor Coverings	8	45.00	360.00		360.00	Non
24 Paint	Painting	9	50.00	450.00		450.00	Non
25 Cleanup	Cleanup & Restoration	10	45.00	450.00		450.00	Non

The estimate should total $5,525.

17. Type **Bates: Kitchen remodel** in the Memo field.

18. Click **Save & Close** for the estimate and then close the Customer Center.

REINFORCE YOUR SKILLS 9-2

Create a Progress Invoice Based on an Estimate

In this exercise, you will create a progress invoice to charge for the remodel plans that have been completed.

1. Choose **Customers→Create Invoices** and then choose **Bates Tania: Remodel Kitchen** as the Customer:Job.

2. Click the estimate for **01/07/2020** in the Available Estimates window and click **OK**.

3. Choose to create the invoice for **selected items or different percentages** and then click **OK**.

4. Click the **Show Quantity and Rate** and **Show Percentage** checkboxes to deselect them if necessary.

5. Type **1200** in the **Amount** column for the first line (01.4 Remodel Plans) and click **OK**. (You can adjust the column widths by dragging between the column borders.)

6. Click **OK** in the **Zero Amount Items** window.

   Note that, after that selection is made, everything will fill into the Create Invoices window.

7. Choose **Due On Receipt** as the terms and set the date to: **012220**

8. Click **Save & Close** and choose not to have the terms permanently changed.

Collect a Customer Deposit

In this exercise, you will help Angela to collect a deposit from Tania Bates for $2,000 toward the remainder of the work. These funds will be held in a liability account until they are earned, at which time you will create a progress invoice to record the income. There is already a Customer Deposits account set up, so you will begin by creating the two items you will use for the actual deposit.

1. Choose **Lists→Item List**.
2. Choose **Item→New→Other Charge** named: `Cust Dep`
3. Leave the Description blank so you can fill it in on each invoice, change the Tax Code to **Non** and direct it to the **2200•Customer Deposits** account, and click **Next**.

   The New Item window appears.
4. Choose to create a new Payment item named: `Payment`
5. Type `Customer Payment` as the Description for the new item and then click **OK**.
6. Close the Item List.

Collect the Deposit

7. Choose **Customers→Create Invoices** and then choose **Bates, Tania: Remodel Kitchen** as the Customer:Job.
8. Click **Cancel** in the Available Estimates window as you are not ready to invoice for the remaining work.
9. Ensure the date is set to **01/22/2020** and then enter the deposit and payment using this illustration.

ITEM	QUANTITY	DESCRIPTION	RATE	AMOUNT	TAX
Cust Dep.			2,000.00	2,000.00	Non
Payment		Customer Payment		-2,000.00	

10. Type `Customer Deposit: Remodel Kitchen` in the Description field.
11. Type `Bates: remodel $2,000 deposit` in the Memo field and then click **Save & New**.

Apply the Customer Deposit to a Progress Invoice

Angela has now completed the kitchen remodel and will invoice Tania to record the earned income, utilizing the deposit. The Create Invoices window should still be open. If not, choose Customers→Create Invoices.

12. Choose **Bates, Tania: Remodel Kitchen** as the Customer:Job.
13. Click the estimate for **01/07/2020** in the Available Estimates window and click **OK**.
14. Click **OK** to Create an invoice for the remaining amounts of the estimate.
15. Set the date of the invoice to **02/22/2020** and enter **02-1055** in the Invoice # field.
16. Scroll down in the item area of the invoice and then enter the customer deposit in the line below *25 Cleanup*, choosing **Cust Dep** as the Item.

17. Type **Customer Deposit Applied** for the Description and type **-2000** in the Amount column.

    The Balance Due should be $2,325 after deducting the $2,000 deposit.

18. Click **Save & Close**.

REINFORCE YOUR SKILLS 9-4

Assess Finance Charges

In this exercise, you will assess finance charges for customers with overdue invoices. The finance charge preferences have already been set up for the company, so you will not need to complete that step.

1. Choose **Customers→Assess Finance Charges**.

2. Type **013120** as the Assessment Date and then tap Tab.

   Two invoices are selected to have finance charges assessed.

3. Click **Assess Charges**.

REINFORCE YOUR SKILLS 9-5

Enter Time Tracking Data and Produce a Paycheck

In this exercise, you will enter time spent on a job by Clark Mitchell and then create a paycheck for him.

1. Choose **Employees→Enter Time→Use Weekly Timesheet**.

2. Use this information to enter the time worked for the week of **Jan 27 to Feb 2, 2020**:

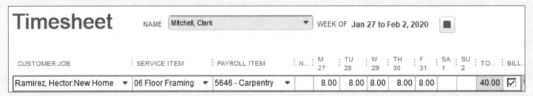

3. Click **Save & New**.

4. Use this information to enter the time worked for the week of **Feb 3 to Feb 9, 2020**:

5. Click **Save & Close**.

6. Choose **Employees→Pay Employees**.

7. Use the **calendar** icon to change the Pay Period Ends date to **02/09/2020** and click **Yes** in the Pay Period Change window.

8. Change the Check Date to **02/11/2020**.

9. Click in the **checkmark** ✓ column to the left of **Mitchell, Clark** and then click **Continue**.

10. Review the paycheck you are about to create using time data and then click **Create Paychecks**.

11. Close the Confirmation and Next Steps window.

Display Reports for Estimates and Time Tracking

In this exercise, you will help Angela to create estimate and time tracking reports.

1. Choose **Lists→Chart of Accounts**.
2. Click in the **Look for Account Name or Number** field, type **Estimates**, and click **Search**.
3. Right-click the **Estimates** account and choose **QuickReport: 4•Estimates** from the bottom of the pop-up menu.
4. Set the date range to **All**.

   On the report, review the estimates that have been created; the one you entered is at the bottom.

5. Close the Account QuickReport and the Chart of Accounts windows.

View the Progress Invoicing of an Estimate

You will now run a report that will show you the percentage of the estimates that have been invoiced.

6. Choose **Reports→Jobs, Time & Mileage→Job Progress Invoices vs. Estimates**.
7. Type **a** to set the date range to All.

   Notice the estimate you created and the amount that has been invoiced.

8. Close the Job Progress vs. Estimates window, choosing not to memorize the report.

Create a Time by Job Summary Report

Finally, you will create a report that shows time spent on Hector Ramirez' New Home job.

9. Choose **Reports→Jobs, Time & Mileage→Time by Job Summary**.
10. Type **a** to set the date range to All.

    Scroll down to view the time data for the new home job for Hector Ramirez. The image shows the detail for each job collapsed, except for the Ramirez, Hector:New Home job.

Quality-Built Construction Chapter 9
Time by Job Summary
All Transactions

	Feb 22, 20
▶ Cruz, Albert:Cottage - New Construction	2,160.00
▶ Escalona, Heather:House-New Construction	2,501.00
▶ Hamby, Shane:Cottage - New Construction	2,321.00
▶ Molotsi, Hugh	16.00
▶ Molotsi, Hugh:Second Story Addition	2,113.00
▼ Ramirez, Hector:New Home	
06 Floor Framing	80.00
Total Ramirez, Hector:New Home	80.00

11. Close the Time by Job Summary report, choosing not to memorize the report, and then close the company file.

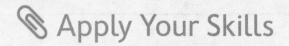 Apply Your Skills

You have decided that it is advantageous to do estimates and progress invoicing for Wet Noses Veterinary Clinic as well as to start job tracking. You realize the importance of this aspect of doing business to ensure you are really profitable on the jobs you are taking on. Now you will take the necessary steps to start using these features. The password for all files unless otherwise stated is Password1. After starting QuickBooks, remember to toggle to Pro as necessary.

APPLY YOUR SKILLS 9-1

Set the Preferences and Create a New Job

In this exercise, you will set the necessary preferences to be able to use QuickBooks' estimating and progress invoicing features. Then you will create a new "job" for Amy Ridgeway's new kitten, Autumn.

1. Start QuickBooks 2019.
2. Open **AYS_A1_Chapter09 (Company)** or restore **AYS_A1_Chapter09 (Portable)** from your file storage location and save your file as: `AYS_A1_Chapter09 Wet Noses Clinic`
3. Edit the Preferences to create estimates and do progress invoicing for the company.

Create a New Job

Now that the preferences have been set, you will create the job for Amy's new kitten.

4. Create a new job for Amy Ridgeway called: `Cat-Autumn`

   Dr. James has decided that it is not important for her to track "job status" for her customers, so you will leave the fields on the Job Info tab blank.

5. Leave the company file open.

Create an Estimate for a Job

In this exercise, you will create an estimate for Amy Ridgeway so she can see the full cost for all of the services for her new kitten. She needs to bring in the kitten to be spayed, tested for FIV and feline leukemia, and vaccinated, but she is concerned about the total cost and needs to budget the services.

1. Create an estimate on **071523** for **Amy Ridgeway: Cat-Autumn**, using the items displayed in the illustration. Click **OK** in the Tax Codes window, if necessary.

ITEM	DESCRIPTION
New Patient	New Patient Exam
Vaccine	Vaccine Injection Fee
Pre-A Blood Wk	Pre-Anesthesia Blood Work
Spay Cat	Feline Spay Procedure
IV Fluids	Intravenous Fluids
Pain Meds	Pre- & Post-Surgical Pain Medication
FIV/FeLV	FIV/Feline Leukemia Test
F Leuk	Feline Leukemia Vaccine
Feline DHC	Feline DHC Vaccine
Rabies	Rabies Vaccine
Rev-Cat/Sm Dog	Revolution-Cat/Small Dog

Remember that all service and non-inventory items are not taxable; only inventory items are taxable.

2. Click **Save & Close**.

3. Run the Estimates by Job report for the dates **07/01/2023** to **07/31/2023**.

4. Click the **Excel** Excel ▾ button and export this list to a new worksheet, saving the worksheet to your file storage location as: **CH9_A2 Estimates by Job**

5. Close the report, choosing not to memorize it, and close Excel. Leave the company file open for the next exercise.

Create a Billable Expense

In this exercise, you will create a bill to be charged back to Amy for the expense of the anesthesiologist hired to perform the spaying procedure for Amy's cat. You have already informed Amy of this charge.

1. Create a bill for **Peters, Samantha**, a new vendor, using a new expense account numbered **66600** and the Account Name **Medical Professionals** and this information to complete the bill:

   • Date: **071823**

   • Ref. No.: **Anes 01**

   • Amount Due: **250**

- Terms: **Net 30**

- Memo: `Ridgeway, Cat-Autumn, Spay`

- Copy the bill memo to the Expense tab Memo field

- Customer: **Ridgeway: Cat-Autumn**

- Ensure the **Billable** column is checked

2. Click **Save & Close** and click **Yes** to accept the payment terms.

3. Close the company file.

Create an Invoice from the Estimate

Amy Ridgeway has decided to get Autumn the care she needs in phases. Now you will create a progress invoice for the first set of items.

4. Create an invoice based on the **07/15/2023** estimate for Amy Ridgeway: Cat-Autumn, choosing the option that will allow you to determine which items to invoice.

5. In the Specify Invoice Amount for Items on Estimate window, click in the **Show Percentage** checkbox and then type **100** in the Curr % column to include these items: New Patient, Spay Cat, IV Fluids, Pain Meds, and Vaccine on the invoice.

6. Click **OK**.

Tip! After you enter 100 in the Curr % column for the first item, you can use the down arrow ⬇ key to move down the column to enter the percentages for the other four items.

7. Read the warning message; click **OK** in the Zero Amount Items window.

The Billable Time/Costs window appears because the anesthesiologist was entered as billable against this job.

8. Click **OK** to select the outstanding billable time and costs to add to the invoice.

9. Click the **Expenses** tab and click in the checkmark column to the left of **07/18/2023** for **Peters**, **Samantha** and then click **OK**.

10. Scroll down to see the entry on the last line of the invoice and then set the date to **07/19/2023** and the invoice # to **180**.

11. Click **Save & Close** on the invoice.

The invoice is created for the customer. The rest of the estimate will still be available, from which you can create future invoices.

12. Run the **Job Estimates vs. Actuals Detail** report for **Ridgeway, Amy:Cat-Autumn**.

13. Click the **Excel** | Excel ▾ | button and export this list to a new worksheet, saving the worksheet to your file storage location as: `CH9_A3 Job Estimates vs. Actuals`

14. Run the **Job Profitability Detail** report for Amy Ridgeway's cat, Autumn.

15. Click the **Excel** | Excel ▾ | button and export this list to a new worksheet, saving the worksheet to your file storage location as: `CH9_A3 Job Profitability`

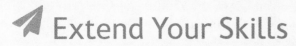
Extend Your Skills

Before You Begin: Open **EYS_Chapter09 (Company)** or restore **EYS_Chapter09 (Portable)** from your file storage location.

You have been hired by Arlaine Cervantes to help her with her organization's books. She is the founder of Niños del Lago, a nonprofit organization that provides impoverished Guatemalan children with an engaging educational camp experience. You have just sat down at your desk and opened a large envelope from her with a variety of documents and noticed that you have several emails from her as well. It is your job to sort through the papers and emails and make sense of what you find, entering information into QuickBooks whenever appropriate and answering any other questions in a word-processing document saved as:

EYS1_Chapter09_LastnameFirstinitial

Remember, you are digging through papers on a desk, so it is up to you to determine the correct order in which to complete the tasks.

- Handwritten receipt: Dated 9/19/2019 for a $500.00 donation from Matthew Drill to purchase food for a camp to be offered in December 2019. Sticky note from Arlaine on the receipt: Can you please figure out a way to account for this donation since the food will not be purchased and consumed until December?

- Handwritten estimate for Expanding Opportunities Together: Dated 9/17/2019 for 50 scarves and 35 handbags. (Expanding Opportunities Together is another nonprofit that is looking to help us raise funds by purchasing and reselling the goods we get from the women in Guatemala.) Each of the products was on a separate line, and both at 25 percent off regular retail.

- Message from Arlaine: "We should probably think about what we should do if customers do not pay their bill on time…. Can we assess finance charges in QuickBooks? If so, please set it up so we charge 12 percent interest on overdue invoices. I think we need to have a nice grace period, though, so please set that at 30 days. Don't worry about charging a minimum finance charge or charging interest on overdue finance charges."

- Printed email: Received the contract from Expanding Opportunities Together. Could you please bill them for 50 percent up front?

- Scribbled note from Arlaine: Is there a report you can create for me that will show how much of the estimate has been invoiced?

10 Customizing and Integrating in QuickBooks

Finally, the artist in you gets to have some fun! It's time to learn about customizing QuickBooks forms and reports to look professional and work best for your company. In this chapter, you will customize reports to include pertinent information and make them look more attractive. You will also customize customer and vendor profile lists, create custom fields, and create a custom invoice template. In addition, you will see how well QuickBooks integrates with Microsoft Office to help you manage your company's data.

LEARNING OBJECTIVES

▸ Use Customer & Vendor Profile Lists

▸ Create and use custom fields

▸ Customize reports and graphs

▸ Create custom templates

▸ Integrate with Microsoft Office

Project: Average Guy Designs

With Guy being a designer, he really wants to jazz up his QuickBooks forms and correspondence. Guy would like to learn how the lists and custom fields can be utilized for his business and is interested in using Word and Excel seamlessly with QuickBooks. You will be in charge of adding some finesse to Average Guy Designs' company reports and templates.

Average Guy Designs
110 Sampson Way
Bayshore, CA 91547

Invoice

Date	Invoice #
11/16/2023	10026

Bill To

Tim's BBQ Palooza
Tim Laughlin
8 College Drive
Berkeley, CA 94608

P.O. No.	Terms	Due Date	Project
	Net 30	12/16/2023	

Description	Qty	Rate	Amount
Website Design Work	1	125.00	125.00

You can customize your templates to make them more appealing.

Working with Customer & Vendor Profile Lists

When Guy created his new QuickBooks company and chose a type of company on which to base it, QuickBooks created a generic Chart of Accounts and populated the Customer & Vendor Profile Lists with entries relevant to his chosen company type. You have already seen many of these profile lists in the forms and lists you have worked with in this book.

Look at the profile lists that QuickBooks provides to track customer and vendor information, as well as the examples of forms and lists in which you may find them appearing as fields.

PROFILE LISTS AND WHERE THEY APPEAR	
Name of List	**You may find this list as a field on...**
Sales Rep List	Customer & Job List (Additional Info tab)
	Create Invoices form
Customer Type List	Customer & Job List (Additional Info tab)
Vendor Type List	Vendor List (Additional Info tab)
Job Type List	Customer & Job List (Job Info tab)
Terms List	Vendor List
	Create Invoices form

(cont'd.)

PROFILE LISTS AND WHERE THEY APPEAR	
Name of List	**You may find this list as a field on...**
Customer Message List	Enter Sales Receipts form
Payment Method List	Receive Payments form
Ship Via List	Create Invoices form (product or custom template)
Vehicle List	Enter Vehicle Mileage window

Designating Sales Reps in QuickBooks

For many businesses, being able to track sales by employee or representative is important, and QuickBooks provides a way to track this information by providing a Sales Rep List as one of the Customer & Vendor Profile Lists. Sales Reps may be employees, a partner in the business, or independent contractors to whom you issue 1099s. You will manage this list the same as you do other lists in QuickBooks, and you can choose to display this field on forms and reports. There are even pre-set reports that allow you to determine sales by reps.

Making the Lists Work for You

Using the Customer & Vendor Profile Lists can help you in many ways. You can even use a list for a purpose other than that for which it was intended. For instance, your company may not ship products, so you have no need for the Ship Via field. You can use this field to track an additional aspect of your company. You cannot create new profile lists, so you need to maximize the lists QuickBooks provides by modifying them to track all information needed by your company.

There are two main benefits of fully utilizing these lists. The first is that they can be included on reports and used to filter the reports. For example, you can use the Customer Type to display only residential customers on your Profit & Loss Report or Customer reports to conduct a focused marketing effort. The second benefit is that they can be used to customize form templates.

 Lists→Customer & Vendor Profile Lists

DEVELOP YOUR SKILLS 10-1

In this exercise, you will work with the Customer Message, Vendor Type, and Customer Type Lists. You can use these procedures with any other profile list as well. You will set up three employees for Average Guy Designs. The password for all files unless otherwise stated is Password1. *Leave the file open unless otherwise instructed.*

1. Start QuickBooks 2019 and toggle to Pro, if necessary.
2. Choose **File→Open or Restore Company**.
3. Open **DYS_Chapter10 (Company)** or restore **DYS_Chapter10 (Portable)** from your file storage location and save your file as: **DYS_Chapter10 Average Guy Designs**

Edit a Profile List Entry

4. Choose **Lists→Customer & Vendor Profile Lists→Customer Message List**.
5. Double-click **Thank you for your business.**

6. Replace the current message with: **We truly appreciate your business.**

7. Click **OK** to save the new message.

   Now you can select this message on the Create Invoices and Enter Sales Receipt forms that you create for your customers.

8. Close the Customer Message List window.

Create New Profile List Entries

You will now add a new vehicle to the Vendor Profile List and a new type to the Customer Type List.

9. Choose **Lists→Customer & Vendor Profile Lists→Vehicle List**.

10. Click the **Vehicle** drop-down arrow ▼ and choose **New**.

11. Enter **2013 Vespa** as the new vehicle, click **OK**, and then close the Vehicle List.

12. Choose **Lists→Customer & Vendor Profile Lists→Customer Type List**.

13. Click the **Customer Type** drop-down arrow ▼ and choose **New**.

14. Enter **From Website** as the new type, click **OK**, and then close the Customer Type List.

    You will now edit Mary Jones' customer record to reflect that she learned of the business from the website.

15. Choose **Customers→Customer Center**.

16. Double-click **Jones, Mary** in the Customers & Jobs List at the left.

17. Click the **Additional Info** tab.

18. Set the Customer Type to **From Website** and click **OK**.

    Leave the Customer Center open.

Delete a Profile List Entry

It has been decided that it's not necessary to have both Suppliers and Supplies on the Vendor Type List, so you will delete one.

19. Choose **Lists→Customer & Vendor Profile Lists→Vendor Type List**.

20. Single-click **Suppliers**.

21. Click the **Vendor Type** drop-down arrow ▼ and choose **Delete Vendor Type**; click **OK** to confirm the deletion.

    In this case you were able to delete the Vendor Type. If an entry in any Type List has been used in at least one transaction, you will not be able to delete it; you should make it inactive instead.

22. Close the Vendor Type List.

Creating Custom Fields

You will work with many forms in QuickBooks, and you may choose to send some of these forms to customers and vendors. QuickBooks provides many standard forms (such as invoice, purchase order, and sales receipt), but you can also create your own forms or modify the standard Intuit forms. To use custom fields on a form, you must create your own form rather than use one of the standard forms provided by QuickBooks. You can also make a copy of a standard Intuit form and customize it.

Custom fields for names include customers/jobs, vendors, and employees and can be created in the same window, which is accessible from any of these three lists. Custom fields for items must be set through the Item List. All types of custom fields can be used on multiple forms once they are created. These fields can also be included on reports or just used to store additional information, such as favorite brand, which might be useful if you are a fashion retailer and want to be able to produce a list of customers who all like the same brand for an event. Consistency in entries is the key to using these types of fields!

Adding Custom Fields

Before you can use custom fields in reports, you must first set them up in the lists where they belong.

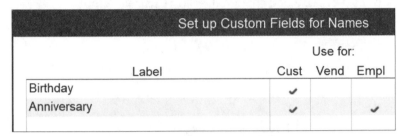

Set up Custom Fields for Names			
		Use for:	
Label	Cust	Vend	Empl
Birthday	✔		
Anniversary	✔		✔

The Set up Custom Fields for Names window allows you to create custom fields for three lists: Customers & Jobs, Vendors, and Employees.

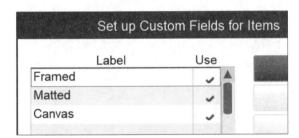

Set up Custom Fields for Items		
Label	Use	
Framed	✔	
Matted	✔	
Canvas	✔	

You must set up all custom fields for items in a separate window.

Note! Custom fields are available for all types of items except for subtotals, sales tax items, and sales tax groups.

Customers→Customer Center: [open customer record]→Additional Info→Define Fields

Lists→Item List: [edit item]→Custom Fields

DEVELOP YOUR SKILLS 10-2

In this exercise, you will fill in Chris Nelson's customer type and create custom fields to track additional information for future use on custom templates.

1. With the Customer Center open, double-click **Nelson, Chris** in the Customers & Jobs List at the left, scrolling down, if necessary.

2. Click the **Additional Info** tab.

3. Choose **From Website** as the Customer Type.

4. Click the **Define Fields** button in the Custom Fields section of the window.

5. Use this information to set up two custom fields:

Set up Custom Fields for Names			
		Use for:	
Label	Cust	Vend	Empl
Birthday	✔		
Anniversary	✔		✔

Ⓐ Label (first row): **Birthday** and check to Use for: **Cust**

Ⓑ Label (second row): **Anniversary** and check to Use for: **Cust** and **Empl**

6. Click **OK**; click **OK** again to acknowledge the prompt that you can use custom fields in templates, if necessary.

7. Click in the **Birthday** field and type **05/21/69** to enter Chris Nelson's date of birth.

8. Click **OK** to accept the changes and then close the Customer Center window.

Create and Fill an Item Custom Field

You will now add a custom field for items and use it on a non-inventory item.

9. Choose **Lists→Item List**, resizing the window, if necessary.

10. Double-click **Art Work** to open the Edit Item window.

11. Click the **Custom Fields** button and then click **OK** to continue to the Custom Fields for Art Work window.

12. Click the **Define Fields** button.

13. Use this information to add the custom fields:

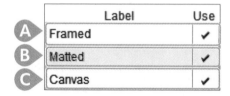

Label	Use
Framed	✔
Matted	✔
Canvas	✔

Ⓐ Label (first row): **Framed** (and check **Use**)

Ⓑ Label (second row): **Matted** (and check **Use**)

Ⓒ Label (third row): **Canvas** (and check **Use**)

14. Click **OK** and then **OK** two more times, closing the Information and Custom Fields for Art Work windows.

You have created the custom fields but did not type in any data here because you will add it to the individual forms instead. If you wish, you can type the custom field information into the Custom Fields for Art Work window and it will then appear on each form or report you create that displays the field.

15. Click **OK** one last time to close the Edit Item window and then close the Item List.

Setting Price Levels

There are many instances when a business may wish to charge different prices. Perhaps a customer is a dealer of your product or a high-volume customer to whom you wish to give a better price. Using price levels is a way you can customize the varying prices without having to manually type it on your sales forms. When a price level is set and associated with a customer or job, it will automatically fill in on forms or future transactions (although you can manually change what fills in, if needed). A price level can also be set directly on the form without editing the customer's record. Price levels require that the items in the Item List have prices set. Quick-Books will calculate the price level according to the price already set.

With all versions of QuickBooks, the price level can be set by a fixed percentage. If you are working with a Premier or higher version of QuickBooks, you can also set price levels per item. Before setting up price levels, you need to make sure that the preference is turned on in QuickBooks.

Note! Although you can use a discount to reduce a price, price levels might be better because discounts are not linked to individual customers or jobs.

Fixed Percentage Price Levels

The fixed percentage price level lets you decrease or increase the items being charged to a customer or job by a specific percentage amount. For instance, you may wish to decrease all items purchased by nonprofit agencies by 10 percent or customer's purchases by 5 percent.

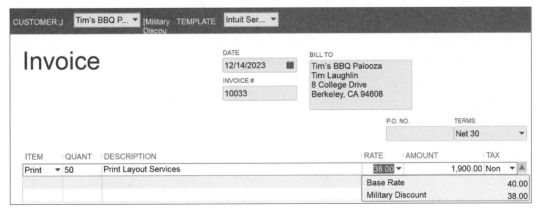

When price levels are set up, you can choose from them in the Rate field on sales forms.

Per-Item Price Levels

If you use the Premier version or above option, you can create specific dollar amounts for items or groups of items that you can associate with selected customers or jobs. For instance, you may wish to charge Evelyn Huff $50 per hour for basic video editing services rather than the standard $55 per hour rate.

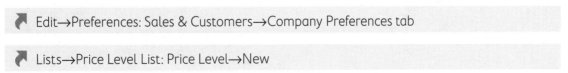

Edit→Preferences: Sales & Customers→Company Preferences tab

Lists→Price Level List: Price Level→New

DEVELOP YOUR SKILLS 10-3

In this exercise, you will first set a fixed percentage price level of 5 percent less than the "normal" price as a military discount. You will assign a price level to Tim's BBQ Palooza, as its owner is a retired Marine. You will then create an invoice utilizing the new price level on the company's next job. Price level preferences have already been turned on.

1. Choose **Lists→Price Level List**.
2. Click **Price Level** button at the bottom of the window and then choose **New**.

Note! If you are using a Premier version, you will need to ensure that Fixed % is the Price Level Type selected.

3. Use this information to set a new price level:
   - Price Level Name: **Military Discount**
   - This price level will: **decrease** item prices by **5.0%**
4. Click **OK** and close the Price Level List.

Assign a Price Level to a Customer

5. Choose **Customers→Customer Center**.
6. Double-click **Tim's BBQ Palooza** and then click the **Payment Settings** tab.
7. Click the **Price Level** drop-down arrow ▼, choose **Military Discount**, and click **OK**.
8. Right-click **Tim's BBQ Palooza** and choose **Add Job**.
9. Type **Print Menus** as the Job Name and click **OK**.
10. Click **New Transactions** and then choose **Invoices**.
11. Use this information to complete the invoice:
    - Date: **121423**
    - Item: **Print**
    - Quantity: **50**
    - Rate: Click the **Rate** drop-down arrow ▼ and notice the Base Rate is 40 and the Military Discount Rate is 38; tap [Esc] to keep the Military Rate
    - Customer Message: **We truly appreciate your business.**
    - Memo: **Tim's BBQ: Print Menus**
12. Click **Save & Close** to record the invoice; close the Customer Center window.

BEHIND THE SCENES BRIEF

11000•Accounts Receivable DR 1900.00; **48800•Print Layout Income CR <1900.00>**

Setting Billing Rate Levels

Available only in Premier editions of QuickBooks (Contractor, Professional services, and Accountant editions as well as Enterprise), billing rate levels are used when you have employees or vendors performing the same job at different levels of expertise and you want to bill accordingly. When you've set up the billing rate level, you will go to the specific employees or vendors and choose the appropriate level.

When setting up billing rates, you can either set a fixed hourly rate that would be used for all service items, employees, and vendors with this billing rate level or set a custom hourly rate for one or more service items. The service items must be set up as two-sided items. When used with a time sheet, the time can then be billed back to the customer at the adjusted hourly rate.

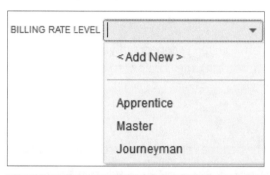

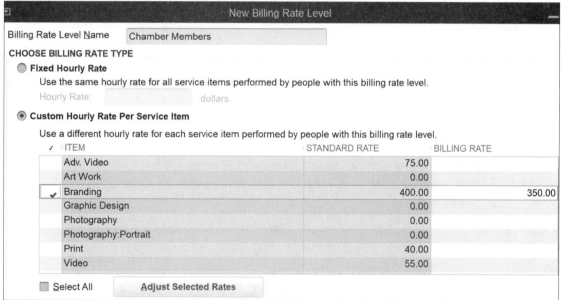

Create new billing rate levels with a fixed hourly rate or custom hourly rates by service item. In this example, Guy decided to give a special deal to fellow chamber members who wanted a full branding package.

Customizing Reports and Graphs

Customization takes place on many fronts, and customizing the reports that you produce is important for business analysis.

You may find yourself asking:

- Which accounts should I display?

- What information do I need to filter out?

- What header and footer information should I include?

- How do I want my fonts and numbers to look?

Display Properties

The Display tab of the Modify Report window allows you to change aspects of your report such as the dates it represents, your reporting basis (cash or accrual), the columns to display, and subcolumn preferences.

Report Date Range

Each preset report has a default date range displayed when the report is first created. The date can either be:

- When your reporting period ends, such as a balance sheet report created "As of June 30, 2023."

- For a range of days, such as a profit & loss report created for June 1–30, 2023.

The date range is determined by the type of report you produce.

Accrual vs. Cash Basis Reporting

There are two methods of accounting from which you can choose for your company:

- **Accrual Basis:** Income is recorded when a sale is made, and expenses are recorded when incurred. This method is used often by firms and businesses with large inventories; it's required for publicly traded companies.

- **Cash Basis:** Income is recorded when cash is received, and expenses are recorded when cash is paid. This method is commonly used by small businesses and professionals.

You enter data into QuickBooks the same way regardless of whether you use the cash or accrual basis of accounting. When you create your reports, you can easily switch between cash and accrual basis. When you first create a QuickBooks company, the default for reports is to use the accrual basis. You can set your company's default report basis in the report section of the Edit Preferences window.

If you operate using the cash basis, you will not need to display Accounts Receivable and Accounts Payable on your financial statements. These are only displayed when transactions have happened and cash has yet to change hands.

> **FLASHBACK TO GAAP: REVENUE & CONSISTENCY**
>
> Remember that publicly traded companies are required to use the accrual basis of accounting (revenue) and that companies need to use the same accounting principles and methods from year to year (consistency).

Report Columns and Subcolumns

Each preset report displays certain default columns. You can change the columns to make your report more useful. For instance, you can choose to display multiple months on a Profit & Loss report to compare income and expenses in different reporting periods.

Some reports allow you to add subcolumns to further analyze your data. The use of columns and subcolumns to stratify data can be a very valuable way to help you to analyze and scrutinize your company's financial data.

This is an example of subcolumns that can be added to a report. The subcolumns available differ based on the report displayed.

Filtering Reports

Reports, unless customized, will display all data for accounts, customers, or any other category. But you can apply a filter on a report that will let you choose what information to include, thereby "filtering out" the rest. Filters can be applied to any report, and the report you run determines the specific information that can be filtered. You are also able to filter transaction reports for text that is contained in custom fields, if those fields are on the forms for the transactions included in the report.

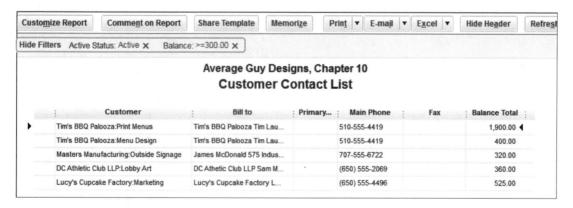

Formatting Fonts and Numbers

Formatting deals with the appearance of the report; it has nothing to do with the data contained within it. You will change the report's font(s) and the way numbers are displayed in the following exercise.

For example, QuickBooks displays its preset reports in the default font. You can make many choices as to the characteristics of the font in your report, such as the font name, style, color, and size. When you have negative numbers in your report, they can be displayed in a variety of ways, such as in parentheses or with a minus sign.

You can also choose how QuickBooks will display all numbers in your report. The options available are displayed in the illustration to the right.

Edit→Preferences: Reports & Graphs→Company Preferences tab

Reports→Company & Financial→[select report]: Customize Report

DEVELOP YOUR SKILLS 10-4

In this exercise, you will create and customize a Profit & Loss report. Guy spoke with his accountant and determined that Average Guy Designs uses the cash basis for reporting. You will begin by changing this default for the company file.

1. Choose **Edit→Preferences**.
2. Click the **Reports & Graphs** category on the left side of the window.
3. Click the **Company Preferences** tab and then choose **Cash** in the Summary Reports Basis section.
4. Click **OK** to save the new preference.

Add a Filter

You will first run the preset Profit & Loss Standard report and then apply a filter to the report to show only income accounts.

5. Choose **Reports→Company & Financial→Profit & Loss Standard**.
6. Use this information to set a custom date range:
   - From: **120123**
   - To: **123123**
   - Click the **Refresh** button on the toolbar, resizing the report window to view all the data
   You will see the Profit & Loss report displayed for December 2023.
7. Click the **Customize Report** button on the report toolbar.
8. Follow these steps to apply a filter that will include only income accounts on the report:

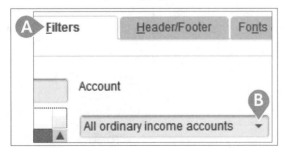

Ⓐ Click the **Filters** tab.

Ⓑ Choose **All Ordinary Income Accounts** as the Account.

9. Click **OK**.

You will now see the report with no expense accounts shown.

Change the Font and Number Formatting

Now you will spruce up the report by changing the way the font and numbers appear.

10. Click the **Customize Report** button on the report toolbar and then click the **Fonts & Numbers** tab in the Modify Report: Profit & Loss window.

11. Use this information to change the formatting:

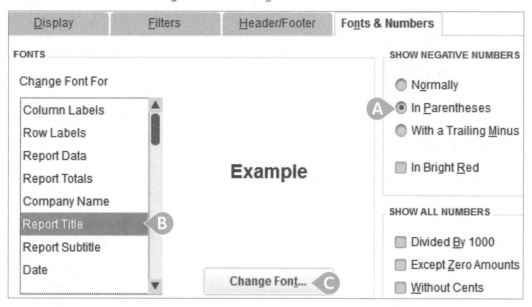

Ⓐ Show Negative Numbers: **In Parentheses**

Ⓑ Change Font For: **Report Title**

Ⓒ Click the **Change Font...** button

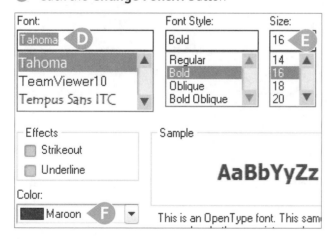

Ⓓ Font: **Tahoma**

Ⓔ Size: **16**

Ⓕ Color: **Maroon**

12. Click **OK** in the Report Title window.

13. Click **Yes** to change all related fonts and then click **OK**.

   You will see the font formatting changes that you just made. Leave the report open; you will continue to customize it in the next exercise.

Additional Report Formatting Options

You have learned to choose many report customization options. Now you will learn to create a header and footer to your specifications and to memorize and recall a report.

Header and Footer Options

All preset QuickBooks reports display the default headers and footers. You can change the information included and how it is formatted on the Header/Footer tab of the Modify Report window.

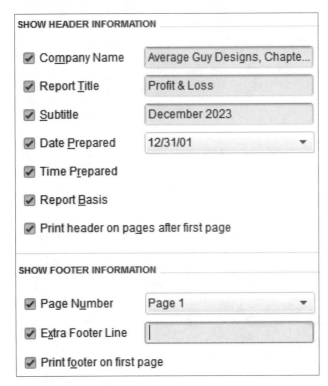

Page Layout

You can choose to use the default standard report layout or to use left, right, or centered alignment.

Memorizing Reports

After you have created a report with your chosen settings, you may wish to save the report options so you can easily produce the same report again. The process of saving the settings of a report is called *memorizing* a report, and it is available for all reports. The memorizing feature memorizes the format of the report, not the data contained within it. This means that when you open a memorized report, it will contain your most recently entered data.

To recall the memorized report, you can choose it from the Memorized Report List.

Memorized Report Groups

QuickBooks allows you to organize your memorized reports into groups. There are six preset groups (accountant, banking, company, customers, employees, and vendors), and you can choose to create your own. When you memorize a report, you can place it in a group immediately or later.

Batch Processing of Reports

If you have a group of reports that you run together on a regular basis, you may wish to process them as a batch to save time. You will first need to set the reports you wish to process together as a memorized report group, and then you will be able to process them all at once.

The Process Multiple Reports window allows you to choose which group of reports to process as a batch. You can set the date range in this window, too, if you need to change it from the range that was memorized.

Specialized Reports

QuickBooks offers many ways that you can report on your transactional data and examine the health of your business. Not only can you schedule reports to be sent to your email regularly, but you can also comment on reports and then share them within your organization, as well as contribute and share reports across the QuickBooks community.

Scheduled Reports

As a business owner, it is important to continually monitor and analyze your company's financial data. QuickBooks facilitates this by allowing you to schedule reports to be sent regularly by email. You can choose which reports to send and the frequency by which they are sent.

> **Note!** To use the Schedule Reports feature, you must have Outlook open if you use it to email through QuickBooks. In addition, you must close other company files and keep your computer on, with sleep mode turned off.

Commented Reports

You can view, add, or delete comments to any report, thus creating a Commented Report that you can save, print, or share. When you do add comments to a report, QuickBooks saves a snapshot of the report at that time into the Commented Reports List.

Contributed Reports

You can customize or create your own reports to meet a specific need. If that report can be beneficial to others, you can add it to Contributed Reports by clicking Share Template on the report toolbar. When sharing the template, the data doesn't get transmitted; only the template for the report is shared. It's a great way to help the QuickBooks community! It's free to share and free to use contributed reports.

Industry Specific Reports

There are several Industry Specific Reports listed under the Contributed tab of the Report Center menu, including many Job Costing Professional Services reports, Construction reports, and Retail reports.

> Reports→Memorized Reports→Memorized Report List *or* Commented Reports *or* Process Multiple Reports

---

DEVELOP YOUR SKILLS 10-5

In this exercise, you will make additional custom changes in the report and memorize the final product. You will then add comments to and save the report.

The Profit & Loss Standard report should still be open. If not, repeat Develop Your Skills 10-4 to produce the report.

1. Click the **Customize Report** button on the report toolbar.
2. Use this information to make the changes to the header and footer:
   - Click the **Header/Footer** tab
   - Company Name: **Average Guy Designs**
   - Report Title: **Income Report**
   - Date Prepared: Click to uncheck the box
   - Alignment: **Left**
3. Click **OK**.

   Look at the changes you have made to your report.

Change How Columns Are Displayed

Now you will modify the report so it separates the income by each two-week period.

4. Click the **Customize Report** button on the Report toolbar.

5. Click the **Display Columns By** drop-down arrow ▼ in the Columns section and choose **Two Week**.

6. Click **OK**.

   QuickBooks displays the Income Report that you have customized.

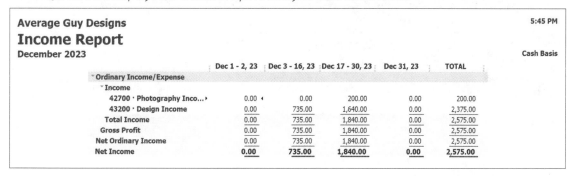

Average Guy Designs							5:45 PM
Income Report							
December 2023							Cash Basis
		Dec 1 - 2, 23	Dec 3 - 16, 23	Dec 17 - 30, 23	Dec 31, 23	TOTAL	
▾ Ordinary Income/Expense							
▾ Income							
42700 · Photography Inco...▸		0.00 ◂	0.00	200.00	0.00	200.00	
43200 · Design Income		0.00	735.00	1,640.00	0.00	2,375.00	
Total Income		0.00	735.00	1,840.00	0.00	2,575.00	
Gross Profit		0.00	735.00	1,840.00	0.00	2,575.00	
Net Ordinary Income		0.00	735.00	1,840.00	0.00	2,575.00	
Net Income		**0.00**	**735.00**	**1,840.00**	**0.00**	**2,575.00**	

Memorize a Report

Now that the report is the way you want it, you will memorize it for easy recall.

7. Click the **Memorize** button on the report toolbar.

8. Use this information to memorize the report and place it in a group:

   • Name: **Income Report**

   • Click to place a checkmark in the **Save in Memorized Report Group** checkbox

   • Save in Memorized Report Group: **Company**

9. Click **OK** and then close the Income Report window.

Process Multiple Reports

You will now process a batch of reports from the Company group.

10. Choose **Reports→Memorized Reports→Memorized Report List**.

11. Scroll down to the group header *Company*, right-click it, and choose **Process Group**.

    In the Process Multiple Reports window, you will see that the report you just memorized, Income Report, is included in this group.

12. Click **Display** to process the batch of reports.

    QuickBooks will produce all of the reports in the Company group for the date ranges displayed. If your report windows are maximized, you'll only see the top-most report. Restore the top-most window to see all of the report windows. Change the date ranges as desired.

13. Choose **Window→Close All**.

Create a Commented Report

You will add a comment to a report and save it in the Commented Reports List.

14. Choose **Reports→Company & Financial→Profit & Loss Standard**.

15. Set the date range:

- From: **120123**

- To: **123123**

16. Click **Refresh**, resize the report to see all the data, and then click the **Comment on Report** button on the report toolbar.

17. Follow these steps to complete a commented report:

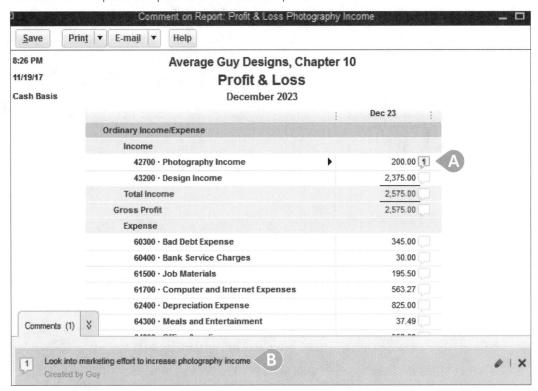

- Ⓐ Click in the comment balloon.

- Ⓑ Type the comment in the 1 field: **Look into marketing effort to increase photography income**

18. Click **Save** in the Comments area to save the comment.

19. Click **Save** on the toolbar, enter **Profit & Loss Photography Income Concerns** as the report name, and click **OK**.

20. Click **OK** to acknowledge the commented report was saved and then close the report window; finally, close the Profit & Loss report, choosing not to memorize it.

This saves your report in the Commented Reports List, which you can view from the Reports menu.

Creating Custom Forms

Before you customize your forms, think about what you want them to do for you:

- Do you want to include custom fields?
- Do you want to include a company logo?
- What do you want the forms you will be sending out to your stakeholders to say about your company?
- How much detail do you want to include?
- What size fields will you need?

Templates

A template is a specific form format (with no data) on which you can base future forms. Quick-Books provides several templates, but you can also create custom templates to meet the needs of your unique company or create templates for preprinted forms. All templates available for a particular type of form are available from the drop-down list at the top of the form. Changing templates for a transaction that has already been entered will not change the information recorded in the transaction, even if the field is not visible on the new form.

Creating a Custom Template

When you choose to create a custom template, you begin by specifying information in the Basic Customization window. This window also provides a preview of how the template looks as you make changes to the various fields and information.

Adding a Company Logo to Templates

QuickBooks allows you to further personalize your templates by including your company logo. When you add a logo to your template, the image file will be stored in the folder where your company file is located. To add a logo or picture on a template, the company file must be located on the computer's hard drive or on a shared server. It will not work if your company file is located on a flash drive.

The Manage Templates Window

It is in the Manage Templates window where you will assign a name for your new template. You can also access additional templates online from this window. When you click the Download Templates button, QuickBooks launches a web browser and displays the QuickBooks website from which you can choose additional templates available to you.

Using Custom Fields in Forms and Reports

You need to create your own custom form template to utilize the custom fields you set up earlier in this chapter. You can choose to add the custom field information for customers, jobs, vendors, and employees on the Header tab of the Additional Customization window. To add the custom fields for items, you must use the Columns tab. It is up to you to determine whether the various fields will be displayed on the screen, on the printed form, on both, or in neither place.

If you wish to display custom fields on reports, you can choose to display them in the Screen and/or Print boxes on the Columns tab of the Modify Report window.

When creating a template, you can choose to see a field on the screen, printed on the form, in both places, or not at all.

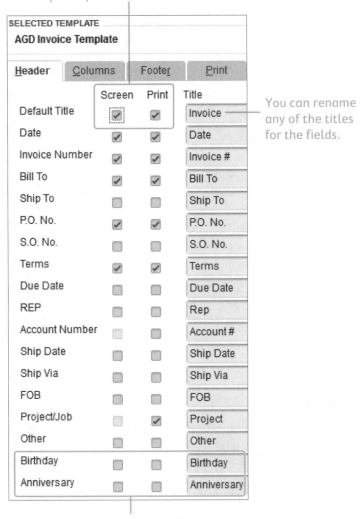

You can rename any of the titles for the fields.

You can include your custom fields on your new template.

The Layout Designer Window

QuickBooks allows you to determine not only what is included on a template, but also where it will be placed. You can move fields and labels around your template and change the size of fields in the Layout Designer window. Each element on the template is termed an "object" in the Layout Designer window, and you can use some standard techniques to select, move, and resize all objects. The Snap to Grid feature ensures that all objects line up to a grid for which you can specify the spacing. In addition, you will see two shadows where the standard envelope windows are located so you can make sure to line up the addressees and return addresses properly.

Lists→Templates

In this exercise, you will create a template for the company.

1. Choose **Lists→Templates**.
2. Click the **Templates** drop-down arrow ▼ and choose **New**.
3. Ensure **Invoice** is the type of template selected; click **OK**.
4. Click the **Manage Templates** button in the Basic Customization window.
5. Replace the default template name at the top right with **AGD Invoice Template** and then click **OK** to return to the Basic Customization window.

Change the Color Scheme of the Template

You will now change the template and company name color.

6. Click the **Select Color Scheme** drop-down arrow ▼, choose **Green**, and click the **Apply Color Scheme** button.

   You can see the new color in the preview area on the right side of the window.

Add Customization

Now it is time to decide which customer and item fields you wish to include on the new template.

7. Click the **Additional Customization** button at the bottom of the window.
8. Click to place a checkmark in the **Due Date** checkbox in the Print column.

   A Layout Designer window appears to let you know how you can make changes to the way in which the new field will be laid out on the template.

9. Click in the checkbox for **Do not display this message in the future** and tap Enter.
10. Use this information to continue to customize your template:

    • Header tab: Scroll down, if necessary, and click to place checkmarks in the **Screen** column for both **Birthday** and **Anniversary**.

    • Columns tab: Scroll down, if necessary, and click to place checkmarks in the **Screen** column for **Framed**, **Matted**, and **Canvas**.

    Notice the order column; it shows the order in which the columns will appear on the invoice from left to right.

11. Click **OK** in the Additional Customization window.
12. Feel free to play around and customize your template further, including using the Layout Designer.
13. When you are finished customizing your template, click **OK** in the Basic Customization window and close the Templates window.

Integrating with Microsoft Office

QuickBooks works very well with a variety of Microsoft Office Suite programs. For instance, you can import and export lists from Outlook, export reports to Excel, import list entries from Excel, and merge data from QuickBooks with a Word document to produce letters. There are also a large number of apps available that integrate seamlessly with QuickBooks.

> **Note!** Integrated applications are software products created by independent developers and industry experts. Examples include Time Tracking, Inventory Tracking, Customer Relationship Management, and Managing Recurring Invoices and Payments. These apps can be controlled and restricted through the Integrated Applications Company Preferences tab. They are available through the QuickBooks Marketplace for a fee. Go to apps.com to learn more.

Sending Letters with Word

There are a large number of letter templates in Word, or you can customize your own. After you have prepared your letter, QuickBooks will launch Word and merge your QuickBooks data into the letter for you.

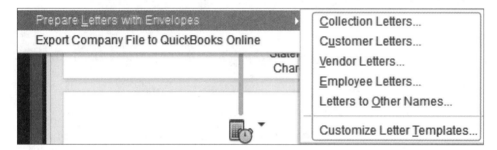

The option to create letters with Word is accessible from the Company menu.

Exporting QuickBooks Reports to Excel

While there are many reports provided for you in QuickBooks, you may want more control over how you manage and display your QuickBooks data. To analyze your QuickBooks data more effectively, you may wish to export it to Microsoft Excel, a spreadsheet program, so you can use the advanced features available in it. QuickBooks makes it very easy to export and update a report.

QuickBooks allows you to easily export a report or update an existing spreadsheet by clicking the Excel button on a report's toolbar.

Updating Excel Reports

You can update reports exported to Excel without having to reformat all the data each time a new entry has been made in QuickBooks. The formatting changes that you make to your Quick-Books data will be "memorized" in Excel, so when you export that same report in the future, you will be able to update an existing worksheet. Use this process to avoid going in and changing all of the formatting each time you export the report. Some of the formatting options that will be memorized for you are report titles, new formulas, row and column headers (both font changes and new header names), and inserted columns and rows.

You can initiate the updating of an exported report from the report window in QuickBooks or from the Excel window while viewing the report.

You can click the Excel button and choose Create a New Worksheet to display the Send Report to Excel window.

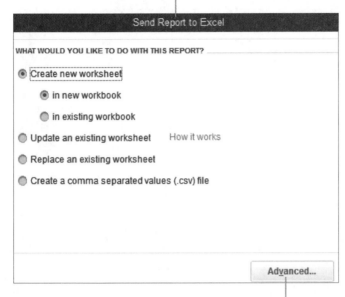

The Advanced button leads to options to help control how data is exported to Excel.

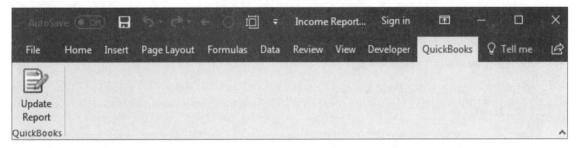

When working in Excel with a spreadsheet containing data that has been exported from QuickBooks, you can update the spreadsheet using the QuickBooks tab from within Excel.

Company→Prepare Letters with Envelopes→Customer Letters

Reports→Memorized Reports

Note! To learn more about how to work with your report in Excel, you may want to check out a Labyrinth Learning Excel textbook for the version you are using (2019, 2016, 2013, etc.).

In this exercise, you will produce letters for your customers, Olivia York and Hernando Diaz, to say Happy Birthday!

To complete this exercise, you must have a copy of Microsoft Word installed on your computer. If you do not have Word installed, skip this exercise and continue to the next topic.

1. Choose **Company→Prepare Letters with Envelopes→Customer Letters**.

2. Click **Copy** to place a copy of the QuickBooks letter templates in your company file folder, if necessary.

   The Letters and Envelopes window will appear, asking you to choose the recipients. By default, all customers are selected.

3. Follow these steps to select two customers:

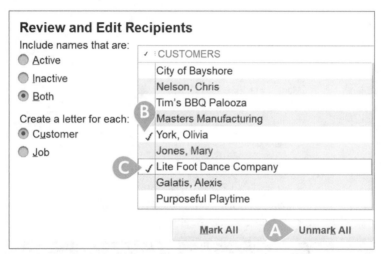

   Ⓐ Click **Unmark All**.

   Ⓑ Click to select **York, Olivia**.

   Ⓒ Click to select **Lite Foot Dance Company**.

4. Click **Next**.

   You will now have a chance to choose from a template or to create or edit your own template.

5. Scroll down in the list of letter templates, click **Customer birthday** to choose that template, and click **Next**.

6. Use this information to set how you want to sign off on the letters:

   • Name: `Guy Marshall`

   • Title: `Graphic Designer and Owner`

7. Click **Next**.

QuickBooks will create the letters and launch Microsoft Word for you. You may have to switch to Microsoft Word to see the letters. If required information was missing from your customer record(s), you would see a QuickBooks Information Is Missing window explaining how to resolve the issue.

Warning! At the time of this writing, there is a bug preventing QuickBooks from launching Word 2019. If this happens to you, continue on to step 12.

Average Guy Designs. Chapter 10
110 Sampson Way
Bayshore, CA 91547

November 20, 2023

Olivia York
1021 Miller St.
Medford, OR 97504

Dear Olivia,

Happy Birthday!

Please accept our wishes for an enjoyable day and a prosperous year.

We also want to take this opportunity to thank you for your business. Customers like you make it all worthwhile.

Congratulations again,

Guy Marshall
Graphic Designer and Owner
Average Guy Designs. Chapter 10

---

8. You may have to switch back to QuickBooks and then read the information regarding how to print the letters and envelopes and then click **Next**.

The Envelope Options window will appear.

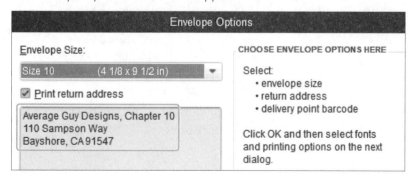

9. Click **OK** in the Envelope Options window.

The envelope will appear in Word.

10. If necessary, switch back to Word; in the Envelope Options window there, click **Cancel** since you don't need to print practice envelopes!

11. Close all Word windows and then click **Cancel** in the QuickBooks Letters and Envelopes window.

Export a Report to Excel

Now you will export the report you memorized earlier to Excel. To complete this task, you will need to have Microsoft Excel 2007 or later installed on your computer. If you do not have Excel installed, or if you have been exporting reports to Excel as a part of the AYS exercises for QuickGrader and have this task down, then you can continue on to the next section.

12. Choose **Reports→Memorized Reports→Memorized Report List**. Right-click the **Income Report** and choose **Generate Report: Income Report**.

13. Click the **Excel** button on the report toolbar and then choose **Create New Worksheet**.

14. Ensure that your report data will be used to **create a new worksheet in a new workbook**.

15. Click **Export**.

16. Choose **File→Save As** from the Excel Ribbon.

17. Navigate to your file storage location and save the report as: **Income Report**. Click **Yes** in the Microsoft Excel window.

> **Note!** To learn more about how to work with your report in Excel, you may want to utilize a Labyrinth Learning Excel textbook for the version you are using (2019, 2016, 2013, etc.).

18. Close the Microsoft Excel window.

19. Close the Income Report and Memorized Report List window in QuickBooks.

Using Excel to Import Multiple List Entries into QuickBooks

Another very valuable role that Microsoft Excel can play with your QuickBooks work is that it can be used to help you to import multiple list entries. You will want to make sure that you start with an Excel worksheet that is set up with the correct fields for importing so the import process goes smoothly.

	A	B	C	D	E	F	G	H	I	J	K	L	M
1	Vendor Name	Company Name	Mr./Ms.	First Name	M.I.	Last Name	Main Phone	Fax	Alt. Phone	E-mail	Address 1	Address 2	Address 3
2													
3													
4													
5													
6													
7													

Here is an example of how you would want to set up your Excel spreadsheet in order to be able to import multiple vendors seamlessly into QuickBooks.

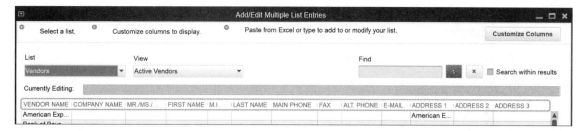

Notice how the names of the columns (the fields) in the QuickBooks Add/Edit Multiple List Entries window matches with those in Excel.

You can add multiple list entries to five of the lists within QuickBooks:

- Customers

- Vendors

- Service Items

- Inventory Parts

- Non-Inventory Parts

 Lists→Add/Edit Multiple List Entries

DEVELOP YOUR SKILLS 10-8

In this exercise, you will use the Add/Edit Multiple List Entries method to enter vendors into QuickBooks. The method that is used here can be used with the other four lists that allow multiple entries to be imported into QuickBooks as well.

Before You Begin: *You will need to have Microsoft Excel installed on your computer to complete this exercise, as well as a basic knowledge of how Excel works. If you do not have both of these, move on to Tackle the Tasks or close QuickBooks.*

1. Choose **Lists→Add/Edit Multiple List Entries**.

2. Choose **Vendors** as the List you wish to add additional entries to.

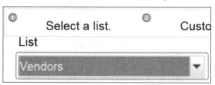

3. Navigate to your file storage location and then double-click **Vendor List.xlsx** to open it and Excel.

4. Select cells **A2** through **O9** and then tap $\boxed{\text{Ctrl}}$ + $\boxed{\text{c}}$ to copy the information to your computer clipboard.

   Make sure that you select only the data, not the column headers, from Excel.

5. Switch back to **QuickBooks**, scroll down to the bottom of the **Vendors List**, and click in the line directly below **USPS**.

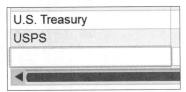

6. Tap Ctrl + v to paste the information from Excel into QuickBooks.

7. Click **Save Changes** and then click **OK** in the Record(s) Saved window.

8. Close the Add/Edit Multiple List Entries window and then close Excel.

9. Close all windows, keeping the company file open if you are continuing on to Tackle the Tasks, or close it if you are done with the chapter.

Tackle the Tasks

Now is your chance to work a little more with Average Guy Designs and apply the skills that you have learned in this chapter to accomplish additional tasks. You will use the same company file you used in the Develop Your Skills exercises throughout this chapter. Complete the following tasks, referring back to the concepts in the chapter as necessary. If you are using the trial software for this course on your computer or in a lab at school, you must toggle to the Pro edition every time you start QuickBooks.

Delete Profile List Entries	Delete Retail and Wholesale from the Customer Type List.
Customize a Report	Create a Balance Sheet Standard report and choose for it to display only assets. Customize it as you like. Set the date as of December 31, 2023, and then memorize it as: Assets Report
Create a Custom Form	Create a new template for sales receipts. Save it as AGD Cash Sales and then customize it as you see fit.
Create a Letter	Create a thank you letter to Ms. Evelyn Huff using the "Thanks for business (service)" template. In the Word document, edit the letter offering 10% off services through December 2023.

Self-Assessment

Check your knowledge of this chapter's key concepts and skills using the Self-Assessment quiz here, in your ebook, or in your eLab course.

1. Before you can use custom fields in reports, you must first set them up in the Item List. *True False*

2. Formatting deals with the appearance of the report, not with the data contained within it. *True False*

3. You can customize your own Word template to use with your QuickBooks data. *True False*

4. After you set your company's default report basis, you cannot change it on individual reports. *True False*

5. You can filter to display only income accounts on a report. *True False*

6. When you memorize a report, you are memorizing both the data and the formatting. *True False*

7. You can use a Customer & Vendor Profile List for a purpose other than that for which it was intended. *True False*

8. You must create your own form template to display custom fields. *True False*

9. You must memorize a report before you can process it with a batch of reports. *True False*

10. To analyze your QuickBooks data more effectively, you may wish to export it to Microsoft Excel. *True False*

11. When you memorize a report, which of these attributes would NOT be the same each time you recall the report?
    A. The company name in bold
    B. The accounts displayed
    C. The accounting basis of the report
    D. The balance of the accounts on the report

12. The option to create letters from Word is accessible from the _____ menu option.
    A. File
    B. Company
    C. Customers
    D. Reports

13. For which type of item can a custom field be set up?
    A. Sales tax group
    B. Subtotal
    C. Service
    D. Sales tax item

14. If you operate using the cash basis of accounting, which account will you NOT need to display on your balance sheet?
    A. Accounts Receivable
    B. Prepaid Rent
    C. Company Checking Account
    D. American Express Credit Card

Reinforce Your Skills

Angela Stevens would like to customize her QuickBooks company file for Quality-Built Construction. She will create custom fields and list entries, create custom price levels and integrate with Microsoft Office. You will be working with a QuickBooks Sample Company File in this exercise. The date will automatically be set to December 15, 2018. The password for all files unless otherwise stated is Password1. Leave the company file open unless otherwise instructed. If you are using the trial software on your computer or in a lab at school, remember to toggle to the Pro edition every time you start QuickBooks.

REINFORCE YOUR SKILLS 10-1

Create and Populate Custom Fields

In this exercise, you will create and populate a custom field.

1. Choose **File→Open or Restore Company**.
2. Open **RYS_Chapter10 (Company)** or restore **RYS_Chapter10 (Portable)** from your file storage location and save your file as: **RYS_Chapter10 Quality-Built Construction**
3. Click **OK** to acknowledge you are opening a sample file.
4. Choose **Employees→Employee Center**.
5. Double-click to open **Mitchell, Clark** for editing.
6. Click the **Additional Info** tab and then click the **Define Fields** button.

   Note that there are already three custom fields set up for customers and four for employees. You will create one more.

7. Type **Certification** as a label and then place checkmarks in the **Vend** and **Empl** columns to the right of the label.
8. Click **OK** twice to accept the new custom field.
9. Click in the **Certification** custom field for Clark Mitchell, type **Welding**, and click **OK**.
10. Close the Employee Center.

    The custom field will now be available for all vendors and employees.

REINFORCE YOUR SKILLS 10-2

Add and Modify Profile List Entries

In this exercise, you will create a new profile list entry and then modify one. Angela has just joined the Chamber of Commerce, so you decide to track customers that come to you through her Chamber participation.

1. Choose **Lists→Customer & Vendor Profile Lists→Customer Type List**.
2. Click the **Customer Type** button and choose **New**.
3. Type **From Chamber** and click **OK**.
4. Close the Customer Type List window.

Modify a Profile List Entry

5. Choose **Lists→Customer & Vendor Profile Lists→Customer Message List**.

6. Right-click **All work is complete!** and then choose **Edit Customer Message**.

7. Add to this message by clicking after *"All work is complete!"* and then pressing the [spacebar] and typing: **We appreciate your business and your prompt payment.**

8. Click **OK**; close the Customer Message List.

REINFORCE YOUR SKILLS 10-3

Create a New Fixed Percentage Price Level

In this exercise, you will turn on the Price Levels function and will create a new fixed percentage price level.

1. Choose **Edit→Preferences**.

2. Click the **Sales & Customers** category and then click the **Company Preferences** tab.

3. Click to choose **Enable Price Levels** and click **OK**; click **OK** again, allowing QuickBooks to close all open windows, if necessary.

4. Choose **Lists→Price Level List**.

5. Click the **Price Level** drop-down arrow ▾ and click **New**.

6. Name the fixed % price level **Military Discount** and choose to **decrease** item prices by a fixed amount of **10 percent**.

7. Click **OK** to save the new price level and then close the Price Level List.

Create an Invoice for a Military Customer

Quality-Built Construction has a new customer, Zoe Minch, who is a captain in the Marine Corps Reserve. She has contracted with you to build a new house for her. While she was in the office, she saw your custom coffee tables and purchased one. You will create an invoice for her using the military price level.

8. Choose **Customers→Customer Center**.

9. Create a new customer, **Minch, Zoe**. On the Payment Settings tab, set the Price Level for this customer to **Military Discount** and then click **OK** to complete the new customer record.

Now you will create an invoice for Zoe Minch's purchase.

10. Choose **Customers→Create Invoices** and then choose **Minch, Zoe** as the Customer:Job.

11. Set the date as **03/25/2020** and then choose **Coffee Table** as the Item.

12. Click the drop-down arrow ▾ in the Rate column, verify that **Military Discount** is the rate for Zoe, and then click **Save & Close** and close the Customer Center window.

Customize a Profit & Loss Report and Export to Excel

In this exercise, you will create a customized Profit & Loss report for Quality-Built Construction and export it to Excel.

1. Choose **Reports→Company & Financial→Profit & Loss Standard**.
2. Set the dates from **010119** to **123119** and then click the **Refresh** button on the Report toolbar.

Change the Columns Displayed

You will now display the columns by quarter across the top of the report.

3. Click the **Customize Report** button on the toolbar; choose the **Display** tab, if necessary.
4. Locate the Columns section of the window and choose to display the columns across the top by **Quarter**; click **OK**.

   This report will allow you to compare the income and expenses from quarter to quarter.

Change the Formatting for the Header

You will now customize the formatting of the report.

5. Click the **Customize Report** button on the toolbar and use this information to customize the report:
   - Display the **Header/Footer** tab.
   - Change the report title to: **Profit & Loss by Quarter**
   - Change the Alignment to **Left**.
   - Display the **Fonts & Numbers** tab.
   - Make any changes you like to the formatting of the fonts and numbers.
6. Click **OK** to save your changes.
7. Memorize the report, naming it **Profit & Loss by Quarter** and saving it in the **Company** group.
8. Click the **Excel** ⌄ button and export this report to a new worksheet, saving the worksheet to your file storage location as: **CH10_R4 Profit and Loss by Quarter 2019**
9. Close Excel and the Profit & Loss by Quarter report.

Modify the Custom Estimate

In this exercise, you will create an appealing estimate template for Quality-Built Construction. You can make changes to a template directly from an open form, and that is the approach you will use to modify the estimate template.

1. Choose **Customers→Create Estimates**.
2. Ensure that **Custom Estimate** is the template displayed.

3. Click the **Formatting** tab of the ribbon and then click **Manage Templates**. Click **OK** in the Manage Templates window.

   The Basic Customization window displays.

4. In the Company & Transaction area of the window, choose to include the **Phone Number**.

5. Click **OK** in the Layout Designer window, choosing to not have it appear again in the future.

6. Choose to include the **Web Site Address**.

7. Change the font and color scheme of the template to your liking.

8. Click the **Additional Customization** button.

9. On the Footer tab, add a Plain Text message that is to be printed: `We stand behind all work that we do. Please let us know if you are not fully satisfied so that we can have a chance to make you happy.`

Use Layout Designer

Finally, you will open the form in Layout Designer and make a few more changes.

10. Click the **Layout Designer** button.

11. Scroll down; select and move the **Phone #** and **Web Site** objects to the top of the form. (Hint: Hold `Shift` to select multiple objects and move them simultaneously.)

12. Move and adjust these and any other objects around as you see fit.

13. When you have the template just right, click **OK** to save your changes.

14. Click **OK** in the Additional Customization window and then click **Print Preview** to see what the customize estimate will look like. Close the Print Preview and the Basic Customization windows to save the changes to the template.

15. Close the Create Estimates window and close your file.

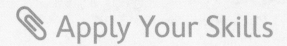# Apply Your Skills

Wet Noses Veterinary Clinic will create some customizations to the QuickBooks company file. This will help collect more relevant data to report on when analyzing the business and will enhance the customer forms. The password for all files unless otherwise stated is Password1. After starting QuickBooks, remember to toggle to Pro as necessary.

APPLY YOUR SKILLS 10-1

Create Custom Fields

In this exercise, you will create a custom field and populate it for a customer.

1. Choose **File→Open or Restore Company**.
2. Open **AYS_A1_Chapter10 (Company)** or restore **AYS_A1_Chapter10 (Portable)** from your file storage location and save your file as: **AYS_A1_Chapter10 Wet Noses Clinic**
3. Open the customer record for **Becky Karakash:Dog-Spencer** and then click the **Additional Info** tab and the **Define Fields** button.
4. Add these labels for customers (Cust): **Species**, **Breed**, **Color**, and **Gender**
5. Click **OK** twice to add the new custom fields.
6. Fill in the custom fields for Spencer using this information:
   - Species: **Canine**
   - Breed: **Golden Retriever**
   - Color: **Light Brown**
   - Gender: **Male**
7. Click **OK** to close the Edit Job window and close the Customer Center.

APPLY YOUR SKILLS 10-2

Customize a Profit & Loss Report

In this exercise, you will help Sadie create a customized Profit & Loss report.

1. Choose **Reports→Company & Financial→Profit & Loss Standard**.
2. Set the dates from **050123** to **053123** and click the **Refresh** button on the Report toolbar.

Change the Columns Displayed

You will now display the columns by week across the top of the report.

3. Click the **Customize Report** button on the toolbar and choose the **Display** tab, if necessary.
4. Locate the Columns section of the window and choose to display the columns across the top by **week**; click **OK**.

   This report will allow you to compare the income and expenses from week to week.

Change the Header Formatting

Sadie doesn't like the look of the default header, and she needs your help to get it just right.

5. Click the **Customize Report** button on the toolbar and then display the **Header/Footer** tab.

6. Change the report title to **Profit & Loss by Week** and change the Alignment to **Left**.

7. Display the **Fonts & Numbers** tab, make any desired changes to the formatting of the fonts and numbers, and click **OK** to save your changes.

8. Memorize the report into the **Company** group, naming it: **Profit & Loss by Week**

9. Click the **Excel** [Excel ▾] button and export this report to a new worksheet, saving the worksheet to your file storage location as: **CH10_A2 Profit and Loss by Week**

10. Close Excel and the report. Keep the company file open for the next exercise.

APPLY YOUR SKILLS 10-3

Modify the Custom Sales Receipt

In this exercise, you will create an appealing sales receipt for Wet Noses. You can make changes to a template directly from an open form, and that is the approach you will use to modify the sales receipt template.

1. Choose **Customers→Enter Sales Receipts**.

2. Click the **Formatting** tab, click **Manage Templates**, and click **OK**.

3. In the Company & Transaction Information area of the window, choose to print the company **Phone Number** and **Fax Number**.

   Close the Layout Designer window, choosing to not have it appear again in the future.

4. Change the font and color scheme of the template to your liking.

5. Click the **Additional Customization** button and, on the Footer tab, add a long text that is to be printed: **We care about your pets! Please let us know if you see anything out of the ordinary for your pet so that we may help as early as possible.**

Use Layout Designer

Finally, you will open the form in Layout Designer and make a few more changes.

6. Click the **Layout Designer** button.

7. Scroll down; select and move the **Phone #** and **Fax #** objects to the top of the form.

8. Move any other objects around as you see fit and click **OK** to save your changes when you have the template as you like it.

9. Click **OK** in the Additional Customization and the Basic Customization windows to save the changes to the template.

10. On the Main tab, click the **Save** drop-down arrow ▾ and choose **Save as PDF**, saving the file to your file storage location as: **CH10_A3 Sales Receipt**

11. Close all windows and the company file.

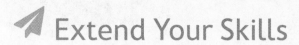

Extend Your Skills

Before You Begin: Open **EYS_Chapter10 (Company)** or restore **EYS_Chapter10 (Portable)** from your file storage location.

You have been hired by Arlaine Cervantes to help her with her organization's books. She is the founder of Niños del Lago, a nonprofit organization that provides impoverished Guatemalan children with an engaging educational camp experience. You have just sat down at your desk and opened a large envelope from her with a variety of documents and noticed that you have several emails from her as well. It is your job to sort through the papers and emails and make sense of what you find, entering information into QuickBooks whenever appropriate and answering any other questions in a word-processing document saved as:
EYS1_Chapter10_LastnameFirstinitial. Remember, you are digging through papers you just dumped out of an envelope and addressing random emails from Arlaine, so it is up to you to determine the correct order in which to complete the tasks.

- Note: The invoice that we send out is so boring looking…. Would you please fancy it up a bit, add a picture (as a logo) that relates to Guatemalan culture and make it a bit more colorful? Also, please include our U.S. office phone number on the invoice.

- Printed copy of Balance Sheet report: A note on the report reads, "Please change the font on this report and make the title align to the right. Make the color of the heading match the color on the new invoice template. Memorize it or something so it will be easy for you to run it next time with the same look."

- Note from Arlaine: Please send letters to all of our donors thanking them for their support during 2019 and inviting them down to visit the camp.

- Note from Arlaine: I would like to indicate the color of the scarves that we sell on our sales forms. Is there a way to add this information? Can you make it appear on the new invoice template that you created?

11

Introducing the Accounting Cycle and Using Classes

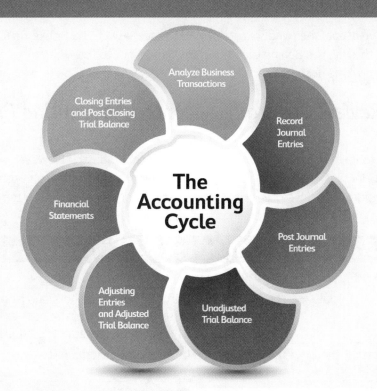

The Accounting Cycle

- Analyze Business Transactions
- Record Journal Entries
- Post Journal Entries
- Unadjusted Trial Balance
- Adjusting Entries and Adjusted Trial Balance
- Financial Statements
- Closing Entries and Post Closing Trial Balance

In this chapter, you will learn about the accounting cycle and review generally accepted accounting principles (GAAP) in QuickBooks. Throughout this chapter, you will work in depth on the first three steps of the accounting cycle while exploring how classes can be used to help with the process. Using classes in QuickBooks allows you to classify transactions to give you more data with which to manage your business. Wrapping up this chapter, you will have the opportunity to learn about and produce a Statement of Cash Flows. This report is generally produced in the next to last step of the accounting cycle, but we will run the report for perspective and to gain more understanding of the process.

LEARNING OBJECTIVES

▸ Work with the accounting cycle and GAAP

▸ Utilize class tracking in transactions and reports

▸ Create a Statement of Cash Flows

📁 Project: Average Guy Designs

In this chapter, you will continue working with Average Guy Designs as you go a step past "behind the scenes" and look at the steps of the accounting cycle. There are seven accounting cycle steps, and you will work closely with the first three steps as well as with classes. Finally, you will examine the cash flow for the business and the profit & loss by class by using QuickBooks reports.

The Accounting Cycle and GAAP

Now we will dive deeper into what occurs behind the scenes in QuickBooks. So far you have had a glimpse of this through the Behind the Scenes and Flashback to GAAP features of this book. Next, we will look at how the accounting cycle and GAAP apply to QuickBooks users.

Time to Review Generally Accepted Accounting Principles (GAAP)

Every industry follows standards and best practices for that industry. However, when it comes to accounting principles, they are the same across industries. GAAP are rules used to prepare, present, and report financial statements for a variety of entities. As GAAP attempt to achieve basic objectives, they have several assumptions, principles, and constraints.

GENERALLY ACCEPTED ACCOUNTING PRINCIPLES (GAAP)	
Principle	**Description**
Business entity principle	The business is separate from the owners and from other businesses. Revenues and expenses of the business should be kept separate from the personal expenses of the business owner.
The assumption of the going concern	The business will be in operation indefinitely.
Monetary unit principle	A stable currency is going to be the unit of record.
Time-period principle	The activities of the business can be divided into time periods.
Cost principle	When a company purchases assets, it should record them at cost. For example, an item worth $750 bought for $100 is recorded at $100.
Revenue principle	Publicly traded companies must record when the revenue is realized and earned, not when cash is received (accrual basis of accounting).
Matching principle	Expenses need to be matched with revenues during the same accounting period. This principle allows for a better evaluation of the profitability and performance (how much did you spend to earn the revenue?).
Objectivity principle	The statements of a company should be based on objectivity.
Materiality principle	When an item is reported, its significance should be considered. An item is considered significant when it would affect the decision made regarding its use.

(cont'd.)

GENERALLY ACCEPTED ACCOUNTING PRINCIPLES (GAAP)	
Principle	**Description**
Consistency principle	The company uses the same accounting principles and methods from year to year.
Prudence principle	When choosing between two solutions, the one that will be least likely to overstate assets and income should be selected.

The Accounting Cycle and Fiscal Period

Accounting records are kept and used to produce financial information. The records are kept for a period of time called a *fiscal period,* which can be any length of time. It may be a month or even a quarter of the year. Most businesses use a year as their fiscal period. A business does not need to use the dates January 1 through December 31 as its fiscal period. Many businesses start their fiscal period in February and end in January. Local government and educational institutions often use a fiscal period that begins July 1 and ends June 30.

The accounting cycle is a series of steps that help the business to keep its accounting records properly during the fiscal period. Prior to the steps outlined below, you should make sure to collect source documents and verify the financial information (which is sometimes considered a first step).

The Steps of the Accounting Cycle

1. Analyze the business transactions.
2. Record the business transactions (both debit and credit parts) in a journal.
3. Post each journal entry to the ledger accounts.
4. Prepare the unadjusted trial balance.
5. Prepare adjusting entries and run an adjusted trial balance.
6. Generate the financial statements.
7. Prepare closing entries and the post-closing trial balance.

This information is used by:

- Business owners needing to know how the business is doing.

- Banks considering lending money to a business owner; they need to know how the business is doing financially.

- Government, when assessing taxes on small businesses; it needs to know how much revenue the business is generating.

QuickBooks takes care of a lot of the steps behind the scenes. But you still need to exercise some common sense to avoid possible future trouble.

Throughout this chapter, we will look at the first three steps of the accounting cycle and how you and QuickBooks can work as a team to ensure your books accurately document what is happening behind the scenes.

Collecting and Verifying Source Documents

To complete the first step in the accounting cycle and analyze transactions, you must first ensure that the information on source documents is recorded correctly in QuickBooks. Source documents take many forms. Whether it is a receipt, check stub, utility bill, memo documenting the transaction, or another document, it is up to you to verify the information on it. QuickBooks makes it easy for you to keep track of source documents through the Doc Center feature.

The QuickBooks Doc Center

The Doc Center feature provides you with the ability to store your source documents electronically, attaching them to the transactions or list entries to which they belong. QuickBooks allows you to enter documents into the Doc Center through a variety of methods, including:

- Via the drag-and-drop method from Windows Explorer or Outlook

- From a scanner

- From another storage location accessible by your computer

While it is convenient and affordable to utilize the Doc Center, the files contained within it are not secure, so you need to take additional precautions when storing documents with sensitive information. You may wish to consider a third-party secure document management service that interfaces well with the QuickBooks Doc Center and provides security features to protect sensitive information if that's a concern.

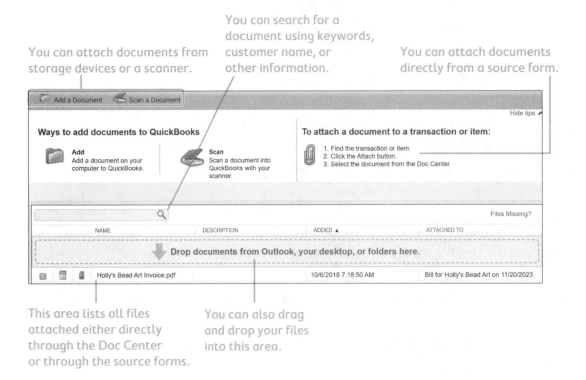

You can attach documents from storage devices or a scanner.

You can search for a document using keywords, customer name, or other information.

You can attach documents directly from a source form.

This area lists all files attached either directly through the Doc Center or through the source forms.

You can also drag and drop your files into this area.

Document Details

You can add different details to help you keep track of this document.

DOCUMENT NAME	Holly's Bead Art Invoice.pdf
TITLE	Holly's Bead Art Invoice, 11-20-23
DESCRIPTION	
KEYWORDS	holly, inventory, bill (Comma separated)
COMMENTS	

ADDED BY	**Guy**
DATE	**10/6/2018 7:18 AM**
SIZE	**34.6 KB**
FORMAT	**Adobe Acrobat Document**

You can add additional details regarding the document as well as viewing the date/time stamp of when it was added.

Company→Documents→Doc Center

DEVELOP YOUR SKILLS 11-1

In this exercise, you will add a document to the Doc Center and then attach it to a QuickBooks transaction. The password for all files unless otherwise stated is Password1. *Leave the company file open unless otherwise instructed.*

1. Start QuickBooks 2019; toggle to Pro, if necessary.

Add a File to the Doc Center

2. Choose **File→Open or Restore Company**.
3. Open **DYS_Chapter11 (Company)** or restore **DYS_01_Chapter11 (Portable)** from your file storage location and save your file as: **DYS_Chapter11 Average Guy Designs**
4. Choose **Company→Documents→Doc Center** and then resize the window.
5. Click **Add a Document** at the top of the window and then browse to your file storage location and double-click **Holly's Bead Art Invoice.pdf**.
6. Click the **Holly's Bead Art Invoice.pdf** checkbox, click the **View Details** button, and enter the following information:
   - Title: **Holly's Bead Art Invoice, 11-20-23**
   - Keywords: **holly, inventory, bill**
7. Click **Save & Close** and then close the Doc Center.

Attach the File to a Transaction

8. Choose **Vendors→Enter Bills**.

9. Click the **Previous** button until you see the bill from **Holly's Bead Art dated 11-20-23** displayed.

10. Click the **Attach File** button on the Ribbon and then choose to attach from the Doc Center.

    The Select Doc Center Documents window will appear.

11. Resize the **Select Doc Center Documents** window so you can see the Attach button, click the checkbox to the left of the **Holly's Bead Art Invoice**, and then click **Attach**.

12. Close the Attachments window and then click **Save & Close**.

> **Warning!** When you attach a document, QuickBooks creates an Attach folder with subfolders for the added documents. Do not delete these folders unless you've removed the documents from the Doc Center first.

Cycle Step 1: Analyze Business Transactions

After you have compiled and verified the source documents (receipts, bills, etc.), you are ready to analyze the transactions QuickBooks style. When you perform this analysis, you will need to answer the following questions from the perspective of *your business*:

- Which accounts are involved and what type are they?

- Is each account increased or decreased?

- Which account(s) is/are debited and for what amount?

- Which account(s) is/are credited and for what amount?

- What does the completed entry look like?

The good news here is that in the Behind the Scenes feature throughout this book, you have been seeing this analysis in action. You will now perform it for yourself!

DEVELOP YOUR SKILLS 11-2

In this exercise, you will analyze transactions. You will take a look at a variety of transactions and analyze each one in the table displayed below. You can download and print Analyze Business Transactions.docx from your file storage location if you do not wish to write in the book.

1. Complete this table by answering the questions about each transaction in the spaces provided.

	Invoice #10024	Sales Receipt #1	Bayshore City Water Co. dated: 12/14/2023 Amount: 525.37	Payment received, invoice: 10024 Date: 11/16/2023	Deposit to checking: 11/19/2023
1. Which accounts are involved? What type are they?					
2. Is each account increased or decreased?					
3. Which account(s) is/are debited and for what amount?					
4. Which account(s) is/are credited and for what amount?					

Note! The last question of "What does the completed entry look like?" is not included because you are using the completed entry in order to answer the rest of the questions!

Working with Classes

Classes and subclasses provide an additional way to track information about transactions. They allow you to keep an eye on particular segments of your business (such as new construction vs. remodel), tracking income and expenses for each. This way, if you wanted to evaluate which segment of the business was most profitable, it would be easy to do because transactions containing class information can easily be displayed on reports. Class tracking is a tool for you to use with your unique business. What you want to see on your reports is how you should base your class tracking. Classes can help you during the accounting cycle by running class reports or adding a class to existing reports. It provides another level of analysis.

When the class tracking preference has been enabled, QuickBooks will add class fields to many forms and registers such as the Create Invoices form, Enter Bills form, and reports. You can also run specific class reports such as the Profit & Loss by Class.

Similar to other lists such as the Vendor Type List, you can't delete a class that has been used in any transaction. Classes can be edited much the same way that you edit other list entries.

A Class Example

After discussions were held with the company's CPA, it was understood that Guy was already using Customer Type to track customer acquisition methods (website, referral, etc.). Upon careful thought, it was decided that it would be more meaningful to use classes to track an aspect of the business for which QuickBooks doesn't provide a list. Guy has already set up six main classes to track the main lines of income that Average Guy Designs' work falls into. An Overhead class needs to be created as a catchall for overhead income and expenses.

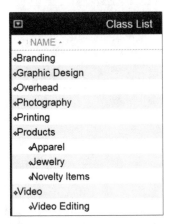

Classes are set up in the Class List. They track a specific aspect of the business. They are flexible in that you can choose how to (and whether to) use the feature for your unique company.

Planning for Class Tracking

Just as when you create a new company in QuickBooks and you take time to plan what you need the company to do for you, you need to do the same before you begin to track classes in QuickBooks. You will want to think about what type of reporting you need for your company and exactly what information you need to display on your reports.

When you are setting up classes for your own company, make sure to also create a class for any type of transaction that doesn't apply to one of your named classes (such as "Overhead" or "Administrative"). This is important because you want to make sure that you apply a class to every transaction involving an income and/or expense once you set up your company to track classes.

Using Classes for Profit Center Reporting

Many businesses use classes for profit center reporting. A profit center is a sector of a business for which income and expenses are tracked separately so that its individual profitability can be determined. One type of business that often relies on profit center reporting, to ensure that the entire business is operating efficiently, is farming.

Utilizing Subclasses

Even though you are allowed to use classes to track only a single aspect of your business, you can use subclasses to classify your data further. For instance, a restaurant can set up "main" classes to track income and expenses by location and then list food, bar, and catering as subclasses under each location (main class).

> **Tip!** Do not use classes to track more than one aspect of your business. If you need additional tracking, use subclasses. If you use classes to track more than one aspect, it will render the class data meaningless.

DEVELOP YOUR SKILLS 11-3

In this exercise, you will verify class tracking is turned on and modify the class list. The work of setting up the main classes has already been done for you, so you will be creating subclasses and then creating the Overhead class.

1. Choose **Edit→Preferences**.
2. Follow these steps to confirm the class tracking preference is turned on:
   - Click the **Accounting** category.
   - Click the **Company Preferences** tab.
   - Ensure there is a checkmark in the **Use class tracking for transactions** option box.
   - Click **OK**.

   Once you turn on this preference, QuickBooks adds class fields to many forms and registers such as the Create Invoices and Enter Bills forms. You can also run reports such as the Profit & Loss by Class.
3. Choose **Lists→Class List**.
4. Click the **Class** button and choose **New**.
5. Type **Apparel** in the Class Name field.
6. Click the **Subclass of** checkbox, click the drop-down arrow ▼, choose **Products**, and click **Next**.
7. Type **Jewelry** for the Class Name. Click the **Subclass of** checkbox, click the drop-down arrow ▼, choose **Products**, and click **Next**.
8. Type **Novelty Items** for the Class Name. Click the **Subclass of** checkbox, click the drop-down arrow ▼, choose **Products**, click **OK**, and then click **Next**.
9. Type **Overhead** for the Class Name, click **OK**, and then close the Class List.

Applying Classes to Transactions

If you decide to use classes, they should be applied to all transactions involving an income and/or expense account. This can be done through most forms, registers, or journal entries. With the exception of several class tracking reports, you can customize reports to add the class field and also create budgets based on them. You can also apply classes to payroll transactions—either to a whole paycheck or to individual earning items.

You can find the class field in sales forms such as Create Invoices, Create Purchase Orders, and on expense forms such as Pay Bills.

> **Note!** A Customer Deposit does not need to have a class assigned to it because it does not affect the income statement.

Consistent Class Applications

When you begin using class tracking, it is important to consistently apply a class to every transaction that deals with income and expense accounts so that your data, and therefore reporting, is meaningful. If you apply classes to only some transactions and then create a report to show the profitability by class, the information will be skewed. This is why it is important to create a class (such as Overhead) for transactions that don't fit one of your main classes.

Cycle Step 2: Record Journal Entries

When you enter a transaction in a QuickBooks form (Invoice, Bill, etc.), QuickBooks performs the work behind the scenes for you by including the necessary general journal information. In other words, it uses the correct accounts and moves the money accordingly along with the memos and other information that you've entered into the form. When entering any transaction, you must ensure that you are following GAAP. If you were doing this by hand, you would need to enter:

- The date of the transaction

- The account names and amounts of each of the debit and credit parts

- A reference to the source document or a brief explanation

In QuickBooks, you need to ensure that your items are set up properly (i.e., routed to the right accounts) so the proper accounts will be debited and credited in the journal that is kept behind the scenes for you.

Average Guy Designs, Chapter 11
Journal
All Transactions

Trans #	Type	Date	Num	Name	Memo	Account	Debit	Credit
1	Transfer	01/01/2023			Funds Tran...	30000 · Opening Balance Equity		5,432.67
					Funds Tran...	10000 · Checking	5,432.67	
							5,432.67	5,432.67
2	Deposit	11/30/2023			Account Op...	10200 · Savings	7,382.35	
					Account Op...	30000 · Opening Balance Equity		7,382.35
							7,382.35	7,382.35
3	Invoice	11/01/2023	10001	Huff, Evelyn:Holida...		11000 · Accounts Receivable	105.00	
				Huff, Evelyn:Holida...	T-shirt and...	43200 · Design Income		105.00
							105.00	105.00
4	Invoice	12/03/2023	10002	Hakola, Ashley:W...		11000 · Accounts Receivable	120.00	
				Hakola, Ashley:W...	Design of w...	43200 · Design Income		120.00
							120.00	120.00
5	Invoice	12/03/2023	10003	Lucy's Cupcake F...		11000 · Accounts Receivable	400.00	
				Lucy's Cupcake F...	Branding fo...	43200 · Design Income		400.00
							400.00	400.00

QuickBooks keeps a journal for you as you enter each transaction. Note the first five transactions that were entered into the Average Guy Designs company file.

Cycle Step 3: Post Journal Entries

In the third step of the accounting cycle, you find the entries that were entered into the general journal posted to the individual ledger accounts. This step is done entirely behind the scenes for you (thank you, QuickBooks!). From the Chart of Accounts, you can double-click to view a register for a balance sheet account and a QuickReport for any income or expense account to see the transactions affecting the account. When you view these registers and QuickReports, you will be able to see that the amounts have been properly posted from transactions to the underlying accounts.

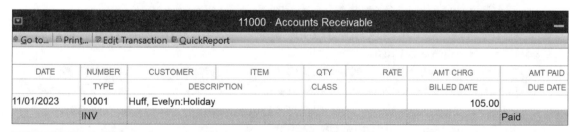

Notice that the third transaction entered in the journal can be found in both the Accounts Receivable register and on the Design Income Account QuickReport.

DEVELOP YOUR SKILLS 11-4

In this exercise, you will create two invoices and one bill, applying classes to each.

1. Choose **Customers→Create Invoices**.
2. Use this information to complete the first invoice:
   - Customer:Job: **City of Bayshore:Branding**
   - Click **Cancel** to close the Available Estimates window, if necessary
   - Click the **Class** drop-down arrow ▼ and choose **Novelty Items** under Products
     Selecting class from the top of the form will apply that class to all items on the Invoice.
   - Date: **121523**
   - Terms: **Net 30**
   - Item 1st Line: **Coasters**; Quantity: **100**
   - Item 2nd Line: **Sm Tiles**; Quantity: **100**; Description: `Calligraphy: City of Bayshore on each tile`
3. Choose any customer message and type `City of Bayshore: Novelty Products` in the Memo field.
4. Click **Save & New** and click **Yes** on the Information Changed window.

   Second invoice:

5. Use this information to complete the second invoice, choosing the class on each line item instead of at the top of the window:
   - Customer:Job: **Jones, Mary**
   - Date: **121523**
   - Item 1st Line: **Graphic Design**; Quantity: **3**; Rate: **55**; Class: `Graphic Design` (close the Price Levels window, if necessary)
   - Item 2nd Line: **Video**; Quantity: **4**; Class: `Video Editing`
6. Choose a customer message, type `Jones M:design, video` in the Memo field, and then click **Save & Close**.

BEHIND THE SCENES BRIEF

   11000•Accounts Receivable DR 3,332.31; **43200•Design Income CR <165.00>, 48900•Video Editing Income CR <220.00>; 41300•Novelty Sales CR <2699.00>; 25500• Sales Tax Payable CR <248.31>**

Apply Classes to an Expense Transaction

You need to purchase some materials for the photo shoot, so you will use the company credit card. While at the store, you will also purchase supplies for the office.

7. Click the **Enter Credit Card Charges** ▭ task icon in the Banking area of the Home Page.
8. Ensure the **21000•RiverBank Visa** credit card account is chosen and then use this information to complete the transaction:
   - Purchased from: `One Click Photo Supply` (tap ⏴Tab⏵ and then choose to **Quick Add** as a **Vendor**)

- Date: **121823**
- Ref No: **One Click01**
- Amount: **146.79**
- Memo: **Supplies for photo shoot & general office**
- Expenses tab line 1: Account: **61500•Job Materials**; Amount: **103.67**; Memo: **Dog House poster for shoot**; Customer Job: **JLR Doggie Playhouse:New Business Kickoff Campaign**; **Billable**; Class: **Photography**
- Expenses tab line 2: Account: **64900•Office Supplies**; Amount: **43.12**; Memo: **Sharpies, Paper Cutter**; Class: **Overhead**

The amount for the second line will fill in for you by subtracting the amount in the first line from the total.

> **BEHIND THE SCENES BRIEF**
>
> 61500•Job Materials DR 103.67; 63000•Office Supplies DR 43.12; **21000•RiverBank Visa CR <146.79>**

9. Click **Save & Close**.

Running Class Reports

The goal of using class tracking is so that you can produce reports that will focus on the areas of the business that you decided were important to track. They will help you determine profitability in those classes and could assist you in making decisions on the future direction of the company.

The Profit & Loss Unclassified Report

This report will display any transaction amount that does not have a class associated with it. Running this report periodically is a method by which you can ensure that you won't miss any transactions. It is then easy to use the QuickZoom feature to drill to the unclassified transactions (source documents) and assign a class to them.

The Profit & Loss by Class Report

When you've applied classes to all your transactions, running this report will display the net income (loss) by class broken down by income and expenses and categorized by class. If there are unclassified transactions, you will have a column before the Total column displaying the total amount that has not been classified for each account. You can drill down to the source documents through this report so you can assign classes to the transactions.

🏹 Reports→Company & Financial→Profit & Loss Unclassified

🏹 Reports→Company & Financial→Profit & Loss by Class

In this exercise, you will run a Profit & Loss Unclassified report and then apply classes to a number of transactions.

1. Choose **Reports→Company & Financial→Profit & Loss Unclassified**.

Apply Class Information to an Invoice

2. Change the date range to **From: 110123 To: 123123**, click the **Refresh** button on the toolbar, and resize the window to view the data.

   This report will list unclassified transactions. You will use QuickZoom to drill down to an invoice and add the class.

3. Mouse over the 43200•Design Income amount (6,835.00) and then double-click using the QuickZoom tool.

   A Transaction Detail by Account report appears, displaying all the transactions for this account and listing the Invoice numbers.

4. Locate and then double-click with the QuickZoom pointer on the **Invoice #10025** for the **Masters Manufacturing** line to drill down to the source document (invoice).

   Although there is only one item on this invoice, you will have to assign the class on the line item as you cannot do it for the entire transaction after it has been saved for the first time.

5. Choose **Graphic Design** in the Class field for the item.

ITEM	QUANT	DESCRIPTION	RATE	AMOUNT	CLASS	TAX
Web		Website Design Work	125.00	125.00	Graphic Design	Non

6. Click **Save & Close**; click **Yes** to record the transaction.

7. Refresh the Transaction Detail by Account report.

   Invoice #10025 should no longer be listed because it now has a class applied to it.

8. Close the Transaction Detail by Account and the Profit & Loss Unclassified reports, choosing not to memorize the reports.

9. Choose **Reports→Company & Financial→Profit & Loss by Class**.

10. Change the date range to **From: 110123 To: 123123** and click the **Refresh** button on the toolbar. Leave the report open.

    The Design Income amount should now be listed under the Graphic Design column.

Apply Classes to an Existing Expense Transaction

11. Choose **Reports→Company & Financial→Profit & Loss by Class** if it is not still open.

12. Change the date range to **From: 120123 To: 123123**, click the **Refresh** button on the toolbar, and resize the window to view the data.

13. Locate and then double-click the amount for 68610•Gas & Electric: Utilities ($82.37) to open the Transactions Detail by Account report.

14. Double-click the NoCal Gas & Electric Bill on 12/15/2023 to open the bill (source document).

15. Click in the **Class** column on the Expenses tab and then choose **Overhead**.

16. Click **Save & Close** and then click **Yes** to record the transaction. Click **Yes** to refresh the report.

    Notice that the class now appears on the Transaction Detail by Account report.

17. Close the Transaction Detail by Account report, choosing not to memorize it.

18. Refresh the Profit & Loss by Class report and take a look at the Overhead column to see the amount from the bill you just classified.

19. Close the Profit & Loss by Class report, choosing not to memorize it.

The Balance Sheet by Class Report

The Balance Sheet by Class report is available for those who are using a Premier or Enterprise version of QuickBooks. In this report, each class appears as a column. This is not a basic report for novice users to use, as it may display unexpected results at times, and the ability to understand and fix these anomalies requires a solid accounting background.

Adding a Class Field to Reports

Many reports can be customized to have the class included on them. On some reports, you can also use the class as a filter to focus on one or more classes at a time.

Running the Journal Report

If you wish to see your company's transactions displayed in the general journal, you can run a report to display this information. You can also add the class field to the Journal report in order to get a better picture of your company's information.

 Reports→Accountant & Taxes→Journal

DEVELOP YOUR SKILLS 11-6

In this exercise, you will run the Journal report and add the class field to the report. You will also use the Class field as a filter on the journal report.

1. Choose **Reports→Accountant & Taxes→Journal** and then click **OK** in the Collapsing and Expanding Transactions window, if necessary.

2. Use the date range **120123** to **123123** and refresh the report, resizing the window to view the report data.

3. Click the **Customize Report** button, type **cl** in the Search Columns field, choose **Class**, and click **OK**.

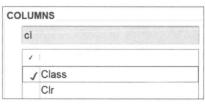

4. Scroll down to see transaction #149.

Note this transaction is for the City of Bayshore Invoice that you entered. You'll also see Mary Jones' Invoice for Graphics Design and Video Editing as transaction #150 below it.

Average Guy Designs, Chapter 11
Journal
December 2023

Trans #	Type	Date	Num	Name	Memo	Account	Class	Debit	Credit
125	Deposit	12/02/2023			Deposit	10000 · Checking		2,000.00	
					Add funding...	32000 · Owners E...			2,000.00
								2,000.00	2,000.00
149	Invoice	12/15/2023	10034	City of Bayshore:B...	City of Bays...	11000 · Accounts...	Products:Novelty Items	2,947.31	
				City of Bayshore:B...	Set of 4 Coa...	41300 · Home Decor	Products:Novelty Items		1,500.00
				City of Bayshore:B...	Set of 4 Coa...	12100 · Inventory ...	Products:Novelty Items		793.00
				City of Bayshore:B...	Set of 4 Coa...	50000 · Cost of Go...	Products:Novelty Items	793.00	
				City of Bayshore:B...	Calligraphy: ...	41300 · Home Decor	Products:Novelty Items		1,199.00
				City of Bayshore:B...	Calligraphy: ...	12100 · Inventory ...	Products:Novelty Items		530.00
				City of Bayshore:B...	Calligraphy: ...	50000 · Cost of Go...	Products:Novelty Items	530.00	
				State Board of Equ...	San Tomas ...	25500 · Sales Tax...	Products:Novelty Items		248.31
								4,270.31	4,270.31
150	Invoice	12/15/2023	10035	Jones, Mary	Jones M:des...	11000 · Accounts...		385.00	
				Jones, Mary	Graphic Des...	43200 · Design Inc...	Graphic Design		165.00
				Jones, Mary	Basic Video...	48900 · Video Edit...	Video:Video Editing		220.00
				State Board of Equ...	San Tomas ...	25500 · Sales Tax...		0.00	
								385.00	385.00
151	Credit Card Char...	12/18/2023	One ...	One Click Photo Su...	Supplies for...	21000 · RiverBank...			146.79
				JLR Doggie Playho...	Dog House f...	61500 · Job Mater...	Photography	103.67	
				One Click Photo Su...	Sharpies, Pa...	64900 · Office Sup...	Overhead	43.12	
								146.79	146.79

QuickBooks keeps a journal for you as you enter each transaction. Note the three transactions that were entered into the Average Guy Designs company file.

5. Click the **Sort By** drop-down arrow ▼ at the top of the window and select **Class** to sort by class.

6. Click the **Customize Report** button and then the **Filters** tab.

7. Follow these steps to filter the report by the Novelty Items class:

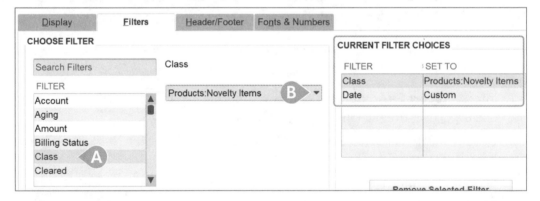

Ⓐ Click **Class** in the Filter list.

Class will now appear as the field to be filtered by (to the right of the Search Filters field.)

Ⓑ Click the **All Classes** drop-down arrow ▼ and choose **Novelty Items** under Products.

The Current Filter Choices section displays the selected filter.

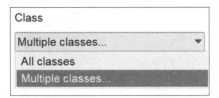

8. Click **OK**.

   You are viewing only transactions for the period 12/01/2023–12/31/2023 that have been assigned the class Novelty Items. You can see why it's important to assign classes to all transactions if you decide to use class tracking.

9. Close the Journal report, choosing not to memorize it.

Producing a Statement of Cash Flows

The Statement of Cash Flows is a financial report that has been required under GAAP since 1987. You have already seen Balance Sheet and Profit & Loss reports, but this report plays an important part in showing how viable a company is in the short term. This helps a variety of stakeholders to see whether the company will be able to pay its bills, payroll, and other expenses. It also indicates the financial health of the company.

While the Profit & Loss report looks at the total amount of income coming in and the expenses going out, the Statement of Cash Flows specifically looks at the cash inflows and outflows during a period of time. If you remember from GAAP, corporations are required to use the accrual basis of accounting that records when income and expenses are accrued rather than when cash is exchanged. The Statement of Cash Flows essentially translates the company's data from accrual to cash basis so that an understanding of how the company is operating and how cash is being handled can be reached.

FLASHBACK TO GAAP: REVENUE PRINCIPLE

Remember that publicly traded companies must record when revenue is realized and earned (accrual basis of accounting), not when cash is received (cash basis).

Method of Reporting

QuickBooks uses the indirect method when creating a Statement of Cash Flows. This means that net income is the starting point for the report; you make adjustments for the non-cash transactions from there. Basically, you will take a net income generated using the accrual basis of accounting and convert it to the cash basis by adding increases to current liability accounts and subtracting increases to current asset accounts.

FLASHBACK TO GAAP: CONSISTENCY

Remember that this means that the company uses the same accounting principles and methods from year to year.

Sections of the Statement of Cash Flows Report

Note! It's important to ensure the accuracy of the Statement of Cash Flows, meaning that all transactions to receive payments, pay bills, and deposit funds should be performed before running the report.

There are three sections of the Statement of Cash Flows that organize your company's financial information:

- **Operating:** In this section, you take the activities that result from the normal operation of the business and convert them to the cash basis. These types of activities may include such things as sales receipts, production costs, advertising, payroll, and expenses for services performed.

- **Investing:** In this section, you will account for fixed assets that are bought or sold, loans that you have issued, and other payments that are not related to the normal operation of the business (e.g., payments related to a merger).

- **Financing:** In this section, you take into account such items as cash from investors (company stock and bond transactions) and dividends that are paid.

Average Guy Designs, Chapter 11
Statement of Cash Flows
December 1, 2023 through February 28, 2024

	Dec 1, '23 - Feb 28, 24
OPERATING ACTIVITIES	
Net Income	1,166.80
Adjustments to reconcile Net Income	
to net cash provided by operations:	
11000 · Accounts Receivable	-5,142.31
12100 · Inventory Asset	1,323.00
13300 · Prepaid Insurance	-700.00
20000 · Accounts Payable	773.59
21000 · RiverBank Visa	146.79
25500 · Sales Tax Payable	223.47
Net cash provided by Operating Activities	-2,208.66
INVESTING ACTIVITIES	
15000 · Furniture and Equipment	-12,039.00
16000 · Vehicles	825.00
Net cash provided by Investing Activities	-11,214.00
FINANCING ACTIVITIES	
26000 · Loan - Equipment (Comp Syste...	8,950.00
28300 · Loan - Furniture (Office)	2,639.00
32000 · Owners Equity	2,000.00
Net cash provided by Financing Activities	13,589.00
Net cash increase for period	166.34
Cash at beginning of period	12,191.24
Cash at end of period	**12,357.58**

The Statement of Cash Flows allows you to view the company financials "as if" you were using the cash basis of accounting and will be produced using the indirect method as shown above. It helps to determine the "liquidity" of your company.

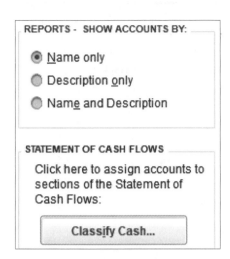

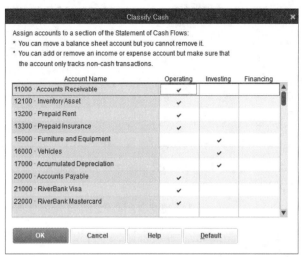

The Statement of Cash Flows section on the Company Preferences tab of the Reports & Graphs category contains the Classify Cash button. Choose this if you want to assign accounts to different sections of the report.

Forecasting Cash Flow

This report is important because it is one of the main financial statements used to get approved for a loan, to attract shareholders, or to demonstrate the financial health of your company. You can also use it internally to help guide decisions that you have to make for your company by giving you a tool by which you can forecast the cash that is and will be flowing into and out of your company.

The Cash Flow Forecast report will show you a forecast of cash flow. The date range for this report will be in the immediate future.

Average Guy Designs, Chapter 11 **Cash Flow Forecast** **January 2024**					
	Accnts Rece...	Accnts Paya...	Bank Accnts	Net Inflows	Proj Balance
Beginning Balance	4,120.00	1,799.95	13,441.33		15,761.38
Jan 1 - 6, 24	0.00	0.00	-1,050.00	-1,050.00	14,711.38
Week of Jan 7, 24	360.00	0.00	0.00	360.00	15,071.38
Week of Jan 14, 24	2,947.31	0.00	0.00	2,947.31	18,018.69
Week of Jan 21, 24	0.00	0.00	0.00	0.00	18,018.69
Jan 28 - 31, 24	220.00	0.00	0.00	220.00	18,238.69
Jan 24	3,527.31	0.00	-1,050.00	2,477.31	
Ending Balance	7,647.31	1,799.95	12,391.33		18,238.69

The Cash Flow Forecast report gives you a glimpse of what you can expect your cash flow to look like in the near future based on the data in your company file now.

> ↗ Reports→Company & Financial→Statement of Cash Flows *or* Cash Flow Forecast

> ↗ Edit→Preferences | Reports & Graphs→Company Preferences tab

In this exercise, you will produce a Statement of Cash Flows and create a report that will be used internally to make some decisions for the company. Payments received, deposits made, and most outstanding bills have already been recorded for this exercise. There will still be some outstanding transactions as is normal for most businesses.

1. Choose **Reports→Company & Financial→Statement of Cash Flows**.

   QuickBooks will display the Statement of Cash Flows report with a default date range of This Fiscal Year-to-date.

2. Use the date range **120123** to **022824** and then refresh the report.

   Notice the three main sections of the report: Operating Activities, Investing Activities, and Financing Activities.

3. Close the report window, choosing not to memorize it.

Run a Cash Flow Forecast Report

The next report will look at the cash flow forecast for the immediate future.

4. Choose **Reports→Company & Financial→Cash Flow Forecast**.

   QuickBooks will display the Cash Flow Forecast report with a default date range of Next 4 Weeks.

5. Use the date range **010124** to **013124** and then refresh the report.

6. Close the report window, choosing not to memorize it.

The Accounting Cycle in Practice

In theory, there are particular things that you should be doing on a daily, weekly, monthly, and quarterly basis. These practices will help to ensure both the accuracy of your reports and that you are not missing something. By coming up with a routine, you will also be more aware of any potential cash flow problems. These are some tasks that you should stay on top of to make QuickBooks work for you.

- Know what's in your bank accounts at the start of every business day.

- Make sure all transactions are recorded. This includes cash sales, bills paid, checks deposited, and orders placed. Run payroll on time and save and scan any related documents, such as receipts, into the Doc Center.

- Run reports such as the Unpaid Bills Detail, Open Invoices, A/R Aging Detail, Unbilled Costs by Job, and any other reports that will aid in pointing you to a potential issue.

- Depending on what these reports tell you, take action either by paying your vendors, making collection calls, or sending statements. Don't forget your tax bill!

- Try to estimate your cash flow for the near future. What will you need to spend? Can you make payroll?

- Make sure you reconcile your bank and credit card accounts on a monthly basis. It is also a good idea to run a trial balance on a monthly basis.

- If you're maintaining Inventory, make sure that it's accurate. Again, cash flow is important. Stocking too much can hurt your cash flow. Not having enough to sell can hurt your bottom line.

- Run your Profit & Loss report and Balance Sheet reports fairly often. They tell the bigger picture.

Tackle the Tasks

Now is your chance to work a little more with Average Guy Designs and apply the skills that you have learned in this chapter to accomplish additional tasks. You will use the same company file that you used for the DYS exercises. Enter the following tasks, referring back to the concepts in the chapter as necessary. If you are using the trial software for this course on your computer or in a lab at school, you must toggle to the Pro edition every time you start QuickBooks.

Analyze Transactions	Answer these questions about invoice 10035, which you produced in this chapter, using the file **TTT_Chapter11 Analyze Business Transactions.docx**. Save the file as: `CH11_TTT Analyze Business Transactions` • Which accounts are involved and what type are they? • Is each account increased or decreased? • Which account is debited and for what amount? • Which account is credited and for what amount?
Apply Classes to Transactions	The City of Bayshore requested a new job that you will name Posters. Write a check from the 10000•Checking Account on 12/17/2023 to Graphic Supply Shoppe for job materials for the City of Bayshore in the amount of $156.29. Memo for check and Expenses tab: City of Bayshore: Poster job materials Choose to pass on the expense to the customer job and assign Graphic Design as the class. Create an invoice for Ashley Hakola, Job:Wedding using Video Editing as the class on 12/29/2023 for six hours of Video, Basic Video Editing Services and two hours of Adv. Video. Memo: Hakola:Wedding, video editing
Produce a Class Report	Produce a Profit & Loss by Class report for December 2023.
Create a Statement of Cash Flows	Create a Statement of Cash Flows for the date range of 11/01/2023 through 12/31/2023.

Self-Assessment

Check your knowledge of this chapter's key concepts and skills using the Self-Assessment quiz here, in your ebook, or in your eLab course.

1. Class tracking in QuickBooks should be used to track different types of customers. *True   False*

2. The accounting cycle is a series of steps that helps a business keep its accounting records properly during the fiscal period. *True   False*

3. Classes can be used to track particular segments of your business. *True   False*

4. Classes can be used by companies to track multiple profit centers. *True   False*

5. While in a source document such as an invoice or bill, a file can be attached. *True   False*

6. You can customize a report to add the Class field or filter by class. *True   False*

7. A Statement of Cash Flows essentially translates a company's data from accrual to cash basis. *True   False*

8. You would find company stock transactions in the operating section of the Statement of Cash Flows report. *True   False*

9. The GAAP are rules used to prepare, present, and report financial statements. *True   False*

10. The Cash Flow Forecast report is used to show cash flow for prior quarters. *True   False*

11. Classes are most efficiently used to:
    A. Track types of customers
    B. Track additional information for one purpose
    C. Assign accounts to customers
    D. Record information about one customer

12. Which report would you run to easily apply classes to unclassified transactions?
    A. Profit & Loss by Class
    B. Balance Sheet by Class
    C. Class Change
    D. Profit & Loss Unclassified

13. Which of these is NOT a question you would ask when analyzing your business transactions during the first step of the accounting cycle?
    A. Which account is credited and for what amount?
    B. What is the source document for the transaction?
    C. Is each account increased or decreased?
    D. What does the completed entry look like?

14. Which of these is an activity that you would find in the Financing section of the Statement of Cash Flows report?
    A. Dividends that are paid
    B. Production costs
    C. Assets that the company bought
    D. Payroll costs

Reinforce Your Skills

Emily Holly is beginning to review the end of quarter reports and has also decided to start using Class tracking for the next quarter for her company, Electrical Energy. You will be assisting Emily by running the appropriate reports and setting up the classes. The password is Password1. Leave the company file open unless otherwise instructed. If you are using the trial software on your computer or in a lab at school, remember to toggle to the Pro edition every time you start QuickBooks.

REINFORCE YOUR SKILLS 11-1

Analyze Transactions

In this exercise, you will analyze transactions to help you understand the accounting concepts "behind the scenes." Remember that you can run a Journal report to see all transactions.

1. Start Quickbooks 2019 and toggle to Pro, if necessary.

2. Choose **File→Open or Restore Company**.

3. Open **RYS_Chapter11 (Company)** or restore **RYS_Chapter11 (Portable)** from your file storage location and save your file as: **RYS_Chapter11 Electrical Energy**

4. Open **RYS_Chapter11 Analyze Business Transactions.docx** from your file storage location and save your file as: **CH11_RYS Analyze Business Transactions**

5. Complete this table by answering the questions about each transaction in the spaces provided here or in **CH11_RYS Analyze Business Transactions**.

	Invoice #FC 2	Sales Receipt dated 04/20/2023	Bill dated 04/16/2023 for Four Brothers Hardware	Payment received, Chai, Linda: New Home, invoice # Chai 01, 04/24/2023, 1,200.00	Deposit made to checking on 04/26/2023
1. Which accounts are involved and what type are they?					
2. Is each account increased or decreased?					
3. Which account is debited and for what amount?					
4. Which account is credited and for what amount?					

Track and Use Classes

In this exercise, you will turn on the class tracking feature and set up additional classes. Emily has decided to start tracking classes as of October 1, 2023.

1. Choose **Edit→Preferences**.
2. Choose the **Accounting** category and then click the **Company Preferences** tab.
3. Click the **Use Class Tracking for Transactions** checkbox and click **OK**.
4. Choose **Lists→Class List**.

   Take a look at the classes that have already been set up for the company by default.

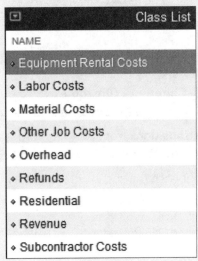

5. Close the Class List window.

Use Classes in Transactions

Now that class tracking is turned on, you will begin to use classes in all transactions. In this section of the exercise, make sure to enter the correct class for each transaction. Choose Save & Close after entering the details of each transaction.

6. Enter these transactions, using the appropriate class(es) for each:

   - On **10/03/2023**, you purchased office supplies for **$98.64** at **Priceco** (add as new **Vendor**). You paid with your **East River Visa** card. (Hint: Choose **Banking→Enter Credit Card Charges**.) Enter the memo: **Office Supplies** for the charge and the expense. Assign the **64900•Office Supplies** account and the **Overhead** class.

   - On **10/28/2023**, you received a bill from **Four Brothers Hardware** for **$349** for material costs billable to **Chai, Linda:New Home** job. Assign a Ref. No., and the terms for the bill are **Net 15**. Use **Material Costs** for the class, and the Memo for both bill and expense should be: **Chai: Primer and Paint** (Hint: Choose **Vendors→Enter Bills**.)

   - On **11/16/2023**, **Oceans, Peggy** (new drywall subcontractor) submitted an invoice for you to pay for **$350**. Assign a Ref. No., and the terms for the bill are **Net 15**. The account should be **53600•Subcontractors Expense**. Use **Subcontractor Costs** for the class, and the Memo for both bill and expense should be: **Oceans: Drywall installation** (Hint: Choose **Vendors→Enter Bills**.)

- On **11/06/2023**, **Hiroki Akiyamai** hired you to do a small three-hour wiring job that day at $50/hour and paid the entire amount with check number **1992**. Assign **Revenue** as the class and enter **Akiyamai: Wiring** as the memo. (Hint: Choose **Customers→Enter Sales Receipts**.)

REINFORCE YOUR SKILLS 11-3

Create a Cash Flow Report

In this exercise, you will look at how the company's cash flow has been for October–December 2023.

1. Choose **Reports→Company & Financial→Statement of Cash Flows**.
2. Use the date range **100123** to **123123.**
3. Look at the cash flow for Electrical Energy, Inc., for the period and then close the Statement of Cash Flows window, choosing to not memorize the report.
4. Close the company file.

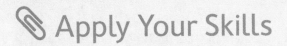 Apply Your Skills

Dr. James has asked you to take control over analyzing and entering transactions. She has also asked you to set up class tracking and produce reports based on class, jobs, and forecasting. She is looking to you as the lead in helping her determine the health of the company. The password for all files is Password1. After starting QuickBooks, remember to toggle to Pro as necessary.

APPLY YOUR SKILLS 11-1

Analyze Transactions

In this exercise, you will analyze a variety of transactions. You may download and print a copy of the table shown here if you do not wish to write in the book or if you are using the ebook.

1. Start QuickBooks 2019 and toggle to Pro, if necessary.

2. Choose **File→Open or Restore Company**.

3. Open **AYS_A1_Chapter11 (Company)** or restore **AYS_A1_Chapter11 (Portable)** from your file storage location and save your file as: `AYS_A1_Chapter11 Wet Noses Clinic`

4. Open **AYS_A1_Chapter11 Analyze Business Transactions.docx** from your file storage location and save it as: `CH11_A1 Analyze Business Transactions`

5. Complete the table by answering the questions about each transaction in the spaces provided here or in **CH11_A1 Analyze Business Transactions**. (Hint: Use Sort By to locate the transactions.)

	Invoice #176, dated 06/22/2023	Sales Receipt #6, dated 06/04/2023	Bill dated 07/21/2023 for Wyland Broadband	Payment received on Invoice #177, dated 07/15/2023	Deposit made to checking on 04/29/2023 for $50,000.00
1. Which accounts are involved and what type are they?					
2. Is each account increased or decreased?					
3. Which account is debited and for what amount?					
4. Which account is credited and for what amount?					

6. Save and close **CH11_A1 Analyze Business Transactions.docx**. Leave the company file open.

APPLY YOUR SKILLS 11-2 [QG]

Use Classes to Track Why Customers Visit

Dr. James has decided that she wishes to know a bit more about what brings her customers through her doors. In this exercise, you will help her to use classes to track this aspect of her business by creating classes and applying them on source documents.

1. Turn on the class tracking preference.

2. Set up four new classes: **Routine/Scheduled**, **Emergency**, **Product Sales**, and **Overhead**

3. Choose the appropriate QuickBooks window to record these transactions, making sure to apply the classes that you have created:

   - On **070123**, enter a bill for the monthly rent for **$2,300** payable to Oberg Property Management.

   - On **070123**, Chris Lorenzo brought in his cat, Jaguar, who was having a hard time breathing. Create invoice #181 for the visit and charge him for an Exam, a Venipuncture, and a CBC Chem.

   - On **070223**, you received bill **#77-9-57** from Seattle Vet Supply for **$3,787.49** (**$1,946.72** for medical supplies, **$994.22** for medicines, and **$846.55** for vaccines). The terms for the bill are Net 15. All of these items are used in the practice for a variety of procedures and ailments.

   - On **070223**, Teresa Martinez brought in her cat, Pinkie, for her annual exam, a rabies shot, and one Revolution Cat/Small Dog. She paid the same day with check number **2627**.

   - On **070523**, you received a bill from Brian's Pet Taxi for **$56** for transporting Steve Gaines' injured dog Jasper to your office (you will need to create a new expense account called **Pet Transportation using 64500 as the number**). You will pass this expense to the dog's owner.

   - On **070523**, Toni Wagner brought in her dog, Arizona, for an exam and paid in cash.

4. Run the **Profit & Loss by Class** report for: **07/01/2023** to **07/10/2023**

5. Click the **Excel** [Excel ▾] button and export this list to a new worksheet, saving it to your file storage location as: **CH11_A2 Profit and Loss by Class**

6. Close the company file.

Customize a Report and Run a Report to Display Transactions Without Classes

Now that you've been using classes, you will run some reports to see how you can better determine where the company's profits and/or losses are coming from. In this exercise, you will classify some transactions that were missed. You will also look at the future cash flow for the upcoming months August and September.

1. Choose **File→Open or Restore Company**.

2. Open **AYS_A3_Chapter11 (Company)** or restore **AYS_A3_Chapter11 (Portable)** from your file storage location and save your file as: `AYS_A3_Chapter11 Wet Noses Clinic`

3. Run the **Profit & Loss Unclassified** report for the date range: **07/01/2023–07/31/2023**

4. Add the **Overhead** class to the **60000•Advertising and Promotion** transaction in the amount of **$135**. Choose to refresh the report after recording the transaction. The **60000•Advertising and Promotion** account should no longer be displayed.

5. Run the **Item Profitability** report in the **Jobs, Time & Mileage** category, dated **07/01/2023** to **08/31/2023**.

6. Customize the report filter by **Class**, choosing **Routine/Scheduled** as the filter to display.

7. Click the **Excel** [Excel ▾] button and export this report to a new worksheet, saving it to your file storage location as: `CH11_A3 Item Profitability by Class`

8. Run the **Cash Flow Forecast** report for the date range **08/01/2023** to **08/31/2023** and displayed in one-week periods.

9. Click the **Excel** [Excel ▾] button and export this report to a new worksheet, saving it to your file storage location as: `CH11_A3 August Forecast Cash Flow`

10. Close the company file.

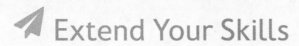
Extend Your Skills

Before You Begin: Open **EYS_Chapter11 (Company)** or restore **EYS_Chapter11 (Portable)** from your file storage location.

You have been hired by Arlaine Cervantes to help her with her organization's books. She is the founder of Niños del Lago, a nonprofit organization that provides impoverished Guatemalan children with an engaging educational camp experience. You have just sat down at your desk and opened a large envelope from her with a variety of documents and noticed that you have several emails from her as well. It is your job to sort through the papers and emails and make sense of what you find, entering information into QuickBooks whenever appropriate and answering any other questions in a word-processing document saved as:
EYS1_Chapter11_LastnameFirstinitial. Remember, you are digging through papers you just dumped out of an envelope and addressing random emails from Arlaine, so it is up to you to determine the correct order in which to complete the tasks.

- Credit card receipt: From Crafters Supply Warehouse, dated 9/2/2019 in the amount of $1,200 for the purchase of supplies for the camp.

- Message from Arlaine: "Can you set up a way for us to easily give a 25 percent discount to resale customers on a per-invoice basis?"

- Note from accountant: "Please develop a system to keep better track of source documents. You can do it electronically or 'physically,' but we need the backup documentation organized."

- Scribbled on a scrap of paper: Can we keep track of the funds that come in and go out for different purposes? Is there some sort of feature that would let us track income and expense by, let's say, Food-Camp, Building-Camp, Supplies-Camp, General Use, Administrative Costs?

- Handwritten donation receipt dated 9/5/2019: For camp supplies in the amount of $775 from Sharona Duke. Make sure you indicate that it is for camp supplies on the sales receipt.

- Scribbled note from Arlaine: "I would like to see what our cash flow is for July. Is there a report that will provide me with this information? What if I wanted to see what a prediction of cash flow for September 2019 might look like? Is there an easy way to do that in QuickBooks?"

QUICKBOODS
DESKTOP 2019

12 | Reporting, Adjusting Entries, and Closing the Books

It is now time to wrap up all you have learned and finish out the accounting cycle. In this chapter, you will work through the last four steps of the cycle as you close out the fiscal period. You will dive in and look a bit more closely at what's behind the scenes by making general journal entries as well as inventory adjusting entries. You will also produce the major end-of-period financial reports—Trial Balance, Worksheet, Income Statement, Statement of Owner's Equity, and Balance Sheet. Finally, you will learn what closing the books looks like in QuickBooks.

LEARNING OBJECTIVES

▸ Prepare a Trial Balance report

▸ Make general journal entries

▸ Adjust inventory

▸ Create financial statements

▸ Close the books in QuickBooks

📂 Project: Average Guy Designs

Guy has asked you to close Average Guy Designs' books for the fiscal year 2023. You will begin the process by creating a Trial Balance report, which will tell you whether the debits and credits are equal and will display the balances of each account. Then it will be time to take a look at what a "pen-and-paper" worksheet includes and how the information flows from column to column through it.

Next, you will look behind the scenes at the Make General Journal Entries window, where you will enter adjusting entries for depreciation and the Opening Balance Equity account. Any necessary inventory adjustments will also be made.

DATE	12/31/2023 📅	ENTRY NO.	45					
ACCOUNT	DEBIT	CREDIT	MEMO		NAME		BILLABLE?	CLASS
62400 · Depreciation Expense	332.42		Record 1Q 2023 Depreciation					Overhead
17000 · Accumulated Depreciation ▾		332.42	Record 1Q 2023 Depreciation		▾			Overhead

Adjusting entries are made in the Make General Journal Entries window. Debits are entered first.

When the adjusting entries have been posted, it will be time to create Average Guy Designs' financial statements for the year.

Average Guy Designs Chapter 12
Summary Balance Sheet
All Transactions

	Dec 31, 23
▼ ASSETS	
▼ Current Assets	
Checking/Savings ▸	30,412.52 ◂
Other Current Assets	5,494.50
Total Current Assets	35,907.02
Fixed Assets	6,806.58
TOTAL ASSETS	42,713.60
▼ LIABILITIES & EQUITY	
▼ Liabilities	
▼ Current Liabilities	
Accounts Payable	995.36
Credit Cards	471.79
Other Current Liabilities	27.08
Total Current Liabilities	1,494.23
Long Term Liabilities	6,689.00
Total Liabilities	8,183.23
Equity	34,530.37
TOTAL LIABILITIES & EQUITY	42,713.60

The Balance Sheet is one of the main financial statements. Here you are viewing a Summary Balance Sheet, which includes less detail.

Closing the Books in QuickBooks

The last four steps of the accounting cycle deal with "closing" the books at the end of a fiscal period. At the end of the fiscal year QuickBooks uses the fiscal year information based on what you entered when you first created your company. This information can be viewed through the My Company window accessed from the Company menu.

You can set a closing date in QuickBooks, although QuickBooks will perform year-end adjustments automatically based on your fiscal year. You will learn how to set a closing date in QuickBooks at the end of this chapter, after you have explored the rest of the accounting cycle.

The Final Steps of the Accounting Cycle

The final steps result in your company books being closed for the past fiscal period and prepared for the next one. For many companies, the last steps of the accounting cycle are carried out by an accountant. A company needs to decide whether it will use an accountant to close the books or if it is something that it will take on.

So far, in your path through the accounting cycle, you have ensured that source documents are available and organized before analyzing and recording transactions (QuickBooks posted them in a journal and to ledger accounts behind the scenes). Now you will prepare reports to show how your company performed for the fiscal period and close out temporary accounts. As you explore these final steps, you will be seeing how QuickBooks addresses each of them.

Permanent Accounts

Accounts for which the ending balance for one fiscal period is the opening balance for the next are called permanent accounts. These are also called the balance sheet accounts. Similar to your personal checking account, you wouldn't zero out your account at the end of each year; it continues on from one accounting period to the next!

Temporary (aka Nominal) Accounts

Not all accounts are permanent! Called temporary, or nominal, the income and expense accounts are zeroed out at the end of each fiscal period, with the amounts moving into an equity account as either a net income (if income was greater than expenses) or a net loss (if expenses exceeded income for the period). An example of a Temporary account is a Sales account.

The Income Summary Account

If you were doing paper-based accounting, you would use an Income Summary account to "clear out" the temporary account balances and move the lump sum to an equity account. QuickBooks doesn't actually create an Income Summary account, but it takes the net income or loss resulting from the balances in your income and expense accounts and moves them to the capital/equity account for you. You will learn more about this temporary account as we progress through this chapter.

QuickBooks' Automatic Year-End Adjustments

Specific tasks are performed automatically behind the scenes at the end of your fiscal year, such as:

- Closing out temporary accounts by moving the balances to a "virtual" income summary account

- Determining a net income or loss for the company to be displayed on the balance sheet for the last day of the fiscal year, after transferring the balances from the temporary accounts

- Automatically transferring the net income or loss from the last day of the fiscal period to the Retained Earnings account on the first day of the new fiscal period

The result of this behind the scenes action is that you will start off the new fiscal year with a net income of zero (and a zero balance in each of the temporary accounts).

 Company→My Company: Edit→Report Information

DEVELOP YOUR SKILLS 12-1

In this exercise, you will verify that the correct month is set as the first month of the fiscal period for Average Guy Designs. The password for all files unless otherwise stated is Password1. *Leave the company file open unless otherwise instructed.*

1. Start QuickBooks 2019 and toggle to Pro, if necessary.

2. Choose **File→Open or Restore Company**.

3. Open **DYS_Chapter12 (Company)** or restore **DYS_Chapter12 (Portable)** from your file storage location and save your file as: **DYS_Chapter12 Average Guy Designs**

4. Choose **Company→My Company**.

5. Click the **Edit** ✎ button at the top-right corner of the My Company window.

6. Click **Report Information** and then verify that *January* is displayed as the first month in the company's fiscal year.

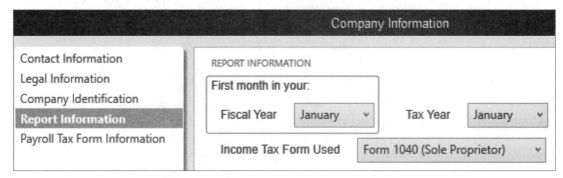

7. Click **OK** in the Company Information window; close the My Company window.

Preparing for Year-End Reporting

When you are doing pen-and-paper accounting, you must prepare a Trial Balance report to ensure that the debits and credits are equal. Preparing a Trial Balance report involves taking all of the ledger accounts and their balances and displaying them on one report to ensure debits equal credits. When you use QuickBooks, though, you cannot record a transaction if the debits and credits are not equal, so a more useful purpose for the Trial Balance report is to use it to prepare for adjusting entries. These same steps should be performed when closing any period.

QuickBooks Reporting Capabilities

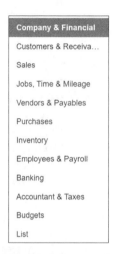

As you have seen, QuickBooks provides users with a large number of reports that they can use to tell the story of their business in a variety of ways. In addition, there are reports contributed by other users that you may find of value. All of these reports are organized into twelve categories.

Custom Reports

If you are not able to find the perfect report for your business, Quick-Books allows users to create custom summary and detail reports. The software provides a window that guides you through the decision of which custom report to create.

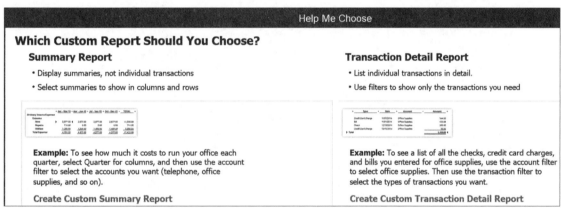

Cycle Step 4: Unadjusted Trial Balance

In the third step of the accounting cycle, QuickBooks posted the amounts from the journal that documents all transactions to individual account ledgers behind the scenes. Step 4 of the accounting cycle involves creating a Trial Balance report. QuickBooks Pro allows you to create a Trial Balance report, and, if you have the Premier Accountant edition, you can create a Working Trial Balance report as well. This initial trial balance is termed an "unadjusted" trial balance as it is prior to performing any necessary adjusting entries. You will complete adjusting entries later in this chapter.

In traditional accounting, a Trial Balance is a report that adds up all the debits and credits so mistakes can be traced if debits don't equal credits. Because QuickBooks always adds correctly, you do not need to do a trial balance. Nevertheless, QuickBooks provides a Trial Balance report if you want to see your data in this format.

The Trial Balance report lets you look at the ending balance of every account in the Chart of Accounts for a chosen period of time. You can use it to help guide you as you create adjusting entries. You can use the QuickZoom feature to find the source of the amount of the transactions on the report.

Average Guy Designs Chapter 12
Trial Balance
As of December 31, 2023

	Dec 31, 23	
	Debit	Credit
28300 · Loan - Office Furniture		2,639.00
30000 · Opening Balance Equity		22,815.02
41100 · Clothing		177.00
41200 · Accessories		120.00
42700 · Photography Income		2,414.00
43200 · Design Income		10,215.00
48900 · Video Editing Income		7,521.00
48910 · Returned Check Charges		40.00
49000 · Less Discounts Given	16.70	
50000 · Cost of Goods Sold	148.50	
60300 · Bad Debt Expense	345.00	
60400 · Bank Service Charges	39.50	
61500 · Job Materials	463.57	
61700 · Computer and Internet Expenses	728.44	
63300 · Insurance Expense	475.49	
64300 · Meals and Entertainment	206.72	
64900 · Office Supplies	478.81	
66100 · Company-Paid Benefits	203.50	
66200 · Company - Paid Taxes	188.20	
66300 · Gross Wages	2,460.00	
67100 · Rent Expense	2,200.00	
67200 · Repairs and Maintenance	314.44	
67500 · Shipping Expense	18.49	
68610 · Gas & Electric	82.37	
TOTAL	51,485.25	51,485.25

A Trial Balance report compiles all of the accounts in your ledger into a report that verifies that debits equal credits. This figure displays a Trial Balance report before adjustments have been made.

Preparing a Worksheet

In pen-and-paper accounting, a worksheet is a report that you create to assist you with preparing the year-end financial statements. The worksheet has five sets of debit and credit columns that represent the following sections (displayed from left to right):

• Trial Balance

• Adjustments

• Adjusted Trial Balance

- Income Statement

- Balance Sheet

The information from the Trial Balance report is displayed in the Trial Balance section. You would work across the worksheet as adjustments are made and then recorded in the Adjusted Trial Balance section. Finally, the amounts from the Adjusted Trial Balance would be transferred to the Income Statement and Balance Sheet sections, based on which accounts would be found on each one.

Because QuickBooks does this behind the scenes, there is no worksheet for you to physically produce.

 Reports→Accountant & Taxes→Trial Balance

DEVELOP YOUR SKILLS 12-2

In this exercise, you will create a Trial Balance report for Average Guy Designs for the 2023 year.

1. Choose **Reports→Accountant & Taxes→Trial Balance**.

2. Set the date range from **010123** to **123123** and then refresh the report.

   This report displays all the accounts in your Chart of Accounts and the current balance for each. The debits and credits are in balance.

3. Close the Trial Balance report, choosing not to memorize it.

Digging in Behind the Scenes with Adjusting Entries

QuickBooks has been performing Journal Entries all along as you enter transactions, whether you are depositing funds or paying bills. However, there may be times when you have to make your own adjusting journal entries, especially before closing the books for a period.

The Accounting Cardinal Rule: Debits and Credits Must Always Be Equal

When you venture into the General Journal Entry window, you will see a Debit column and a Credit column. As you create your journal entries, you must make sure that the debits equal the credits. (Don't worry! QuickBooks will not let you record a transaction until you get this right.)

Note! Depending on the version of QuickBooks you are using, the Make General Journal Entries window may look a bit different. The images in this text are from the Pro version.

Making Journal Entries

If you are familiar with manual accounting, you will notice that the Journal report shows the entries as they would appear in the pen-and-paper journal used in manual accounting. You can run this report if you want to see all transactions made within a certain period. It can also be useful in trying to locate problems.

Trans #	Type	Date	Num	Name	Memo	Account	Debit	Credit
						Average Guy Designs Chapter 12		
						Journal		
						December 22 - 29, 2023		
40	Sales Receipt	12/22/2023	2			12000 · Undeposit...	200.00	
					Photography...	42700 · Photograp...		200.00
				State Board of Equ...	San Tomas ...	25500 · Sales Tax...	0.00	
							200.00	200.00
42	Payment	12/23/2023	470	Mary Jones		12000 · Undeposit...	270.00	
				Mary Jones		11000 · Accounts...		270.00
							270.00	270.00
43	Invoice	12/23/2023	10020	Olivia York:Project...		11000 · Accounts...	200.00	
				Olivia York:Project...	Print Layout...	48800 · Print Layo...		200.00
				State Board of Equ...	San Tomas ...	25500 · Sales Tax...	0.00	
							200.00	200.00

The Journal report shows all transactions made in QuickBooks, including adjusting entries if any, made through the Make General Journal Entries window. This illustration displays transactions for a period in December 2023.

General Journal Entries are not to be taken lightly. These types of entries are used when there is no other way of fixing the issue as a way of balancing the books but are also made for the reasons listed in Cycle Step 5. There are times when making a journal entry is part of the process in keeping the books.

When making a general journal entry, two lines will be used. Debit entries are listed first, followed by credit entries.

Cycle Step 5: Adjusting Entries and Adjusted Trial Balance

Adjusting entries are made at the end of an accounting period to bring some of the general journal account balances up to date so they will be correct on the financial statements. Some examples of adjusting entries that are often made are:

- Updating the book value of fixed assets by recording depreciation for the fiscal period

- Updating prepaid accounts (other current assets) by transferring the amount used in the fiscal period to an expense account

- Transferring balances out of the Opening Balance Equity account to their correct "resting place"

After the adjusting entries have been made, an adjusted trial balance is prepared. This report can be created in the Premier Accountant edition, and will show the three columns in the report as illustrated.

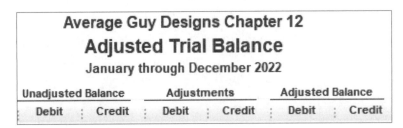

Average Guy Designs Chapter 12					
Adjusted Trial Balance					
January through December 2022					
Unadjusted Balance		Adjustments		Adjusted Balance	
Debit	Credit	Debit	Credit	Debit	Credit

Adjusting Inventory Quantity/Value on Hand

There may be times when you have inventory that is no longer in sellable condition. These items should be removed from inventory and the amount expensed. Other times you may need to adjust the value of your inventory because of obsolescence or for another reason. Or, you may need to adjust both the quantity and the value of your inventory.

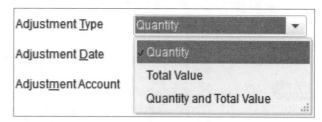

In the Adjust Quantity/Value on Hand window, you can choose the type of the adjustment via a drop-down list.

Adjusting the Quantity of Your Inventory

You can either enter the new quantity on hand, which might be the best choice if you have just conducted an annual inventory, or the quantity difference, which works well if you know how many items you have to remove. If you choose to enter the quantity difference, make sure to enter a minus sign in front of the number to show a decrease in the number of items.

Adjusting the Value of Your Inventory

If you don't need to adjust the quantity of your inventory but rather need to adjust the value of your inventory, you can use the same window. QuickBooks Pro and Premier use the average cost method of inventory valuation. You can adjust the average cost per inventory item by adjusting the total value of the inventory. Obsolescence or an incorrect beginning cost for inventory may require you to take this step.

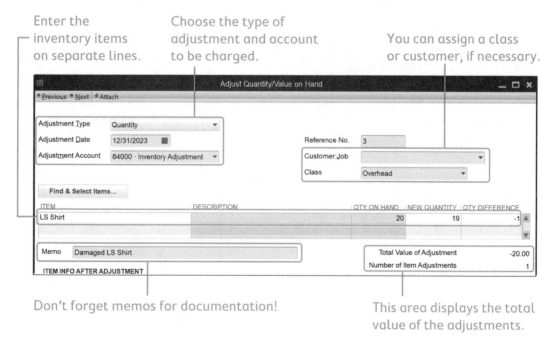

Enter the inventory items on separate lines.

Choose the type of adjustment and account to be charged.

You can assign a class or customer, if necessary.

Don't forget memos for documentation!

This area displays the total value of the adjustments.

Accounting for Depreciation

Previously, you learned about fixed assets and the fact that you don't expense them when purchased, but rather over the life of the asset. You should enter a depreciation transaction for your fixed assets for every fiscal period in which you produce financial statements. For small businesses, this is typically at the end of a fiscal year.

The depreciation adjusting entry can be made in the Make General Journal Entries window. It affects the expense account that tracks depreciation and the accumulated depreciation fixed asset contra account. When you make this transfer, the current book value of your fixed assets will be displayed correctly, meaning that the credit amount in the accumulated depreciation contra account will decrease the total value of the company's fixed assets (which have a debit normal balance).

Note! After adjusting entries have been entered into QuickBooks (Premier Accountant edition), you can create an Adjusted Trial Balance report, which shows the beginning balance, adjustments, and ending balance for each account. These ending balances are used in the financial statements. This report also represents one of the sections of the worksheet that illustrates the fifth step of the accounting cycle.

In QuickBooks Pro, after adjusting entries are made, you can create another Trial Balance report, which reflects the adjusted amounts.

BEHIND THE SCENES

When making an adjusting entry for depreciation, you debit the Depreciation Expense account and credit the Accumulated Depreciation account. Remember that Accumulated Depreciation is a fixed asset contra account. By crediting it, you are decreasing the value of the fixed assets.

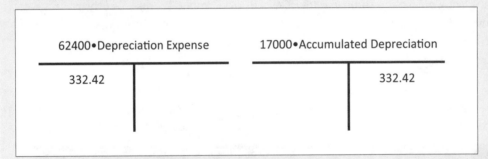

Behind the scenes in an inventory adjustment, you remove the items from the Inventory Asset account and enter them as an Inventory Adjustment to Cost of Goods Sold for the company.

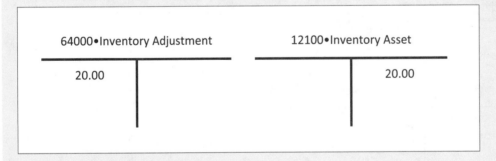

🔥 Vendors→Inventory Activities→Adjust Quantity/Value on Hand

🔥 Company→Make General Journal Entries

🔥 Reports→Inventory→Physical Inventory Worksheet

You have completed a physical inventory count and need to make sure that the items on hand match the count in QuickBooks. In this exercise, you will make any necessary inventory adjustments. You will begin by creating an inventory report to assist you with your physical inventory count.

1. Choose **Reports→Inventory→Physical Inventory Worksheet**.

   At this time, you would normally print the worksheet and manually enter the inventory count.

Average Guy Designs Chapter 12
Physical Inventory Worksheet
November 29, 2023

Item	Description	Preferred Vendor	Quantity On Hand	Physical Count
Coasters		Hartwell Designs	0	0
Earrings	Designer Earrings	Holly's Bead Art	22	21
LS Shirt		Allisons Fox Desig...	20	18
Scarf		Knit a Bit	25	24
Sm Tiles		Hartwell Designs	0	0
T-Shirt	Allison's original design...	Allisons Fox Desig...	19	19

You will now use information from the physical inventory count to adjust Average Guy Designs' inventory. LS Shirt is off by one due to the accidental damage and disposal of an item. In addition, Guy just told you that he created a gift basket for a local Chamber event to advertise the company's services.

2. Close the Physical Inventory Worksheet window, choosing not to memorize the report, if necessary.

Adjust the Inventory

3. Click the **Inventory Activities** task icon drop-down arrow ▼ in the Company area of the Home Page and then choose **Adjust Quantity/Value On Hand**.

4. Use this information to make the first inventory adjustment:
   - Adjustment Type: **Quantity**
   - Adjustment Date: **123123**
   - Adjustment Account: **Inventory Adjustment**

5. Use this information to complete the first inventory adjustment:
   - Class: **Overhead**
   - Item: **LS Shirt**
   - New Quantity: **19** (then tap ⌈Tab⌉ to calculate the Qty Difference)

   You could also type -1 in the Qty Difference column and then the New Quantity would automatically adjust.

6. Memo: **Damaged LS Shirt**

   Notice the Total Value of Adjustments is -20.00 at bottom of window and Quantity on Hand dropped to 19.

7. Click **Save & New**.

You will now mark the three items that Guy included in the gift basket out of inventory.

8. Use this information to record the second inventory adjustment:

   • Adjustment Date: **123123**

   • Adjustment Account: **Advertising Expense** (then tap [Tab])

9. Click **Set Up** to set up this new account using this information:

   • Account Type: **Expense**

   • Number: **60100** (then click **Save & Close** to create the new account)

   You will now complete the second inventory adjustment. Notice that you cannot select a separate class for each item. Therefore, you will need to make two adjustments, as you do not want to choose a parent class that has subclasses.

10. The class for the first adjustment: **Products: Jewelry**

    • Item and New Quantity: **Earrings** and **21**

    • Memo: **Included in Chamber gift basket**

    The adjustment should match the figure below.

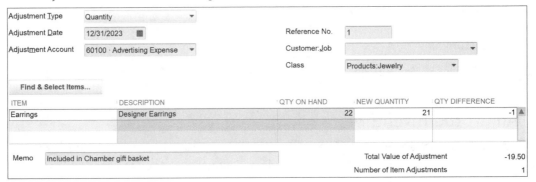

11. Click **Save & New**.

12. Use the following information for the final adjustment:

    • Account: **60100•Advertising Expense**

    • Class: **Products: Apparel**

    • Item and New Quantity (first line): **Scarf** and **24**

    • Item and New Quantity (second line): **LS Shirt** and **18**

    • Memo: **Included in Chamber gift basket**

13. Click **Save & Close**.

14. Choose **Reports→Inventory→Inventory Stock Status by Item** and then type **a** to show all dates and see the updated report.

15. Close the report, choosing not to memorize it.

Record the Vespa Depreciation for the Year

The vehicle costs $4,500 and will depreciate over four years, the expected amount of time you will use it. After four years, it will be worth $1,200. Thus, the vehicle will depreciate $825 per year for four years. (This is using the straight-line method of depreciation—$4,500-$1,200=$3,300. A total of $3,300 is what will depreciate over the next four years—$3,300/4=$825 per year for four years. The $1,200 value after four years was determined previously.)

Note! You should contact your accountant to determine the depreciation method and amount that are best for your company.

In this exercise, you will record the depreciation and memorize the depreciation transaction.

16. Choose **Company→Make General Journal Entries** from the menu bar.

17. Click the **Previous** ◀ button a few times to take a look at how transactions that you have entered are displayed in the general journal; click **New** 🔳 to start a new entry.

18. Use this information to enter the first year's depreciation:

- ⓐ Date: **123123**
- ⓑ First Account Line: **62400•Depreciation Expense**
- ⓒ Debit: **825**
- ⓓ Memo: **Record Vespa depreciation**
- ⓔ Second Account Line: **17000•Accumulated Depreciation**
- ⓕ Credit: **825**
- ⓖ Memo: **Record Vespa depreciation**

19. Click **Memorize** on the Ribbon.

20. Use this information to memorize the transaction:

- Name: **Annual Depreciation Vespa**
- Select **Automate Transaction Entry**
- How Often: **Annually**
- Next Date: **123124**
- Number Remaining: **3**

21. Click **OK**, click **Save & New**, and then click **OK** again, if necessary.

> **BEHIND THE SCENES BRIEF**
>
> 62400•Depreciation Expense DR 825.00; **17000•Accumulated Depreciation CR <825.00>**

Record the Transfer of Funds Between Equity Accounts

Finally, in the last segment of this exercise, you will transfer funds from the Opening Balance Equity account to Owner's Equity (Retained Earnings).

22. Use this information to record the journal entry:

    - Date: **123123**
    - First Account Line: **30000•Opening Balance Equity**
    - Debit: **22815.02**
    - Memo: **Owner's Equity**
    - Second Account Line: **32000•Owners Equity**
    - Memo: **Owner's Equity Transfer**

23. Click **Save & Close** to record the journal entry; click **OK** to post to the **Retained Earnings** account.

> **BEHIND THE SCENES BRIEF**
>
> 30000•Opening Balance Equity DR 22,815.02; **32000•Owners Equity CR <22,815.02>**

Preparing Financial Statements

After the adjusted entries have been made, it is time to move on to producing the financial statements for the company. Financial statements are very important in that they can be used both internally and externally to learn about the financial health of a company. Internally, reports are used by management to make decisions regarding operations. It is beneficial to not only look at the current year's statements, but also compare them to the statements from the previous fiscal year. Externally, the financial statements are used in a variety of capacities such as to determine whether money should be lent to a company, whether a business is profitable, and whether to purchase stock in a company.

> **FLASHBACK TO GAAP: OBJECTIVITY**
>
> Remember that a company's statements should be based on objectivity.

Cycle Step 6: Financial Statements

The next step in the accounting cycle requires that financial statements be produced. These three statements must be produced: Income Statement (also known as the Profit & Loss report), Statement of Owner's Equity, and Balance Sheet.

Some users of your company's financial data may also need a Statement of Cash Flows.

The Income Statement

The Income Statement (aka the Profit & Loss report) displays the income and expenses generated over a specific period of time. In this case, the net income or net loss will tell a story about the financial health of the company. When using pen-and-paper accounting, the values to be displayed on the Income Statement will come from the Income Statement section of the worksheet.

The Income Statement will have either two or three sections. If the company deals with inventory, then a Cost of Goods Sold section will be displayed along with the Income and Expense sections.

FLASHBACK TO GAAP: MATCHING

Remember that you are to match the expenses to revenues within the same fiscal period. The Income Statement helps you to make sure this happens.

The Income Statement is made up of temporary accounts. Therefore, it will begin each fiscal year with all accounts displaying a zero balance because the previous period's amounts will have been transferred to the Retained Earnings account as either a net income or a net loss.

Analyzing the Income Statement

There are different measures used to analyze a company's health using the income statement, and the measure used will depend on the purpose of the analysis. The Statement of Cash Flows is a more reliable report in many instances, but the Income Statement can still be a useful tool for analyzing aspects of the business such as:

- Ratios to measure profitability (gross margin %, net income %)
- Growth trend analysis (earnings vs. expenses)
- Comparison to similar businesses
- Return on investment

The Balance Sheet

The Balance Sheet displays the permanent accounts, which make up the elements of the accounting equation (Assets = Liabilities + Equity). It reflects the financial condition of a business on a particular date. In pen-and-paper accounting, the values for the Balance Sheet come from the Balance Sheet section of the worksheet.

FLASHBACK TO GAAP: TIME PERIOD

Remember that the activities of the business can be divided into time periods.

Just as the Income Statement is not a perfect tool for analyzing a business, the Balance Sheet is not always the right tool. It can, though, be useful for looking at:

- Ratios to measure profitability, liquidity, and financial strength in the long run (current ratio, quick ratio, return on assets, and return on equity)
- Comparison of assets to liabilities over time
- Working capital (current assets less current liabilities)
- Leverage (debt/worth)

The Statement of Owner's Equity

The Statement of Owner's Equity shows the capital at the beginning of the fiscal period, any additional investments as well as draws by the owner, the net income or loss, and the ending amount.

The amounts on the Statement of Owner's Equity come from two sections of the pen-and-paper worksheet. The net income or loss comes from the Income Statement section, and the beginning capital, investments, and draws come from the Balance Sheet section.

QuickBooks does not provide this as a report for you. One way to look at the change in owner's equity from one fiscal period to another is to customize a Balance Sheet Previous Year Comparison report by filtering it to show only equity accounts.

Creating Reports to Compare Data from Previous Fiscal Periods

QuickBooks provides ready-made reports to help you compare company financial information from the current and previous fiscal periods. The Profit & Loss Previous Year Comparison and Balance Sheet Previous Year Comparison reports show the dollar values for each year and detail the change in amount and percentage.

In addition to the preset reports available in QuickBooks to compare data, you can also customize summary reports to show the same previous period information.

 Reports→Company & Financial→Profit & Loss Standard *or* Balance Sheet Standard *or* Balance Sheet Prev Year Comparison

---

DEVELOP YOUR SKILLS 12-4

In this exercise, you will create financial statements for Average Guy Designs. The first report you will create is the Income Statement for the year.

1. Choose **Reports→Company & Financial→Profit & Loss Standard**.
2. Set the date range from **010123** to **123123**, refresh the report, and then resize the window to view the data.
3. Click the **Customize Report** button on the toolbar.
4. Click the **Header/Footer** tab and then change the report title to **Income Statement** and click **OK**.

   Notice the Depreciation Expense of $825 under the Expense section of the report. The Owner's Equity will not show up on this report.

5. Close the Profit & Loss report, choosing not to memorize it.

Run a Balance Sheet Report

Now you will produce the Balance Sheet report for the period ending December 31, 2023.

6. Choose **Reports→Company & Financial→Balance Sheet Standard**.
7. Set the As of date to **123123** and refresh the report.

   You will now see a basic Balance Sheet report with both the Accumulated Depreciation and the Owner's Equity displayed.

8. Close the Balance Sheet report, choosing not to memorize it.

Create a Report That Shows the Equity Account Information from Two Periods

Next, you will create a report that shows the change in equity information from one period to the next. This is what will simulate the Statement of Owner's Equity report.

9. Choose **Reports→Company & Financial→Balance Sheet Prev Year Comparison**.

10. Click the **Customize Report** button.

11. Enter these dates: **123122** to **123123**.

12. Follow these steps to modify the report to show the change in equity accounts:

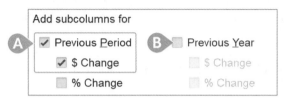

(A) Click to select **Previous Period** and **$ Change**.

(B) Click to de-select **Previous Year**.

13. Click the **Filters** tab, ensure **Account** is the Filter selected, and then choose **All equity accounts**.

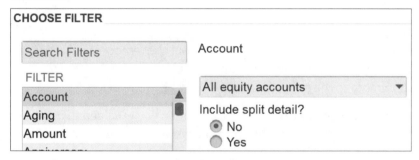

14. Click the **Header/Footer** tab, change the **Report title** to `Equity Previous Year Comparison`, and then click **OK**.

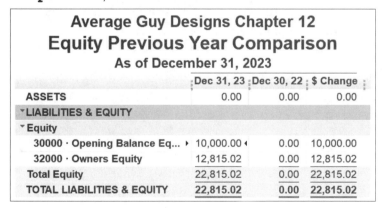

Average Guy Designs Chapter 12 Equity Previous Year Comparison As of December 31, 2023	Dec 31, 23	Dec 30, 22	$ Change
ASSETS	0.00	0.00	0.00
LIABILITIES & EQUITY			
Equity			
30000 · Opening Balance Eq... ▸	10,000.00 ◂	0.00	10,000.00
32000 · Owners Equity	12,815.02	0.00	12,815.02
Total Equity	22,815.02	0.00	22,815.02
TOTAL LIABILITIES & EQUITY	22,815.02	0.00	22,815.02

The report displays the balances for the equity accounts on 12/30/2022 (you entered 12/31/2022 as the date, but the report will show one day prior) and 12/31/2023 as well as the dollar change. In this scenario, the company was not operating on 12/30/2022, but it still shows the change in equity from one year to the next!

15. Close the **Balance Sheet Prev Year Comparison** report window, choosing not to memorize the report.

Wrapping Up the Accounting Cycle and Closing the Books

To wrap up the accounting cycle, you need to "zero out" the temporary accounts and move the resulting net income or net loss to a permanent account (specifically an equity account) to begin the next fiscal year. In addition to moving the net income or net loss to the equity account, you also need to bring the account that tracks owner's draw or shareholder distributions to zero.

Cycle Step 7: Closing Entries and Post-Closing Trial Balance

In pen-and-paper accounting, there are five tasks involved in the final step of the accounting cycle.

1. Transfer the ending amounts from all of the income accounts to the Income Summary account.

2. Transfer the ending amounts from all of the expense accounts to the Income Summary account.

3. Transfer the amount in the Income Summary account to the capital account.

4. Transfer the amount in the owner's draw account to the capital account (Retained Earnings).

5. Create a post-closing trial balance report.

Each of these tasks results in journal transactions that close out the temporary accounts and move the amounts to Income Summary. Then a transaction is recorded that transfers the amount from Income Summary to the capital account. Take note of the following:

• If the balance in the Income Summary account is a credit, then you will need to debit it and credit the capital account. This signifies that the company has experienced a net income.

• If the balance in the Income Summary account is a debit, then you will need to credit it and debit the capital account. This signifies that the company has experienced a net loss.

When you close the books in QuickBooks, all of this is done for you behind the scenes. This step will result in either an increase or decrease in the capital account balance based on whether the company saw a net income or a net loss and the amount of funds the owner(s) drew from the company.

The final report that you will create is a post-closing Trial Balance that shows all temporary accounts with a zero balance. This report also allows you to check for one last time that debits and credits are equal. You should have only permanent accounts displayed in the post-closing Trial Balance.

If you choose not to close the books, these year-end adjustments will be made automatically:

- Income and expense accounts will be zeroed out.

- Net income will be adjusted so that the Equity section of the balance sheet will display a line for net income as the same as it was on the last day of the prior year.

- Retained earnings will be increased by the prior year's net income and then decreased by the same amount (so you start with net income of zero for new period.)

Setting a Closing Date

As you know, you are not required to close the books in QuickBooks. When you close the books by setting a closing date, QuickBooks does the following for you:

- Transfers the net income or net loss to Retained Earnings

- Restricts access to transactions prior to the closing date by requiring a password

After you close the books, you can run the Condense Data Utility, which cleans up your data.

Only the company file administrator can set a closing date and allow or restrict access to prior-period transactions by user.

SETTING A CLOSING DATE IN QUICKBOOKS

Pros	Cons
You can restrict access to prior-period transactions by setting a password.	You can't easily access all of the details from previous-period transactions.
You can create a closing date exception report that displays any modified transactions that are dated on or before the closing date.	You can't create reports that compare transaction data from prior periods.
Transactions can't be changed without your knowledge. Users would need the closing date password and permissions.	

↗ Company→Set Closing Date

Here is an example of the final step of the accounting cycle. You can see that $100,000 of income will move into the Income Summary account as well as $50,000 of expenses. This results in a $50,000 credit balance that, when transferred to the capital account, will represent a net income of $50,000. In addition, you can see how the owner draw of $10,000 affects the capital account.

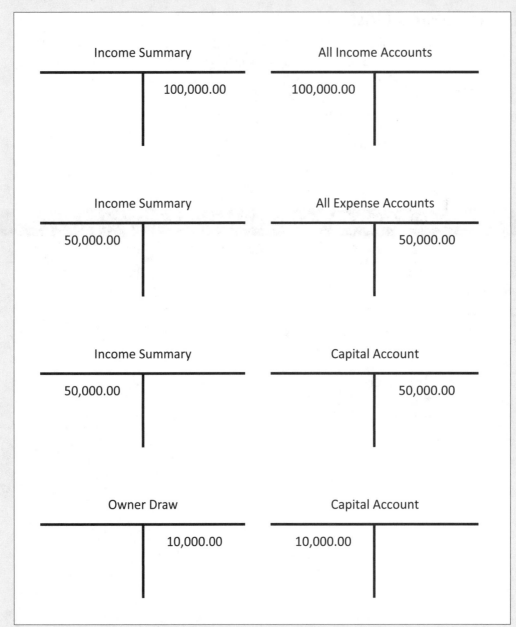

The net effect behind the scenes is a zero balance in the Income Summary account, all the income accounts, all the expense accounts, and the Owner Draw account. There will be a net increase (credit) in the capital account of $40,000.

In this exercise, you will set a closing date and password for the Average Guy Designs QuickBooks company file.

1. Choose **Company→Set Closing Date** and then click the **Set Date/Password** button in the Preferences window.

   The Set Closing Date and Password window appears.

2. Use this information to set the closing date and password:

   - Click the checkbox to **Exclude estimates, sales orders, and purchase orders from closing date restrictions**
   - Closing Date: **123123**
   - Closing Date Password: **123**

   > *Note!* When closing the books, you can choose not to include transactions that do not affect what happens "behind the scenes" by excluding estimates, sales orders, and purchase orders. If you are not sure what decision to make for your own company, check with an accountant. Also, remember to set a strong password to use for the company file. A simple one is used here as a basic example.

3. Click **OK** in the Set Closing Date and Password window and then close the Preferences window.

Working with a Company File After Closing

After you have set a closing date, there is one additional step to the accounting cycle. It has to do with creating another Trial Balance report. You also may choose to clean up your company's data after you close the books by condensing the company file.

In this exercise, you will run the Trial Balance for 2023 and then again for the first day of 2024. In the report for 2023, you will see the entries you made for Accumulated Depreciation, Owners Equity, and Inventory Adjustment. In the report for 2024, you will see how QuickBooks has closed the books for you at the end of your fiscal period.

1. Choose **Reports→Accountant & Taxes→Trial Balance**.

2. Set the **Dates** from **010123** to **123123** and then click the **Refresh** button.

   Notice the amounts in Accumulated Depreciation, Owners Equity, and Inventory Adjustment.

3. Change the **Dates** to **010124** to **010124** and then click the **Refresh** button.

   You can see that QuickBooks has closed out all of the temporary accounts and transferred the net income to Owners Equity.

4. Close the Trial Balance report, choosing not to memorize it.

Correcting Transactions from a Closed Period

After a password has been set for a closed period, you will need to enter it if you need to change or add a transaction in the prior period.

> **Tip!** If you are using the Premier Accountant edition, you can produce the Closing Date Exception report that shows any transactions dated on or before the closing date that were entered after you set the closing date.

The Audit Trail

The audit trail feature of QuickBooks allows you to track every entry, modification, or deletion to transactions in your file. The audit trail feature is always on to make sure that an accurate record of your QuickBooks data is kept. The audit trail does not track changes to lists, only to transactions. This can help you to research transaction history and determine whether certain types of fraudulent activity are occurring. To view the audit trail, you can run a QuickBooks report called "Audit Trail," which is available from the Accountant & Taxes category of the Report Center.

Condensing the Company File

After you have closed the books, you may decide to condense your company file. This process also gives you choices to delete transactions from before the company closing date that are no longer needed and create "summary" transactions to take their places. Types of transactions that will not be summarized are:

- Those with open balances or that are linked to others with open balances

- Any that have not been reconciled or cleared

- Any that are marked "To be printed"

QuickBooks will not remove any payroll transactions for the current calendar year because of payroll tax reporting requirements. Condensing the file is also a way of reducing a large company file that has accumulated a lot of data over the years.

> **Warning!** Condensing your company data has huge implications, so make sure you understand what you are doing before you perform this operation.

After you have decided on what to clean up during the condensing process, QuickBooks will:

1. Create a copy of the company file, which will be in its original state prior to the condensing process. The name of the file will include the date and the word "copy" appended to the end. The location of the copy will also be displayed.

2. Verify the integrity of your company file.

Remember that transactions dated after your company closing date will not be affected by the clean-up process.

During the process you will be asked for:

- The date to use to remove transactions

- How you want inventory to be handled (Summarize inventory transactions or Keep inventory transaction details)

- Which transactions to remove, such as uncleared bank and credit card transactions, and time and mileage activities to name a few

- Which list entries to remove, if any, such as accounts, classes, and completed To Do notes

An advantage to condensing the company file is that it will also remove list entries that have not been used after the prior period. When all of the transactions for a particular list entry have been deleted or summarized, you can then delete the list entry.

> **Tip!** Make sure that you have completed all year-end activities before you clean up your company file, such as producing W-2s, W-3s, and 1099-MISC forms.

> ➚ File→Utilities→Condense Data

NEW! 2019 QuickBooks now allows you to reduce your company size without removing any data through Data File Optimization. Essentially, QuickBooks will remove the information in the Audit Trail from a previous period, which decreases the size and may help your company to run more smoothly because of a decreased size. Don't worry, though, QuickBooks will prompt you to save a copy of you file with the audit trail intact before this process so you can go back to it and view the Audit Trail, if needed.

Working with an Accountant's Copy

If your accountant needs to make adjustments to your QuickBooks file, but you do not want to lose access to it while it is being adjusted, you may want to create an accountant's copy file. Your accountant can make the needed adjustments, and you can at least keep up with your daily transactions.

However, there are some tasks that you *cannot* do while your accountant is working on your file, such as:

- Edit or delete accounts

- Add, edit, or delete transactions dated on or before the dividing date

- Reconcile an account

Just as with setting a closing date, only the company file administrator can create an accountant's copy. When the accountant's copy is created, QuickBooks appends the date and time the file was created to the filename (e.g., QuickBooks2019 Acct Transfer Dec 04,2019 08 20 PM). The extension will be .QBX.

The Dividing Date

When you create an accountant's copy, you must set a dividing date. The dividing date determines the fiscal period that the accountant will be working on. The accountant will be able to work on transactions prior to that date, and you will be able to continue to work entering transactions after that date. Be careful when setting this date to ensure that your accountant will have the access needed and that you will still be able to modify recent transactions, if necessary. If your accountant is making adjusting entries, it makes sense to set the dividing date as the last day of the previous fiscal year.

 Best Practice

It is generally best to set the dividing date about two weeks after the last day of whichever fiscal period you need. Typically, it will be the end of a quarter. This way the accountant can move transactions between the two periods, if needed.

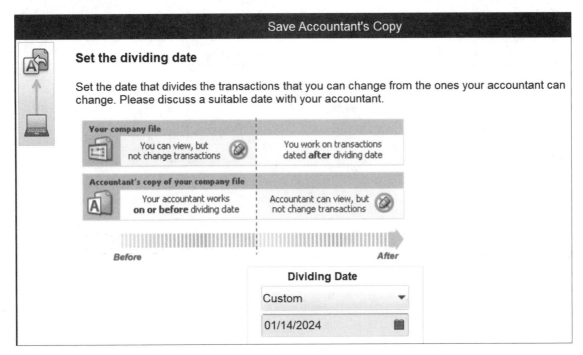

The dividing date will determine the date from which your accountant can make changes to your company file. It also dictates your own access to your company file.

Managing Accountant's Copies

You will encounter four tasks when working with accountant's copies: saving, sending, importing, and removing restrictions. All of these are accessible through the File option on the menu.

- **Saving an accountant's copy of the file:** You have two options. The first option is to create an accountant's copy, which enables you and the accountant to work independently and you to import the accountant's changes later. The second option is to create a portable or backup file if the accountant needs to set up the books, do daily bookkeeping, or work on payroll. You won't be able to work on the file until the accountant is finished, or you will have to manually enter the changes later.

- **Sending the file:** You can email the file or save it to a CD or other storage media to provide your accountant with the file. You can also use the Intuit's Accountant's Copy File Transfer service. This option, found under File→Send Company File→Accountant's Copy→Send to Accountant, requires Internet access, as the file will be uploaded to Intuit's web server. Your accountant will receive an email with a link to download the file.

> **Warning!** If you use the File Transfer service, the company file will not be available during the process of creating and uploading the file. The file will show "(Accountant's Changes Pending)" on the title bar. You must wait for the process to be finished.

- **Importing the file:** When you receive the file back from your accountant, you must import the accountant's changes into your company file. When you do this, you will be prompted to create a backup copy of your file. This is important in case the import is not successful—you will still have a workable copy of your company file. During the import process, it will be up to you to accept all or none of the changes into your company file and to view the notes left for you from your accountant.

- **Removing restrictions on your file:** To cancel an accountant's copy, you must choose to remove restrictions. If you do this, though, you will not be able to import the accountant's copy changes. On the other hand, if you accidentally create an accountant's copy file, just cancel it to work with your file in normal mode.

Reports→Accountant & Taxes→Audit Trail

File→Send Company File→Accountant's Copy

DEVELOP YOUR SKILLS 12-7

In this exercise, you will correct a transaction from a closed period and produce an Audit Trail report.

Guy realized that invoice #10001, dated 12/01/2023, should have been dated 12/10/2023. You will first correct the invoice.

1. Choose **Edit→Find** and then click the **Simple** tab, if necessary.
2. Type **10001** in the Invoice # field and click **Find**.
3. Click the **Go To** button.

    Invoice #10001 was already selected, so when you clicked Go To, QuickBooks opened the Create Invoices window with it displayed.

4. Change the date to **121023** and type **Huff: holiday reunion** in the Memo field.
5. Click **Save & Close** to record the new date for the invoice; click **Yes** to make the change to the transaction.

    A QuickBooks window appears that lets you know that you are making a change to a transaction from a closed period. To bypass this window and make the change, you need to enter the closing date password.

6. Type **123** and click **OK**.
7. Close the Find window.

Create an Audit Trail Report

You will now look at the Audit Trail report, which will show the change you just made to invoice #10001.

8. Choose **Reports→Accountant & Taxes→Audit Trail**.
9. Ensure the Date Entered/Last Modified is set to **Today**.
10. Click the **Customize Report** button and then click the **Filters** tab.
11. Scroll down and choose **Memo** as the filter; type **Huff: holiday reunion** in the Memo field.
12. Click **OK** to see the filtered report.

13. Scroll down, if necessary, until you can see the documentation of the change that you just made to invoice #10001.

Average Guy Designs Chapter 12
Audit Trail

Num	Entered/Last Modified	Last modified by	State	Date	Name	Memo	Account	Split	Amount
Transactions entered or modified by Guy (Admin)									
Invoice 10001									
10001	12/02/2017 21:19:48	Guy (Admin)	Latest	*12/10/2023*	Evelyn Huff:Project #1	*Huff: holid...*	11000 · Accounts...	-SPLIT-	105.00
					Evelyn Huff:Project #1	*T-shirt and...*	43200 · Design Inc...	11000 · Acc...	-105.00
					State Board of Equaliza...	San Tomas ...	25500 · Sales Tax...	11000 · Acc...	0.00
10001	12/02/2017 12:40:48	Guy (Admin)	Prior	12/01/2023	Evelyn Huff:Project #1		11000 · Accounts...	-SPLIT-	105.00
					Evelyn Huff:Project #1	T-shirt and i...	43200 · Design Inc...	11000 · Acc...	-105.00
					State Board of Equaliza...	San Tomas ...	25500 · Sales Tax...	11000 · Acc...	0.00

The Audit Trail report reflects Invoice 10001 with a date change. The entry date will differ from yours.

The Audit Trail report shows the prior and most current versions of a transaction.

14. Close the Audit Trail report window, choosing not to memorize it.

Tackle the Tasks

Now is your chance to work a little more with Average Guy Designs and apply the skills that you have learned in this chapter to accomplish additional tasks. You will use the same company file you used in the Develop Your Skills exercises throughout this chapter. If you are using the trial software for this course on your computer or in a lab at school, you must toggle to the Pro edition every time you start QuickBooks. Enter the following tasks, referring back to the concepts in the chapter as necessary. Use **TTT_Chapter12 Worksheet** for this section and save it as: `CH12_TTT Worksheet Answers`

Create a Balance Sheet Report as of 03/31/2023	
Calculation	**Answer**
Quick ratio: (current assets − inventory)/current liabilities	
Return on assets: net income/total assets	
Working capital: current assets − current liabilities	

Create an Income Statement Report for the Period 01/01/2023–03/31/2023	
Calculation	**Answer**
Gross profit margin: (revenue − COGS)/revenue	
Operating profit margin: revenue − expenses related to day-to-day operations of the business	
Net profit margin: net income/revenue	

Self-Assessment

Check your knowledge of this chapter's key concepts and skills using the Self-Assessment quiz here, in your ebook, or in your eLab course.

1. An example of an adjusting entry is one that updates the value of a fixed asset.   *True   False*

2. An Income Summary account is used to clear out permanent account balances.   *True   False*

3. QuickBooks will not allow you to record a transaction for which debits do not equal credits.   *True   False*

4. QuickBooks provides a worksheet to use when preparing financial statements.   *True   False*

5. When you account for depreciation, the account Accumulated Depreciation is credited.   *True   False*

6. A permanent account is one for which the ending balance for one fiscal period is the opening balance for the next.   *True   False*

7. The Income Statement shows the balance of permanent accounts as of a certain date.   *True   False*

8. Analyzing the Balance Sheet will allow you to calculate the gross margin percentage.   *True   False*

9. The Income Statement is a financial report that displays the income and expenses over a specific period of time.   *True   False*

10. One of the advantages of closing the books in QuickBooks is that you can restrict access to prior-period transactions by setting a password.   *True   False*

11. A general journal entry is made for what reason?
    A. Record end-of-year fixed asset depreciation
    B. Adjust an inventory quantity
    C. Adjust owner's equity
    D. Any of these options

12. An adjusting entry may allow you to complete which of these transactions?
    A. Enter a bill from a vendor.
    B. Record depreciation for a fiscal period.
    C. Create a sales receipt to record the daily sales.
    D. Record a deposit into the Checking account.

(cont'd.)

13. Which report allows you to track every entry, modification, or deletion to transactions in your file?
    A. Closing Date Exception report
    B. Post-Closing Trial Balance report
    C. Accountant's Copy report
    D. Audit Trail report

14. Which of these does QuickBooks NOT do for you automatically at the end of the fiscal year?
    A. Transfer net income or net loss to Retained Earnings
    B. Ensure you start the new fiscal year with zero balances for the permanent accounts
    C. Close out temporary accounts
    D. Allow you to start the new fiscal year with a net income of zero

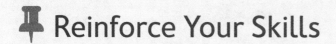

Reinforce Your Skills

Emily Holly from Electrical Energy has asked you to prepare for closing her company's books by running the end-of-period financial reports and making adjusting entries. You will then close the books and make a correction to a transaction from the prior period. The password for all files unless otherwise stated is Password1. Leave the company file open unless otherwise instructed. If you are using the trial software on your computer or in a lab at school, remember to toggle to the Pro edition every time you start QuickBooks.

REINFORCE YOUR SKILLS 12-1

Work with the Trial Balance Report

In this exercise, you will create a Trial Balance report for Electrical Energy.

1. Start QuickBooks 2019.
2. Choose **File→Open or Restore Company**.
3. Open **RYS_Chapter12 (Company)** or restore **RYS_Chapter12 (Portable)** from your file storage location and save your file as: **RYS_Chapter12 Electrical Energy**
4. Choose **Reports→Accountant & Taxes→Trial Balance**.
5. Set the date range from **010123** to **123123** and then refresh the report.

   The Trial Balance report for the fiscal year displays.
6. Close the Trial Balance report, choosing not to memorize it.

REINFORCE YOUR SKILLS 12-2

Create an Adjusting Entry and Inventory Adjustment

In this exercise, you will make an adjusting entry to record depreciation for 2023. Then you will record an inventory adjustment to account for LED Track Lighting that was damaged.

1. Choose **Company→Make General Journal Entries**; click **OK** in the Assigning Numbers to Journal Entries window.
2. Type **123123** as the date.
3. Debit **Depreciation Expense** for **500**, typing **2023 Depreciation** as the Memo and choosing **Overhead** as the Class.
4. Credit **Accumulated Depreciation** for **500**, copying the memo from the first line and using the same class.
5. Click **Save & Close** to record the transaction.
6. Click in the checkbox to not display the message in the future and click **OK** in the Tracking Fixed Assets on Journal Entries window.

Make an Inventory Adjustment

Next you will create an inventory adjustment to deduct the damaged LED Track Lighting from inventory.

7. Choose **Vendors→Inventory Activities→Adjust Quantity/Value on Hand**.

8. Type **123123** as the Adjustment Date and tap Tab.

9. Type **Inventory Adjustment** in the Adjustment Account field, tap Tab, and click **Set Up** to set up the new account.

10. Set the Account Type as **Expense** and the **Number** as **62200**; click **Save & Close**.

11. Choose **Material Costs** as the class.

12. Choose to reduce the number of LED Track Lighting in inventory by one (**−1**) in the Qty Difference column and then click **Save & Close**.

REINFORCE YOUR SKILLS 12-3

Produce Financial Statements

In this exercise, you will produce an Income Statement and Balance Sheet for Electrical Energy.

1. Choose **Reports→Company & Financial→Profit & Loss Standard**.

2. Set the date range from **010123** to **123123** and then refresh the report.

   The Profit & Loss report displays for 2023. You will now change the report title to Income Statement.

3. Click the **Customize Report** button.

4. On the Header/Footer tab, change the Report Title to **Income Statement** and click **OK**.

5. Click the **Memorize** button on the toolbar, type **Income Statement 2023** as the report name, and click **OK**; close the report window.

Create a Balance Sheet Report

6. Choose **Reports→Company & Financial→Balance Sheet Standard**.

7. Change the As of date to **123123** and refresh the report.

8. Click the **Memorize** button, type **Balance Sheet as of 12/31/2023** as the report name, and click **OK**; close the report window.

   To see the memorized reports list, choose Reports menu→Memorized Reports→Memorized Report List.

REINFORCE YOUR SKILLS 12-4

Close the Books

In this exercise, you will set a closing date for Electrical Energy's QuickBooks company file.

1. Choose **Company→Set Closing Date**.

2. Click the **Set Date/Password** button on the Company Preferences tab of the Accounting section.

   The Set Closing Date and Password window appears.

3. Click in the checkbox to **Exclude estimates, sales orders, and purchase orders from closing date restrictions**.

4. Use this information to complete the Set Closing Date and Password window:

   - Closing Date: **123123**

   - Closing Date Password: **789**

5. Click **OK** to set the closing date and password and then click **OK** in the Preferences window.

Make a Correction to a Transaction from a Prior Period

In this exercise, you will make a correction to a transaction from a closed period. Emily realized that she needs to change the amount of the bill dated 12/12/2023 for Con Edison to $264.03. You will make that change now.

1. Choose **Edit→Find**.

2. Choose **Bill** as the Transaction Type and **Con Edison** as the Vendor; click **Find**.

   You will see all of the bills for the vendor displayed at the bottom of the window.

3. Double-click the bill for **12/12/2023**.

   The Enter Bills window will open with the selected bill displayed.

4. Change the Amount on the bill to **$264.03** (both in the top and bottom portions of the window) and click **Save & Close**; click **Yes** to record the transaction.

   A QuickBooks window appears, asking for you to enter the closing date password in order to make the change.

5. Type **789** and click **OK**.

6. Close the Find window and close the company file.

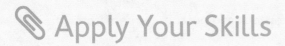

Apply Your Skills

Wet Noses Veterinary Clinic is ready to close the books for the fiscal year. To do so, you will create a Trial Balance report, work with Journal Entries, close the books, and create an Accountant's copy of the QuickBooks company file. After starting QuickBooks, remember to toggle to Pro as necessary.

APPLY YOUR SKILLS 12-1 `QG`

Create a Trial Balance Report

In this exercise, you will help Dr. James create a Trial Balance report for her veterinary clinic.

1. Choose **File→Open or Restore Company**.
2. Open **AYS_A1_Chapter12 (Company)** or restore **AYS_A1_Chapter12 (Portable)** from your file storage location and save your file as: **AYS_A1_Chapter12 Wet Noses Clinic**
3. Choose **Reports→Accountant & Taxes→Trial Balance**.
4. Set the date range to cover the month of May 2023.

   The trial balance report for the one-month period of May 2023 displays.
5. Click the **Excel** ⌐Excel ▾⌐ button and export this report to a new worksheet, saving the worksheet to your file storage location as: **CH12_A1 Trial Balance**
6. Close the Trial Balance report, choosing not to memorize it.

APPLY YOUR SKILLS 12-2 `QG`

Enter Journal Entries

In this exercise, you will create adjusting entries. Dr. James has invested in the company by purchasing furniture and equipment. You will first enter a general journal entry to record a fixed asset investment, the furniture and equipment that Dr. James provided to the company. You will then need to enter the depreciation transaction for the fixed assets.

1. Open the **Make General Journal Entries** window and click **OK** in the Assigning Numbers to Journal Entries window.
2. Create a transaction dated **05/01/2023** that debits **Furniture and Equipment** and credits the **Partner 1 Equity** account for **$16,320**, entering **Record fixed asset investment** as the Memo; click **Save & New**. Click **OK** in the Tracking Fixed Assets on Journal Entries window, choosing to not display the message in the future.

   You will now help Sadie record the depreciation for the month.
3. Create a transaction dated **05/31/2023** that debits **Depreciation Expense** and credits the **Accumulated Depreciation** account for **$128**. Use **Record May 2023 Depreciation** as the Memo; click **Save & Close**.
4. Create a QuickReport that will show the change in Partner 1 equity from **04/30/2023** to **05/31/2023**.
5. Create a **Profit & Loss Standard** report for the month of May.
6. Click the **Excel** ⌐Excel ▾⌐ button and export this report to a new worksheet, saving the worksheet to your file storage location as: **CH12_A2 May 2023 Profit and Loss**

7. Close the Excel and report window.

8. Create a **Balance Sheet Summary** report as of May 31, 2023.

9. Click the **Excel** `Excel ▾` button and export this report to a new worksheet, saving the worksheet to your file storage location as: `CH12_A2 May 2023 Balance Sheet Summary`

10. Close the window and close the company file.

APPLY YOUR SKILLS 12-3

Close the Books

In this exercise, you will close the books and create an Accountant's Copy of the file.

1. Open the **Preferences** window with the Accounting category and the Company Preferences tab displayed.

2. Choose to set the closing date and password; choose to exclude estimates, sales orders, and purchase orders from closing date restrictions.

3. Enter **05/31/2023** as the Closing Date and then use **123** as the Closing Date Password.

Create an Accountant's Copy

Next you will create an accountant's copy that your accountant can use to view your company data and make adjusting entries.

4. Choose **File→Send Company File→Accountant's Copy→Save File** and then click **Next**.

5. Choose **Accountant's Copy** and then click **Next**.

   If using the Premier Accountant edition, the menu command will be File→Accountant's Copy→Client Activities→Save File.

6. Set a custom Dividing Date of **053123** and then click **Next**.

   If you are completing this exercise prior to 05/31/2023, you will not be allowed to set the closing date (because it is in the future).

7. If you see the Warning window, click **OK** if you had selected today's date or a date in the future to be the dividing date and then choose to **Cancel** the Save Accountant's Copy window. If there's no Warning window, click **OK** (so that QuickBooks can close all windows and save your file), choose your default file storage location, and then click **Save**.

   You now have a file that you can send to your accountant.

8. Close the company file.

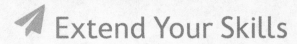 Extend Your Skills

Before You Begin: Open **EYS_Chapter12 (Company)** or restore **EYS_Chapter12 (Portable)** from your file storage location.

You have been hired by Arlaine Cervantes to help her with her organization's books. She is the founder of Niños del Lago, a nonprofit organization that provides impoverished Guatemalan children with an engaging educational camp experience. You have just sat down at your desk and opened a large envelope from her with a variety of documents and noticed that you have several emails from her as well. It is your job to sort through the papers and emails and make sense of what you find, entering information into QuickBooks whenever appropriate and answering any other questions in a word-processing document saved as: **EYS1_Chapter12_LastnameFirstinitial**

Remember, you are digging through papers on a desk, so it is up to you to determine the correct order in which to complete the tasks.

- Note from Arlaine: I know that the end-of-period accounting for not-for-profits is a bit different than what is done for "regular" for-profit businesses. Will you please research the differences for me and report back?

- Scribbled note from Arlaine: Please create a Balance Sheet report as of 8/31/2019, change the name of it to **Statement of Financial Position**, and export it to Excel. Save the Excel file as: **SFP, 8-31-19**

13 | Bringing It All Together!

I n this chapter, you will synthesize all you have learned in Unit 1 (Chapters 1–5) and Unit 2 (Chapters 6–10) in two separate projects. You will look at the information that has been compiled for an expanding auto-detailing business and then process it in QuickBooks.

📂 Project 1: Keeping the Books for June 2019

Martin Beatty has owned and operated a small automobile detailing business, Rugged Cross Auto Detailing, out of his home for the past three-and-a-half years. His business has grown, and he is no longer able to serve his customer base from his converted garage facility. Martin is looking for a commercial building to lease from which he can run his business. When the move is complete, Martin plans to employ four full-time detailing specialists. Martin's wife, Bridget, manages the bookkeeping. At a small-business seminar she recently attended, Bridget learned about QuickBooks and is now ready to start using it.

Your instructor may assign this as an individual or a group project. If you complete the project individually, you will assume all roles. If you're working in a group, your first task is to determine who will serve in each of these three roles:

- Administrator Ⓐ
- Accounts Receivable Representative Ⓡ
- Accounts Payable Representative Ⓟ

You will be keeping the books for the company for June 2019, which will be broken down into "sessions." At the end of each session, you will produce "deliverables" for evaluation. You will not be given specifics in many cases, just as you would not be given specifics when working with your own company. You may need to add new customers, vendors, or other information "on the fly" and use your own problem-solving and reasoning skills. Use QuickBooks' help and search features as needed. Now, let's get started!

Session #1: The Company File and Lists

Ⓐ The Administrator is responsible for creating the new company file. If you are working in a group, set yourself up as the administrator and your teammates as additional users. Grant permissions for each user account based on the responsibilities of each position. (You may wish to review the entire project to determine the access needed.) Since you may be entering transactions that occurred in the past, make sure to turn off the Date Warning preferences. Examine the Chart of Accounts to ensure there is an appropriate income account for each type of service Rugged Cross Auto Detailing provides as well as an expense account for non-inventory items (i.e., Job Materials). Delete the unnecessary accounts. Finally, set up the bank and credit card accounts.

Ⓡ The Accounts Receivable team member is responsible for setting up the customers. In addition, you will need to set up the service items that will be displayed on invoices and sales receipts.

Ⓟ The Accounts Payable team member is responsible for setting up the vendors. In addition, you will need to populate these profile lists: Vendor Type List, Customer Type List, Payment Type List, and Terms List. Finally, you will assist the Administrator by setting up the non-inventory items.

Session #1 Data

COMPANY GENERAL INFORMATION

Business Name	Rugged Cross Auto Detailing
Industry	Automotive Sales or Repair
Business Type	Sole Proprietorship
Employer Identification Number (EIN)	#99-9999999
Business Address	18071 Hamburg Avenue, Anaconda, MT 59711
Phone	(406) 555-5192
Fax	(406) 555-3172
Fiscal Year	June
Tax Year	January
Tax Form	1040 (Sole Proprietorship)
QuickBooks Start Date	06/01/2019
Basis	Cash
State ID	#999-9999-9

BANK ACCOUNTS

Account Name	Account Number	Opening Balance	Opening Balance Date
Checking: Deer Lodge County Credit Union	Acct. #4673-85	$13,265.72	5/31/2019
Savings: Deer Lodge County Credit Union	Acct. #4673-02	$42,105.01	5/31/2019
Credit Card: Copper City Bank Visa	Acct. #4000 9999 7777 3333	$0	5/31/2019

CHART OF ACCOUNTS

Delete the Equipment Rental account and add these accounts.

Account	Account Type
Cleaning Service Income	Income
Detailing Service Income	Income
Repair Service Income	Income
Job Materials	Expense

CUSTOMER TYPES/SUBTYPES

These lists contain the needed customer types (business/personal) and subtypes. Delete any other customer types not currently needed.

Business

- Chamber (of Commerce)
- From Ad
- Internet
- Referral
- Other

Personal

- From Ad
- Internet
- Referral
- Other

VENDOR TYPES

- Insurance
- Suppliers
- Tax Agency

- Utilities
- Other

PAYMENT METHODS

- American Express
- Cash
- Check
- Debit Card
- Discover

- Gift Card
- In-Kind (Other payment type)
- MasterCard
- Visa

TERMS LIST ENTRIES

- Due on Receipt
- Net 15
- Net 20

- Net 30
- 1% 10 Net 25
- 2% 15 Net 30

CUSTOMERS

Name/ Company	Address	Phone	Terms	Customer Type
John McNay	2118 Hagen St. Anaconda, MT 59711	(406) 555-2195	Due on Receipt	Personal: Referral
Dan Greany	102 Copper Rd. Anaconda, MT 59711	(406) 555-6103	Due on Receipt	Personal: Internet
Dan Thomas	1407 West 4th St. Opportunity, MT 59711	(406) 555-1254	Net 20	Personal: From Ad
Annette Helsper	1305 West 3rd St. Anaconda, MT 59711	(406) 555-5928	Due on Receipt	Personal: Referral
Pam Swanson	246 Birch St. Deer Lodge, MT 59722	(406) 555-6203	Net 15	Personal: Referral
Mike McCollough	955 Eagle Mtn. Dr. Anaconda, MT 59711	(406) 555-1093	Net 20	Personal: Internet
Larry Bloodneck	1104 East Park St. Philipsburg, MT 59858	(406) 555-3397	Due on Receipt	Personal: Internet
Mark Biggs	496 Mt. Baldy Rd. Anaconda, MT 59711	(406) 555-5981	Due on Receipt	Personal: From Ad
Sean Murphy	1106 West Park St. Anaconda, MT 59711	(406) 555-1942	Due on Receipt	Personal: From Ad
Leslie McGrevy	507 West 3rd St. Silver Bow, MT 59750	(406) 555-8851	Net 15	Personal: Internet
Anaconda Car Sales/ Rashid Jamal	4201 East 6th St. Anaconda, MT 59711	(406) 555-9441	1%10 Net 25	Business: Referral
Jenson Auto Wholesalers/ Erika Jenson	331 Pine St. Anaconda, MT 59711	(406) 555-7344	2%15 Net 30	Business: Referral

VENDORS

Name/ Company	Address	Phone	Account No. / Payment Terms	Type
Sullivan Insurance Co./Colleen Sullivan	206 West 4th St. Anaconda, MT 59711	(406) 555-2195	B22931 / Net 30	Insurance
Smelter City Power and Gas/Ron Johnson	201 West 3rd St. Anaconda, MT 59711	(406) 555-4431	129-774 / Net 15	Utilities
Crown Property Management/ Brian Sanders	4213 Salem St. Anaconda, MT 59711	(406) 555-7534	C420 / Due on Receipt	Other
Anaconda Water Works/ Dennis Thomas	1104 West 4th St. Anaconda, MT 59711	(406) 555-3842	5529-1 / Due on Receipt	Utilities
Butte Waste Management/ Teresa Moore	666 Hellsgate Ln. Butte, MT 59701	(406) 555-6666	NTGD00 / Net 15	Utilities
McCarthy Automotive Supply/Patsy McCarthy	1900 Butte Hill Rd. Phoenix, AZ 85001	(480) 555-2235	VW-112 / Due on Receipt	Suppliers
Hamill Car Detail Supplies/Katlin Hamill	24567 Danny Boy Way Corona, CA 92877	(951) 555-9988	921-ZP / Net 15	Suppliers
PriceCo			Due on Receipt	Suppliers
Deer Lodge County Treasurer/ Regina Parsons	County Courthouse 800 Main St. Anaconda, MT 59711	(406) 555-3732	999-99-9999 / Due on Receipt	Tax Agency

MENU OF SERVICES (SERVICES ARE NON-TAXABLE)

Individually Priced Repair Services

- Rock Chip Windshield Repair $55
- Automotive Paint Sealant $125
- Paint Over Spray Removal $25
- Paint Touch Up $20

Individually Priced Cleaning Services

- Hand Wash $20
- Hand Wash with Interior $35
- Electronic Odor Elimination $25
- Shampoo Carpet $60
- Shampoo Upholstery $50
- Engine Clean $45
- Exterior Polish & Wax $75
- Exterior Wax $45
- Water Spot/Tar Removal $15

Individually Priced Detailing Services

- Vinyl/Leather Treatment $25
- Tire/Bumper Dressing $15
- Shampoo Trunk $25

Packaged Cleaning Services (prices are for a small car/large car)

Paint Protection:
Thorough hand washing and drying, followed by application of a protective sealant $90/$125

Packaged Detailing Services (prices are for small car/large car)

Full Interior/Exterior Detailing:
Hand washing and drying, as well as machine buffing and waxing of exterior; interior cleaning, shampooing, with leather and glass protection applied $180/$225

Full Exterior Detailing:
Hand washing and drying, as well as machine buffing and waxing of exterior $160/$180

Interior Detailing:
Interior cleaning and shampooing, with leather and glass protection applied $100/$140

NON-INVENTORY PARTS (NON-TAXABLE)

Set up the following items, directing them to the Job Materials Expense account:

Item	Description	Price
Brushes	Sold as an assortment of sizes	$19.99
Rags	Sold in a 50-rag bundle	$39.99
Buckets	Sold in a 3-pack package	$18.49
Water Hose	50-foot hose	$17.99
Paper Hand Towels	Sold in a pack	$13.56
Mimi's Upholstery and Carpet Cleaner	Sold by the case	$60.00
Jack's Superior Exterior Car Wash Cleaner	1-gallon jug	$13.99

Session #1: Deliverables

Submit the following as directed. If your class is using Quick Grader, be sure to export the report to Excel.

- **Project1-1-1** QG **:** A report displaying the Chart of Accounts

- **Project1-1-2** QG **:** A report displaying the customers' names, Bill To addresses, phone numbers, and types

- **Project1-1-3** QG **:** A report displaying the vendors' names, account numbers, Bill From addresses, phone numbers, and types

- **Project1-1-4** QG **:** A report displaying the Terms Listing

- **Project1-1-5:** A report displaying the Items Listing (columns should be Item, Description, Type, and Price)

Session #2: Day-to-Day Work

Ⓐ The Administrator is responsible for making all deposits, receiving all payments on accounts, and entering credit card charges.

Ⓡ The Accounts Receivable team member is responsible for entering all invoices and cash sales.

Ⓟ The Accounts Payable team member is responsible for entering and paying all bills, and for writing and printing all checks.

Session #2: Data

Monthly Diary

Saturday, June 1, 2019

- Using a Service Invoice template, sold a Rock Chip Windshield Repair service to Larry Bloodneck on account using invoice #19-101.

- Received cash from Dan Greany for both Hand Wash with Interior and Electronic Odor Elimination services.

- Received a check (#429) from Sean Murphy for Hand Wash and Engine Clean services.

- Received a utility bill from Smelter City Power and Gas for $142.09, for service through 5/27/19, Ref #0519-129-774.

- Used the Visa card to purchase printer ink from PriceCo for $42.99.

- Wrote a check to Crown Property Management for $1,500 for June rent, to be printed later.

 CHECK FIGURE *Checking $11,765.72 • A/R $55.00 • A/P $142.09 • Visa $42.99*

 You can easily find your figures to compare these to in your Chart of Accounts!

Monday, June 3, 2019

- Received cash from Chris McCartney for a Hand Wash with Interior service.

- Received a check (#1465) from Dan Thomas for an Automotive Paint Protection service for a large SUV.

- Received a utility bill from Butte Waste Management for $74.00, for June 2019 service, Ref #NTGD00-0619.

- Received a bill from Hamill Car Detail Supplies for $60.00 for a case of Mimi's Upholstery and Carpet Cleaner, Ref #6376-18.

    Use the Items tab (not the Expense tab) to record this and future purchases of non-inventory job materials.

Tuesday, June 4, 2019

- Received a bill from Sullivan Insurance Co. for $154.30, Ref #MT-737-06, for quarterly business insurance.

    Ensure the Expense tab is displayed.

- Purchased water, soda pop, and snacks for the waiting room at Thompson's Grocery with credit card for $36.55, and these items are considered office supplies.

- Sold a Hand Wash with Interior service to John McNay on account using invoice #19-102.

- Received check #777 from Billy Mercedes for a Full Exterior Detailing service for a small car.

Wednesday, June 5, 2019

- Purchased a sound system and charging station for the lobby from Electronics Wizardry for $359.36 using the company Visa card; assign to Shop Expense.

- Sold a Paint Touch Up to Anaconda Car Sales on account using invoice #19-103.

- Received a bill from Hamill Car Detail Supplies for $38.48 for a package of Brushes and a 3-pack of Buckets.

- Invoiced Jenson Auto Wholesalers for five small car Full Interior/Exterior Detailing services using invoice #19-104.

Thursday, June 6, 2019

- Sold a Full Interior/Exterior Detailing service for a large SUV to Mike McCollough on account using invoice #19-105.

- Received a bill from McCarthy's Automotive Supply for $55.96 for four gallons of Jack's Superior Exterior Car Wash.

    Recall that this is a job material and is, therefore, recorded on the Items tab.

Friday, June 7, 2019

- Invoiced Anaconda Car Sales for four small vehicle and one large vehicle Full Interior/Exterior Detailing services, using invoice #19-106.

- Received check #2503 for $55.00 as payment on account from Larry Bloodneck; apply to invoice #19-101.

- Received a bill from WebWorks for a year's worth of Internet hosting (Computer & Internet) for $600, terms Net 15, Ref #RC-Annual 19

- Received a check (#435) from Sean Murphy for a Hand Wash service.

Saturday, June 8, 2019

- Purchased a carpet for the lobby from Superior Interiors using the company Visa for $189.45; this is considered a Shop Expense.

- Sold an Automotive Paint Protection service for a large vehicle to Leslie McGrevy on account using invoice #19-107.

- Sold an Automotive Paint Protection for a large vehicle to Larry Bloodneck on account using invoice #19-108.

- Received check #1668 for $900.00 as payment on account from Jenson Auto Wholesalers; apply to invoice #19-104.

- Paid all bills in Accounts Payable; checks are to be printed.

- Printed all checks in the queue using check #1800 as the first check number.

> **Tip!** Print the checks to PDF so they are created and assigned a number in your account, while saving on paper and ink.

- Deposited all funds held in Undeposited Funds into Checking.

 CHECK FIGURE *Checking $12,060.89 • A/R $1,475.00 • A/P $0 • Visa $628.35*

Monday, June 10, 2019

- Debit card charge of $38.44 at Simpson's Pizzeria for a customer appreciation lunch (Meals & Entertainment); use DB as the check number.

- Sold a Hand Wash with Interior service to John McNay using invoice #19-109.

- Sold an Interior Detailing package for a large car to Roxy Holden [1065 West Park St., Anaconda, MT 59711; (406) 555-1579] on account using invoice #19-110, terms Net 15.

- Received check #332 for $35.00 as payment on account from John McNay; apply to invoice #19-102.

- Received check #3355 for $20.00 as payment on account from Anaconda Car Sales; apply to invoice #19-103.

Tuesday, June 11, 2019

- Received check #446 from Logan Webb for a Hand Wash with Interior service.

- Sold a Full Exterior Detailing service package for a large SUV to Dan Thomas on account using invoice #19-111.

- Sold a Paint Touch Up service to Kristin Newberg [675 10th St., Anaconda, MT 59711; (406) 555-9821] on account using invoice #19-112, terms Net 15.

- Received check #781 for $225.00 as payment on account from Mike McCollough; apply to invoice #19-105. `

Wednesday, June 12, 2019

- Received a bill from Anaconda Water Works for $63.20, Ref #54698-0619.

- Invoiced Jenson Auto Wholesalers for two small vehicle and two large vehicle Full Interior/ Exterior Detailing services using invoice #19-113.

- Sold a Hand Wash with Interior service to Dan Greany on account using invoice #19-114.
- Received check #2139 for $125.00 as payment on account from Larry Bloodneck; apply to invoice #19-108.
- Used the company Visa to purchase office supplies for $29.78 at Office Superstore.

Thursday, June 13, 2019
- Sold Mark Biggs a Full Exterior Detailing for a small car on account using invoice #19-115; Mark then paid with check #577 for $160 later in the day.
- Sold a Hand Wash to Annette Helsper on account using invoice #19-116.
- Received check #6028 for $140.00 as payment on account from Roxy Holden; apply to invoice #19-110.
- Received a check (#438) from Sean Murphy for a Hand Wash.

Friday, June 14, 2019
- Received a cash payment from James Hakola for a Hand Wash and Exterior Polish & Wax services.
- Sold Hand Wash and Engine Clean services to Katie Fox [1644 Henderson Avenue, Anaconda, MT 59711; (406) 555-4312] on account using invoice #19-117, terms Net 15.
- Sold Hand Wash and Engine Clean services to Pam Swanson on account using invoice #19-118.
- Received a bill from Hamill Car Detail Supplies for $27.12 for 2 packs of Paper Hand Towels.
- Received check #899 for $180.00 as payment on account from Dan Thomas; apply to invoice #19-111.
- Received check #1012 for $125.00 as payment on account from Leslie McGrevy; apply to invoice #19-107.

Saturday, June 15, 2019
- Received check #3362 from Anaconda Car Sales for $700 on account.
- Sold a Hand Wash with Interior service to John McNay on account using invoice #19-119.
- Invoiced Anaconda Car Sales for two small vehicle and three large vehicle Full Interior/Exterior Detailing services using invoice #19-120.
- Received check #341 for $35.00 as payment on account from John McNay; apply to invoice #19-109.
- Wrote a $95.00 check to Martinez Janitorial, LLC for office cleaning (Repairs & Maintenance); set check to be printed.
- Paid all bills in Accounts Payable; checks to be printed.
- Printed all checks in the queue using the next available check number, #1807.
- Deposited all funds held in Undeposited Funds into Checking.

 **CHECK FIGURE** *Checking $13,732.13• A/R $2,330.00 • A/P $0 • Visa $658.13*

Monday, June 17, 2019

- Wrote a check to Sullivan Insurance Co. for $100, debiting the Insurance Expense account; to be printed.

- Received check #2664 for an Interior Detailing package for a small car from Annette Helsper.

- Invoiced Leslie McGrevy for an Interior Detailing package for a large car using invoice #19-121.

Tuesday, June 18, 2019

- Received check #2121 for $65.00 as payment on account from Pam Swanson; apply to invoice #19-118.

- Invoiced Jenson Auto Wholesalers for one small vehicle and three large vehicle Full Interior/Exterior Detailing services using invoice #19-122.

- Received a bill from McCarthy's Automotive Supply for $95.95 for 4 gallons of Jack's Superior Exterior Car Wash and a bundle of Rags.

- Received check #1676 for $810.00 as payment on account from Jenson Auto Wholesalers; apply to invoice #19-113.

Wednesday, June 19, 2019

- Sold a Full Interior/Exterior Detailing service for a small car to Larry Bloodneck on account using invoice #19-123.

- Received check #1427 for $65.00 as payment on account from Katie Fox; apply to invoice #19-117.

- Received a check (#441) from Sean Murphy for a Hand Wash.

Thursday, June 20, 2019

- Sold a Full Exterior Detailing package for a large vehicle to Alison Mandish on account using invoice #19-124, terms Net 15.

- Sold Hand Wash and Exterior Polish & Wax services to Lucky Rogers [898 8th St., Anaconda, MT 59711; (406) 555-2632] on account using invoice #19-125, terms Net 20.

- Received a bill from Hamill Car Detail Supplies for $60 for a case of Mimi's Upholstery and Carpet Cleaner.

- Received check #3099 for $20.00 as payment on account from Annette Helsper; apply to invoice #19-116.

- Used the company Visa to purchase a banner for advertising from Brag About It! for $65.03.

Friday, June 21, 2019

- Received check #1020 for $140.00 as payment on account from Leslie McGrevy; apply to invoice #19-121.

- Sold a Hand Wash with Interior service to John McNay on account using invoice #19-126.

- Received check #350 for $35.00 as payment on account from John McNay; apply to invoice #19-119.

Saturday, June 22, 2019

- Invoiced Anaconda Car Sales for one small vehicle and three large vehicle Full Interior/Exterior Detailing services using invoice #19-127.

- Received check #2150 for $180.00 as payment on account from Larry Bloodneck; apply to invoice #19-123.

- Paid all bills in Accounts Payable; checks to be printed.

- Printed all checks in the queue using the next available check number, #1810.

- Deposited all funds held in Undeposited Funds into Checking.

 CHECK FIGURE *Checking $14,911.18 • A/R $3,220.00 • A/P $0 • Visa $723.16*

Monday, June 24, 2019

- Invoiced Jenson Auto Wholesalers for six small vehicle and one large vehicle Full Interior/Exterior Detailing services using invoice #19-128.

- Received check #507 for $180.00 as payment on account from Alison Mandish; apply to invoice #19-124.

- Invoiced Pam Swanson for Exterior Polish & Wax using invoice #19-129.

- Received cash from Sally Cassen for a Hand Wash with Interior service.

- Received check #2721 for $35.00 as payment on account from Dan Greany; apply to invoice #19-114.

Tuesday, June 25, 2019

- Sold a Paint Protection package service for a small car to Leslie Golden [1001 Crescent Lane, Anaconda, MT 59711; (406) 555-3478 on account using invoice #19-130, terms Net 20.

- Sold Hand Wash with Interior and Exterior Wax services to Mike McCollough on account using invoice #19-131.

- Received check #925 for $20.00 as payment on account from Kristin Newberg; apply to invoice #19-112.

Wednesday, June 26, 2019

- Received a check (#443) from Sean Murphy for a Hand Wash and Engine Clean.

- Received check #3378 for $1,035.00 as payment on account from Anaconda Car Sales; apply to invoice #19-120.

- Purchased water and candy (Office Supplies) at Thompson's Grocery with credit card for $14.95.

Thursday, June 27, 2019

- Sold Hand Wash with Interior and Exterior Wax services to Billy Mercedes on account using invoice #19-132.

- Sold Hand Wash and Tire/Bumper Dressing services to Roxy Holden on account using invoice #19-133.

Friday, June 28, 2019

- Received check #1689 for $855.00 as payment on account from Jenson Auto Wholesalers; apply to invoice #19-122.

- Received a bill from Hamill Car Detail Supplies for $55.48 for miscellaneous supplies (Shop Expense).

- Received check #1691 for $1,305.00 as payment on account from Jenson Auto Wholesalers; apply to invoice #19-128.

Saturday, June 29, 2019

- Paid all bills in Accounts Payable; checks to be printed.

- Wrote a check to Martin Beatty for $3,000 as an owner's draw; to be printed.

- Printed all checks in the queue using the next available check number, #1813.

- Deposited all funds held in Undeposited Funds into Checking.

 CHECK FIGURE *Checking $15,385.70 • A/R $1,455.00 • A/P $0 • Visa $738.11*

Session #2: Deliverables

Submit the following as directed. If your class is using Quick Grader, be sure to export the report to Excel.

- **Project1-2-1** QG : A report displaying the summary of the balance each customer owes and if the balances are current or overdue, as of June 30, 2019

- **Project1-2-2** QG : A report displaying the transactions that Rugged Cross has had with each vendor for the month of June 2019

- **Project1-2-3** QG : A report displaying the details of all deposits, including the payments that make up each one for the month of June 2019

Session #3: Wrap It Up

Ⓐ The Administrator is responsible for setting up all accounts and items necessary for this session's transactions, producing balance sheet and profit & loss reports, and customizing the company's reports. You are also in charge of reconciling the bank and credit card statements.

Ⓡ The Accounts Receivable team member is responsible for accounting for any checks returned for nonsufficient funds (once the items and accounts are set up), sending out customer statements, editing/fixing invoices and payments on account, and writing off bad debt.

Ⓟ The Accounts Payable team member is responsible for issuing customer refunds, accepting vendor refunds, and editing/fixing bills and bill payments.

Session #3: Data

Scenarios

- On 6/27/19, Billy Mercedes upgraded his service to a Full Interior/Exterior Detailing service for his small car. Correct invoice #19-132 to reflect this change.

- You were reviewing your source documents and realized that the bill from Anaconda Water Works dated 06/12/2019 for $163.20 was incorrectly entered into QuickBooks for $63.20.

- You received a damaged case of Mimi's Upholstery and Carpet Cleaner (six of the twelve bottles were damaged) from Hamill Car Detail Supplies. The vendor issued you a credit on 6/30/19 for $30 (use a quantity of 0.5 on the Items tab to arrive at this amount) to account for the damaged goods, REF #CR1-921-ZP. You will use this credit when paying a future bill to the vendor.

- On June 19, 2019, you received the following notice from the bank: Check #577 for $160.00 from Mark Biggs was returned for nonsufficient funds. A $25 fee has been charged to your account. Pass this charge on to the customer.

Once you have finished dealing with the preceding scenarios, complete these tasks on 6/30/2019:

- Pay all bills in Accounts Payable; checks to be printed.

- Print all checks in the queue using the next available check number, #1815.

- Deposit all funds held in Undeposited Funds into Checking, if necessary.

 CHECK FIGURE *Checking $15,100.70 • A/R $1,740.00 • A/P −$30.00 • Visa $738.11*

Bank Statement

Use this bank statement to reconcile the checking account for June 2019. You *must* create the detailed reconciliation report requested for the Project1-3-1 deliverable immediately after the reconciliation, as you will only be able to produce a PDF report and therefore won't be able to export to Excel after the fact.

Deer Lodge County Credit Union
687 Copper Road
Anaconda, MT 59711

Statement of Account Prepared For:

Rugged Cross Auto Detailing
18071 Hamburg Avenue
Anaconda, MT 59711

Account Number: 4673-85
Statement Period: June 1 - 30, 2019

Total Deposits:	8,280.00	Total Payments:	6,197.04
Beginning Balance:	$13,265.72	Ending Balance:	15,348.68

Transactions:

Date	Transaction type	Payment	Deposit	Balance
5/31/2019	Beginning Balance			$13,265.72
6/4/2019	Check #1800	1,500.00		11,765.72
6/7/2019	Check #1802	98.48		11,667.24
6/8/2019	Deposit		1,420.00	13,087.24
6/8/2019	Check #1804	142.09		12,945.15
6/8/2019	Check #1805	154.30		12,790.85
6/10/2019	Check #1801	74.00		12,716.85
6/10/2019	POS Debit Card	38.44		12,678.41
6/14/2019	Check #1806	600.00		12,078.41
6/15/2019	Deposit		1,895.00	13,973.41
6/16/2019	Check #1803	55.96		13,917.45
6/19/2019	NSF Check	160.00		13,757.45
6/19/2019	NSF Fee	25.00		13,732.45
6/20/2019	Check #1808	63.20		13,669.25
6/21/2019	Check #1807	95.00		13,574.25
6/22/2019	Deposit		1,435.00	15,009.25
6/24/2019	Check #1809	27.12		14,982.13
6/28/2019	Check #1812	95.95		14,886.18
6/29/2019	Check #1811	60.00		14,826.18
6/29/2019	Deposit		3,530.00	18,356.18
6/30/2019	Check #1814	3,000.00		15,356.18
6/30/2019	Service Charge	7.50		15,348.68
	Ending Balance			15,348.68

Credit Card Statement

Use this credit card statement to reconcile the credit card account for June 2019. Choose to enter a bill (dated 06/30/19) for a payment to be made later for the total amount owed to the vendor.

You *must* create the summary reconciliation report requested for the Project1-3-2 deliverable immediately after the reconciliation, as you will only be able to produce a PDF report and therefore won't be able to export to Excel after the fact.

Copper City Bank Visa
552 West 3rd Street
Anaconda, MT 59711

Credit Card Statement Prepared For:
  Rugged Cross Auto Detailing
  18071 Hamburg Avenue
  Anaconda, MT 59711

Account Number: XXXX XXXX XXXX 3333

Statement Period: June 1 - June 30, 2019

Total Charges:	$738.11	Total Credits:	$0.00
Beginning Balance:	$0.00	Ending Balance:	$738.11

Transactions:

Date	Description	Charge	Credit	Balance
	Beginning Balance			$0.00
6/1/2019	PriceCo	42.99		$42.99
6/3/2019	Thompson's Grocery	36.55		$79.54
6/6/2019	Electronics Wizardry	359.36		$438.90
6/9/2019	Superior Interiors	189.45		$628.35
6/14/2019	Office Superstore	29.78		$658.13
6/23/2019	Brag About It!	65.03		$723.16
6/29/2019	Thompson's Grocery	14.95		$738.11
	Periodic Finance Charge	0		$738.11
	Ending Balance			$738.11

Session #3: Deliverables

Submit the following as directed. If your class is using Quick Grader, be sure to export the report to Excel.

- **Project1-3-1** QG: A report displaying details of the reconciled checking account as of June 30, 2019

- **Project1-3-2** QG: A report displaying a summary of the reconciled credit card account as of June 30, 2019

- **Project1-3-3** QG: A report displaying transaction details and balance owed to each vendor as of June 30, 2019

- **Project1-3-4** QG: A report displaying the amount owed by each customer as of June 30, 2019

- **Project1-3-5:** A graph displaying the sales by item for June 2019

- **Project1-3-6** QG: A report displaying company net income for the month of June 2019

- **Project1-3-7** QG: A report displaying the balances of all assets, liabilities, and equity accounts as of June 30, 2019

📂 Project 2: Keeping the Books for July 2019

Now that the move is complete and business has picked up, Martin will be employing four full-time detailing specialists. In addition, customers have been asking about purchasing the products he uses on their cars, so he will begin to purchase and resell them. You will now be helping Bridget keep the books for the month of July 2019 and will assist with month-end reporting.

Your instructor may assign this as an individual or a group project. If you complete the project individually, you will assume all roles. If you're working in a group, your first task is to determine who will serve in each of these three roles:

- Administrator Ⓐ
- Accounts Receivable Representative Ⓡ
- Accounts Payable and Payroll Representative Ⓟ

You will be keeping the books for the company for July 2019, which will be broken down into "sessions." At the end of each session, you will produce "deliverables" and provide them to your instructor for evaluation. Save these deliverables as PDF files or print them, depending on the instructions you are given. You will not be given specifics in many cases, just as you will not be given specifics when working with your own company. You may need to add new customers, vendors, or other information "on the fly" and use your own problem-solving and reasoning skills. Use QuickBooks' help and search features as necessary.

Note! If you completed Project 1, you have two choices: 1) begin this project by opening your final company file from Project 1, or 2) restore the Project 2-Rugged Cross Auto Detailing (Portable) file. The password for the file is *Password1*.

Session #1: The Company File and Lists

Ⓐ The Administrator is responsible for setting up all fixed asset and liability accounts (including fixed asset items), preparing for the company to track petty cash, and preparing to assess finance charges. If you are working in a group, set yourself up as the administrator and your teammates as additional users. Grant permissions for each user account based on the responsibilities of each position. (You may wish to review the entire project to determine the access needed.) Since you will be entering transactions that occurred in the past, make sure to turn off Date Warning.

Ⓡ The Accounts Receivable team member is responsible for setting up the sales tax and inventory items, setting up a method for receiving electronic payments, preparing for estimates and progress invoicing, and setting up the price levels. The service items will have no tax code assigned once the sales tax preference is turned on, so you will need to assign "Non" to each. (Hint: You can quickly accomplish this by using the Add/Edit Multiple Entries window and choosing to "copy down.")

(P) The Accounts Payable team member is responsible for setting up employees and preparing to track payroll. Rugged Cross uses an outside payroll service, so you will not need to turn on payroll. In addition, you will need to set up the company to be able to track prepaid insurance and prepaid rent.

Session #1: Data

Employees

Set up these employees.

Joey Conlon	**Piper Wyatt**	**Don Hermansen**	**Natalie Monk**
1086 Jefferson Way Anaconda, MT 59711	706 Chestnut St. Anaconda, MT 59711	1206 West Park St. Silver Bow, MT 59750	304 Alder St. Anaconda, MT 59711
(406) 555-2196	(406) 555-3486	(406) 555-2122	(406) 555-1309
SSN: 123-45-6789	SSN: 234-56-7891	SSN: 345-67-8912	SSN: 456-78-9123
Gender: Male	Gender: Female	Gender: Male	Gender: Female
DOB: 11/10/1976	DOB: 4/13/1987	DOB: 6/14/1980	DOB: 4/29/1989
Married	Single	Domestic Partner	Single
US Citizen: Yes	US Citizen: Yes	US Citizen: Yes	US Citizen: Yes
Ethnicity: White	Ethnicity: American Indian	Ethnicity: White	Ethnicity: Asian
Disabled: No	Disabled: No	Disabled: Yes	Disabled: No
I-9: Yes	I-9: Yes	I-9: Yes	I-9: Yes
Miliary Service: No	Military Service: Yes, Reserve	Military Service: No	Military Service: No

Payroll Information

Add the required vendors, payroll expense and payroll liability accounts, and items.

- Federal taxes are to be paid to the US Treasury, 2020 Lucille Lane, Washington DC 20039.

- State taxes are to be paid to the State of Montana Treasurer, 1600 Montana Avenue, Helena, MT 59604.

- Payment for employee health benefits is to be paid to Employee Health Co., 976 Lyle Drive, Billings, MT 59101.

> *Note!* Do NOT use this information when completing payroll for your own company, as this information is provided only as a learning tool. You must find the information that applies to your company based on its location.

Finance Charge Information

- Annual interest rate: 12%

- Minimum finance charge: $1.00

- Grace period: 30 days

- Finance Charge Account: Finance Charges (Account Type: Other Income)

- Do not assess on overdue finance charges

- Calculate charges from due date

Sales Tax Information

> **Note!** There is no sales tax in Montana. However, because it's important to know how to deal with this feature in QuickBooks, a fictitious sales tax rate and vendor are being used in this project. When working with your own company file, learn and follow the laws in your jurisdiction.

The sales tax in Deer Lodge County is 4.25% and is payable to the Deer Lodge County Treasurer.

Make all non-inventory parts non-taxable and all inventory parts taxable. All services are non-taxable. All customers should be taxable. It is up to you to verify that the correct tax rate is applied for each sale.

Fixed Assets and Liabilities

All fixed asset items were purchased new prior to your QuickBooks start date. Set up all fixed assets as fixed asset items. Enter the cost in the appropriate fixed asset account and long-term liability loan account (if appropriate). All fixed asset loans are to be set up as long-term, regardless of the remaining balance.

Because these purchases were made before this year, when entering the loans for the assets, the Opening Balance Equity account will be debited when you enter the opening balance for the loan. You will be entering the balance as of 5/31/19, the day before your QuickBooks company started.

Use the Furniture and Equipment fixed asset account for all items except for the vehicle. For the vehicle account, create a new fixed asset account called Vehicles to track it and all future vehicles.

Fixed Asset Name	Purchase Date	Description	Cost	Associated Long-Term Liability?	Loan Account Vendor/ Balance (as of 5/31/2019)
Auto Buffer	11-9-2017	DeWalt, model V654N	$400	No	
Injection Steam Cleaner	9-25-2017	DupRay, model V-45664-FV	$1,499	Yes, Equipment Loan	ABC Equipment Loans/ $762.49
Industrial Vacuum	5-14-2018	Attix 12 RDF High Suction, model 12990	$598	No	
Air Compressor	6-14-2017	Hitachi, model HRGH-5460	$395	No	
Window Repair Kit	5-21-2016	New Haven, Resin Injection, model GL 578	$499	No	
Power Washer	8-3-2017	McCullough, model XF2-3	$295	No	
Computer System	2-4-2019	Dale Computers, model FFX-3911	$2,500	Yes, Computer Loan	Dale Computers/ $1,942.94
Copier/Fax/ Scanner	2-4-2019	PH, model 5399	$600	No	
Ford F-150	1-30-2018	2017 Ford F-150, VIN # 302LF3118JQA920	$25,300	Yes, Ford Loan	Snake- City Auto Finance/ $20,135.20

Products for Sale

All inventory items are taxable. Use Cost of Goods Sold as the COGS account, Inventory Asset as the asset account, and Product Sales as the income account. Use the same description for purchases and sales.

Item Name	Description	Cost	Preferred Vendor	Sales Price	Reorder Point
Wash Mitts	Micro Fiber Wash Mitts, 3-pack	3.48	Hamill Car Detail Supplies	12.95	10
Dry Towels	Micro Fiber Dry Towels, 3-pack	2.25	Hamill Car Detail Supplies	10.95	10
Window Cleaner	Jasper's 14 oz. Window Cleaner	1.37	Jasper Jones Auto Detail LLC	4.95	15
Glass Polish	Jasper's 8 oz. Glass Polish	2.59	Jasper Jones Auto Detail LLC	8.95	10
Paste Wax	Rosey's Exterior Paste Wax	5.25	Rosey & Girls Auto Supply	18.95	7
Interior Cleaner	Jasper's 16 oz. Interior Cleaner	3.89	Jasper Jones Auto Detail LLC	12.95	10
Vinyl Rubber Dressing	Rosey's 8 oz. Vinyl/ Rubber Dressing	3.55	Rosey & Girls Auto Supply	11.95	7
Leather Conditioner	Rosey's 6 oz. Leather Conditioner	4.27	Rosey & Girls Auto Supply	12.95	5
Wheel Rim Polish	Rosey's 16 oz. Wheel-Rim Polish/Cleaner	3.50	Rosey & Girls Auto Supply	9.95	5
Rubbing Compound	Rosey's 12 oz. Rubbing Compound	5.03	Rosey & Girls Auto Supply	14.95	7

Session #1: Deliverables

Submit the following as directed. If your class is using Quick Grader, be sure to export the report to Excel.

- **Project2-1-1** [QG]: A report displaying the Chart of Accounts (columns should be Account, Type, and Balance Total)

- **Project2-1-2** [QG]: A report displaying the stock status of all inventory items as of 7/1/2019

- **Project2-1-3** [QG]: A report displaying the company's employees (columns should be Employee, SS No., Phone, and Gender)

- **Project2-1-4** [QG]: A report displaying all fixed asset items (columns should be Item, Purchase Date, Purchase Description, Account, and Cost)

Session #2: Day-to-Day Work

(A) The Administrator is responsible for making all deposits, receiving all payments on account, entering credit card charges, entering fixed asset and long-term liability transactions, paying the sales and payroll taxes owed, turning on preferences, preparing the company to receive discounted payments (by creating a Cash Discount expense account), paying for prepaid expenses, and creating the Prepaid Rent (an Other Current Asset) account.

(R) The Accounts Receivable team member is responsible for entering all sales transactions (including estimates) and passing on expenses to customers. Remember that all customers pay tax on inventory items but not on service items.

(P) The Accounts Payable team member is responsible for all payroll transactions, entering and paying all bills, purchasing and receiving inventory, and printing all checks.

Session #2: Data

Monthly Diary

Monday, July 1, 2019

- You forgot that you agreed to a special pricing of $150 for the Full Interior/Exterior Detailing service for small cars on invoice #19-104. Correct this error for the customer on 7/1/2019, using CR1 as the credit number. They have chosen to retain the overpayment to use on a future invoice.

- You ran a special for Interior Detailing services on June 17 for $75 for any size car. The sale price was not reflected in the cash sale for Annette Helsper. Since the customer has already paid for the service, you will need to issue her a printed refund check for the difference on 7/1/2019 using CR2 as the credit number. Leslie McGrevy took advantage of the same offer and was invoiced (#19-121) for the services using CR3 as the credit number. She has chosen to retain the overpayment for future services.

- Wrote a check to Crown Property Management for $8,700 for July–December 2019 rent (for a discounted amount of $1,450/month). Set Prepaid Rent up as an Other Current Asset.

- Received a bill from Smelter City Power and Gas for $137.52 for June 2019 power bill, REF #0619-129-774.

- Received check #461 in the amount of $55.00 from Logan Webb for Rock Chip Windshield Repair service.

- Received check #355 for $35 as payment on account from John McNay; apply to invoice #19-126.

- Invoiced Anaconda Car Sales for 4 small vehicles and 3 large vehicles Full Interior/Exterior Detailing services using invoice #19-136.

> **Tip!** Make sure to type the correct invoice number and replace the credit memo numbering!

- Received $125 in cash from Sally Cassen for Paint Protection service for a large van.

- Created PO #101 made out to Jasper Jones Auto Detail LLC for 30 Window Cleaner, 25 Glass Polish, and 25 Interior Cleaner.

- Created PO #102 made out to Hamill Car Detail Supplies for 20 Wash Mitts, 20 Dry Towels.

- Created PO #103 made out to Rosey & Girls Auto Supply for 15 Paste Wax, 15 Vinyl Rubber Dressing, 10 Leather Conditioner, 10 Wheel Rim Polish, and 15 Rubbing Compound.
- Chose to have QuickBooks show the Reminders List when opening a company file and ensured that "Inventory to Reorder" is included as a list.

Tuesday, July 2, 2019

- Received a bill from Butte Waste Management for $74.00 for July 2019 service, REF #NTGD00-0719.
- Received $60 in cash from Katie Fox for a Hand Wash with Interior and an Electronic Odor Elimination service.
- Purchased office supplies from Office Superstore for $109.74 using the company Visa card.
- Received check #3392 for $957.80 as payment on account from Anaconda Car Sales; apply to invoices #19-106 and #19-127; invoice #19-127 was paid within the discount period, so apply the discount (create a Less Discounts Given contra account).
- Sold Engine Clean and Hand Wash services to Alison Mandish on account using invoice #19-137.
- Received check #1984 from James Hakola for a Full Exterior Detailing service for a small car.
- Received check #1642 from Stephen Markle for a Full Interior and Exterior Detailing service for a small car.
- Sold Hand Wash with Interior and Paint Protection services for a VW Beetle to Helen Firth for cash.

Wednesday, July 3, 2019

- Received a bill from Sullivan Insurance Co. for $154.30 for monthly business insurance, REF #MT-737-07.
- Received a bill from McCarthy's Automotive Supply for $311.87 for 8 gallons of Jack's Superior Exterior Car Wash and 5 bundles of Rags.
- Wrote a check to be printed for $216 to Dale Computers as payment on the computer loan.
- Received a check (#1579) from Jenna Matthews for a Paint Protection service for a small car.
- Invoiced Jenson Auto Wholesalers for 7 small cars and 2 large cars Full Interior/Exterior Detailing services using invoice #19-138; apply the available credit of $150.00 to the invoice.
- Received check #3396 for $1,381.05 as payment on account from Anaconda Car Sales, which should be applied to invoice #19-136. It was paid within the discount period.
- Invoiced Sofia Harrison for a Hand Wash with Interior and Upholstery Shampoo services using invoice #19-139; permanent terms are Net 20.
- Received 20 Wash Mitts and 20 Dry Towels from Hamill Car Detail Supplies with the bill, which included a $15 shipping fee. Create a Shipping Expense account.
- Received check #801 for $90.00 as payment on account from Leslie Golden; apply to invoice #19-130.

Friday, July 5, 2019

- Received 30 Window Cleaner, 25 Glass Polish, and 25 Interior Cleaner from Jasper Jones Auto Detail LLC without the bill.

- Received a check (#622) from Felicity York for a Rock Chip Repair service.

- Received a check (#449) from Sean Murphy for Hand Wash and Engine Clean services as well as a package of Wash Mitts and Window Cleaner. Make sure to collect Deer Lodge County sales tax for the inventory items!

- Received check #510 for $65.00 as payment on account from Alison Mandish; apply to invoice #19-137.

- A new customer, Dee Motor Company [515 Main St., Anaconda, MT, 59711; (406) 555-6000], has asked Martin for an estimate of what it would cost to have the 15 Honda Civics they just acquired at auction given a Full Interior/Exterior Detailing package.

- Received check #1168 for $95.00 as payment on account from Lucky Rogers; apply to invoice #19-125.

- Received check #783 for $80.00 as payment on account from Billy Mercedes; apply to invoice #19-132.

- Invoiced Annette Helsper for a Hand Wash with Interior service as well as a package of Wash Mitts 3-pack, a Dry Towel 3-pack, Window Cleaner, and Interior Cleaner; invoice #19-140.

- Invoiced Skye Simpson [3011 Santa Rosa St., Anaconda, MT, 59711; (406) 555-9975 for a Paint Protection service for a large car as well as a package of Dry Towels and Interior Cleaner; invoice #19-141; with permanent terms Net 15.

Saturday, July 6, 2019

- Received a bill from Hamill Car Detail Supplies for $120.00 for 2 cases of Mimi's Upholstery and Carpet Cleaner.

- Received cash from Cynthia Clackamas for a Hand Wash with Interior and Electronic Odor Elimination services, as well as a package of Wash Mitts, pack of Dry Towels, Window Cleaner, and Glass Polish.

- Received check #1707 for $1,525.80 as payment on account from Jenson Auto Wholesalers; apply to invoice #19-138. It was paid within the discount period.

- Received all items on PO#103 from Rosey & Girls Auto Supply with the bill, which includes a $19 shipping fee.

- Received check #790 for $80.00 as payment on account from Mike McCollough; apply to invoice #19-131.

- Invoiced Pam Swanson for a Hand Wash with Interior and Rock Chip Repair services as well as a package of Wash Mitts, Interior Cleaner, Vinyl/Rubber Dressing, and Rubbing Compound; invoice #19-142.

- Invoiced Dan Thomas for a Hand Wash service with Interior service as well as Dry Towels, Rubbing Compound, Vinyl/Rubber Dressing, and Leather Conditioner; invoice #19-143.

- Paid all bills in Accounts Payable. Checks are to be printed.

- Printed all checks in the queue, using the next available check number, 1816.

- Deposited all funds held in Undeposited Funds into Checking.

 CHECK FIGURE *Checking $9,525.37 • A/R $876.50 • A/P $173.10 • Visa $109.74*

Monday, July 8, 2019

- Purchased water, soda pop, and snacks for the waiting room from Thompson's Grocery with credit card for $41.92. Apply to Office Supplies.

- Received check #844 for $85.00 as payment on account from Sofia Harrison; apply to invoice #19-139.

- Invoiced Anaconda Car Sales for 4 small vehicles and 5 large vehicles Full Interior/Exterior Detailing services using invoice #19-144.

- Sold a Hand Wash with Interior service and Vinyl/Rubber Dressing to John McNay using invoice #19-145.

- Received check #2130 for $180.00 as payment on account from Pam Swanson; apply to invoices #19-129 and #19-142.

- Received check #6031 for $35.00 as payment on account from Roxy Holden; apply to invoice #19-133.

- Received a check (#257) from Zoe Christopher for Paint Protection for a large car and Automotive Paint Sealant services as well as a package of Dry Towels, Paste Wax, Interior Cleaner, and Leather Conditioner.

- Wrote a check to be printed later to ABC Equipment Loans for $52.75 for payment on the Equipment Loan.

Tuesday, July 9, 2019

- Received check #918 from Millie Hannan for a Paint Protection service for a small car as well as Dry Towels, Glass Polish, Paste Wax, Vinyl/Rubber Dressing, and Leather Conditioner.

- Received check #2132 for $40.04 as payment on account from Pam Swanson; apply to invoice #19-142.

- Invoiced Chris McCartney for a Full Interior/Exterior Detailing service for a Mazda Miata using invoice #19-146.

- Received cash from Stacy Rollins for an Interior Detailing service for a small car, Leather Conditioner, and Rubbing Compound.

Wednesday, July 10, 2019

- Invoiced Jenson Auto Wholesalers for 8 small car Full Interior/Exterior Detailing services using invoice #19-147.

- Received check #3112 for $78.58 as payment on account from Annette Helsper; apply to invoice #19-140.

- Received check #917 for $87.96 as payment on account from Dan Thomas; apply to invoice #19-143.

- Received a bill from McCarthy's Automotive Supply for $111.92 for 8 gallons of Jack's Superior Exterior Car Wash.

- Invoiced Meryl Eastwood [1631 Harmony Lane, Anaconda, MT, 59711; (406) 555-9346 for Rock Chip Repair and Hand Wash services as well as a package of Wash Mitts, Dry Towels, Glass Polish, Wheel-Rim Polish, and Interior Cleaner; invoice #19-148. The permanent terms are Net 20.

- Received cash from Anderson Craig for Hand Wash with Interior and Exterior Polish and Wax services as well as Vinyl/Rubber Dressing and Leather Conditioner.

- Received check #3404 for $1,826.55 as payment on account from Anaconda Car Sales; apply to invoice #19-144. It was paid within the discount period.

- Use company credit card at Butte Ford for chrome exhaust tips in the amount of $106.47; the job materials expense is to be passed on to John McNay on his next invoice.

Thursday, July 11, 2019

- Received check #2017 for $149.92 as payment on account from Skye Simpson; apply to invoice #19-141.

- Purchased a 2016 Blue Ford Econoline van to provide mobile detailing services; dealer is Butte Ford. The purchase price was $29,000 plus 4.25% sales tax; down payment is 10% of base cost from Checking. Check #1826 was handwritten for the down payment; the remainder of the amount was financed through Copper City Bank at 4.9%. The purchase price includes a 3-year warranty. Due to the fictional timeframe that this project operates in, the Loan Manager will not be able to be utilized. However, your instructor may choose to assign loan terms and ask you to use this feature. You should create a fixed asset item named "Ford Econoline Van" for the van that includes the purchase price plus the sales tax. You will also need a Long Term Liability account for the new loan using the price (including tax) less the down payment.

- Invoiced Kristin Newberg for a Full Exterior Detailing service on a small car, a package of Dry Towels, Paste Wax, Vinyl/Rubber Dressing, and Leather Conditioner; invoice #19-149.

- Invoiced Dan Greany for a Full Interior/Exterior Detailing service on a large car; invoice #19-150.

- Received a check (#3427) from Wayne Rink for a Full Exterior Detailing for a small car, Vinyl/Rubber Dressing, and Leather Conditioner.

- Received check #362 for $47.46 as payment on account from John McNay; apply to invoice #19-145.

- Received a check (#453) from Sean Murphy for a Hand Wash service.

Friday, July 12, 2019

- Received a bill from Hamill Car Detail Supplies for $100.68 for 3 packs of Paper Hand Towels and a case of Mimi's Upholstery and Carpet Cleaner.

- Received check #782 for $180.00 as payment on account from Chris McCartney; apply to invoice #19-146.

- Received a bill from Anaconda Water Works for $185.61, for June 2019 water bill, REF #77-65331.

- Received a bill from Jasper Jones Auto Detail LLC for all items on PO#101. The items were received into inventory on July 5.

- Invoiced Katie Fox for an Interior Detailing service on a small car, a package of Dry Towels, Vinyl/Rubber Dressing, and Leather Conditioner; invoice #19-151.

- Dee Motor Company liked the estimate they received and have decided to go with Rugged Cross for the detailing service; invoice them for 50% of the total amount up front using invoice #19-152.

Note! Make sure progress invoicing is "on" in the company preferences.

- Received check #1718 for $1,411.20 as payment on account from Jenson Auto Wholesalers; apply to invoice #19-147. It was paid within the discount period.

- Received a check (#377) from Ricky Ricardo for a Hand Wash with Interior and Exterior Wax services as well as a package of Wash Mitts, Interior Cleaner, Vinyl/Rubber Dressing, and Rubbing Compound.

- Be sure you have set up a Payroll Liabilities (Other Current Liability) account, as well as new accounts for Gross Wages, Company-Paid Taxes, and Company-Paid Benefits (as subaccounts of Payroll Expenses).

- Using this table from the outside payroll service, generated paychecks for all employees for the first two weeks of the month (check/pay period end date 7/12/2019).

	Joey Conlon	Piper Wyatt	Don Hermansen	Natalie Monk	Totals
Gross Wages	$1,120.00	$1,220.00	$1,100.00	$1,120.00	$4,560.00
Federal Taxes W/H (Employee)	$116.43	$180.78	$113.30	$131.66	$542.17
State Taxes W/H	$46.58	$52.58	$45.38	$46.58	$191.12
Net Pay	$956.99	$986.64	$941.32	$941.76	$3,826.71
Federal Taxes Owed (Co.)	$85.68	$93.33	$84.15	$85.68	$348.84
State Taxes Owed (Co.)	$24.64	$26.84	$24.20	$24.64	$100.32
Company Benefits Owed	$400.00	$350.00	$400.00	$400.00	$1,550.00

- Printed the four paychecks but NOT the rest of the checks in the queue; use the next check number available (#1827) as the first check number.

- Created these checks to be printed: 1) federal taxes, 2) state taxes, 3) employee health insurance

Saturday, July 13, 2019

- Created a $95.00 check for Martinez Janitorial, LLC, for office cleaning (to be printed). The expense should be charged to the Repairs and Maintenance expense account.

- Received cash from Carlos Espinosa for both an Interior Detailing for a small car and Electronic Odor Elimination services as well as Dry Towels, Interior Cleaner, Vinyl/Rubber Dressing, and Leather Conditioner.

- Invoiced Anaconda Car Sales for 7 small vehicles and 2 large vehicles Full Interior/Exterior Detailing services using invoice #19-153.

- Sold a Hand Wash service to John McNay using invoice #19-154 (don't forget to include the exhaust tips that were purchased for him).

- Paid all bills in Accounts Payable; checks are to be printed.

- Printed all checks in the queue using the next available check number, 1831.

- Deposited all funds held in Undeposited Funds into Checking.

 CHECK FIGURE *Checking $4,819.06 • A/R $4,119.09 • A/P –$30.00 • Visa $258.13*

Monday, July 15, 2019

- Received check #164 from Jennie Newport for a Paint Protection service for a large car, a package of Wash Mitts, Dry Towels, Window Cleaner, Glass Polish, and Vinyl/Rubber Dressing.

- Received check #932 for $217.13 as payment on account from Kristin Newberg; apply to invoice #19-149.

- Invoiced Larry Bloodneck for a Hand Wash with Interior and Exterior Wax services using invoice #19-155.

- Received check #2735 for $225.00 as payment on account from Dan Greany; apply to invoice #19-150.

- Received cash from Sydney Crawford for a Paint Protection service for a large car, Dry Towels, Window Cleaner, Interior Cleaner, and Vinyl/Rubber Dressing.

Tuesday, July 16, 2019

- Invoiced Jenson Auto Wholesalers for 6 small car Full Interior/Exterior Detailing and 4 large car Full Interior/Exterior Detailing services; invoice #19-156.

- Received check #2323 for $133.12 as payment on account from Meryl Eastwood; apply to invoice #19-148.

- Received a bill from McCarthy's Automotive Supply for $139.90 for 10 gallons of Jack's Superior Exterior Car Wash.

- Received $196.16 in cash from Tinie Kelly for a Hand Wash with Interior and Exterior Polish and Wax services as well as Dry Towels, Window Cleaner, Interior Cleaner, 2 Vinyl/Rubber Dressings, and 2 Rubbing Compounds.

- Received check #5482 for $1,350.00 as payment on account from Dee Motor Company; apply to invoice #19-152.

- Ran an Inventory Stock Status by Item report dated 07/16/2019 to determine if any inventory needed to be reordered.

- Using the next available PO, ordered any inventory that had dropped below the reorder point, making sure that the amount ordered resulted in the number being 10 items above the reorder point number.

Thursday, July 18, 2019

- Invoiced Fajer Alghanim [1893 Mountain Vista Dr., Anaconda, MT, 59711; (406) 555-3399] for a Full Exterior Detailing service for a small car, a package of Wash Mitts, Dry Towels, Window Cleaner, Interior Cleaner, and Vinyl/Rubber Dressing; invoice #19-157. Permanent terms Net 15.

- Received check #3417 for $1,692.90 as payment on account from Anaconda Car Sales; apply to invoice #19-153. It was paid within the discount period.

- Invoiced Mike McCollough for Rock Chip Repair, Engine Clean, and Hand Wash services using invoice #19-158.

- Received check #1350 for $137.37 as payment on account from Katie Fox; apply to invoice #19-151.

- Received a check (#458) from Sean Murphy for Hand Wash and Engine Clean services as well as Dry Towels, Interior Cleaner, Glass Polish, and 3 Rubbing Compounds.

Friday, July 19, 2019

- Received a bill from Hamill Car Detail Supplies for $118.47 for 2 packages of Brushes, a case of Mimi's Upholstery and Carpet Cleaner, and a 3-pack of Buckets (these items were not on a PO).

- All of the Civics have been detailed for Dee Motor Company; invoice them for the remaining amount due using invoice #19-159.

- Invoiced Roxy Holden for a Hand Wash with Interior service as well as a package of Wash Mitts, Glass Polish, Interior Cleaner, Leather Conditioner, and Wheel-Rim Polish/Cleaner; invoice #19-160.

- Received check #1730 for $1,940.40 as payment on account from Jenson Auto Wholesalers; apply to invoice #19-156. It was paid within the discount period.

- Received cash from Cathy Jefferson for Paint Protection service for a small car, Dry Towels, 2 Window Cleaners, 2 Glass Polishes, and 2 Wheel-Rim Polish/Cleaners.

- Used the company credit card to purchase a wheel cover from Park Motors for $89.72, to be passed on to Leslie McGrevy on her next invoice. The expense should be applied to Job Materials.

Saturday, July 20, 2019

- Invoiced Anaconda Car Sales for 4 small vehicles and 5 large vehicle Full Interior/Exterior Detailing services using invoice #19-161.

- Received check #2173 for $80.00 as payment on account from Larry Bloodneck; apply to invoice #19-155.

- Sold a Hand Wash with Interior service and Rubbing Compound to John McNay using invoice #19-162.

- Received a check (#947) from Jim McMinnville for a Hand Wash and Engine Clean as well as Dry Towels and a Wheel-Rim Polish Cleaner.

- Received check #799 for $120.00 as payment on account from Mike McCollough; apply to invoice #19-158.

- Received all inventory items ordered on July 16th from each vendor, with the bills.

- Paid all bills in Accounts Payable; checks are to be printed.

- Printed all checks in the queue using the next available check number, #1840.

- Deposited all funds held in Undeposited Funds into Checking.

 CHECK FIGURE *Checking $11,213.45 • A/R $3,903.29 • A/P –$30.00 • Visa $347.85*

Monday, July 22, 2019

- Received check #1623 for $216.03 as payment on account from Fajer Alghanim; apply to invoice #19-157.

- Invoiced Tammy Cadwell [1625 Ridge Route Dr., Anaconda, MT, 59711; (406) 555-7635 for Paint Protection for a small car and Automotive Paint Sealant services as well as a package of Wash Mitts, Dry Towels, Window Cleaner, Interior Cleaner, Vinyl/Rubber Dressing, and Wheel-Rim Polish/Cleaner; invoice #19-163. Permanent terms Net 20.

- Invoiced Lucky Rogers for a Hand Wash with Interior and Exterior Polish and Wax services as well as a package of Wash Mitts, Dry Towels, Window Cleaner, Glass Polish, Vinyl/Rubber Dressing, and Rubbing Compound; invoice #19-164.

- Received check #5499 for $1,350.00 as payment on account from Dee Motor Company; apply to invoice #19-159.

- Received a check (#1365) from Robin Poway for Paint Protection service for a Honda Accord (small car) and Automotive Paint Sealant services as well as Dry Towels and 2 Vinyl/Rubber Dressings.

Tuesday, July 23, 2019

- Invoiced Jenson Auto Wholesalers for 5 small car Full Interior/Exterior Detailing and 5 large car Full Interior/Exterior Detailing services; invoice #19-165.

- Received check #371 for $177.06 as payment on account from John McNay; apply to invoices #19-154 and #19-162.

- Invoiced Alison Mandish for a Hand Wash with Interior service, a package of Wash Mitts, Dry Towels, Interior Cleaner, Leather Conditioner, and Rubbing Compound; invoice #19-166.

- Received a bill from McCarthy's Automotive Supply for $125.91 for 9 gallons of Jack's Superior Exterior Car Wash.

- Received cash from Samuel Beacon for a Hand Wash service, Dry Towels, Window Cleaner, Interior Cleaner, and Rubbing Compound.

- Received check #6052 for $95.20 as payment on account from Roxy Holden; apply to invoice #19-160.

- Ran an Inventory Stock Status by Item report dated 07/23/2019 to determine if any inventory needed to be reordered.

- Using the next available PO, ordered any inventory that is at or below the reorder point, making sure that the amount ordered resulted in the number being 10 items above the reorder point number.

Wednesday, July 24, 2019

- Invoiced Leslie Golden for a small car Full Interior/Exterior Detailing service, a package of Wash Mitts, Window Cleaner, Wheel-Rim Polish/Cleaner, and Interior Cleaner; invoice #19-167.

- Received a check (#641) from LaShonda Rimes for a Hand Wash with Interior and Exterior Hand Wax services as well as Dry Towels, Glass Polish, Paste Wax, 2 Vinyl/Rubber Dressings, and 2 Leather Conditioners.

- Received check #1182 for $177.45 as payment on account from Lucky Rogers; apply to invoice #19-164.

- Received a check (#462) from Sean Murphy for a Hand Wash service, Paste Wax, Interior Cleaner, Vinyl/Rubber Dressing, and Rubbing Compound.

- Received check #3429 for $1,826.55 as payment on account from Anaconda Car Sales; apply to invoice #19-161. It was paid with the discount period.

- Invoiced Dee Motor Company for 7 small cars and 2 large cars Full Interior/Exterior Detailing services; invoice #19-168. Permanently change the terms in the customer record to be 1% 10 Net 25.

Thursday, July 25, 2019

- Received a bill from Hamill Car Detail Supplies for $180 for 3 cases of Mimi's Upholstery and Carpet Cleaner (the items are not on a PO).

- Received check #1749 for $1,984.50 as payment on account from Jenson Auto Wholesalers; apply to invoice #19-165. It was paid within the discount period.

- Invoiced Margaret Miller [395 3rd St., Anaconda, MT, 59711; (406) 555-0123] for an Interior Detailing for a small car and Electronic Odor Elimination services, Dry Towels, Interior Cleaner, and Leather Conditioner; invoice #19-169. Permanent terms Net 20.

- Received cash from Emilio Estrella for a Hand Wash with Interior and Carpet Shampoo services, as well as Dry Towels, Paste Wax, and Vinyl/Rubber Dressing.

- Invoiced Leslie McGrevy for a Hand Wash with Interior service using invoice #19-170. Included the billable wheel cover expense (purchased on July 20). Also applied the $65.00 credit to the invoice.

- Wrote a check payable to Snake-City Auto Finance for $267 as payment on the Ford F-150 loan, to be printed.

Friday, July 26, 2019

- Invoiced Anaconda Car Sales for 3 small vehicles and 7 large vehicles Full Interior/Exterior Detailing services using invoice #19-171.

- Received check #523 for $102.50 as payment on account from Alison Mandish; apply to invoice #19-166.

- Received all items ordered on 7/23/2019 from each vendor, with the bills.

- Sold a Hand Wash with Interior service and Wheel-Rim Polish/Cleaner to John McNay using invoice #19-172.

- Using this table from the outside payroll service, generated paychecks for all employees for the first two weeks of the month (pay period end date 7/26/2019).

	Joey Conlon	Piper Wyatt	Don Hermansen	Natalie Monk	Totals
Gross Wages	$1,232.00	$1,220.00	$1,210.00	$1,120.00	$4,782.00
Federal Taxes W/H (Employee)	$133.95	$180.78	$136.02	$131.66	$582.41
State Taxes W/H	$53.30	$52.58	$51.98	$46.58	$204.44
Net Pay	$1,044.75	$986.64	$1,022	$941.76	$3,995.15
Federal Taxes Owed (Co.)	$94.25	$93.33	$92.57	$85.68	$365.83
State Taxes Owed (Co.)	$27.10	$26.84	$26.62	$24.64	$105.20
Company Benefits Owed	$400.00	$350.00	$400.00	$400.00	$1,550.00

- Printed the four paychecks but NOT the rest of the checks in the queue; use the next check number available (#1843) as the first check number.

- Created checks to be printed: 1) federal taxes, 2) state taxes, and 3) employee health insurance

Monday, July 29, 2019

- Invoiced Billy Mercedes for a Hand Wash with Interior, Exterior Wax services, as well as Dry Towels, Paste Wax, Interior Cleaner, and Leather Conditioner; invoice #19-173.

- Received check #5512 for $1,692.90 as payment on account from Dee Motor Company; apply to invoice #19-168. It was paid within the discount period.

- Invoiced Frances Tuscan [675 Arbor Rd., Anaconda, MT, 59711; (406) 555-9321 for a Full Exterior Detailing service for a large car, a package of Wash Mitts, Dry Towels, Window Cleaner, Interior Cleaner, and Vinyl/Rubber Dressing; invoice #19-174. Permanent terms Net 15.

- Received a check (#729) from Phoebe Martinez for a Full Exterior Detailing for a large car, Dry Towels, Window Cleaner, Interior Cleaner, and Wheel-Rim Polish/Cleaner.

Tuesday, July 30, 2019

- Received check #1052 for $59.72 as payment on account from Leslie McGrevy; apply to invoice #19-170.

- Paid all bills in Accounts Payable; checks are to be printed.

- Deposited all funds held in Undeposited Funds into Checking.

- Paid all sales taxes collected during the month of July to Deer Lodge County Treasurer.

- Wrote a check to Martin Beatty for $3,000 as an owner's draw, to be printed.

- Printed all checks in the queue using the next available check number, #1847.

 CHECK FIGURE *Checking $9,177.04 • A/R $3,486.93 • A/P –$30.00 • Visa $347.85*

Session #2: Deliverables

Submit the following as directed. If your class is using Quick Grader, be sure to export the report to Excel.

- **Project2-2-1** QG : A report displaying all open invoices as of July 31, 2019

- **Project2-2-2** QG : A report displaying the transactions Rugged Cross has had with each vendor in July 2019

- **Project2-2-3:** A report displaying a summary of the total sales by item for July 2019

- **Project2-2-4** QG : A report displaying the amount of each paycheck issued in July 2019

> **Tip!** You didn't use the QuickBooks payroll features, so you will NOT use the reports listed under Employees & Payroll to create this report.

- **Project2-2-5:** A graph displaying income and expenses by account for June and July 2019

- **Project2-2-6:** A report displaying the Items List (columns should be Item, Description, Type, Price, and Sales Tax Code)

- **Project2-2-7** QG : A report displaying the customers and their contact information and balance owing (columns should be Customer, Main Phone, and Balance Total)

- **Project2-2-8** QG : A report displaying the Chart of Accounts (columns should be Account, Type, Balance Total, and Description)

Session #3: Wrap It Up

Ⓐ The Administrator is responsible for setting up all accounts necessary for the transactions in this session and for customizing the company's reports.

Ⓡ The Accounts Receivable team member is responsible for producing the balance sheet and profit & loss reports. You will also account for bad debts and prepaid rent.

Ⓟ The Accounts Payable team member is responsible for making any inventory adjustments.

Session #3: Data

- On July 30, 2019, you learned that Mark Biggs has filed for bankruptcy, so you wrote off the balance he owes as bad debt using the credit memo method using BD-01 as the number.

- Using the register, transferred $1,450 from Prepaid Rent to Rent Expense for August rent (date the transaction 7/31/2019).

- Set up the rent transfer to occur automatically on the first of the month for the next four months, beginning on 9/1/2019.

- Customized the balance sheet standard and profit & loss standard reports to make them more visually appealing.

- Used the physical inventory worksheet provided to make needed inventory adjustments.

Rugged Cross Auto Detailing
Physical Inventory Worksheet
July 31, 2019

Item	Description	Preferred Vendor	Quantity On Hand	Physical Count
Dry Towels	Micro Fiber Dry Towels, 3-pack	Hamill Car Detail Supplies	5	5
Glass Polish	Jasper's 8 oz. Glass Polish	Jasper Jones Auto Detail LLC	15	15
Interior Cleaner	Jasper's 16 oz. Interior Cleaner	Jasper Jones Auto Detail LLC	14	13
Leather Conditioner	Rosey's 6 oz. Leather Conditioner	Rosey & Girls Auto Supply	9	9
Paste Wax	Rosey's Exterior Paste Wax	Rosey & Girls Auto Supply	8	8
Rubbing Compound	Rosey's 12 oz. Rubbing Compound	Rosey & Girls Auto Supply	16	14
Vinyl Rubber Dressing	Rosey's 8 oz. Vinyl/Rubber Dressing	Rosey & Girls Auto Supply	7	7
Wash Mitts	Micro Fiber Wash Mitts, 3-pack	Hamill Car Detail Supplies	18	17
Wheel Rim Polish	Rosey's 16 oz. Wheel-Rim Polish/Cleaner	Rosey & Girls Auto Supply	12	12
Window Cleaner	Jasper's 14 oz. Window Cleaner	Jasper Jones Auto Detail LLC	15	14

Session #3: Deliverables

Submit the following as directed. If your class is using Quick Grader, be sure to export the report to Excel.

- **Project2-3-1** QG : A standard Balance Sheet Standard report dated July 31, 2019 (cash basis)

- **Project2-3-2** QG : A standard Profit & Loss Standard report for July 2019 (cash basis)

QUICKBOOKS DESKTOP 2019

A | Need to Know Accounting

E ven though QuickBooks does everything for you "behind the scenes," it is important that you have a basic understanding of what is happening to your books.

In this Appendix, you will learn about the basic financial statements important to any business and the accounts that appear on these reports. You will also learn about the double-entry accounting system and the debits and credits that must always be equal.

LEARNING OBJECTIVES

▸ Working with financial statements

▸ Debits and credits: the double-entry accounting system

▸ Finding additional accounting resources

Working with Financial Statements

There are two main reports that a company will produce periodically to illustrate its financial well-being.

- A Balance Sheet report displays all of the holdings of the company along with the debts as of a particular date.

- An Income Statement, otherwise known as a Profit & Loss report, displays the income and expenses for a specified period of time.

Understanding the accounts that make up each of these reports is key to understanding your company's books.

The Accounting Equation and the Balance Sheet

The first equation you need to learn when it comes to accounting is simply termed the accounting equation:

Assets = Liabilities + Equity

This means that if you take all of your company's debt and add any investments (equity), you will have a value equal to all of the assets that your company owns.

A balance sheet is a financial statement that displays all asset, liability, and equity accounts (the balance sheet accounts). Take a look at the following illustrations to see how the accounting equation works and is represented in a Balance Sheet.

Average Guy Designs Chapter 12
Balance Sheet
As of December 31, 2023

	Dec 31, 23
ASSETS	
Current Assets	
Checking/Savings	
10000 · Checking	25,782.41
10200 · Savings	3,382.35
10400 · Money Market	1,000.00
10500 · Petty Cash	247.76
Total Checking/Savings	30,412.52
Other Current Assets	
12100 · Inventory Asset	1,225.00
13200 · Prepaid Rent	3,500.00
13300 · Prepaid Insurance	700.00
Total Other Current Assets	5,425.00
Total Current Assets	35,837.52
Fixed Assets	
15000 · Furniture and Equipment	2,639.00
16000 · Vehicles	4,500.00
17000 · Accumulated Depreciation	-664.84
Total Fixed Assets	6,474.16
TOTAL ASSETS	**42,311.68**
LIABILITIES & EQUITY	
Liabilities	
Current Liabilities	
Accounts Payable	
20000 · Accounts Payable	995.36
Total Accounts Payable	995.36
Credit Cards	
21000 · Sunriver Credit Union Visa	471.79
Total Credit Cards	471.79
Other Current Liabilities	
24000 · Payroll Liabilities	24.60
25500 · Sales Tax Payable	2.48
Total Other Current Liabilities	27.08
Total Current Liabilities	1,494.23
Long Term Liabilities	
26000 · Loan -Vehicles (Vespa - 1)	4,050.00
28300 · Loan - Office Furniture	2,639.00
Total Long Term Liabilities	6,689.00
Total Liabilities	8,183.23
Equity	
30000 · Opening Balance Equity	-2,815.02
32000 · Owners Equity	25,630.04
Net Income	11,313.43
Total Equity	34,128.45
TOTAL LIABILITIES & EQUITY	**42,311.68**

The upper section (Assets) represents the left side of the accounting equation and displays all assets. The lower section (Liabilities) represents the right side of the accounting equation and displays all liabilities and equity accounts. Notice how the Total Assets = Total Liabilities & Equity ($42,311.68).

The Income Statement (aka Profit & Loss Report)

The accounts that you find on the Income Statement (or Profit & Loss report) are income and expense. In the illustration you can view an Income Statement and the accounts that appear on it.

The total of all your income accounts less your COGS accounts will result in your Gross Profit.

The Total Expense is totaled below the Gross Profit.

Average Guy Designs Chapter 12
Profit & Loss
January 2023

	Jan 23
▼ 41000 · Product Sales	
41100 · Clothing	150.00
Total 41000 · Product Sales	150.00
43200 · Design Income	740.00
48900 · Video Editing Income	250.00
49000 · Less Discounts Given	-14.08
Total Income	**1,125.92**
▼ Cost of Goods Sold	
50000 · Cost of Goods Sold	75.00
Total COGS	**75.00**
Gross Profit	**1,050.92**
▼ Expense	
60400 · Bank Service Charges	30.00
64300 · Meals and Entertainment	135.48
64900 · Office Supplies	83.59
67200 · Repairs and Maintenance	314.44
▼ 68600 · Utilities	
68610 · Gas & Electric	82.37
Total 68600 · Utilities	82.37
Total Expense	**645.88**
Net Ordinary Income	**405.04**
Net Income	**405.04**

The difference between the Gross Profit and Total Expense results in the Net Income (or Net Loss if the expenses are greater than the income).

Debits and Credits: The Double-Entry Accounting System

There is another equation in accounting that is paramount for us to keep in mind: Debits must always equal credits!

Accounts are often displayed in a "T" format in accounting (which you can see in all of the Behind the Scenes sections of this book).

Account Name	
Debit Side	Credit Side

The T-accounts allow you to place the name of the account on the top, account debits on the left side, and account credits on the right side. This means that the left side (debits) across all T-accounts must always equal the right side (credits) across all T-accounts when entering accounting transactions (hence the term "double-entry").

In order to understand debits and credits a bit better, we will now look at the types of accounts and their normal balances.

Types of Accounts and Normal Balances

We have looked at the two main financial statements and the types of accounts included in each. The balance sheet is comprised of asset, liability, and equity accounts. The income statement is comprised of income and expense accounts. Before we look deeper into each account type, it is important to understand normal balances.

Each type of account must have a normal balance of either a debit or a credit. The normal balance is the side that will increase the amount of the account. Assets and expenses both have debit normal balances and will increase when debited and decrease when credited. Liabilities, equity, and income all have credit normal balances and will increase when credited and decrease when debited.

The concept of normal balances makes sense if you think of the balance sheet. Assets with a debit normal balance must equal the sum of the liabilities and equity, which both have a credit normal balance. Think of this as the marriage of the accounting equation and the fact that debits must equal credits!

The following table describes the primary account types and their normal balances:

Account Type	Description
Assets	An asset is anything that a company owns or monies that are owed to the company. Examples of assets are checking accounts, accounts receivable, and vehicles. Assets have a debit normal balance.
Liabilities	A liability is something that a company owes, such as an auto loan or a credit card balance. Liabilities have a credit normal balance.
Equity	Equity accounts are both investments into the company (Owner's Equity or Stockholder's Equity) and the net income or loss from the operation of a business (Retained Earnings). Equity accounts have a credit normal balance.
Income	Income accounts reflect the sales and fees earned during an accounting period. Income accounts have a credit normal balance.
Expenses	Expense accounts record the expenditures that a company accrues while conducting business. Expense accounts have a debit normal balance.

The Trial Balance Report

At the end of an accounting cycle, a Trial Balance report is prepared that shows all accounts affected during the cycle. The balance of each account is entered in the appropriate column based on its normal balance. The net income or net loss is the difference between income and expenses. If the income is greater than the expenses, an excess credit balance will result and will increase the equity account (a net income). If the expenses are greater than the income, an excess debit balance will result and will decrease the equity account (a net loss).

Average Guy Designs Chapter 12
Trial Balance
As of December 31, 2023

	Dec 31, 23	
	Debit	Credit
10000 · Checking	10,226.64	
10200 · Savings	3,382.35	
10400 · Money Market	1,000.00	
10500 · Petty Cash	247.76	
11000 · Accounts Receivable	15.00	
12000 · Undeposited Funds	0.00	
12100 · Inventory Asset	1,364.00	
13200 · Prepaid Rent	3,500.00	
13300 · Prepaid Insurance	700.00	
15000 · Furniture and Equipment	2,639.00	
16000 · Vehicles	4,500.00	
20000 · Accounts Payable		1,770.36
21000 · Sunriver Credit Union Visa		471.79
24000 · Payroll Liabilities		24.60
25000 · Customer Deposits	0.00	
25500 · Sales Tax Payable	0.00	
26000 · Loan -Vehicles (Vespa - 1)		4,050.00
28300 · Loan - Office Furniture		2,639.00
30000 · Opening Balance Equity		22,815.02
41100 · Clothing		150.00
41200 · Accessories		120.00
42700 · Photography Income		200.00
43200 · Design Income		3,658.84
48900 · Video Editing Income		250.00
49000 · Less Discounts Given	16.70	
50000 · Cost of Goods Sold	133.50	
60300 · Bad Debt Expense	345.00	
60400 · Bank Service Charges	39.50	
61500 · Job Materials	683.70	
61700 · Computer and Internet Expenses	728.44	
63300 · Insurance Expense	475.49	
64300 · Meals and Entertainment	206.72	
64900 · Office Supplies	478.81	
66100 · Company-Paid Benefits	203.50	
66200 · Company - Paid Taxes	188.20	
66300 · Gross Wages	2,460.00	
67100 · Rent Expense	2,200.00	
67200 · Repairs and Maintenance	314.44	
67500 · Shipping Expense	18.49	
68610 · Gas & Electric	82.37	
TOTAL	**36,149.61**	**36,149.61**

The debits and credits in a Trial Balance report must be equal.

Self-Assessment Answer Key

Chapter 1: Introducing QuickBooks Pro

Item	Answer	Heading or DYS
1	False	Determining the Edition
2	True	Types of Tasks
3	False	Accrual vs. Cash Basis Accounting
4	False	Types of QuickBooks Files
5	True	Types of QuickBooks Files
6	True	Opening and Restoring QuickBooks Files
7	True	The QuickBooks Icon Bar
8	True	The QuickBooks Icon Bar
9	False	Updating Your QuickBooks Company File
10	C	Backup Location
11	A	Types of QuickBooks Files
12	A	Opening and Restoring QuickBooks Files
13	B	Following a Transaction Path (in Sale of Camera diagram)

Chapter 2: Working with Customers

Item	Answer	Heading or DYS
1	False	Chapter 2 Title Page
2	True	Delete a Customer
3	True	Creating Items
4	False	Create a Sales Receipt for a Customer
5	True	Creating Invoices
6	True	Entering Customers Not Already on the Customers & Jobs List
7	True	Voiding vs. Deleting Transactions
8	False	The Find Feature
9	True	Receiving Payments
10	True	Invoice Status Tracker
11	B	Creating Invoices
12	A	The Undeposited Funds Account
13	D	Creating Invoices
14	D	The Search Feature

Chapter 3: Working with Vendors

Item	Answer	Heading or DYS
1	True	Creating a New Vendor
2	False	Creating a New Vendor
3	False	Deleting a Vendor
4	True	Entering Bills
5	True	Payment Details
6	False	Writing and Printing Checks
7	False	Writing and Printing Checks
8	False	QuickZoom
9	False	Merge Duplicate Vendors
10	False	The Profit & Loss (P&L) Report
11	A	Paying Bills
12	B	The Vendor Center
13	C	Deleting a Vendor

Chapter 4: Performing Bank Tasks

Item	Answer	Heading or DYS
1	False	Making Deposits
2	False	Behind the Scenes under Making Deposits
3	False	Type of Account and Normal Balance
4	False	Working with an Account Register
5	False	Double-Clicking Accounts and "QuickBooks Responses" table
6	True	Importing Banking Transactions into QuickBooks
7	True	Reconciling Accounts
8	False	The Chart of Accounts
9	True	Problem Resolution Process
10	False	Reconciliation Reports
11	A	Problem Resolution Process
12	D	Making Deposits
13	A	Balance Sheet Reports

Chapter 5: Creating a Company

Item	Answer	Heading or DYS
1	False	Choosing Your Start Date
2	True	Start Setup
3	False	"Anatomy of a QuickBooks Chart of Accounts" table
4	False	Moving and Sorting Accounts Within the List
5	True	Editing Your QuickBooks Preferences
6	True	How Many Companies Should You Create?
7	True	The Report Center
8	True	Advanced Setup/EasyStep Interview
9	True	Setting Up Users
10	True	Setting Up Users
11	False	Subaccounts
12	A	"Anatomy of a QuickBooks Chart of Accounts" table
13	B	Working with QuickBooks in a Multi-User Environment"
14	D	"Account Types and Numbering Conventions" table
15	B	Account Types and Numbering

Chapter 6: Managing Physical Inventory

Item	Answer	Heading or DYS
1	False	Creating Purchase Orders
2	True	Non-Posting Accounts
3	False	Should I Use QuickBooks to Track My Company's Inventory?
4	True	Show Lowest Subaccount Preference
5	False	"Inventory Reports and Their Purposes" table
6	True	Sales Tax Items and Groups
7	True	Note! after Behind the Scenes under Send a Batch of Forms
8	True	The Shipping Manager
9	True	Working with Electronic Customer Payments/Wire Transfers
10	False	Tracking Sales
11	A	Should I Use QuickBooks to Track My Company's Inventory?
12	D	Inventory Reports and Their Purposes
13	B	Note! under Discount Payment Terms
14	D	Non-Posting Accounts

Chapter 7: Working with Balance Sheet Accounts and Budgets

Item	Answer	Heading or DYS
1	False	Memorizing Transactions
2	False	Tracking Petty Cash
3	True	Tracking Petty Cash
4	True	Depreciation
5	True	Accumulated Depreciation
6	False	Setting Up a Long-Term Liability
7	True	Retained Earnings
8	True	Paying Down the Other Current Asset Account
9	True	Recording Methods
10	True	Budgeting and Predicting in QuickBooks
11	C	Tracking Petty Cash
12	D	Working with Other Current Assets
13	B	Depreciation
14	B	Opening Balance Equity

Chapter 8: Using QuickBooks for Payroll

Item	Answer	Heading or DYS
1	True	Payroll Items
2	False	Working with Employees in QuickBooks
3	True	Payroll Recordkeeping in QuickBooks
4	True	Setting Employee Defaults
5	True	Workers' Compensation Insurance
6	True	Working with Payroll Schedules
7	False	The Pay Payroll Liabilities Window
8	False	Information to Track
9	False	Working with Employees in QuickBooks
10	False	"Common Payroll Errors and Their Fixes" table
11	B	Payroll Items
12	C	Behind the Scenes Brief in DYS 8-5
13	B	Tracking and Paying Payroll Liabilities
14	C	1099-MISC and 1096

Chapter 9: Job Costing, Creating Estimates, and Time Tracking

Item	Answer	Heading or DYS
1	False	Creating an Estimate for a Job
2	False	Create a Progress Invoice
3	True	Methods of Entering Time
4	False	Passing on Expenses to Customers
5	True	Creating an Estimate for a Job
6	False	Unearned Income
7	True	Unearned Income
8	False	Tracking Mileage
9	False	Assessing Finance Charges and Producing Statements
10	False	Creating Statements for Customers
11	D	Jobs, Time & Mileage Tracking Report
12	B	Job Profitability
13	A	Tracking Mileage
14	A	Customer Deposits

Chapter 10: Customizing and Integrating in QuickBooks

Item	Answer	Heading or DYS
1	False	Adding Custom Fields
2	True	Formatting Fonts and Numbers
3	True	Sending Letters with Word
4	False	Accrual vs. Cash Basis Reporting
5	True	Filtering Reports
6	False	Memorizing Reports
7	True	Making the Lists Work for You
8	True	Creating Custom Fields
9	True	Batch Processing of Reports
10	True	Exporting QuickBooks Reports to Excel
11	D	Memorizing Reports
12	B	Sending Letters with Word
13	C	Note! under Adding Custom Fields
14	A	Accrual vs. Cash Basis Reporting

Chapter 11: Introducing the Accounting Cycle and Using Classes

Item	Answer	Heading or DYS
1	False	A Class Example
2	True	The Accounting Cycle and Fiscal Period
3	True	Working with Classes
4	True	Using Classes for Profit Center Reporting
5	True	The QuickBooks Doc Center
6	True	Adding a Class Field to Reports
7	True	Producing a Statement of Cash Flows
8	False	Sections of the Statement of Cash Flows Report
9	True	Time to Review Generally Accepted Accounting Principles (GAAP)
10	False	Forecasting Cash Flow
11	B	A Class Example
12	D	The Profit & Loss Unclassified Report
13	B	Cycle Step 1: Analyze Business Transactions
14	A	Sections of the Statement of Cash Flows Report

Chapter 12: Reporting, Adjusting Entries, and Closing the Books

Item	Answer	Heading or DYS
1	True	Cycle Step 5: Adjusting Entries and Adjusted Trial Balance
2	False	The Income Summary Account
3	True	Preparing for Year-End Reporting
4	False	Preparing a Worksheet
5	True	Accounting for Depreciation
6	True	Permanent Accounts
7	False	The Balance Sheet
8	False	The Balance Sheet
9	True	The Income Statement
10	True	Setting a Closing Date
11	D	Cycle Step 5: Adjusting Entries and Adjusted Trial Balance
12	B	Cycle Step 5: Adjusting Entries and Adjusted Trial Balance
13	D	The Audit Trail
14	B	Cycle Step 7: Closing Entries and Post-Closing Trial Balance

Glossary

accountant's copy A special copy of your Quick-Books file that can be created if your accountant needs to make adjustments to your QuickBooks file, but you do not want to lose access to it while it is being adjusted

accounting cycle A series of steps to help a business keep its accounting records properly during the fiscal period

accrual basis In the accrual basis of accounting, income is recorded when the sale is made and expenses are recorded when accrued; often used by firms or businesses with large inventories

activities Affect what is happening behind the scenes; can be easily input into forms, such as invoices or bills

Adjusted Trial Balance A listing of all the company accounts contained in the general ledger that has been prepared after adjusting entries are posted for an accounting period; this is an internal document and not a financial statement

assets Anything owned by a company or that is owed to a company; items such as a checking account, a building, a prepaid insurance account, or accounts receivable

audit trail Allows you to track every entry, modification, or deletion to transactions in your file; accessed through the Accounting category in the Report Center or the Report option on the menu bar

average cost method A method of inventory tracking in which the value of the inventory is determined by dividing the total value of the inventory by the total number of inventory items

bad debt Funds owed to you that are not collectable and need to be written off

Balance Sheet A report that displays all assets, liabilities, and equity as of a specific date; it focuses on income and expenses for that period

balance sheet accounts The asset, liability, and equity accounts, such as bank, credit card, current liabilities (sales tax payable and payroll liabilities), accounts receivable, accounts payable, and retained earnings

Balance Sheet by Class report A balance sheet report in which each class appears as a separate column; should be used only by expert users

batch A group of customers that a user can create similar invoices for at one time

batch timesheets A feature that allows you to create timesheets for multiple employees who work the same hours on the same jobs and using the same payroll item(s)

behind the scenes The accounting that QuickBooks performs for you when you enter transactions

bounced checks Checks returned by the bank due to non-sufficient funds in the account; also called "NSF" checks

cash basis In the cash basis of accounting, income is recorded when cash is received and expenses are recorded when cash is paid; commonly used by small businesses and professionals

Cash Flow Forecast A report that gives you a glimpse of what you can expect a company's cash flow to look like in the near future based on current data in the company file

centers QuickBooks has four centers—Customer, Employee, Report, and Vendor—that allow you to view the Customers & Jobs, Employee, and Vendor lists; access QuickBooks reports; and view snapshots of information (of an individual customer, vendor, or employee)

company setup Takes you through the steps necessary to set up a new company in QuickBooks

Company Snapshot A window that offers a quick view of your company's bottom line in one convenient place

Contributed reports Reports submitted by another user you can use so you don't have to "reinvent the wheel"; you can also share your custom reports with this feature

contributors Users that share their report templates with the QuickBooks community

cost of goods sold (COGS) The purchase price you pay for items you will use for a job or to create a saleable item, including labor

depreciation A way to match income to expenses—a fixed asset is used to produce income over a period of time, and depreciation allows you to record the appropriate expense for the same period; many small businesses record depreciation transactions just once a year, but they can be entered monthly or quarterly if the business produces financial statements for those periods

draw An owner's withdrawal of funds from the company

edition Intuit creates a multitude of editions (versions) of QuickBooks to choose from: QuickBooks Online, QuickBooks Pro, QuickBooks Premier, and QuickBooks Enterprise

equity accounts Reflect the owner's investment in the company and have a credit normal balance; in a sole proprietorship, equity is what the owner has invested in the company and in a corporation and the equity is what the shareholders have invested in the company

FIFO (first in, first out) An inventory valuation method in which the value of the first inventory brought in is used to determine the COGS, whereas the value of the inventory is based on the inventory purchased last (which more closely resembles the actual replacement cost)

filtering Allows you to include only the essential data in your report; choose to filter out many types of data such as accounts, dollar amounts, and types of customers; allows you to closely examine and report on a specific group of data

fixed asset account A type of account that tracks the activities associated with a fixed asset

fonts QuickBooks displays its preset reports in a default font; you can make many changes to the characteristics of the font in your report, such as the font name, style, color, and size

Forecast A feature that allows you to make predictions about the future; it can be created based on actual figures from the last year or from scratch

Generally Accepted Accounting Principles (GAAP) Rules used to prepare, present, and report financial statements for a wide variety of entities

header and footer Default headers and footers appear on all preset QuickBooks reports; change the information included along with how it is formatted on the Header and Footer tabs of the Additional Customization window

I-9 An IRS form used when hiring employees to verify identity and employment eligibility

Income Statement A financial report that can be found in the Company & Financial category of the Report Finder window; P&L reports reflect all transactions that have affected income and expense accounts within a specified time period (also called a Profit & Loss report)

Item List A list of products and services a company buys, sells, or resells; before an invoice can be generated, items must be created in the Item List as services, non-inventory parts, inventory parts, or other charges

job costing Allows a user to determine the profitability of each job for a customer by tracking by expenses and revenues for the job

Layout Designer A window that provides rulers to line up objects and toolbar buttons to help manipulate your template objects

Lead Center A feature that allows you to track information about potential customers

liabilities Anything owed by the company, such as loans, expenses, or accounts payable

LIFO (Last in, First out) Inventory valuation method in which the value of the last inventory brought in is used to determine the cost of goods sold (COGS), whereas the value of the inventory is based on the inventory purchased earlier in the year

Lists (database) Allows you to store information about customers, vendors, employees, and other data important to your business

logo An image that represents your company; QuickBooks allows you to personalize your templates by including your company logo

Long Term Liabilities account A QuickBooks account that tracks a liability (loan) you do not plan to pay off within the next year

normal balance Each type of account must have a normal balance of either a debit or a credit, and the normal balance is the side that will increase the amount of the account; assets and expenses have a debit normal balance, while liabilities, equity, and income have credit normal balances

online backup QuickBooks offers an online backup option for a monthly fee that is determined based on the amount of room you wish to have available for your backup work

Opening Balance Equity account An equity account created by QuickBooks when you start your first balance sheet account; it allows you to have an accurate balance sheet from the start

outside payroll service A service that runs payroll for a company outside of QuickBooks; the company inputs the information into QuickBooks without using the payroll features

Payroll Liabilities The account in which you hold payroll taxes and other deductions until you are required to pay them

payroll options Intuit provides a variety of options to run your payroll; to view and compare these options, visit the Student Resource Center

permanent account An account for which the ending balance for one fiscal period is the opening balance for the next

petty cash Cash kept by businesses for small expenditures; in QuickBooks, Petty Cash is set up as a bank account in the Chart of Accounts

Profile Lists Lists generated upon company setup that will store customizable information related to the specific list; examples are the Vendor Type List, Payment Method List, and the Sales Rep List

profit and loss (P&L) report A financial report that can be found in the Company & Financial category of the Report Finder window; P&L reports reflect all transactions that have affected income and expense accounts within a specified time period; also called an Income Statement

purchase order A form utilized by many companies to enter items into inventory; it does not affect anything "behind the scenes"

reconciliation The process of matching your QuickBooks accounts to the bank and credit card statements you receive; it is important to make sure that your account records in QuickBooks match those of the bank or credit card company

report A way to display your company information in various ways, such as printed, onscreen, or as a PDF file

resize To change the height or width of an image, window, or object

restored The process of decompressing a QuickBooks backup or portable company file; when you restore a file in the same location with the same name as another file, it will replace that file

sales orders Allow you to manage customer orders of both products and services; available in the Premier and Enterprise editions

source documents Forms used to enter data into QuickBooks, such as Invoices, Sales Receipts, Checks, Bills, Credit Memos; can also include documents stored in the Doc Center, such as a scanned store receipt or an image of a check received

Starter Chart of Accounts During the setup process, QuickBooks asks you to choose the business type that your company most closely resembles (this cannot be changed later); QuickBooks uses your choice to create a Chart of Accounts close to what you need (it will take you less time to edit it to fit your unique business than to start from scratch)

Statement of Cash Flows A report that shows how viable a company is in the short term; demonstrates whether a company will be able to pay its bills, payroll, and other expenses, and also indicates the financial health of the company

Statement of Owner's Equity A report that shows the capital at the beginning of the fiscal period and any additional investments, as well as draws, the net income or loss, and the ending amount

T-accounts A means of displaying an accounting transaction to show that debits equal credits, in which the name of the account is placed on the top of the "T," account debits are on the left side, and account credits are on the right side

temporary account Accounts are zeroed out at the end of each fiscal period, with the amounts from them moving into an equity account as either a net income (if income was greater than expenses) or a net loss (if expenses exceeded income for the period); also called a nominal account

Time Tracking Allows you to create weekly timesheets so you can break down the hours by customer/job or record single activities for a customer/job

Trial Balance A report that adds up the debits and credits at the end of an accounting period so mistakes can be traced if debits don't equal credits

unearned income Funds received from a customer as a deposit or for a gift certificate; these funds should be held in a liability account until they are "earned"

units of measure A feature available in the Premier and higher versions of QuickBooks that allows you to convert units of measure; useful for companies that purchase and sell in different units of measure or need to indicate units on purchase or sales forms

version When referring to software, this is a way to track new developments in software; Intuit creates a new version of QuickBooks each year (such as QuickBooks 2017, 2018, or 2019), and each new version provides additional features that are new for that year

W-4 An IRS form completed by an employee so the employer can withhold the correct federal income tax from the employee's pay

Index